D0758313

Woman's Inhumanity to Woman

WOMAN'S
INHUMANITY
TO WOMAN

Phyllis Chesler

Thunder's Mouth Press/Nation Books
New York

Ma—this book is for you.

CONTENTS

The world into which one was precipitated was terrible, yes. . . . One entered hoping at least for the solidarity of one's companions in misfortune, but the hoped for allies, except in special cases, were not there. . . . This brusque revelation, which became manifest from the very first hours of imprisonment, often in the instant form of . . . aggression on the part of those in whom one hoped to find future allies, was so harsh as to cause the immediate collapse of one's capacity to resist.

—Primo Levi

No one can humiliate you like one of your own.

—Judy Grahn

The black man wants to be white . . . a native is an oppressed person whose permanent dream is to become the persecutor.

—Frantz Fanon

The women who hate me cut me / as men can't . . .

—Dorothy Allison

Most mothers worry when their daughters reach adolescence, but I was the opposite. I relaxed. I sighed with relief. Little girls are cute and small only to adults. To one another they are not cute. They are lifesized.

—Margaret Atwood

INTRODUCTION

Recently, at a literary event, I saw an old feminist friend whom I have known for more than thirty years. She is a celebrated writer, for whom I have great respect. I recently advised her on a matter for which she was very grateful.

"What are you working on?" she asked.

"I'm completing a book about woman's inhumanity to woman. Would you like to see it when it's done?"

"Oh, not me, don't turn to me. I think you should be writing about how men oppress women, not about what oppressed people do in order to survive." She said this smugly, sternly, and sanctimoniously. There was something rigid, brittle, in this otherwise free spirit.

"But," I said, "why not give the book a chance? Why not look at it? If I've taken a wrong turn, you can point me in the right direction."

Stony silence.

"Well, I guess you're right. Maybe I can do that." But she didn't look happy about it.

I am surprised, a bit frightened for my work. Here was a feminist writer who had pre-judged an intellectual work, who was reluctant to even read a book if it did not seem to espouse the party line.

We stood together for awhile. Finally, she said: "I'm not the one for you. I don't want to see your manuscript."

Within months, my friend had changed her mind. "Oh, how clever of you. What you're saying is that women are sexists too."

Are women really sexists? Of course we are. A recent study of 15,000 people in nineteen countries on five continents found that women hold sexist views just as men do. Studies have found that some women are hostile toward women and do not like, trust, respect, or find their statements to be credible. This is hardly surprising since women grow up in the same culture that men do, and thus are not immune to that culture. We live on the same planet; women are not an alien species. To the extent that women are oppressed, we have also internalized the prevailing misogynist ideology which we uphold both in order to survive and in order to improve our own individual positions vis-à-vis all other women.

Recent studies and crime statistics confirm that men are aggressive in direct and dramatic ways. Although most women are not directly or physically violent, women are highly aggressive, but in indirect ways. The targets of such female aggression are not men—but other women and children.

Researchers in Europe, North America, and Australia have found that verbal and indirect aggression among girls and women includes name-calling, insulting, teasing, threatening, shutting the other out, becoming friends with another as revenge, ignoring, gossiping, telling bad stories behind a person's back, and trying to get others to dislike that person. Additionally, the formation of exclusive female dyads and cliques begins early in life. According to the authors Ellen Goodman and Patricia O'Brien, "Cliques are the female equivalent of bullies. Cliques offer security to those who conform, and cause insecurity in those who don't." Author Nancy Friday notes that "boys try the macho, aggressive form of bullying; with girls, bullying means exclusion from their friendship group."

In India, for example, the practice of a mother-in-law dousing her daughter-in-law with kerosene to obtain more dowry-money from the next daughter-in-law, continues. In addition, a recent survey in India confirms that more than fifty percent of the women questioned believe that wife-beating is justified. In Egypt, a recent survey reveals, seven out of ten women believe that female genital mutilation is justified. In parts of China, where a policy of one child per family and a preference for sons over daughters has led to a scarcity of eligible brides, parents routinely pay kidnappers to acquire a daughter-in-law who will produce the desired grandson and labor as her mother-in-law's servant. In Cambodia jealous wives throw acid at their husband's girlfriends—not at their philandering husbands. Some studies suggest that female gossip also plays a role in the "honor killings" of Muslim girls and women in the Middle East.

A recent survey of 500 British women reveals that one third believed that domestic violence was acceptable in certain circumstances and more than half felt it was wrong to end a relationship with a violent partner. In the United States the psychologist Gloria Cowan has been studying women's hostility to women. Such hostility includes a refusal to believe that women are economically discriminated against or are the victims of sexual violence. Cowan's subjects are young and middle-aged, Hispanic–, Native–, Asian–, African–, and white–Americans. She found that a woman's political or economic philosophy does not predict whether she will be hostile toward women. Rather, such hostility is correlated with the believer's own satisfaction or dissatisfaction with herself. Cowan states: "The data indicate that women who are hostile toward other women don't feel good about themselves. They have lower personal self-esteem, optimism, sense of self-efficacy, life satisfaction, and higher objectified body consciousness compared to women who are not hostile toward women."

The fact that someone is a woman does not mean that she likes, trusts, or works well with other women. Although women may be more emotionally expressive and interpersonally sophisticated than men are, some women also dislike and distrust other women. Despite recent advances in women's education and employment, and despite women's liberal voting patterns, research also indicates that many women still dislike a woman leader who has a male style of leadership and prefer a woman homemaker to a woman who has a career.

"Are you still doing that book?" asks my friend the Last Leftist. For nearly twenty years she has asked me this same question almost every time we meet.

"Of course I am," I say.

"I wish you'd give it up," she admonishes me. "This will delight every woman-hater around. You'll be hurt, but you'll hurt other women too."

Hurt women? But I am writing this book in the hope that it will enable women to treat each other with more respect, kindness, compassion, fairness, and civility. Contrary to myth, this is not how most women treat each other. Most women do not hate women; only some do. Most women in fact depend upon other women for emotional and social companionship. But, as men do, women either idealize or demonize women. Most women unconsciously expect other women to mother them and feel betrayed when a woman fails to meet their ideal standards. Most women are no more realistic about women than men are. To a woman other women are (supposed to be) Good Fairy Godmothers, and if they are not they may swiftly become their dreaded Evil Stepmothers.

Paradoxically, many women also have rather low standards for each other; it is a protective device. Women are afraid to ask each other directly for what we want in order to avoid feeling disappointed or shamed when an amiable situational companion refuses to stand by us through a life crisis.

I write this book because I would like to see women treat each other more realistically and therefore in more psychologically radical ways. Such behaviors might include minimizing unrealistic expectations, bonding together despite differences, experiencing disagreements less personally, holding grudges only briefly, not forever, disagreeing without annihilating each other. I would like to liberate women from the bonds of inauthentic "niceness."

Given the reality of female oppression, how women treat each other matters more, not less. I want my readers to acknowledge that what women do or refuse to do for other women matters deeply. I want women to understand that we have real power over each other. I want women to use this power consciously and ethically.

I am not saying that woman's inhumanity to woman is on the same level as man's inhumanity to woman; it is not. But, women have enormous influence over each other; we have the power to encourage each other to either resist or to collaborate with tyranny. Each time one woman tells the truth—ten more do so. Each time one woman fights back, thousands more are encouraged to do so.

As therapists Karen Fite and Nikola Trumbo note, women are not "innocent of the betrayals we commit, but our ignorance of what's going on and why does rob us of the power to act otherwise." Fite and Trumbo understand that one must not "blame the victim" but they would also like to see women "accept responsibility for learning to act otherwise."

Lesbian and philosopher Sarah Lucia Hoagland writes that

if women refuse to uphold "patriarchal standards" then things would change "especially because women will go a long way to please each other or at least not offend each other."

Author bell hooks would like women to "challenge the simplistic notion that man is the enemy, woman the victim." We all have the "capacity to act in ways that oppress, dominate, wound (whether or not that power is institutionalized)." Therefore it is the "potential oppressor within that we must resist."

Physician and author Margarete Mitscherlich suggests that oppressed women's "pressing need to be loved" leads them to staunchly "identify with male laws and prejudices." In Nazi Germany most women did not "distance themselves from the anti-Semitism of the time." Rather, they "identified with the aggressor" and expected each other to obey fascist patriarchal orders. Men alone are not responsible for patriarchy; women are also their willing, even ardent, collaborators. Mitscherlich believes that women can only resist such collaboration by becoming "more conscious of their aggression and (by bearing) their guilt feelings more adequately."

It is impossible to change one's behavior if we do not first name that behavior. By acknowledging the shadow side of female-female relationships, I hope that women can begin to transform envy into compassion, betrayal into cooperation.

"Are you going to name names?" one feminist leader asked worriedly.

"What, and publish the phone book?" I said.

A friend and I were having tea. She asked me: "How can a

woman suddenly turn on you, start bossing you around, humiliate you, rage at you, then act as if it never happened, even insist that it did not happen? Do white women have split personalities? Did something terrible happen to them when they were girls?"

"That's possible," I said, "but, it's no excuse for truly bad behavior."

"This white woman has dedicated her life to anti-racist work. When she lost her temper on our recent trip to Africa, she only lost it with black Africans, not white Africans. I was embarrassed to be traveling with her."

"How did you handle it?" I asked.

"I told her this, but she said that I was over-reacting. She refused to apologize for something she said she did not do. She made me feel crazy. When I tried to talk about it in a small meeting, our Chair (a prominent social activist) just sank down lower and lower in her seat, covered her eyes, unable to confront this woman, even to open a productive dialogue."

We are silent for awhile.

My friend asked me: "Have you run into such things too?"

"Absolutely."

Once, I became very close to someone. She was always under siege. In me, she found an ever-ready heart and ear. I thought she was brilliant, but more important, principled. For years people told me that she was too angry, crazy, and politically dangerous. I did not agree that I should distance myself from her personally. She thundered on the lecture platform, but she was very soft-spoken privately. The intimacy was dear to me. And then there came a day when she turned on me. The details do not matter. What matters is that this woman who conducted herself with pronounced humility as the First among Helpless Victims began to leave murderous messages on my phone machine. The disparity between my friend and this altered voice was frightening and demoralizing. It was as if she had switched into another personality. Thinking of it this way did not make it less troubling, only more troubling.

I asked a friend, "What immediately comes to mind when I say the phrase, woman's inhumanity to woman?"

He said, "Nothing much. Jealousy, maybe."

"And what do you think of when I say man's inhumanity to man?"

"Oh," he responded, "that's a big one. War. Fratricide. Slavery. Greed. Evil."

He does not sound as if he feels personally responsible for the existence of evil in the world. He does not act as if he is about to be punished for it. He automatically assumes that other men are evil, not himself.

Most women have been overly and unfairly criticized. Perhaps women are afraid that if we focus on female misdeeds, collective punishments will be meted out. Perhaps for the same reason women are the first to condemn the next woman for the most minor infraction.

Men are taught that it is normal, even desirable, to compete and disagree with each other; when they do so, they do not personalize the argument nor do they think that a friendship or working relationship will be jeopardized by a strong difference of opinion. Women do.

When I sent an early draft of this manuscript around, an esteemed female colleague said she was afraid to tell me what she really thinks because she respects my work and values her friendship with me too much to risk losing it. Had I not already researched and written this book I might have thought, "How sensitive, how kind, how loyal she is!" But, I've changed. This book has changed me. I tell her that our friendship is not at issue, only the ideas in a book are. Perhaps her criticism might strengthen the work—that is why I've sent it to her. But, I must reassure her that our collegiality and friendship will be able to withstand strong disagreements about important ideas.

The patriarchal nuclear family may not be a safe place for some women, not only because of male domestic violence but because women's hidden war against each other also begins at home. The harm may last a lifetime.

A physician consults me. She wants to publish what she refers to as "shameful" material but is afraid that it might jeopardize her career.

She said, "My mother admired my father and was so dependent on him that when she discovered from the babysitter that he had sexually assaulted both me and my sister, she decided he needed more attention! We were instructed to welcome him at the dinner table and to treat him like a king."

Like so many incest victims, this woman sounds angrier at the mother who failed to protect her than she (dares) sound about the father who raped her.

She said, "I can't understand how a mother could do this. Her own mother, my grandmother, was a beastly, cruel woman. Maybe because of that my mother was dependent on my father's vileness and abuse."

She may be right but she is also blaming another woman, her dead maternal grandmother, for what her father alone has done.

I asked, "Had you tried talking to your mother about this?"

"I did. But she would never say she was sorry about what he'd done or about her failure to help me. Until the day she died she was just jealous of his attention toward me."

I raised this issue unexpectedly at a workshop I gave about something else. One woman immediately protested, tried to stop me from talking. She said, "No, you are absolutely wrong. Women are very supportive of each other. I've experienced this myself. Haven't we all?" She looks around for support.

Within an hour, this woman grew tearful. She admitted, "My mother was my lifelong enemy. She refused to touch me. Now as she lies dying she wants me to be her body servant. I can't do it."

Another workshop member said, "My grandmother used to physically hit my mother. My mother pretended this was not happening."

Women want to believe that they and other women are

"safe." Hence, a woman cannot afford to notice that a woman—her own mother no less—is hitting her.

One of my adult students described her mother as an "eternally competitive sister." She said, "Mom was always happy when people mistook her for my sister. She still is. She kept pushing me to succeed, comparing me, negatively, to relatives who were child prodigies. But she was the one who was holding me back. She made disparaging remarks to me about myself every day, every hour."

Georgetown University Professor of Linguistics Deborah Tannen, author of *I Only Say This Because I Love You: How the Way we Talk can Make or Break Family Relationships Throughout Our Lives*, writes, "Because we want so much to feel that our mothers—and our daughters—approve of us and think well of us, any comment that indicates anything less than complete approval swells in significance, overshadowing everything else. And that is why the criticism I hear from mothers and about mothers is overwhelmingly about criticism."

The patriarchal *extended* family is also not necessarily a safe or welcoming space for all women.

A man tells me that his wife has been over-medicating and starving his disabled mother who lives with them.

"She resents having to take care of her. I'm at my wit's end. Now, my wife's begun to hit her."

Clearly, the burden of caring for a handicapped person has brought out the worst—not the best—in this caretaker.

A concerned son does not view "caretaking" as his responsibility, and while he feels badly, he does not feel guilty. He does not offer to become his mother's caretaker. Leaving his job would plunge the family into dire poverty.

Society—a web of many patriarchal families, both nuclear and extended—does not always welcome all women. A friend tells me that since she became a widow, most of the still-married women in her large religious circle have stopped inviting her to dinner parties and social events.

She said, sadly, "This is not personal. They just can't deal with death. What do you think?"

"These women are trying to hide their husbands away from you," I told her. "They're afraid that you might steal them. Married women treat widowers differently: they look in on them. They say, 'There's always room at the table for an extra man.' "

My friend looks pained, falls silent.

"I've been a lesbian all of my life," another friend told me. "My family always treated me as if I had leprosy. When I finally moved out, my mother would only invite me to family events if I dressed 'normally' and came alone."

"Is this still true today?" I asked.

"Just last week at my nephew's wedding, my sister sat me way in the back with strangers. She did not introduce me to the bride or to the bride's family."

Many women in the workplace continue to treat women in traditional patriarchal ways. One recent study demonstrated that women scientists rejected other female proposals for national science foundation funding more often than male scientists did. Another study showed that women lawyers at a large male-dominated law firm were lethal competitors with other women for the handful of token female slots, but that (good news at last!) women lawyers at a large sex-integrated and woman-friendly firm cooperated, bonded with, mentored each other, and enjoyed working together. According to other research, women of color experience both racism and sexism within corporations.

Many small businesses are owned and run by women in America. According to an in-depth study of one such enterprise, familial dynamics were used to placate and control an all-female staff by maintaining the illusion of being one big happy (but dysfunctional) family. The owner was the "nurturing" mother, her underpaid female employees who received no health benefits were her daughters and each others' sisters. Creativity and dissent were punished, standards were low, verbal humiliation a given. However, losing one's temper, being moody, or bitchy were tolerated. Such passive-aggression was dismissed as "PMS," not as anger over power differences.

A woman told me the following story: "I was an administrative manager. When female vendors or salespeople came to pitch their products to me and to my male coworker, they looked, smiled, addressed their sales pitch to him, even though in most cases, I was the primary decision maker. When male vendors did this, I thought, the habits of male bonding die hard. But when women did this, often cutting me out of the conversation entirely, it was more hurtful."

Although "small," these negative, critical comments at home and at work add up. The cumulative effect of such negative comments, often coupled with the absence of equally small but positive comments—the kinds of positive or comforting things that women might automatically, absentmindedly say to men, but not to other women—also add up. Experienced daily over a lifetime, such verbal interactions can have devastating consequences.

Women who endure such small humiliations daily say that the most lasting and haunting harm resides in growing accustomed to such treatment, in large part because other women insist that you do. After all, *they* have. What's so special about you? Always implied but unspoken: "It could be worse."

I can no longer remain silent about this. Minimizing and denying woman's sexism is what grounded an entire liberation movement—at least, psychologically.

I have remained silent, not only because my feminist colleagues warned me away from this subject, but also because most women learn early on as young girls that it is dangerous to expose that which is covered up and then denied. Your mother, sister, and girlhood friends will ostracize you for it.

While most women envy and compete only with each other—not with men—few women can survive without bonding to at least one or two other women. Women seek female approval as much as they seek male approval. Therefore, most girls and women deny even to themselves that they envy or compete, even indirectly, with those upon whom they also depend.

We live in strange times. On the one hand, an increasing

number of women compete against each other in direct and aggressive ways, both physically and verbally in sports, business, politics, law, journalism, science, medicine, and the arts. On the other hand, even today, many men and women remain ambivalent about or continue to disapprove of the woman who competes in direct and visible ways. (This gets many a good female CEO, politician, or professional athlete in quite a lot of trouble.)

A high-profile feminist editor refused to even look at this manuscript. She said, "You should not be writing this book. Are you ready to sell out, is that why you're doing it?"

I do not want to write this book; I have to write this book.

Once, feminists needed to believe in "us," in women, since no one else did. For a while such faith was heroic, the stuff of which sanity is fashioned. However, to now insist that all women are sisters or that most women including feminists are kind, or even polite to each other, or that such niceties rise to the level of morality or justice is foolish and self-destructive.

Anti-feminists (those who oppose abortion, equal pay for equal work, "working" mothers, same-sex marriage, same-sex adoptions, women in the armed forces, a battered woman's right to self-defense, and who do not believe that women are oppressed or the victims of physical or sexual violence, etc.) will probably have no problem with this book and therein lies the rub, for I do not agree with those who believe that women are all bitches, whores, and lunatics who must be savagely tamed. I do not view women as monsters (career or otherwise), who neglect their children, abuse their husbands, are responsible for male impotence, unemployment, violence and madness, the destruction of the family, the killing of unborn babes, and for hail, famine, and drought as well. In short, I do not think that women should be burned at the stake as witches.

But I no longer share as an article of faith the belief in the power of political-social programming to improve human nature; clearly, I am not the optimist I once was. While I may be something of a lapsed Utopian, I still believe in the importance of political struggle. However, I am now more realistic about how long such struggles may take and more anxious therefore that individual women work every day to strengthen and support each other while they are working to improve woman's fate during the next millennium.

Having more political, economic, or legal power is no guarantee that those who have it will automatically behave in ethical or compassionate ways. Narcissism, greed, envy, and murderousness can be found among both powerful and powerless people; kind, humble, happy, and courageous people exist within every class, race, and gender.

I do not think that human nature and behavior, mental illness, or evil (four very different things) can necessarily be explained away or abolished by a politically or religiously correct position or analysis.

The fight for equality and justice is important in and of itself, because it is right, not because it can guarantee us a pain-free, perfect, brave new world. A beggar freed from poverty may still be a scoundrel, a rich woman may be enlightened and compassionate. A poor woman may love herself and her family and do good deeds on earth, a rich woman may see only herself but she may also hate herself and punish all those who have the power to love. One's character, spirit, outlook, and capacity for ethical behavior may not be totally tied to one's visible, material fortune.

I am not concerned with achieving psychological justice only. Economic justice is just as crucial—maybe even more so. Words alone will not do, nor will mere symbolic gestures. People now understand that only a few people own and control most of the earth's resources; the Masters of the Universe are mainly men. We also know that many global industries are poisoning the atmosphere and human biology, causing illness and death, consigning some workers to a lifetime of brutal working conditions, low pay, overwork, no leisure time, and others to lifetimes of unemployment, self-hatred, and despair.

In this context, what does it mean for a corporate executive who earns ten times what her secretary earns, or for a wealthy socialite whose domestic servants are grossly underpaid, to suddenly become polite and soft-spoken toward their female (or male) employees? It will not solve the suffering born of economic disparity, but it is humane to speak humbly, gently, rather than to yell or be dismissive. Such small changes may make the lives of workers more bearable in psychological terms. It will not solve the larger crisis of economic injustice. Class- and race-based working and living conditions will have to change. Organizing for economic justice remains a continuing problem and priority for both women and men.

However, an increasing number of women are beginning to earn more money, own small businesses, run mid-sized corporations, make a profit, invest money, and give away disposable income. Here is where women can start putting our money down to help other women in concrete ways.[1]

I am not suggesting that suffering and deprivation are good for the human spirit or that it is better to be poor than rich. However, I do suggest that neither left-wing materialist internationalist visions, nor right-wing materialist nationalist visions have been able to deliver a living wage, shelter, healthcare, education, leisure, dignity or freedom to all humanity. I am also suggesting that the human spirit has the power to learn from adversity in remarkable ways.

One friend worriedly told me, "This is such an important topic. You must make your political analysis very clear in every chapter. If women treat each other inhumanely it's because they are oppressed and subordinated by patriarchy, poverty, and racism. Otherwise, feminists will attack the book, our opponents will enjoy watching the cat-fight."

I have been afraid of this too.

My friend said, "What you're saying might be true but it's not totally true and it's also heartbreaking and demoralizing."

For those whose work I cherish and whose principles I share and who fear that the exposure of woman's behavior and internalized self-hatred will be used to crush us further, let me assure them that I remain fully cognizant of the continuing war against women. Perhaps I can persuade my publisher to turn the next four paragraphs into a bookmark with which the reader may mark every troubling chapter to come: a talisman, a reminder, a necessary corrective.

Every day, in the ordinary course of human events, man-made tragedies abound. For example, in the United States, every nine seconds a woman is beaten by her husband; every day, nearly 2000 women are raped mainly by male intimates and acquaintances. Elsewhere in the world, each year an additional two million girls suffer the fate of the twenty-two million women who have preceded them and undergo female genital mutilation. This destroys their capacity for sexual pleasure, sometimes causes sterility, and leads to a lifetime of physical and psychological pain. Every day an increasing number of girls and women are kidnapped or sold into sexual and domestic slavery, are forced to veil themselves, or are psychologically buried alive in other customary ways. Thousands of girls and women are killed each year by their male relatives in family "honor killings."

Despite some truly dazzling advances by a token number of women who have been blessed with a capacity for hard work, as well as by membership in the "right" class, race, religion, family, and geographical region, for most women, conditions of gender apartheid still prevail. Women of this world continue to be deprived of the hope and consolation that educational, religious, medical, legal, and economic opportunities often confer. Every day women are denied abortions or forced by poverty and a total lack of social support to surrender a child for adoption against their will. Mothers unjustly lose custody of their children merely because they are women, not because they are unfit. More often, a mother is expected to rear her child alone, never free of economic worry, abandoned by her child's father and by a society that values motherhood in name only.

In addition to such female-specific hardships, most women must also work for money. Although they may perform the same work as men, they are paid far less. On the job, many women are also forced to endure hostile work environments, or are fired if they allege that such discrimination exists.

For women, war ups the ante: their villages and cities are burned, their men are herded away to be executed, they and their female relatives and neighbors are systematically gang-raped by soldiers, tortured in other ways, sometimes murdered. If they are lucky, or unlucky perhaps, these women are taken along as sex and domestic slaves. Afterwards, especially if their rapists have impregnated them, their families may reject or kill them, or they may kill themselves.

All this I know. And yet there is something else, something more.

While the war against women rages openly, visibly, another quieter war against women is also in progress, one that demoralizes women and makes it difficult for them to bond or to fight back.

Day after day women at all levels of society and on every continent also experience other kinds of indignities. Some woman's mother or her sister continues to criticize her nonstop. She knows that her critic means well and only has her best interests at heart, but the woman still feels unjustly attacked, unloved. A woman discovers that her best friend has been sleeping with her husband for a decade; they now wish to marry. A woman is shunned by her own small social circle; no one will tell her why.

A woman alleges sex discrimination and bravely files a complaint. Her female office-mates stop talking to her, several testify against her. A woman alleges rape. The female jurors on her case don't believe her and in fact, feel more sympathy for the accused rapist whom they exonerate. An almost all-female jury finds a battered woman who has killed in self-defense guilty; at a retrial, an almost all-male jury finds her innocent.

A lesbian is battered by her lover. The police do not know whom to believe; they arrest no one. According to sociologist Claire Renzetti, "One (lesbian) was a diabetic. Her partner never hit her, but forced her to eat sugar. Two women who were disabled reported that their abusers took them to isolated, wooded areas and left them without their wheelchairs."

A teenaged girl is mercilessly taunted about her appearance by her peers; she becomes suicidal. A woman wins a beauty contest and loses her three best friends. A woman wins a major promotion at work. Behind her back, other women say that she is sleeping with the head of the company; this is not true, but the promoted woman feels forever sullied. A female executive treats her female assistants as if they are despised indentured servants—hers to humiliate. A group of female subordinates systematically sabotages their female superior whom they view as too cold, mainly because she is competent and holds them to high standards.

My teenaged interviewee is wired for this subject. She's talking before we even sit down.

"Have you ever seen a waitress rush over to serve a party of boys while a party of girls, who were there first, continue to wait? Or seen a female high school teacher prefer to call on boys and ignore girls' upraised hands, because boys' voices are just so much more noticeable! You ought to see how teenage girls flirt with their male teachers and ignore or verbally denigrate their female teachers."

She doesn't pause for breath.

"Have you ever heard a woman berate and bully her female housekeeper, then become another, nicer person when her guests arrive? Or a saleswoman who, within the same hour, exudes charm toward her male customers, but is irritable, short-tempered, with her female customers?"

Most women shrug these indignities off or minimize them. They do not allow them to enter consciousness.

And I, am I not also guilty of inhumanity toward other woman? Oh, but I am. As the poet Judy Grahn has written, "I have committed indecent acts [toward] women and most of them were acts of omission. I have [allowed] suicidal women to die before my eyes or in my ears or under my hands because I thought I could do nothing."

Have women hurt me? Absolutely. Have I also hurt other women? Absolutely. Did I mean to do so? Probably not. Were my expectations of other women too high? Without doubt.

A friend tells me: "I've also been hurt by women. The fact that I could not hold them accountable for the harm they did was a nightmare. But I still believe that most women are essentially kind."

Gently, she reminds me that people, women especially, need to feel safe.

"Telling women that women cannot be relied on to be good is too frightening a message."

She is right. But she is also wrong. It is irresponsible to tell women that the world is safe when it is not. One must tell women to expect enemy fire down the road and deserters and collaborators within their own ranks. Such information will give women the option of adopting measures of self defense.

I hope this book troubles you. It might also change the way you see things. I must caution you to leave all ideology behind. In a sense, you are about to enter a lesser circle of Hell. I would like you to experience it fully, without denial or despair. Otherwise, you will not yearn enough for change.

I do not want to leave you stunned and without hope. On the one hand, I believe that it will take very little for women to begin to do certain things that will gladden other women's hearts, which will strengthen them. On the other hand, resisting tyranny and conformity, refusing to engage in sexist gossip, slander, and shunning, confronting, or withdrawing from a female bully, are all acts that require enormous courage, self-love, and independence. I believe women can do this. In trying we will also make many mistakes; we will be frustrated repeatedly by our own personal and human limitations.

There are many books that describe women's capacity to mother and care-give in non-violent and generous ways, books about women's morality, interpersonal sensitivity and sophistication, capacity for loyalty to female kin, books about female friendships and supportive working women's networks. This co-existing reality does not contradict what I'm writing about here. Like men, women are complex and diverse, capable of both love and hate, good and evil. Some women behave in very loving ways toward women; some mothers, daughters, sisters, friends, and colleagues have close and supportive relationships; some fail each other totally. Most women probably fall somewhere in the middle.

I am focusing on the shadow side of women's relationships to each other, not on the sunny side. Only a handful of writers have focused on what I bring up here. I am standing on their shoulders—and on the shoulders of many more whose research has also been invaluable.[2]

A peculiar silence surrounds woman's inhumanity to woman. Feminists have mainly remained silent; I have remained silent. Is it simply too painful to remember one's own betrayal at female hands, too difficult to analyze the ways in which women—myself included, collaborate in the undoing of other women; too frightening to face the wrath of women for breaking this particular silence?

This book is shaped by a lifetime of reading and listening to women and by a lifetime of being a woman. I write about my relationship to my own mother and to other women as well; I join my voice to the many other voices here.

This book is neither a feminist treatise nor an attack on First, Second, or Third Wave feminism; it is not an attack on women either. Rather, this is a work about female behavior and its various cultural manifestations. It is an appraisal of the ways in which women, like men, have internalized patriarchal values, and like men are also aggressive, competitive, and envious. This is primarily a psychological and literary work. Its approach is not historical, philosophical, or political.

This book is not for women only. I have yet to meet a man whose wife, girlfriend, sister, daughter, or mother hasn't told him about envy, competition, gossip, and shunning among women, and about the ways in which women deny and silence each other about this.

When I first told friends that I had begun to interview women on this subject, most of them were disapproving. One feminist leader told me that "some of my best friends are women." (Yes, she actually said that.) Another leader said that "I've had a very good relationship with my mother so what you are saying can't be true." Within a decade—it took that long—these same feminists were asking me, repeatedly, where that book of mine was, that they needed it.

The feminists in my generation empowered each other in ways that no one else ever did or could. Many of us believed our own ecstatic rhetoric: we were "sisters." I certainly believed this. I expected so much of other feminists—we all did—that the most ordinary disappointments were often experienced as major betrayals. We expected less of men and forgave them, more than once, when they failed us. We expected far more of other women, who paradoxically had less power to share than men did. We held grudges against other women in ways we dared not do against men. We were not always aware of this.

As feminist women, we knew that we were doomed without sisterhood so we proclaimed it, even in its absence. We wanted to will it into existence, verbally, without wrestling it into being. We didn't understand that the sisterhood we so eagerly proclaimed was, like brotherhood, only an ideal, not yet a reality. We'd have to create sisterhood, daily, against considerable odds, and we'd also have to acknowledge our own sexism as well as our racism, classism, homophobia, etcetera.

Over the years, I have interviewed more than 500 women of all ages, classes, races, sexual persuasions, religions, and professions about this subject. I have also reviewed hundreds, possibly thousands of studies that bear on the subject.

In 1980 I had to explain to women that I wanted them to talk about their inhumanity to each other. By 2000–2001, women were eagerly seeking me out to talk about this. Inexplicably, this tabooed theme has become hot: It's on women's tongues and in the air.

As I listened to women talk, I noted how relieved each one

felt after being able to talk about this subject. I found that I was bearing witness, if only in a small way, to things that had never before been said out loud in a serious voice.

The act of remembering is risky, painful. But once we put something into words or write it down, it doesn't seem as terrible as it may really be, as terrible as we felt it to be at the time. Shame and grief fester in silence. Putting things into words is what makes us human, it is what human beings do.

In the first chapter I explore the anthropological, evolutionary, and psychological research on direct and indirect aggression among women around the world and among female primates. I do not conclude that women are innately or genetically programmed toward aggression. And even if they are, the human enterprise is also about the attempt to resist or transcend our animal natures. I also cite some eerie and interesting parallels between human and primate behavior.

In the second chapter I explore the developmental, cognitive, gender, human aggression, and anthropological research done with children and teenagers in Finland, England, Italy, Poland, Australia, Israel, Japan, and India, and among white girls and girls of color in the United States and Canada.

In the third chapter, I review the research that measures sexism as well as other prejudices, both in the United States and around the world. I also examine more than fifty years of anthropological research on gossip and more recent legal research about jurors.

Like sons, daughters want their mothers' love, approval,

protection, and respect; mothers want the same thing. However, in our time this is often hard to come by. Once, the mother-daughter relationship was the primary social bond; in some ways it still is. Mother-daughter bonding was once the inspiration for sacred rituals of transformation and rebirth. However, mother-blaming has seriously challenged, if not replaced mother-adoration. As an increasing number of daughters strive for new kinds of lives, issues of abandonment, guilt, anger, and regret haunt many mothers and daughters.

We now understand that a mother may verbally, physically, sexually, and psychologically abuse her daughter. She may allow her husband to do so too, and she may eject her victimized daughter, not her violent husband. A "good enough" mother may also humiliate and reject her daughter, treat her coldly, try to break her spirit. Also, in some instances, mothers neglect and sadistically abuse their daughters. In some instances, otherwise good enough mothers also envy and persecute their younger, prettier, talented, and ambitious daughters.

In chapters four, five, and six, I explore fairy tales, myths, and Greek dramatic archetypes, such as the mother-goddess Demeter and her merged daughter Persephone, and Queen Clytemnestra and her matricidal daughter Electra. I do so in order to better understand contemporary mother-daughter relationships and the ways in which they influence adult female-female relationships. I am guided here by the plays of Aeschylus, Sophocles, Euripides, and Eugene O'Neill; the theories of Sigmund Freud, Melanie Klein, Karen Horney, and by

the extraordinary late twentieth-century work of many psychoanalytic theorists and therapists, especially that of British therapist and author Nini Herman.

I also rely upon original interviews, fairy tale scholars, mem-
oirists, and novelists such as Jung Chang, Toi Derricotte,
Daphne du Maurier, Laura Esquivel, Maxine Hong Kingston,
Nancy K. Miller, Toni Morrison, and Alice Walker; literary
critics, poets, and on the autobiographical and biographical
writings of educated and accomplished women. Thus, I quote
from the writings by and about Maria Callas, Camille Claudel,
Jill Ker Conway, Betty Friedan, Charlotte Perkins Gilman,
Vivian Gornick, bell hooks, Doris Lessing, Sylvia Plath, Florence Nightingale, Faith Ringgold, Anne Sexton, Agnes
Smedley, Sojourner Truth, and Edith Wharton, among others.

In chapter seven, I discuss the research on sisters and female
friendships. I again draw upon original interviews, scientific
studies, the biographical writings about "sistered" writing
women such as Jane Austen, Florence Nightingale, and Virginia Woolf, and on the novels of Erica Jong, Judith Rossner,
Jane Smiley, and Amy Tan. Such writings allows us to see that
Asian, African, Hispanic, and white women in America may
have different kinds of mother-daughter and sister-sister relationships.

In chapter eight, I discuss the studies about how women
treat each other in the workplace. I discuss racism and sexism
in corporate, academic, and small business settings. I also draw
upon many interviews and on personal experience. While

women are highly competitive, studies also suggest that women work well together in dyads, in woman-friendly settings, and in ways that recapitulate familial settings. However, many women still have one standard for men in the workplace, another standard for women. Many women still expect women professionals to mother them (hold them to low standards, protect them), rather than to lead them.

In chapter nine, I examine the psychoanalytic and feminist research about women in groups. I rely upon the work of many theorists and therapists, but especially upon that of feminist psychiatrist Teresa Bernardez, psychologist Paula Caplan, psychotherapist Betsy Cohen, and the work of certain feminist theorists and social scientists.

In chapter ten, I discuss whether women in feminist groups have been able to transcend traditional female psychological behaviors. Ideology alone might not be enough to help any human being transcend or resist one's own internalized prejudices. We may each have the most radical or the most humane political or religious philosophy; if we ourselves are not *psychologically* radical and humane, we cannot enact our philosophies.

In addition, I derive some of the lessons to be learned from reading (and from writing) this book. I propose some concrete psychological steps that every woman can take in her daily life that might guide her away from inhumanity toward other women and toward love, compassion, and cooperation. In psychological terms, I would like to see women act generously, not enviously.

I have been working on this book for twenty-one years. I have resisted completing it. I must now let it go. I will miss it. Hopefully others will continue the work I have begun here.

The quiet, daily practice of sisterhood requires kindness, discipline, and self-love. It also requires the capacity to respect, and not violate, another woman's boundaries. Only a woman who maintains her own boundaries can do this. Anti-racist and anti-sexist work requires one to perform daily deeds, not merely to make apocalyptic statements; it is a process, not a dramatic moment.

I would like women to understand that although women love and depend upon each other, we are, collectively, also inhumane, sometimes even cruel and sadistic to each other; and that such cruelty is powerful, painful, and paralyzing. Naming and acknowledging this is the first step to changing it.

Many women tend to choose peace over conflict. This often means accepting the status quo and punishing anyone who dares challenge it. More women also need to choose "justice," which always challenges the status quo and which may be achieved only at considerable cost. Injustice is a given. Ideally, therefore, we must each try to behave in ethical ways in our daily interactions.

It is hard for women to talk about how other women have hurt them and about how they too have mistreated other women. I would like to see women create safe, conversational spaces to do just this, both socially and in the workplace. Focused conversation about this subject is the first step women can take to begin the process of change. Such discussions may be as liberating as the very earliest feminist consciousness raising groups once were.

Cinderella and her Sisters: The Envied and the Envying, by professors Anna and Barry Ulanov, is a psychoanalytic and theological study of envy. The authors note the twentieth century's "endless carnage" and "apparently endless spiral of terrorism," but they also note that people continue to attempt to rescue other people, to do good on earth. "Goodness, finally, comprises the only solace for envy, that same goodness which aroused envy in the first place."

I would like women to treat each other in good ways.

The incomparable French writer Monique Wittig, in *Crossing the Acheron*, presents a Dantean, feminist vision of Hell. Armed and dangerous, Wittig's narrator tours Hell with Manastabal, her angel-guide, her Virgil. She writes:

> Manastabel, my guide, says:
> You showed an absolute lack of morality towards the distressed souls at the central station. I'm guiding you through Hell to the best of my knowledge and keeping your own [soul] in mind. But that gives you no right to crush the souls we encounter with your personal judgement. You can, if you wish, feel delighted over and over again at having deserted and been the runaway slave who ran farther away than anyone else . . . All the same, as long as one has

this privilege it's a poor show if you use it to grind down even further the unfortunate creatures who are deprived of it. For it's a privilege so remarkable that you have to ask forgiveness for possessing it. You can accost the damned souls only with the aim of extricating them from Hell and succeeding in the task at whatever cost. And in doing so you're also working for yourself, for all liberty is precarious and this is the cost of maintaining it.

I hope that my discussion of this subject in no way suggests that I am free or beyond blame, and all other women are enslaved and blame-worthy, for this is not true. To the extent to which I may be more privileged than the next woman, I hope that I have used that privilege in the interests of justice and liberty for us all.

1.

THE ANIMAL WITHIN:

THE FEMALE OF THE SPECIES

Most men are not physically violent. However, the deadliest killers of other human beings on earth are men, not women. Male violence poses a serious threat to human survival and stability. It is, therefore, the recurring, often glorified, subject of literature, cinema, and learned treatises. Because male aggression is both so visible and so deadly, it tends to obscure our view of female violence and aggression, which is more often subtle, less visible, but chronic. Female-female violence has, erroneously, been deemed unimportant because it is unlikely to result in someone's immediate death or serious physical injury.

Male aggression is spectacular, terrifying. Male soldiers enter a village and shoot everyone in sight. Male pilots bomb an entire city from a plane. Male soldiers torture, massacre, and imprison enemy men and systematically rape and gang-rape the enemy's women and children. Individual men dominate others by force and through intimidation. Men, not women, are responsible for ninety percent of the violent crimes in our society. Finally, no more than ten percent of all living men own and control most of the world's resources, thereby condemning all others to lives of poverty and struggle. In comparison, female aggression is barely visible. What can mere women do that is as violent as this?

Women ardently collaborate in the maintenance of this culture. They create homes for such men and socialize children to become—or to marry—similarly successful men. Only the rare woman resists doing so.

British evolutionary psychologist Anne Campbell, who is now affiliated with Durham University, and University of Texas psychologists David H. Buss and Joshua Duntley agree that women sustain and help to reproduce patriarchy, by systematically choosing men with more resources and by "favor[ing] sons over daughters." Buss and Duntley argue that female "co-involvement" was crucial in the creation of patriarchy, since women's evolutionary "preferences [for 'Alpha' mates] thus established an important set of ground rules for men's intrasexual competition." Buss and Duntley contend that "neither men nor women are united with members of their own sex," but, rather, in the main compete with others of their own sex.

Indeed the primary targets of women's aggression, hostility, violence, and cruelty are other women. As most women know, a woman can make life hell, on a moment-by-moment basis, for any other woman whom she envies, fears, or with whom she must compete for resources. For example, older women and all-female cliques tend to bully girls and women into submission; cliques shun any woman whom they view as prettier, smarter, sexually freer, or "different."

Female rivalries tend to support, not disrupt, the status quo. Thus, in order to survive or to improve their own lot, most women, like men, collude in the subordination of women as a class.

In addition to exercising brute economic and physical force, I believe that women *psychologically* tame girls and other women into conformity by threatening to withdraw their considerable capacity for emotional intimacy from any girl or woman whose growth or change of circumstance threatens the status quo. In a sense, women maternally enchant—then terrorize or "turn" upon each other. Fairy tales are fraught with just such Fairy Godmothers and Evil Stepmothers, and should be understood as a history of embattled female relationships and other sudden reversals of blissful, dyadic fortune.

Scientists have only recently begun to study what has been termed "indirect aggression." Female indirect aggression can be very painful psychologically, socially, and economically. Such aggression is both verbal and nonverbal and includes reputation-wrecking gossip and shunning, which may lead to social "death" and, in some cultures, to real death as well.

Because it is so widespread, male aggression is seen as natural; even when it assumes violent and criminal proportions, it is not necessarily regarded as pathological. Most women, on the other hand, do not engage in male-like aggression. When they do, their behavior is deemed unnatural and therefore pathological—even if what a woman has done is kill in order to save her own life. Women who *physically* fight other women—or men—are viewed as having "no class."

Female-female aggression has been less studied, less discussed, and less recognized than male aggression. Perhaps, in a society that values men over women, what women do to each other is simply deemed less important by both men and women. Similarly, in a society that values beige-colored people, what people of other colors do to each other is viewed as less important.

In 1987, University of Western Australia anthropologist Victoria K. Burbank published a study of female aggression in 137 societies: in Asia, India, the Middle East, Africa, Europe, South America, the Caribbean, and among native-Indian tribes in North America. The data she used had been gathered by social scientists over a period of more than a hundred years. Burbank looked only at cases in which women initiated the aggression and where the aggression took place in the context of the home or neighborhood. Burbank found that women engaged in physical, verbal, and indirect aggression "around the world." Women "shriek, scream, scold, revile, and insult their (mainly) female opponents." For example, in 1870 Aymara women were observed "venting their anger" by "kicking apart the clay cooking stoves of their rivals." In 1895 Kashmiri women were described as "famous for their vocabulary of abuse." In 1931 Ona women were observed having "word duels that lasted for several hours." In 1964 a Kapauku woman who was in a dispute with her husband and co-wife was described as "destroying her [rival's] house, uproot[ing] part of the garden, and wreck[ing] the fence." And, in 1974, the data described how a "Ute woman may kill her rival's horse."

Burbank writes that one of the "most striking findings of this survey is that women are by far the most common targets of female aggression. Women are targets in 124, or ninety-one percent of the 137 societies; whereas men are targets (of female aggression) in seventy-four, or fifty-four percent of the 137 societies. Women targeted mainly co-wives, sexual rivals, a wife and 'the other woman,' and women whose relationships are not specified."

Because we do not expect women to be physically aggressive and because both men and women view aggressive behavior in women with great alarm, people tend to view women's aggression as more emotionally and physically out of control than even the deadliest male aggression. To some extent, studies suggest that men are *in control* when they use violence and that women are not. In addition, women will say that they engaged in violence because they *lost control*, not because they used violence to get their way. It is also possible that the out-of-control quality that accompanies women's perceived and experienced outbursts of violence might, according to Campbell, "result either from females' lack of early training in ritualization" or because women are responding to an impetus so strong that it "overcomes their reluctance to engage in physical aggression."

Robin Fox, a professor of Social Theory at Rutgers University, quotes the late, great anthropologist Margaret Mead: "It was a good thing that wars were in the hands of men since, although they were very good at starting them, they were equally adept at knowing how to bring them to an end." According to Fox, Mead thought this was true "because war was always at bottom a status game for men, and men had an inbuilt capacity for ritualizing such games." Women, on the other hand, "would take war far too seriously. They would see it as protecting their children and nothing but a total fight to the death would satisfy them."

Although Mead may have a point, she is also missing something important. Consider what the historical and anthropological record has to tell us about the cruelty, for example, of mothers-in-law toward daughters-in-law in classical Japan, China, and India. In Fox's words, as a rule, the younger women

> came under the strict and punitive rule of their mothers-in-law. [They endured] aggression in the form of constant harassment, abuse, and beatings, [which] was used to "train" these unfortunate girls in the ways of their new households. A girl could only hope to have sons quickly to improve her status and eventually put her in the "mother-in-law" position where she could herself become the aggressor.

According to New York anthropologist Ilsa Glazer, family life was torturous for women in China:

In order to save money, parents who gave up daughters for adoption adopted female infants to replace them. For the same cost of rearing a girl, the adopted daughter could later be married to their son, saving the cost of a wedding. Mothers and adopted daughters conflicted, for it was in the mother's interest to get the maximum work out of her adopted daughter at the least possible cost. Adopted daughters could be sold if need be. Adopted daughters and natural born sisters were "natural enemies." Higher in status, natural daughters commanded the labor power and obedience of adopted daughters. Beatings of younger women by older women were common. Mothers beat daughters-in-law, daughters, and adopted daughters. Slaves were safe targets for women who vented on them the aggression they dared not express in other relationships. Women in weak positions expressed their aggression in violent temper tantrums, by withdrawing labor, or by complaining to women from other households.

A new bride might be more compliant than an older wife or sister-in-law. They vied for their mother-in-law's approval and for property for their own sons. They were, in Glazer's words, "natural enemies." In addition,

mothers-in-law had rights to the labor of daughters-in-law and to their obedience. Since widows were not permitted to remarry, and since daughters-in-law could be sold or pawned, mothers-in-law and daughters-in-law were also "natural enemies."

Today, in India, young brides are sometimes doused with kerosene and set on fire. Mothers-in-law are often involved. In December of the year 2000, one young Indian wife described being repeatedly beaten by both her husband and her mother-in-law for minor infractions. One day, after she had completed all but one of her non-stop, back-breaking chores, her husband flew into a rage over the single chore left undone.

"I had done everything except this," she said. "But he was angry with me. He said I was lazy. He said if he could get another wife, she would do everything." That afternoon, as she walked toward the kitchen, she said, she felt something splash on her back. Then she burst into flames. When she turned around, she saw her mother-in-law holding a kerosene can and her husband with a matchbox.

In addition to such mother-in-law violence toward a daughter-in-law, Burbank notes that "women aggress against their co-wives verbally in twenty-nine percent of the societies and physically in eighteen percent of the societies. Sisters-in-law also "aggress against one another in fourteen percent of the societies; mothers-in law and daughters-in-law are an aggressive dyad in twelve percent of the societies." Interestingly, sisters who are co-wives sometimes live under one roof with relatively little aggression, but co-wives who have not been thus socialized to get along with each other from childhood on, tend to live separately. Even so, "at least twenty percent of the cases of co-wife aggression may be between 'sisters.' "

Clearly—given Burbank's statistics and the examples cited from Japan, China, and India—the cause of women's discontent is not alleviated, and thus chronic frustration and chronic irritability remain. No male-style ritualized ending is possible because no resolution of the problem is possible. The co-wife has come to stay; the sexual rival is preferred; one's own children—and oneself—may sink ever further into poverty, danger, illness, death.

Pulitzer-Prize-winning science writer Natalie Angier does not view women as innocent victims. She writes:

They have complied with customs that control female sexuality, such as infibulation, purdah, and claustration, and they have insisted that their daughters comply as well. They may even be the active agents of such customs.

In Ilsa Glazer's view,

The more subordinate women are to men and the

more dependent they are on patriarchal social struc-
tures, the more injury they inflict on each other.

Whether female-female cruelty is caused by female opportunism or by female captivity, the harm done is real. Often
women are also aggressive in indirect ways.

Indirect (nonphysical) aggression may take many forms. A
woman may refuse to return your smile or to talk to you at all;
this can be quite unnerving to another woman. Or she may bang
the plate down on the table, stalk out of the room, or complain
about you to others behind your back. Indirect aggression is
often "up close and personal." It may be accompanied by a smile
and by earnest denials that one has intended to harm anyone.
Included here are the most hair-raising power struggles
between mothers and daughters and between sisters, as well as
intense competition for a mate among female intimates. Of
course, such competition also takes place between female
strangers.

Some feminists have insisted that women are prisoners of
men or of a patriarchal system and are, therefore, unable to
resist its values and demands. Others, feminists included, have
insisted that both women and men have free will and, as such,
are responsible for their actions, even if they are forced to
engage in an unending war for survival against all others. Thus,
although it is true that women do have many things in
common with others of their gender, this does not mean that
most women are altruistic "sisters." Like men, women belong

to different, often warring classes, races, religions, or political parties. Most women do not identify with or feel compassion for all other women.

Shirley Abbott, the former editor of *Horizon* magazine and an Arkansas native, reviewed two centuries of African-American slave testimonies. She notes that some slaves speak of their white mistresses as "good" or as "merciful Christian women." However, Abbott writes, as a group "White mistresses were demanding, harsh, impatient, capricious, and quick to call for the laying on of the lash. Some were even sadists, with no redeeming qualities."

The writer Alice Walker describes an incident in the 1930s, in which her mother, an impoverished sharecropper in a small Georgia town, walked into town, wearing a used, donated dress and bearing a voucher to obtain food and flour from the Red Cross. When Walker's mother presented her voucher "she was confronted by a white woman who looked her up and down with marked anger and envy."

> "What's you come up here for?" the woman asked.
>
> "For some flour," said my mother, presenting her voucher.
>
> "Humph," said the woman, looking at her more closely and with unconcealed fury. "Anybody dressed up as good as you don't need to come here *begging* for food . . . the *gall* of niggers coming in here dressed better than me!"

Delia Aguilar, a professor of Ethnic Studies and Women's Studies at Bowling Green State University in Ohio, describes her experience teaching feminism to Asian-Pacific women in the Philippines. Initially—and to her consternation—her students proudly espoused a Second Wave, Western, "essentialist" vision of global sisterhood. Aguilar had to remind her students that they were not academic Western women, that they faced other realities which included

> Massive [Asian] rural to urban migration, ever-increasing poverty and homelessness, militarization, dominance of multinationals, [and] external debt, migration overseas as domestics, or . . . staying home to do backbreaking labor . . . low-paid employment on the assembly line; [becoming] mail-order brides or working in the "entertainment industry."

Thereafter, when Aguilar's students identified themselves as feminists, the "tone was not celebratory." They understood that feminist ideology did not change the fact that some women are more privileged than others.

These are only three examples of interpersonal cruelties and structural difference between women who belong to different classes, races, and geographical regions. Where can we find examples of woman's inhumanity to woman within the same race, class, and country? Just about everywhere. Instances abound in our most beloved novels and poems, in countless studies, even in popular plays, musicals, and operas. We rarely notice them. They do not register.

For example, most readers of Nathaniel Hawthorne's *The Scarlet Letter* remember it as being about sexual immorality and hypocrisy among eighteenth-century Puritan Americans. Hawthorne's fictional hero, Hester Prynne, has been tried for the crime of having a child out of wedlock. The male magistrates sentence Prynne to wear a scarlet letter upon her breast. The women in the novel, however, feel that the sentence is too lenient.

"'Goodwives,' said a hard-featured dame of fifty, 'If the hussy stood up for judgement before us would she come off with such a sentence? Marry, I trow not.'" Hawthorne's women feel that the men have been too "merciful." One woman thinks the men should "at the very least [have] put the brand of a hot iron on [her] forehead." Another woman calls for Prynne's death. Hawthorne presents these "dames of elevated rank" as "ugly" and therefore "jealous" of Prynne's beauty and nobility: Prynne refuses to disclose the name of her child's father, a clergyman. Although the women employ Prynne "for her expert sewing," they continue to shun and torment her.

These women are not cruel to Prynne because they fear they will be punished, collectively, for one woman's sin: Prynne alone has already been tried and sentenced. These women are in their fifties; thus they are no longer competing with a much younger Prynne for a mate. Perhaps the women are unhappy and mistakenly assume that Prynne has stolen their happiness;

perhaps they suffer from excessive envy and are using whatever little power they have to inflict pain on a vulnerable innocent. Their cruelty is gratuitous; it does not lessen over time, nor is it ever sated. Prynne's female employers

> were accustomed to distill drops of bitterness into [Prynne's] heart; sometimes through that alchemy of quiet malice, by which women can concoct a subtle poison from ordinary trifles; and sometimes, also, by a coarser expression, that fell upon the sufferer's defenseless breast [like] a rough blow upon an ulcerated wound.

Jane Austen and, in this century, Margaret Atwood have also portrayed the ways in which polite women of the same class and race can destroy each other's reputations and peace of mind, and exploit other women as reproductive and domestic handmaids.

In the essay, "Eye to Eye: Black Women, Hatred, and Anger," the writer Audre Lorde discusses internalized self-hatred and "horizontal hostility" among black women. Lorde is haunted by a black woman library clerk who once kept her waiting, who refused to recognize her. "Otherwise motionless," Lorde writes,

> [the clerk] slowly turns her head and looks up. Her eyes cross mine with such a look of incidental hostility that I feel pilloried to the wall . . . What makes

her eyes slide off of mine? What does she see that angers her so, or infuriates her, or disgusts her? Why do I want to break her face off when her eyes do not meet mine? Why does she wear my sister's face?

The third-generation Japanese-American poet, Janice Mirikitani, describes certain "walls of silence" that limit sympathy between mother and daughter. In "Breaking Tradition," she writes: "My daughter denies she is like me/her secretive eyes avoid mine. I deny I am like my mother." Mirikitani's mother's "defiance [was] smothered," her "passion and loudness wrapped in an obi/her steps confined to ceremony." Mirikitani, the daughter, wants to "break tradition" by inviting *her* daughter into "this room of myself/filled with tears . . . sounds shaken from barbed wire./My daughter denies she is like me/Her secretive eyes are walls of smoke/I do not know the contents of her room . . ."

The popular American opera *Susannah* by composer Carlyle Floyd is based upon the tale of Susannah and the Elders, which is contained in the Biblical *Apocrypha.* Floyd sets his story in the nineteenth-century American South. Susannah's crime? She is young and beautiful. And, since her parents are dead, she is also vulnerable to cruelty. Susannah arouses enormous envy and hatred among the other white women of the town. One townswoman sings: "That pretty a face must hide some evil . . . she'll come to no good." Floyd's chorus of women condemn Susannah to poverty and, ultimately, to madness and prostitution, first, by taking away her babysitting job and second, by shunning her. "You are not welcome here," the women tell her.

Perhaps, plain, unhappy women form groups against pretty or happy women in order to minimize the disadvantage they might otherwise experience in the competition for mates or resources.

According to Indiana sociologist Donna Eder and educational researcher David A. Kinney, white, midwestern teenage girls are attracted to popular and attractive female cheerleaders; they want them as friends for status reasons. However, non-cheerleader teens also resent cheerleaders and view them as stuck up and unfriendly. (The cheerleaders can't "befriend" everyone.) Thus, paradoxically, girls tend not to bond with the cheerleaders in their school.

Girls and women genuinely want to bond with each other; they want each other's intimate companionship and the pleasure and protection it may afford them. Therefore, girls and women tend to deny that they are *also* secretly competitive, envious, and hostile toward other girls and women, including female kin and best friends. After all, (middle-class) girls and woman have been taught that such feelings and behaviors are neither "nice" nor "ladylike" and will lead to their being rejected by other girls and women. Although many women "get even" with other women "behind their backs," most women will not readily admit, even to themselves, that they have behaved badly, nor do they relish being caught in the act or held accountable for it.

Perhaps Simon Fraser University psychologists Marc A. Johnston and Charles B. Crawford are right when they say: "Females may benefit by downplaying their aggressive nature because they will be perceived as more valuable mates and because they will be more accepted within female social groups."

Like men, women are only part angel; another part is pure animal. And, according to primatologists, evolutionary theorists, and comparative psychologists, while it is true that female primates are not as visibly deadly as their male counterparts, female-female aggression among primates is more common and more violent than previously assumed. Let us review some of the research.

For years, female-female aggression among primates was ignored or minimized. According to the anthropologist Sarah Blaffer Hrdy, this occurred partly because male-male competition was even more "startling and overt," but also because "persistent conflicts between females are often more subtle . . . [the] competition is indirect. Two animals who are not even touching or looking at one another may nevertheless be in competition if one of them occupies a place or consumes a resource that would benefit the other." According to Hrdy, "the central organizing principle of primate social life is competition between females and especially female lineages." On the other hand, the core social units among primates are the mother-daughter dyad and the matriline.

According to Anne Campbell's 1999 review of the literature

on aggression, chimpanzees have a "strong mother-child dyad," in which mothers spend about "60% of (their) time foraging for food alone with their infants." In her view, mothers do not "form strong bonds with other adult females and rarely support each other." Frans de Waal, a comparative psychologist and Director of the Yerkes' Living Links Center at Emory University in Atlanta, writes that primate "female hierarchy is rather vague." He notes, however, that some (bonobo) chimpanzees do "form close affiliative bonds with low rates of aggression."

According to Natalie Angier, "females are drawn to other females for strength. The females may be related or they may not be . . . the recurring theme is one of coalition and desire, of an aggressive need for female alliance." Recent research suggests however, that even where females create alliances or, in Angier's words, a "coalition of desire," hierarchy, upheavals, and intra-sex aggression still prevail.

Enormous variation exists among primates. Ongoing methodological problems also exist. Still, most scientists would agree that a female primate must fend off male infanticidal aggression. She does so by mating not only with the alpha male of her own troop but also (secretly) with stranger and low-ranking males who might avoid killing her infant if they remember mating with her. In addition, a female primate will forge alliances with other females against violent males. According to Michigan primatologist Barbara Smuts, female chacma baboons, olive baboons, blue monkeys, vervet monkeys, patas monkeys, and pigtailed macaques

have all been observed to join forces in order to protect themselves from aggressive, especially infanticidal, males.

According to Carole Jahme, the British primatologist and
the author of *Beauty and the Beasts: Woman, Ape and Evolution*,
the bonobo was originally known as a "pygmy chimpanzee."
That term is no longer in use. A bonobo is very different from
a chimpanzee. Some believe that the bonobo is the "closest
living representative of our earliest known ape-hominid
ancestor." In Jahme's words, the bonobo is also

> known as the "make love not war" ape because sex is
> used by bonobos as a substitute for aggression.
> When things get tense between males, they stop
> themselves before things get really nasty and they
> rub their penises together . . . the females have les-
> bian sex, known as genito-genital rubbing, or GG
> rubbing . . . When an adolescent female bonobo
> tries to ingratiate herself into a new group of
> bonobos, she looks for a senior female and tries to
> become her friend. She sits on the periphery of
> things for a while and sizes up who is who in the
> hierarchy. The young female bonobo then tries to
> cement a bond with a high-status older female by
> engaging in homo-erotic acts with her.

Welcomed newcomers are assured of getting "enough
high-calorie food to eat," which will "enable them to start to

cycle, gestate and lactate." Their "lives and their babies' lives depend on having older, influential female friends. It is the powerful force of female bonding in bonobos that prevents (male-perpetrated) infanticide from occurring in this species." Female bonobos form coalitions and support each other. Fights tend to be settled between individuals; no one takes sides, although "mothers are observed supporting their sons in conflicts." Female bonobos will also "gang up and attack lone (violent) males."

According to Jahme, bonobos "openly share food, whereas chimps do not . . . If a male bonobo has found some prized fruit, a young female will encourage him to give it to her in exchange for sex, an offer he cannot refuse."

What makes the cooperating female bonobos fascinating is that they are usually not blood-sisters, but have "evolved a cultural solution to help them through isolation from their kin." Interestingly, an adult *male* bonobo will remain close to his mother throughout her life. Sons, not daughters, babysit or parent their younger siblings. In return, their mothers pass on the incoming, newcomer females to their sons.

But a non-bonobo female primate cannot trust her female allies; even her own mother may turn on her. For example, despite the importance of mother-daughter bonding, if the mother is still breeding when more than one daughter becomes sexually mature, the mother will harass and eject that second daughter as a breeding-competitor. Although female primates tend to "affiliate" more loosely than male primates, they do create dominance hierarchies in which dominant, breeding, females inhibit reproduction in subordinate "helper" females. Among primates, female dominance hierarchies consist of groups of female relatives who support each other against more distant relatives and in which one female matriline supports its members against other matrilines. In a sense, female-female bonding exists because of female-female competition.

University of Minnesota primatologists Anne Pusey and Jennifer Williams, and legendary primatologist Jane Goodall reviewed the data gathered from a thirty-five-year study of chimpanzees. They found that higher-ranking female primates had "significantly higher infant survival, faster maturing daughters, and more rapid production of young." Whether this is due to a reduction in aggression-related stress or to gaining access to better foraging areas, remains unknown.

Harvard University professor of Biological Anthropology Richard Wrangham notes that "in extreme circumstances, female primates can compete as intensively as males." He observes that "captive females" tend to use "male-like behaviorial strategies to gain rank, including opportunistic coalitions and frequent reconciliations." Wrangham is talking about captive primates, not captive women, but perhaps his distinction might apply to human behavior as well.

Free-lance writer Duncan Anderson, in a *Science* magazine article, "The Delicate Sex: How Females Threaten, Starve, and

Abuse One Another," agrees that "most fatal violence in primates is the work of males." But female-female violence among
primates constitutes a close second. Anderson, Hrdy, and
Smuts all note that females of many species—macaques, chimpanzees, baboons, gorillas, langurs, monkeys, marmosets,
tamarins, gelada baboons, sacanna baboons, and talapoin
monkeys—are known to sabotage each other's reproductive
cycles. Female-female aggression (starving, abusing) causes
spontaneous abortions. Hrdy notes that dominant, higher-
ranking female primates overtly harass subordinate females.
Such behaviors are "implicated in delays in maturation, inhibi-
tion of ovulation, or in extreme cases, spontaneous abortion by
subordinates."

Jim Moore, a professor of Anthropology at the University of
California, San Diego, also notes the rivalry between mothers
and non-mothers among female langurs. Non-mothers will
purposefully find and sexually entice a roving bachelor alpha
male to take over their troop, so that he can kill the current
alpha male, and also all pre-existing infants. Thus such a
female langur will effectively "eliminate the infants that would
compete for food with *her* future infants." Samuel K. Wasser,
zoologist, and specialist in obstetrics and gynecology at the
University of Washington, suggests that, since resources are
always scarce,

> . . . maybe mid-ranking females [try] to keep lower
> ranking females from having offspring that would

compete with their own . . . It's often called "aunting behavior." The term is awful. Some of the infant handling is nasty. It's a type of competition. They're picking kids up, dropping them on their heads. Stepping on them. One mother had her kid handled forty times in an hour, by maybe thirty different animals. It died of exposure within two months. I even have cases of female infanticide. One mother picked up another's infant and simply bit it in the head . . . Among baboons, when six or more females are in heat, things get real nasty.

British ecologist Josephine Andrews, now affiliated with the anthropology department at Washington University, reports a case of primate infanticide by a female black lemur in Madagascar. She found that, after an attack by dogs and the subsequent death of the leading female, a fight ensued between two adult females neither of whom was "dominant." As they fought, one female suddenly picked up the other female's infant and "ran back up the mango tree with the screaming infant, shaking it violently from side to side in her mouth, smashing the rib cage, and then held the body while eating some of the entrails." The mother of the dead infant became silent and, although she sat watching the body, she did not ascend the tree to investigate. For the next few days, the female who had lost her infant sat apart from the rest of the group. She did not eat with the others, but waited until they had moved away before feeding. From then on, the killer of the baby lemur and her infant led the troop. The mother of the dead baby trailed some distance behind them.

Many scientists have hypothesized that such infant abuse and infanticide by female primates may be related to female-female competition to attain or reinforce dominance within a troop or is due to direct competition for scarce food resources. In the case of the black lemur infant killing, Andrews notes that the killer thereafter appeared to become dominant over the mother of the dead baby.

According to Allison Jolly, who is affiliated with Princeton's department of Ecology and Evolutionary Biology, although female lemurs "may be assemblages of mother-daughter dyads," they are "capable of high aggression towards other females." Jolly notes that adult females disperse young females by targeting them for aggression and ultimate expulsion. In three studies, which observed troops over a decade, when the second daughter of a dominant female matured, the "dominant female targeted her, and aggression escalated from July until the nulliparious female emigrated in September."

Among ringtails, females have "more aggressive encounters than males. 'Matrilines' can effectively eliminate other 'matrilines.' Female lemurs engage in systematic campaigns against each other." According to Jolly, the "outcome is sometimes wounding, expulsion from the troop, and in extreme cases, death. Female hierarchies are often circular and can be upset from year to year as females attack each other."

According to Hrdy, certain female primates (gorilla and hamadryas baboons) do bond in order to fend off male sexual and physical attacks. However, since infant care is quite labor-intensive, biological mothers also try to enlist other subordinate females in caring for their infants by destroying the subordinate's capacity to mate or to bear infants of her own. Thus, some female primates will sometimes fight *for* each other, but, more often, females fight *against* each other: mother against daughter, higher-ranking female against lower-ranking female, one troop of females against another troop of females. They fight over food, infants, sex, and position in the hierarchy. As female primates jockey for position, they hit, push, pinch, shove, and make faces at each other.

Wendy Saltzman, a primatologist of the Wisconsin Regional Primate Research Center, showed that "if a young female common marmoset responds aggressively to a same sex intruder, this predicts whether she will gain a breeding position in a peer group." University of Wisconsin psychologists Charles T. Snowden and Jennifer J. Pickhard confirm that, although there is more male than female aggression among the cotton-top tamarins, most "aggression [is] between same-sex individuals." They also confirm that "aggressive behavior increases between parents and offspring as helpers seek to become breeders." In Snowden and Pickhard's review of the literature, they suggest that male primate victims of same-sex aggression and ejection from a troop seem to enjoy higher survival rates than those of their female counterparts. (We will discuss what the consequences of being shunned are, in human terms, for girls and women, in the next two chapters.)

Thus, the disadvantage of being a subordinate within an all-female hierarchy may mean that lower-ranking females will never become mothers and will remain perpetual mother's helpers. According to Jahme:

> Marmoset and tamarin monkey groups usually only have one dominant breeding female during the breeding season. The other members of the group help to care for the babies, often twins, that the dominant female produces, the males carrying her babies and subordinate females, possibly aunts, helping to suckle the twins.

In a study of Cebus capucinus primates, University of California anthropologist Joseph H. Manson, Washington University anthropologist Lisa M. Rose, UCLA anthropologist Susan Perry, and University of Pennsylvania psychologist Julie Gros-Louis found that the females bonded and created stable coalitions or genetic and nepotistic alliances. However, "individual competitive ability also affects female dominance rank," and dominance reversals may occur when female-female aggression is intense. Where female bonding and hierarchy remain stable, the dominant females are groomed and supported. Such hierarchical alliances are subject, however, to sudden changes as a function of food distribution, stress, and upheaval of any kind.

According to Jolly, female lemurs regularly kill each others' infants. During intertroop conflicts, or targeting campaigns chases ensue; in terrified flight, a mother may drop her infant. "When an infant is dropped, all females crowd around the peeping infant. If the mother reaches the infant, it almost clings at once to her fur. However, if the mother is subordinate, she may be repeatedly chased away by the dominants within her troop."

Interestingly, Jolly notes that "reconciliation after conflict apparently does not occur" and that, although female lemurs tend to fight alone, they also engage in a subtle "glancing back and forth (in order) to recruit a hesitating ally" in a joint attack. (We will discuss similar behavior among girls and teenagers in the next chapter.)

Although, in many primate species, the females, including mothers and daughters, do cooperate with each other, they also compete with each other in subtle, ambiguous ways. "They cooperate selfishly, and there is a perpetual undercurrent of competition." According to Hrdy, "Infant sharing, with all its complexities, provides a striking illustration of the fine line between cooperation and exploitation, between a female helping a relative in her troop and one helping herself at a relative's expense."

This reads like a fairy tale or a Gothic romance about a spinster aunt or a captive governess.

More extreme anecdotes of female primate infanticide exist. Dian Fossey observed how a dominant female gorilla and her adult daughter, cannibalistically and secretly, fed on the offspring of a lower-ranking female. Jane Goodall described how a dominant chimpanzee female and her adult daughter kidnapped, killed, and cannibalized almost all the infants born to the troop within a three-year period. In the words of Reijo Holmström, an amateur biologist and psychoanalytic-developmental theorist associated with the Department of Psychology at Turku University in Finland, "When the abduction had been successful and feeding on the victim had begun, the victorious female might consolingly touch the deprived mother sitting next to her."

Nice touch.

In an article entitled "Female Aggression among the Great Apes: A Psychoanalytic Perspective," Holmström suggests that the cannibalizing primate might be the progenitor of the "wicked child-eating witch folktales."

Goodall also describes a reign of terror conducted by a "masculine" top-ranked chimpanzee female named Gigi and her partner, Passion, who was her second in command. Together, they completely destroyed a daughter group that had left the troop. On her own, Passion systematically destroyed the offspring of lower-ranking females.

Perhaps these are strange and uncommon occurrences; perhaps they are extreme examples of female-female competition among primates. Perhaps such behaviors are "adaptive." According to Jahme,

Jane Goodall once thought that chimpanzee Passion's infanticidal behaviour was psychotic, but now suspects that Passion's murderous behaviour towards lower-ranking Gilka's babies might not have been pathological, as she first thought, but adaptive. In committing infanticide, high-ranking females reinforce their social rank, killing their infants' competitors and having a meal of fresh meat in one fell swoop. Goodall has seen a number of female chimps behave this way, including Flo's daughter Fifi, observed trying to snatch a baby chimp away from its middle-ranking mother.

Deborah J. Curtis, associated with Zurich University's Anthropological Institute, and Alphonse Zaramody of Mahajanga University's Earth Sciences Department in Madagascar, confirm that "mate monopolization" or "monogamy" among mongoz lemurs exists—but that it seems "more attributable to females, as only [females] exhibit high levels of intrasexual aggression." They note that paternal care of infants was "fairly extensive."

I am neither a primatologist nor an evolutionary theorist, but I cannot let such a tempting observation go by without wondering whether Curtis and Zaramody are, perhaps, suggesting that mongoz lemur females prefer monogamy because it is correlated with male childcare and male protection against both aggressive and infanticidal males and females. If so, this may put an entirely different spin on both the origins and the intentionality of patriarchy.

Curtis and Zaramody published their findings in 1997. Earlier, in 1990, Jane Goodall published her observations about the infanticidal-cannibalistic reign of the chimpanzees Passion and her daughter Pom. Goodall's observations, albeit of only one mother-daughter pair in one troop, also lend some credence to the possibility that the female of the species might have had good reason to initiate or welcome bonding with males for the protection it might afford them and their infants from other females, as well as from murderous stranger-males. According to Goodall, although male chimpanzees will kill infants, they almost never do so in order to eat them. Only certain infanticidal females do.

Goodall observed Passion and Pom devouring the carcass of the infant they'd abducted and killed "slowly and with relish . . . the way normal prey is consumed." The only protection that one mother, Gilka, had was male protection. After having her first infant snatched, killed, and eaten, Gilka gave birth a second time. As Passion approached, staring at Gilka's new infant, Gilka "began to scream loudly, looking back and forth from Passion to the two males. As though they understood what was going on, the males charged over and, one after the other, attacked Passion."

Over time, the unfortunate Gilka would lose three infants to this mother-daughter team; Melissa also lost an infant to them. When Melissa had a second infant, Goodall observed how "she managed to keep close to one of the big males almost all the time." Once Goodall observed Pom making a silent approach. Melissa saw her, "instantly began to scream, loudly and urgently and hurried to sit close to Satan. With one hand laid on the big male's shoulders, Melissa turned and barked her defiance at the younger female."

Why the infanticide and cannibalism? Goodall offers no blanket theory; she merely notes that "after Passion became pregnant herself, the killings stopped and then Pom also became pregnant and was no longer prepared to cooperate with her mother."

Is such behavior due to aberrant, experimenter-induced feeding patterns? Or is this simply an example of how a top-ranking primate female manages to reserve more resources for herself and her children (and future children) by killing infant-competitors in her own troop?

Carole Jahme reminds us that Passion was herself badly beaten by a male chimpanzee, the second-ranked Evered. This brutality was Evered's "reproductive strategy. Through fear he was able to monopolize [Passion's] body during ovulation and later was sure that her baby was his." Evered followed the same strategy with another female. Jahme wonders whether the male brutalizing of females "encourages the females to bully" and further, whether "Passion's beatings could have encouraged her to beat Evered's sister (Gilka) and kill her babies later on."

Some might say that resemblances between primates and human beings must be viewed as poetic metaphor, if for no reason other than that there are many different primate pasts to claim and no certainty about who, precisely, our antecedents are.

And yet, some kind of evolutionary or genetic similarity

between primates and humans does seem to exist. Female primates and female humans may both be genetically predisposed to compete against and dominate other females in order to suppress, severely, the next female's desirability, fertility, live-birth rate. We have seen how primates accomplish this. In a sense, humans do likewise. Advantages of class, caste, race, and geography function in similar ways. For example, I have seen women fight over the same mate or for the same child in truly primal or primate-like ways. As a therapist and expert witness, I have seen post-menopausal mothers sue their own daughters for custody of a grandchild—think of the sensational Gloria Vanderbilt case—and infertile second wives take full charge of the brainwashing and legal campaigns designed to win their new husband's brood (and paycheck) away from a first wife. I have seen adoptive mothers engage in the fiercest of fights against birthmothers who have changed their minds about surrendering children for adoption.

In a sense, bonobos resemble female humans (or vice versa if you will). Both leave their matrilineal homes; both must try to please the highest ranking women, who have always lived in Prince Charming's castle. Uncanny resonances linger on. I have seen human newcomer girls and women who behaved like bonobos entering an established all-female group, in terms of their "grooming upwards" and jockeying for position.

In some ways, human beings resemble flesh-eating, war-waging, female-harassing chimpanzees; in other ways, human beings resemble vegetarian, female-bonded upward-grooming bonobos. In any case, human beings parted company from our primate ancestors more than six million years ago. In those years, in Natalie Angier's view, male humans (unlike male primates) learned to bond brilliantly with each other, and female humans learned to rely on male, not female, protectors. This, Angier believes, is what constituted the patriarchal "revolution."

It is in light of such overwhelming (and interesting) research that Anne Campbell questions the myth of the "coy female" and the myth of the "nonaggressive woman." Campbell writes:

> It is ironic that some of these myths have been supported by the feminist movement, which has tried to insist that women's aggression is exclusively a response to male violence. The idea that females could have survived without the motivation and ability to compete for scarce resources is, from an evolutionary viewpoint, untenable. Nonetheless, it is a viewpoint that is congenial to the continuance of male protection and control over women.

It should come as a relief to all those feminists who demanded that I not write this book that a cursory reading of the primate studies suggests that women are not evil or mad, but may, in fact, simply be "hard-wired" for aggression toward other women. To the extent to which a human being has the capacity to resist or transform our genetic and evolutionary predispositions, women have the same capacity as men. No more, no less.

Just as scientists have readjusted their views of female-female aggression among primates, so too, they have refined their views of female-female aggression among human children and adults. According to Finnish psychologist Kaj Björkqvist, there is no *logical* reason to assume "that females should be less hostile and less prone to get into conflicts than males." Depending on age, economic class, stress, and tribal custom, girls and women will physically and verbally assault each other. In fact, according to Björkqvist, "with respect to interpersonal aggression, same-sex encounters are more frequent than between-sex encounters."

We may remember that anthropologist Victoria Burbank found female "acts of physical aggression, [which ranged] from slaps to murder, in sixty-one percent of the societies." In physical attacks, world wide, women "pinch, scratch, beat with their fists, pull hair, bite, and rip pierced ears. They throw stones, fight with digging sticks, clubs, knives, awls, spears, and knuckle dusters. Some women attack each other with their hands, and nails, and with cactus thorns tied to their wrists." Women also wrestle, kick, and punch. To a lesser extent, women also use "blunt weapons" and "deadly weapons" against other women. Horrifying as all this may sound, women, in comparison to men, inflict relatively minor physical injuries on one another.

In addition to direct, physical aggression, Burbank found verbal aggression in eighty-two percent of the societies. Most often, women "insult, ridicule, or quarrel with other people." According to New York anthropologist Ilsa Glazer Schuster, "educated women in Zambia and in pre- and post-revolutionary China, threaten their rivals over the telephone; poor women bite off pieces of ears and lips or attack with broken bottles." Schuster points out that, for the poor woman, her very survival is at stake.

Today, women participate in and support dowry burnings in India, female genital mutilation in Africa, and, as we shall see, female honor killings in Islamic countries. In addition, jealous wives in Cambodia have increasingly attacked their husbands' young—usually poor—mistresses with acid. One victim of such an attack said, "I have the soul of a dead woman now. My body is alive, but my soul is dead." Wives throw the acid both to disfigure and to torture the mistress for life. The philandering Cambodian husbands are never attacked, nor are their higher-ranking wives punished for their crimes.

Contemporary girls and women also fight each other physically. For example, according to University of Arizona anthropologist Laura L. Cummings, the stereotype of the "passive Mexican and Hispanic woman is both inaccurate and misleading." Cummings studied Mexican female teenage street-fighting gang members in Chihuahua, Chihuahua, Mexico. She found that ritualized fighting exists among girls as well as boys. Although girls tend to fight physically only against other girls, Cummings also found instances in which female gang members will come to the aid of a male gang member who is outnumbered by a rival, male gang and instances in which female gang members will physically prevent one of their own female members from being abducted by a gang of boys.

In Los Angeles, dubbed "the gang capital of the world," Pennsylvania State University educational researcher Mary G. Harris found that Mexican-American girls are accepted into all-girl gangs only if they are able and willing to fight verbally and physically ("take care of business . . . back up their shit"). Girls who want to be protected by a gang but who can't "hold up the hood" are rejected. Harris found that most female gang members had been raped both at home and on the streets, carried weapons, were into serious drug abuse, and had turned to other girls for protection, for the chance to fight back, express anger, and to belong.

Anthropologist Kimberly H. B. Cook studied women in Venezuela. Fighting takes place there in public and is both verbal and physical. According to one informant:

> Women in Margarita are "guapa." When we fight, we punch and tear each other's hair. A long time ago, I had a fight with a woman. I chased her all around the ranchero. When I caught her, I grabbed her by the hair and pushed her face into the mud. She was screaming, but I wouldn't let go. I was stronger and I laughed. She didn't talk to me for years afterwards, but later we became friends again.

Contemporary adult women, in urban public places, also behave in physically aggressive ways. Like men, women sometimes push and shove each other. However, while doing so, unlike men, women tend not to make eye contact with each other.

Florida's Eckerd College anthropologists Nicole J. Hines and Douglas P. Fry studied male and female modes of aggression in Argentina. Hines and Fry describe a street scene in Buenos Aires—the likes of which I have personally observed (and experienced), in bus and airport terminals all over the world.

In the Hines study, "women pushed and shoved each other as they boarded crowded buses, but without making verbal or eye contact with each other." I have seen Caucasian women "accidentally" bumping into each other in airport bathrooms, as if they were off balance or unclear about personal space boundaries. They act as if they do not know where they end and where some other woman starts.

Once, Hines was doing her aerobic workout in Buenos Aires when another woman purposefully placed her exercise step so close that it interfered with Hines' routine. The Argentinian woman neither spoke nor made eye contact with Hines. Even when Hines said, "I'll just move where there is space," the woman made no comment of any kind—which Hines believes is illustrative of how Argentine women can behave aggressively without acknowledging that they are doing so. Although uncomfortable or even frightening, this is fairly harmless physical aggression among women. Even when women are *crimi-*

nally violent, they tend to be violent toward other women, not toward men.

In 1999, British researcher M. J. George found that young, poor women tended to attack each other physically more often than did older or wealthier women. Frequent forms of attack were "pushing, shoving, grabbing, tripping, slapping, kicking, and punching." Such attacks were launched, primarily, by friends and acquaintances against each other.

Anne Campbell, Steven Muncer, and Daniel Bibel view female-female aggression in terms of an all-out struggle for (economic) survival. Campbell and her colleagues note that competition is extreme among prostitutes. Campbell writes, "When the imperative of crack addiction draws women into prostitution, their desperation leads to a deflation of prices charged for sexual services, which creates conflict with other women working the same patch."

My own review of the literature as well as many interviews that I have conducted indicate that prostituted women compete against each other for johns and for pimps; they distrust each other even more than they distrust men; they verbally and physically attack each other and sabotage each other's relationships with both men and other women. Young, very poor, street-prostituted women do not hesitate to employ *direct* verbal and physical aggression against each other. In a 1992 study of street prostitutes, L. Maher and R. Curtis quote a prostituted American:

> Why would you pick up a girl for ten when you can get one for two? . . . I be there for hours and don't

make a dime and here's this filthy bitch (Mindy) making money left and right.

Although some prostitutes do, indeed, look out for each other in terms of spotting a homicidally kinky or freaky john, most impoverished, prostituted women call each other what men call prostitutes: "Cunt, bitch, 'ho, asshole." Prostitutes (like women in general) demean each other on the basis of physical appearance ("She's a dog. She smells. She looks like a monkey. Did she ever see her skinny little ass?"). Prostitutes also "snitch" on each other, set each other up, in order to gain revenge against a prettier or preferred competitor. The setup can lead to savage beatings, mutilations, gang-rapes, and other terrifying punishments meted out by pimps.

In a recent book about legalized prostitution in Nevada, Dr. Alexa Albert describes a prison-like or "zoo-like" environment in which prostitutes are "required to remain on the premises and (are) let out for fresh air breaks only in the enclosed front and back yards." The prostitutes are not allowed to make phone calls; if they have errands in town, they are forced to hire escorts at their own expense. Their rooms are equipped with hidden intercom systems and are continually searched. Nevertheless, the prostitutes describe the brothel as their "family." Like sisters, the prostitutes are very competitive. Albert writes:

> When I asked the women why they hadn't organized
> to form a union or joined together to purchase a

brothel themselves most of the prostitutes rolled their
eyes and said they could never trust another "ho."

In a sense, prostitutes work in a war zone. According to San
Francisco psychologist Melissa Farley, prostituted women suffer
from extreme forms of combat fatigue or post-traumatic stress
disorder; their symptoms include anxiety, depression, insomnia,
nightmares, hallucinations, "flashbacks," and drug and alcohol
addiction.

Street prostitution occupies one of the bottom positions in
global human economics. Anyone who works in this pluto-
nium factory is subject to a particularly savage primate-like
competition for survival. I do not justify the verbal or physical
cruelties of one prostitute toward another, but I can, at least,
understand it. I have a harder time understanding the gratuitous cruelty of non-prostituted women toward prostitutes or
the cruelty of permanently underpaid women workers toward
each other—especially since they know how easy it is to "fall"
and land, hard, at the next lowest rung on the economic (or
sexual) ladder.

A glaring, yet unacknowledged example of women's fiction-
alized cruelty in this regard may be found in the very popular
musical *Les Miserables*, based on Victor Hugo's magnificent
novel. Most people remember both the novel and the musical
as being about bitter poverty, the viciousness of "small" men
who rise, and above all, about a doomed, but inspiring concept
of justice and liberty for all. In the musical, resources are scant,

"life is a struggle, it's a war . . . and the children have got to be fed and you're lucky to be in a job."

I am stunned by the scene in which the women factory workers demand that the factory owner fire the "slut" Fantine because Fantine is the sole support of an illegitimate daughter. The women factory workers show no mercy toward Fantine; in fact, they knowingly condemn Fantine to prostitution, which, morality aside, is usually associated with violence, disease, and early death. Whereas many working-class women are less judgmental about sexual lapses than their bourgeois sisters are, many working-class women, like these in *Les Miserables*, are not. The prostituted women, coarsened by their own experiences, are, in turn, coarse and pitiless toward Fantine; there is no "gentler, woman's way of being" here. It is women, themselves squeezed by adversity, who deal Fantine the final blow.

My point: In a world in which ceaseless male violence and greed are a given, female mercy does not intervene to save or comfort Fantine. Or other Fantines.

Why do women *physically* fight each other? According to Victoria Burbank, more than one third of the time women's fights "revolve around men and their distribution of favors, whether sexual or otherwise." Women fight each other "out of jealousy for the same man" or in competition for survival.

Primates—and young humans who lack verbal skills—will use physical aggression to express themselves or to get their way. They will hit, push, shove, spit, kick, punch, and bite. As children grow, they add verbal aggression to their repertoire.

They will shout and threaten. As children develop further and gain more social intelligence, they begin to employ indirect and nonphysical forms of aggression. From an evolutionary and anatomical point of view, girls and women are less inclined to attack anyone directly, or physically, than boys and men are—unless, as mothers, their offspring are in immediate physical danger. In addition, girls and women are culturally trained to employ indirect methods of aggression, as a low-risk, low-injury, approach.

Girls learn that a safe way to attack someone else is behind her back, so that she will not know who is responsible. This tracks girls and women into lives of chronic gossip and rumor-mongering, but it also allows girls and women to fight without physically killing each other outright. Primate studies show that a female primate's way of fighting might depress or eliminate another female's capacity to reproduce or to adequately feed her offspring; an analysis of class, race, tribal, and geographically based warfare among human beings suggests that human beings may accomplish a similar end.

The damage that women do to each other begins early, in childhood, and has lifelong consequences. Natalie Angier writes boldly about "women's ways" of indirect aggression. She says:

> I'll admit up front that I dislike this form of aggression, and that to mention it is to reinforce clichés about female treachery and female conniving. Yet it

is an aggression that we gals know, because we grew up as girls and we saw it and struggled against it and hated it and did it ourselves. Indirect aggression is anonymous aggression. It is backbiting, gossiping, spreading vicious rumors. It is seeking to rally others against the despised but then denying the plot when confronted. The use of indirect aggression increases over time, not just because girls don't generally use their fists to make their point, but because the effectiveness of indirect aggression is tied to the fluency of a person's social intelligence; the more sophisticated the person, the cleverer her use of the dorsal blade.

What exactly do we know about indirect aggression among girls?

2.

INDIRECT AGGRESSION AMONG GIRLS AND TEENAGERS

In Margaret Atwood's powerful and haunting novel *Cat's Eye*, the narrator, painter Elaine Risly, recalls a pre-adolescence in which her "best [girl] friends" torment and physically endanger her. Elaine obeys them because she wants to belong. After a near-death experience at their hands, Elaine walks away and says:

> They follow along behind me, making comments on the way I walk, on how I look from behind. "Stuck up! Stuck up!" they cry. I can hear the hatred, but also the need. They need me for this, and I no longer need them. I am indifferent to them. There's something hard in me.

Elaine has become hard and mean; in a sense, she has incorporated her tormentors in order to contain them. Now, she has a "mean mouth." She "walks the halls surrounded by an aura of potential verbal danger." Other girls treat her with caution. Elaine notes that "strangely enough, [her] mean behavior doesn't result in fewer friends, but on the surface, more." Elaine never trusts or bonds with women again. She becomes a celebrated painter whom feminists embrace. She still cannot abide being told what to do by other women. Elaine says:

> I avoid gatherings of these women, walking as I do in fear of being sanctified, or else burned at the stake. I think they are talking about me, behind my back. They make me more nervous than ever, because they have a certain way they want me to be, and I am not that way.

Girls and women may have an evolutionary predisposition towards chronic, intra-gender aggression—which patriarchal civilization may further maximize. While girls may be marked by their bond with mothers, whose status and lives depend upon their having a husband and a son (something quite foreign to most primate species), girls are also marked by their earliest encounters with other girls. As Atwood notes, girls may be "cute" to adults but they are "life-sized" to each other.

Daphne Merkin, in her novel *Enchantment*, describes suffering at the hands of a cold and mocking mother, which she understands makes her more vulnerable to similar mistreatment at the hands of other young girls. Her protagonist, Hannah, says,

> I began looking for a way out of the enchantment my mother had put me under—the spell that bound me . . . to her side. Naomi Litt, fellow member of my fifth grade class, became the alternate focus of my dread . . . I thought of Naomi as someone whose affection had to be won over and over again, like my mother's . . . When Naomi had had enough of me, due to some small assertion of will on my part, she would signal to the other girls in the class—followers all—that they were to "get against me."

Hannah must "totally acquiesce" to Naomi's wishes. Otherwise, Hannah will suffer the insomnia and panic that accompanies being ostracized. Like Atwood's narrator Elaine, Merkin's narrator Hannah, learns how to assuage arbitrary cruelty. Hannah says: "I was begging Naomi's forgiveness not for any specific offense I had committed but for the general crime she discerned in my being who I was."

Girls are social beings who need to belong. Studies suggest that girls have a greater need for dyadic and expressive interpersonal intimacy than boys do and are more adept, sooner, at engaging in it. Thus, most girls want a best friend—that is, they want pair-bond intimacy—but they are also attracted to small cliques, three-somes, or loose affiliations. Girls form exclusive, intense, core groups consisting of two or three members. Research suggests that girls care more about being included than they do about whether they are ranked as dominant or subordinate.

Indeed, most girls are terrified of being excluded or rejected. When this happens, a girl experiences social aloneness in the universe. She learns that she has to reinvent herself and form a new group. Sometimes, one simply hasn't the heart to begin anew, to open oneself up to pitiless exclusion again. A subsequent loss is always greater than the previous loss, since each new loss contains within it the first loss as well.

This fear of being cut off, abandoned, losing the female intimates upon whom one depends, explains why many girls try as hard as they do not to upset or disagree with their friends and thus often end up never saying what they really think or feel. On the one hand, this may account for why girls, more than boys, try to engage in socially sanctioned behavior, try to mediate conflict in a creative or constructive way, and try so hard to apologize for, minimize, or justify winning in a competitive game. On the other hand, if a girl cannot say what she really means or feels, this is likely to lead to resentment, superficiality, and repeated friendship failures. As we shall see, girls try to minimize this by choosing friends who look, dress, talk, and think just like themselves.

And still, girls do not exactly trust each other. How can they? They need each other too much, and the price of remaining connected includes perpetual self-monitoring, which impedes spontaneity and passion. Even when a girl is a good self-monitor, she may still lose her place as a best friend or clique-member for reasons that are entirely beyond her control. That is, one girl sprouts breasts, the others don't; one girl is chosen as a cheerleader, the others aren't; one girl's family suddenly becomes very rich—or very poor. Young girls experience the slightest change as very threatening.

British psychologist Anne Campbell notes that girls do not like any girl who "positively assesses herself or explicitly compares herself" with others. Girls find this offensive. Painfully—and almost constantly—girls scrutinize each others' behavior for displays that might be interpreted as showing that one girl is trying to differentiate herself from others in the group. To girls, as research confirms, "belonging" is the most important thing—and in order to belong, each girl must "conform to group expectations while not exceeding them." Of course, boys also need to belong to a group, but, "having achieved this they then strive for public recognition of status within it." Status-seeking girls tend to be rejected or excluded by other girls. As we shall see, girls view members who are in any way better or worse than other group members as less desirable friends. Finally, Campbell points out that naturalistic studies show that "cliques are girls' preferred mode of association." She theorizes that such a preference is "probably the result of a desire to avoid status competition," which might result in being excluded.

As noted, female human beings have the power to include or exclude others—mainly female others—from their group.

When men exclude a woman, it may indeed have dire consequences both economically and socially. However, being excluded by boys and men is not as emotionally devastating to a girl or woman as being excluded by others of her own gender.

Remember that ejection from certain primate troops sometimes leads to the death of the primate ejected, and that mother-daughter pair-bonding is the dominant and most stable primate social bond. Perhaps girls suffer severely from exclusion because, in addition to whatever inclinations we may share with our primate ancestors, we have also experienced our first home on earth as (or in) a woman's body. We know the taste and smell of it. We swam in human female salty waters before we were born. Perhaps other women still signify home, family, safety—or life itself, to both women and men.

Also, like boys, girls have been mothered mainly by women in infancy and childhood. Unlike boys and most men, girls and women continue to socialize mainly with female intimates. Thus, when a girl or a woman is excluded by other girls or women, a more primal and painful terror is evoked. A friendship web, once severed, can rarely be repaired. The raw feelings of hurt and shame, the "backstabbing" rumors, the betrayal of trust, the loss of one's reputation, the sudden falling away of human society, amount to a loss of one's own existential footing. One's exclusion feels akin to eviction from Eden; it is the loss of illusion and innocence. Re-entry, when possible, demands that the shunned woman never hold anyone accountable for what the friend or group has done to her. She must "eat" the history of turned backs and non-invitations, the cult-like closing of female ranks.

What do we know about aggression and hostility in children? Some adults remember; more adults have repressed memories of having been hit, bullied, taunted, or shunned by other children; few among us remember or admit to having *been* or having assisted bullies. However, as the teachers and parents of young children, we have ample opportunity to observe, if not dramas of the magnitude of *Lord of the Flies*, at least the ordinary social interactions of childhood. They will suffice.

In the mid-1980s, when my son was about six years old, he appeared suddenly at my door in a happy little gang of five or six neighborhood boys. They would whoop and holler, rush around, push each other down, and get into verbal and physical fights until they'd exhausted themselves. The next day they'd be at it again. Unlike their female age counterparts, no boy seemed to hold a grudge or remain mad at anyone in the gang. No two boys conspired against a third. While these boys were physically more aggressive than girls, they were also good-natured and emotionally uncomplicated. All they wanted was to be able to play and play again.

Little girls of the same age already had best friends; they were already serially breaking with each other; girls developed new best friends, literally overnight. The girls already seemed hooked into a series of mother/daughter-like dyadic intimacies which, step by step, were allowing them to become more independent of their mothers. At the same time, this method of achieving independence wedded them, fatefully, to a pattern of merging with or breaking from other girls. Once two best friends broke up, they rarely got back together. Instead they tried to turn their respective new best friends against their old ones.

As my son got older, I observed that girls of his same age group were, perhaps, more verbally adept, more subtle, more holistic in their reading of emotional reality than the boys were; however, the girls were less able to bond with a group in as good-natured and thoughtless a manner as the boys. The girls knew each other and were therefore over-concerned about offending one another and of being rejected or excluded as a result. The girls seemed emotionally devious, mainly because they were indirect and very cautious. The girls wanted each others' approval as much as they feared each others' disapproval. An agonizing place to be. The girls seemed to know how important other girls were to them, but they also seemed to know that girls could turn on each other in a flash. Perhaps terror made them sensitive to each other: their perceived social survival was at stake.

Boys, on the other hand, bonded and were loyal to their group, but not to any one particular individual in that group. They didn't know each other that well, nor did they seem to want to.

Over the years, I have interviewed many American teenage girls and boys. Whereas all have agreed that girls can be mean and catty, many have explained that girls are *also* engaged in a positive and complicated process of befriending each other. For example, Clara, who was seventeen at the time of our interview, said:

> I think that women are more obsessed with individuality than men are. In relationships, women want to be known completely by a single best friend, while men are content with "gangs" of others. This constant need for intimacy might be due to lower self-esteem. Women are constantly geared to look for their own flaws, both physically and mentally, and so are more easily impressed with the positive attributes of other women. I also think that, for whatever reason, women are more afraid of being alone than men. Being alone is not only the absence of people, but the absence of understanding. The female systems that are set up: best friend, second best friend, stranger, enemy, provide a girl with both a place and a value. Each girl surveys her fellows and decides who is the best and who is the worst. This allows each girl to wallow in her low self-esteem or to try and boost it. But it becomes a vicious cycle as each girl grows dependent on the others for confirmation of her character.

In 1976, American psychiatrist and feminist therapist Jean Baker Miller proposed a model of female psychology that was distinct from male psychology. By the mid to late 1980s, Harvard educational psychologist Carol Gilligan's 1982 work on the "different" and more "relational" voice of white middle-class girls began to gain academic credibility and visibility. Some feminists used her work as proof that girls and women are both different from and morally superior to boys and men (I am not suggesting that Gilligan and her colleagues foresaw or intended this outcome). However, given my front-row seat as the mother of a young boy, I could no longer pretend that girls were more moral or relational than boys. On the contrary; the girls' desire to please others involved a great deal of self-censorship and an expectation that other girls do likewise. This interfered with a girl's ability to join a group without worrying herself to death over who said what to whom yesterday.

Gilligan's research presents pre-adolescent and adolescent girls as not only morally or relationally heroic, but also as succumbing to a "tyranny of niceness," losing their "voices," becoming tentative, fearful, "inauthentic." At first, this work focused on white middle-class American girls; subsequently, Gilligan and others studied American girls of color and of working-class origin.

As I observed young boys, I began to understand the advantages of male alliances. I was, ever after, unable to agree with the argument that girls bonded better than boys. Differently—yes; but not better. Even when boys and men do not know or like each other, they join forces to save lives, run a business, put out fires, take over a corporation, or wage wars. Girls and women bond brilliantly too—with a small family unit and with a few best female friends. Not on the job. Not among strangers. At least not yet. In a sense, girls may be described as socially interactive among intimates and anti-social among strangers. The reverse may be true for boys.

My observations as a mother have turned out to have a basis in fact. However, had I published this book ten years ago, I would have been able to quote novelists such as Atwood and Merkin, and the early work of psychologists such as Gilligan and Campbell, but I would not have been able to confirm the complex, double-edged realities of friendships among girls with any compelling social-scientific data. I now can. Of course, even in the 1960s, a few signal, isolated studies existed.

For example, in 1966, the California educational psychologist Norma D. Feshbach showed that adult women obtained "higher scores on measures of covert hostility." Feshbach found this consistent with clinical observations that viewed women as "more hostile than men." Feshbach's clinical experts were probably no different from lay people in that they viewed men as naturally aggressive and, therefore, not pathological when they used aggression to assert dominance. Such clinicians might also have viewed female aggression as unnatural and, therefore, pathological or extreme. It is entirely possible that oppressed women *were* more verbally or interpersonally hostile than men.

In the 1960s, when Feshbach published her work, most clinicians did not view women as members of an oppressed or subordinated group, compelled to express their anger in verbal, covert, and indirect ways, nor did clinicians note that the most frequent targets of female indirect aggression were other women.

In 1969 Feshbach studied gender differences in direct and indirect aggression among eighty-four Caucasian first-graders from middle-class backgrounds in Los Angeles. She found that, when a newcomer was introduced into an existing group, within four minutes girls were engaged in indirect aggression toward the newcomer. Girls, significantly more than boys, either ignored, avoided, refused to help, or excluded the newcomer. Feshbach found that gender differences in "direct physical aggression," in which boys excelled, did not exist under all conditions and that, within sixteen minutes, boys were as indirectly aggressive toward newcomers as girls were. Perhaps girls are conditioned to beware of strangers more than boys are.

Feshbach called for further exploration of the "many indirect routes which can be taken to express hostile, aggressive tendencies." It would be almost twenty years before social scientists would pursue this line of research. Although certain primatologists, anthropologists, North American feminist developmental psychologists, and British aggression psychologists had published relevant work in the 1980s, it is really only since 1992 that cross-cultural, developmental research on direct and indirect aggression among children and teenagers has begun to gather a certain formidable momentum.

Two very different kinds of explorations of childhood and

adolescent aggression are currently underway. Beginning in 1982 and continuing into the new millennium, Carol Gilligan (who remains at Harvard but who will be moving to New York University) and her colleagues have been studying the psychological, relational, and moral development of American girls. Gilligan's information is based on interviews and observation; hers is a qualitative approach. Somewhat later in the 1980s, some Finnish psychologists launched an ambitious research program in this area along somewhat different lines. They—and like-minded researchers in England, Australia, America, Canada, and eventually, in Japan, Italy, Poland, Israel, India, and Russia—decided that interviews and self-reports cannot be fully trusted, since both children and adults will lie in order to please an interviewer or to present themselves in a good light. Accordingly, this group has developed and utilized peer estimates to measure direct and indirect aggression in children and teenagers. They have also chosen a more experimental (less qualitative) and cross-cultural approach.

Interestingly, the Europeans, Canadians, and Australians seem not to have read Gilligan's work, nor she, theirs. (At least, they do not make reference to each other in their work.)

The experimental and cross-cultural studies confirm that, in terms of aggression, normal human development seems to evolve from direct physical aggression to verbal and then to social/psychological or indirect aggression. These studies also confirm that female infants and toddlers are as physically aggressive as their same-age male counterparts. As they grow older, however, boys become more significantly aggressive than girls in physical, or direct ways, and they also add verbal and indirect aggression to their repertoire, although more slowly than girls do and in a somewhat different way.

Thus, both primates and young humans who lack verbal skills will, at first, use physical aggression either to express themselves or to get their way. They will hit, push, shove, spit, kick, punch, and bite. As humans develop, they add verbal aggression to their repertoire. They will shout and threaten. Some time between the age of six and eight, girls begin to display social intelligence, and this allows them to effectively employ indirect forms of aggression.

The male of the species tends to be taller, heavier, and stronger than his female counterpart. Therefore, most females tend to rely on non-physical forms of aggression in dealing with males—unless of course, their own infants are being threatened. As we have seen, female primates will physically attack each other and each others' infants. Among human beings, girls and women are culturally trained to employ indirect methods of aggression. This is a low-risk approach.

Girls learn that a safe way to attack someone else is behind her back, so that she will not know who started the attack. On the one hand, this policy dooms girls and women to behavior such as gossip and shunning, which cannot be ritualistically resolved. On the other hand, it also allows girls and women to fight without physically hurting each other.

According to Finnish psychologist Kaj Björkqvist, by the time a girl is eight years old she is unlikely to express frustration and anger toward others *physically*. Girls are, on the other hand, as verbally aggressive as boys. Instead of hitting or shoving, girls will use verbal, nonverbal, and socially manipulative skills to hurt others—mainly other girls. Girls will insult and denigrate each other; they will also hold grudges for a very long time. Björkqvist and others have shown that girls are "significantly more likely than boys to become friendly with someone else as revenge"; and that girls will gossip and suggest the "shunning" of another girl.

According to Björkqvist, indirect aggression is a type of "hostile behavior [that] is carried out in order to harm the opponent, while avoiding being identified as aggressive." Björkqvist and others developed a scale, known as the Direct and Indirect Aggression Scale, which measures *physical aggression* (hitting, kicking, tripping, shoving, pushing, pulling), and *verbal aggression* (yelling, insulting, teasing, threatening to hurt the other, calling the other names), on the one hand, and on the other hand, *indirect aggression* (shutting the other out of the group, becoming friends with another as revenge, ignoring, gossiping, telling bad stories, planning secretly to bother the other, saying bad things behind the back, saying to others: "let's not be with him/her," telling the other's secrets to a third person, writing notes in which the other is criticized, criticizing the other's hair or clothing, trying to get others to dislike the person).

Note that there are many more things to *do* when one is indirectly hostile than when one attacks directly.

Natalie Angier notes that girls find physical fights unsatis-
factory because they are over too quickly:

> To express anger might work if the betrayer accepts
> the anger and responds to it with respect. But if she
> doesn't acknowledge her friend's anger or sense of
> betrayal, if she refuses to apologize or admit to any
> wrongdoing, or if she goes further, walking away or
> mocking or snubbing her friend, at that point a girl
> may aim to hurt with the most piercing and per-
> sistent tools for the job, the psychological tools of
> indirect, vengeful aggression, with the object of
> destroying the girl's position, her peace of mind, her
> right to be. Indirect aggression is akin to a voodoo
> hex, an anonymous but obsessive act in which the
> antagonist's soul, more than her body, must be got
> at, must be penetrated, must be nullified.

From an evolutionary and biological point of view, girls
cannot *physically* afford to risk retaliation by attacking openly;
culturally, physical aggression is not acceptable in girls and
women. Also, girls seem to develop social intelligence before
boys do—and, hence, are capable of engaging in effective
social manipulation. (Alas, boys catch up; many men certainly
have the social intelligence to aggress against others in indirect
ways.)

Girls may use social manipulation to dominate or express

anger because they have learned to do this from their female role models: adult women. In addition, girls may be less physically aggressive than boys because aggression is less tolerated among girls than among boys; either the punishment is harsher or girls are simply not rewarded for being physically aggressive. Anne Campbell believes that aggression in girls is suppressed by being systematically ignored. She writes:

> When girls aggress, nobody notices and nobody reacts . . . Teachers respond to boys when they scream, cry, or whine; they respond to girls when they use gestures, gentle touches, and speech. By the age of two, girls' aggression is much more likely to be ignored by playmates than is boys', and this lack of response is very effective in stopping the behavior. Boys are overwhelmingly more successful than girls in using aggression to gain compliance from another child. So the little girl learns not only that aggression is emotionally dangerous but that it doesn't get her what she wants.

In 1992—the same year as that in which *Of Mice and Women: Aspects of Female Aggression*, the Björkqvist and Niemelä anthology on gender differences in aggression, appeared—Lyn Mikel Brown and Carol Gilligan published *Meeting at the Crossroads: Women's Psychology and Girls' Development*. According to Brown and Gilligan, as (white, middle class) American girls move from a more boisterous childhood into a more feminine pre-adolescence, a "tyranny of niceness" descends. A girl must be nice in order to have friends. At eight, girls are already fearful of being whispered about, laughed at, made fun of, by other eight-year-old girls: " 'Whispering,' 'telling secrets,' and 'making fun of' are ways to prevent girls from risking too much or acting in ways that are too threatening, too different." Brown and Gilligan note that girls quickly and totally "retract . . . strong feelings rather than face the painful consequences (of being ostracized)."

Thus, according to Brown and Gilligan, girls learn that there is "danger in authentic encounters" with other girls. Girls learn how not to disagree or fight in direct or confrontational ways. Jessie, one of Brown and Gilligan's third-grade interviewees, is struggling to learn how to be nice in order to keep friends:

> If Jessie doesn't "cooperate," she fears that she will lose her entire social world [and] also be made to feel guilty . . . "Losing a friend is horrible," Jessie says, "because you wouldn't have a best friend to play with all the time . . . and I don't think you could find a friend just like that person." [Jessie remains] "consumed" by such constraints. Her strong feelings, spoken directly and with passion, can be dangerous since they are disruptive. Signs of disruption—anger and noise, getting riled up and anxious—are cause for being "ignored," left out, abandoned.

According to Brown and Gilligan, by the third grade, expressing a "different" view among girls has already become "too dangerous and risky." A pre-adolescent girl is sometimes willing to speak more directly when only one other girl is present; this changes when a third girl joins them. However, even as girls are learning how to be indirect and nice, they continue to judge one another. Girls are concerned about who is a true friend and who is only faking it. A girl risks losing her entire social world if she dares to think for herself or if she refuses to back her best friend or her clique even when she thinks they are in the wrong. Girls dare not come to the aid of a girl who is being bad-mouthed.

These are, perhaps, girlish lessons that adult women never forget. I do not mean to suggest that girls are horrible and that boys are wonderful. Boys can be quite brutal physically, more toward other boys than toward girls, although toward girls as well, and are socialized to use aggression to get their way. In fact, boys (and men) say they approve of aggression, while girls and women say they do not. Furthermore, girls and women tend to express remorse about using aggression to achieve control. Girls say they feel guilty about having hurt someone and attribute their aggression to losing control. However, this does not lessen their indirect aggression.

The writer, Joyce Maynard, describes her experience of other ten-year-old girls in the 1960s:

We knew each other's faces and bodies and

wardrobes so well that any change was noticed at once, the fuel for endless notes. That's why I dressed so carefully mornings—I was about to face the scrutiny of fifteen gossip-seeking girls, ten only slightly less observant boys ready to imitate my voice and walk . . . At every moment—even at home, with no one but family there—I'd be conscious of what the other kids, The Group, would think if they could see me now.

The African-American actress and writer Anna Deavere Smith describes her fear of other eleven-year-old "white kids." She learns, however, that girls of all colors have their own ways of bullying and beating each other. She recalls how one Jewish girl's refusal to chip in for a Christmas present for the teacher (her parents would not allow her to do so), led to an ugly campaign against her.

A tall, beautiful black girl (who was pregnant and would soon be forced to leave school) began some of the mockery toward Lila . . . I also remember how surprised I was that the Jewish kids (again, the predominant population) began to turn against Lila too . . . No one took her to the schoolyard and threatened to beat her up, no one stuck her head down the toilet, but the daily vote would be taken, the vote (ninety-nine percent) for buying the present . . . Finally, the teacher got wind of the whole thing and shamed us all by saying, as she should have, that in this spirit she didn't really want a Christmas present, and that Lila should not be forced to participate if her religion wouldn't allow it. I remember this story because it was the first time I saw that a beating—even a public beating—could happen without anyone so much as striking a blow.

Most of my own teenage interviewees confirmed that girls can be extraordinarily hostile towards each other. For example, fourteen-year-old Myra described a ninth-grade class trip as follows:

Throughout junior high school I had been traveling with a clique of girls whom I didn't have much in common with and whom I did not feel I could truly speak to. But it was better than being alone. One day, while still on the trip, my 'friends' decided that none of them had much liked Chloe, another girl in our clique. They sat around insulting her and acting as though a three-year-long friendship had been polite pretense. Of course, Chloe had always been one of the two lowest girls in our private caste system. I was the other.

It occurred to Myra that, if she tried to stop this backstabbing she herself might be the "next one burned." Myra had always resented being paired off with Chloe. She began to insult Chloe as a way of getting close to the other girls. Myra was still never completely accepted. A new high-status girl entered the group.

> This girl blatantly disliked me. Whenever my friends were with this girl, I was never allowed to go near them. If I did, the conversation would die out and the girl would glare at me.

Brown and Gilligan, in their 1992 work, describe the price (white) pre-adolescent girls pay for daring to disagree with other girls. They are aware that disagreeing can lead to being "ridiculed, talked about, rejected." The same girls who are so afraid of being rejected are the very girls who, unconsciously, participate in or do not have the courage to resist that very culture of rejection. One of Brown and Gilligan's interviewees, Noura, is seen as speaking for all the girls when she says that her "'friends (who) were talking about people' might then 'talk about me.'" The authors see Noura as "walking on eggshells (among friends) who police her thoughts and feelings."

What about working class, African-, Hispanic-, and Asian-American girls? Do they fall prey to a tyranny of niceness too? Aren't they tougher, more assertive than white and middle-class girls? Indeed, class and race do matter. In 1985, in an article on urban black adolescent females, clinical psychologist Jewelle

Taylor Gibbs suggested that low-income and working-class white adolescent girls might share more of a common language with black girls of the same class than they do with white girls in middle-income groups.

In 1993, anthropologist Signithia Fordham studied "those loud African-American girls [whose] striking visibility and presence proclaimed African-American women's existence, their collective resistance to their socially proclaimed powerlessness, or 'nothingness.' " In Fordham's view, most of her interviewees had "resisted becoming like white, middle-class girls at school." However, Fordham also found that her high-achieving and academically ambitious black girls adopted a deliberate silence in order to deflect the "hostility" and "anger" they expected from both their peers and their teachers. Unlike white middle-class girls, both the African-American and the white girls studied by Gibbs and Fordham tended to maintain a striking ability to express anger and to disagree with each other. A majority did not strive to conform to idealized standards of femininity. They knew that they could never pass for thin, rich, white, and blond.

In 1995, in *Between Voice and Silence: Women and Girls, Race and Relationships*, Jill McLean Taylor, Carol Gilligan, and Amy M. Sullivan studied low-income and minority girls. The authors applied their earlier "voice-centered" methodology to studying a more diverse group of twenty-six urban young girls considered to be at risk either in terms of dropping out of school or of becoming pregnant. They studied, in depth, eight African-American or African-Caribbean girls; the remaining subjects were all from poor or working class families and were of Portugese, Irish, Italian, and Hispanic origin. Taylor's group did not view being "at risk" as proof of either "deficit" or "deviance." They viewed their interviewees as "resilient resisters" who, unlike their white or middle-class counterparts, were not daunted by "the mesmerizing presence of the perfect girl" because they understood they could never become such girls. However, by the ninth grade, these girls (like their white middle-class counterparts), became very much concerned with rumors and gossip. Many began to stay to themselves as a way of dealing with repeated betrayals of trust.

One of my own ninth-grade (thirteen- and fourteen-year-old) interviewees said that she had, at least temporarily, "sworn off" girlfriends. She said:

> I always felt like a third wheel whenever I was with two other girlfriends. Why is it that girls are so mean and catty towards each other when boys aren't like that at all? For a while, now, my best friend is a boy. He isn't as close as a girlfriend can be but he isn't mean and he doesn't gossip. I am never afraid that one day he'll suddenly stop talking to me or that he'll invite everyone else to a party and never mention it to me. Like my girlfriends did.

I am at ease conducting clinical, psychoanalytically oriented interviews. But I have also conducted laboratory experiments, and I understand that each approach has its advantages and limitations. I respect both approaches. Finnish psychologist Karin Österman, on the other hand, does not believe that self-reports are likely to be accurate. Österman found that self-estimates of aggression were significantly lower than peer estimates. This is because aggression is seen as socially undesirable.

Österman and her colleagues at Abo Akadami University, therefore pioneered the use of peer estimate measurements, first, because peers may be able to note subtle behavior that might otherwise go unnoticed and, second, as a way of overcoming cross-cultural differences in what is viewed as hostile behavior—something that will vary from one country to another. In 1994 Österman's group was able to report that there are cultural variations in the levels of childhood aggression, both in boys and in girls, in Japan, Israel, Chicago (among African- and Caucasian-Americans), Warsaw, and Finland (among Finnish and Swedish-speaking children). She found that eight-year-old boys were more physically aggressive than eight-year-old girls. Still, in this particular study, indirect aggression did not yet appear as a significant gender difference. However, Österman found cultural differences *among girls*, but not among boys, in terms of aggressive behaviors.

Österman found that Polish girls believed that physical, verbal, and indirect aggression all are gender-appropriate for girls. The African-American girls from Chicago exhibited the highest self-estimate and peer-level estimates for all three types of aggression—in Österman's view, a "circumstance likely to reflect the fact that they live in a quite violent environment." Interestingly, four years later, in 1998, British psychologists Katy Tapper and Michael Boulton found that while seven- to eleven-year-old British girls *viewed* aggression more negatively than British boys did, the British girls still *behaved* in ways that were as physically and verbally aggressive as British boys. In this study, Tapper and Boulton did not find that girls engaged in more indirect aggression than boys did. Puzzled, the authors conclude that British children may be different from Finnish children.

In 1998, Österman and her colleagues studied 2,094 subjects, aged eight, eleven, and fifteen, in Finland, Israel, Poland, and Italy. The researchers used the DIAS inventory, pioneered by Björkqvist, which measures both direct and indirect aggressive strategies. Österman found that girls of all age groups in all four countries used indirect aggression more than verbal or physical aggression, and that for boys of all age groups in all four countries, indirect aggression was the style least used. In this study, unlike the Tapper and Boulton findings, girls were using indirect aggressive strategies by the age of eight.[1]

Among boys, indirect aggression was the style least used at any age. Eight-year-old boys in all four countries employed this style twenty-six percent of the time; eleven-year-olds, twenty-three percent of the time; fifteen-year-olds, twenty-six percent of the time. This must be compared with fifteen-year-old girls' use of an indirect strategy fifty-two percent of the time. It is important to note that boys did become more verbally aggressive over time.

In 1995, Anne Campbell found that adolescent girls fight over the "management of sexual reputation," over access to "desirable mates," and to "protect established relationships from takeovers by rivals."

In 1999, the New York journalist Leora Tannenbaum interviewed girls and women, myself included, who had been branded as "sluts" from the 1950s through the 1990s, by both boys and other girls. According to Tannenbaum, her interviewees all described two opposite, lingering reactions: that of never having gotten over being taunted and ostracized by other girls and that of having become stronger and more creative because of it.

In the 1980s, when Tannenbaum was a teenager, she "made out" with her best friend's boyfriend. Tannenbaum now admits that she was wrong. However, in her view, her punishment turned out to be far greater than her crime. Rather than confront her privately, to rage or even to announce the end of their friendship, Tannenbaum's friend "transplanted a private issue between the two of [them] into a public arena . . . [In] the space of a few hours [Tannenbaum] had become a 'slut.'" Tannenbaum describes the jeers, turned backs, ridicule, cruelty, scorn, and jokes at her expense, to which she was subjected for the next three and a half years. The teenage Tannenbaum opted for a doubled invisibility. She had already been rendered invisible by being reduced to a slogan, the butt of a dirty joke; now, in addition, she began wearing extra-loose clothing, learned to avoid eye-contact with other teenagers at her school, tried to hide, cried a lot, and studied even harder. "My intellect became a form of damage control."

Tannenbaum's contemporary teenage interviewees confirmed that a similar, mean misogyny still exists among girls. Teenage girls described being taunted, falsely accused, cursed, and even physically attacked by other girls. They described their best friends as having started false rumors about them in order to cover up their own forbidden sexual activity. One African-American interviewee described being falsely taunted as "gay" because she dressed in a (white) Ivy League fashion. She said: "Guys and girls both did it, but girls were worse. They did it right to my face."

Two of Tannenbaum's eighth-grade interviewees, Rosalina, a Hispanic-American girl from Oakland, and Shawna, her African-American friend, were brutally gang-raped by their male classmates. Afterwards, the rapists' "regular girlfriends," mainly other Latina teenagers, accused the rape victims of trying to steal their boyfriends. "They'd go, 'Hey, bitch. Why are you sleeping with my boyfriend?'" The regular girlfriends then physically, but not sexually, attacked the rape victims. Rosalina viewed the attacks as due to "resentment" because she was "sexually active," and her Catholic-repressed attackers may have wanted to be—but were not.

Such stories are horrifying and very sad. What may we conclude? That nice girls are not necessarily nice at all—and that most girls know this; that girls are as misogynistic as boys; that among middle-class white girls, girlish training, which includes prohibitions against physical aggression and against appearing too openly competitive or hostile, drives the open expression of anger and hostility inward, where it festers and explodes in other, more acceptable indirect ways; that working-class Hispanic- and African-American girls are, anecdotally, more physically, verbally, and indirectly aggressive than their middle-class white counterparts—a finding confirmed by Österman's 1994 study.

The teenage girls who engage in policing, shaming, and ostracizing other teenage girls are not exactly passive victims, but are in fact each of them actively protecting her own self-interest. Many teenage girls—especially those cowed by the tyranny of niceness—do not, apparently, stand up to teenage boys (or to other girls) lest they in turn, one by one, get similarly targeted. Teenage girls understand that any lower-ranking girl can, potentially, be targeted for either direct or indirect aggression (or both), and that, once targeted, she's entirely on her own. Such cowardice amounts to complicity in the sacrifice of other girls, one by one, for the sake of one's own safety.

But how, exactly, do girls bad-mouth and ostracize other girls? How do they "do the thing they do"? And, what, if anything, are the consequences of such indirect aggression? Some British, Australian, Candian, and American researchers have begun to answer these questions.

For example, in 1995, Donna Eder, an Indiana professor of sociology, and David A. Kinney, an urban-education researcher, studied seventh- and eighth-grade (twelve to thirteen years old) Caucasian working-class students in a midwestern location. Boys achieved popularity and status among their peers by becoming top athletes; girls achieved popularity and status either by becoming cheerleaders—or by establishing friendly relations with the few girls who already had guaranteed positions in the top (cheerleader) group.

Eder and Kinney found that girls knew that friendship with a popular cheerleader was crucial to their own status; thus, cheerleaders were highly sought after as friends. However, since a cheerleader cannot choose *everyone* as a best friend, cheerleaders, paradoxically, became resented as much as they were sought after. Among girls, but not boys, "greater popularity could decrease rather than increase status among peers." In fact, girls who were popular in the seventh grade were not necessarily popular in the eighth grade; there seemed to be no positive carryover effect. The researchers believe that this may "reflect the resentment process . . . [in which 'popular' girls] become viewed as being 'snobbish' or 'stuck up,'" which leads to a "withdrawal of friendship offers."

Thus, according to Eder and Kinney, a girl may have a "high degree of popularity or visibility in a school, and, at the same time, may experience a decrease in peer status in terms of friendship relations." Since friendship and dyadic intimacy are so important to girls, these results suggest that social status often come at a high price.

In 1998, Canadian psychologists Joyce F. Benenson and Deborah Bennaroch explored similar themes among seventh- and eighth-grade Caucasian adolescents in Montreal. They wanted to understand the role of same-sex friendship in the lives of boys and girls. They questioned their subjects about romantic relationships, scholastic competence, athletic competence, popularity, attractiveness, and close friendships. Boys cared more about their athletic performance; girls cared more about close friendships. Girls cared "significantly more than boys did about their friends' having boyfriends/girlfriends if they did not have one, about their friends' being more popular than they were, about their friends' being more attractive than they were, and about their friends having more close friends than they had." In short, girls were upset if their friends were in any way superior to them.

The authors suggest that "achievement" might be more difficult to "integrate" into friendships among girls than among boys. "Because of the dyadic and intimate nature of girls' friendships, differences in status in an important domain might create tension." Although dyads may be tense, they alone may be able to satisfy a girl's need for total equality all the time, which can often be achieved only through the creation of uniformity and conformity. In a sense (shades of our primate ancestors!) if a girl is not getting groomed, if she doesn't feel that she's part of the in-crowd, she may not care about the spoils, or status, or about any larger principle. She will leave, and try to form a new, more reciprocal dyad.

Boys may not have the same need for interpersonal or dyadic intimacy that girls do. Boys tend to disclose less to other boys than girls disclose to each other. In the Eder and Kinney study, boys did not mind if their friends were superior in certain areas, including the area of athletic performance, the one thing boys cared about deeply. These boys felt they gained status when someone in their group won.

Although an increasing number of girls have begun to participate in team (not individual) sports, most girls still do not compete as a group against another group of girls. Many girls still demand an egalitarian, dyadic reciprocity and are, therefore, more threatened by the slightest change in status. The dyad is the female equivalent of the hierarchically structured boys club. A change in status of one member of the dyad may mean that the entire club is endangered. According to Benenson and Bennaroch, "If a friend is succeeding in school, then the friend might be spending more time studying, or if the friend has a boyfriend, then she might be abandoning other friends to spend time with her boyfriend." By contrast, boys who are members of the same group feel enhanced by the achievement of any other group member, even if he is a close friend.

Girls fear that a too successful (or a more successful) best friend might abandon the friendship. Thus, a girl may congratulate her friend on her friend's success, but she may also feel less positive about herself. Some girls wrote, spontaneously, that they would be unhappy with their friends' superior success. "I would act like I don't really care, but I would really"; "I would be happy for them, probably be miserable for awhile, though"; "I would be upset"; "I would tell 'em how I feel if they ignore me." Girls wrote that they would complain, be upset, jealous, get depressed, sit and binge, give up on the friendships. Some girls said that they "would try to become more popular themselves by getting to know the individuals who made their close friends more popular."

No boy thought of doing this.

Do the European and American studies of Caucasian children also reflect the lives of African-American children? The answer, tentatively, seems to be: quite possibly yes.

In 1990, a South Carolina anthropologist, Marjorie Harness Goodwin, studied poor, black, Philadelphia school children, between the ages of four and fourteen. She chose to focus on those between the ages of nine and fourteen. Goodwin did not do an experimental or laboratory study, nor did she solicit peer or teacher estimates. Rather, she observed and audio-taped real ("natural") interactions over time, as they unfolded in ordinary settings. Goodwin analyzed the structure of the verbal and non-verbal exchanges. Goodwin's study describes what exactly girls do when they gossip, how they do it, and to whom they do it.

When boys have a dispute, they tend to confront each other in the here-and-now and resolve matters by physical force, intimidation, or through boasting or an exchange of insults. Girls "do not generally utilize direct methods" in a dispute. They avoid making "explicit statements about one's [own] achievements." To do so would indicate that a girl thinks she's cute, or above another. This would violate the egalitarian ethos of the girl-group. Rather than directly confronting one another, girls instead discuss their grievance about another girl only in that party's absence. A girl will tell elaborate stories in order to "instigate a future confrontation" (the girls themselves have coined this phrase), with the absent individual, and in so doing, to organize allies for that.

Thus, if Alice has offended Betty, Betty will tell Carolyn and Diane about it—but in such a way as to enlist Carolyn and Diane against Alice, by persuading them that Alice has, indeed, not only unfairly offended Betty, but offended Carolyn and Diane as well. Of course, Alice might have done no such thing. Betty will "carefully manage" how she presents "past" events. She will do so in order to gain the support of a clique imbued with "righteous indignation," which will then assist Betty in any future confrontation with Alice or in a decision to shun Alice. Betty must accomplish this without appearing to intend to.

Let's assume that Alice has, really, offended Betty. It is still considered an actionable offense for Betty to talk about Alice behind her back; thus Betty has to do so carefully so as to protect herself from being accused of telling either the truth, a half-truth, or a clever lie behind Alice's back. Betty must tell her instigatory story without Carolyn and Diane's becoming aware that Betty is personally—or unfairly—trying to hurt or get back at Alice. According to Goodwin, Betty does this by implicating "her recipient . . . so that both are equally guilty and equally vulnerable." Betty will also wait until Carolyn or Diane "implicates herself first." Once Carolyn and Diane have been properly "briefed," a coalition of what the girls call "two against one . . . is established." Once two or more girls believe that an absent Alice has acted offensively, this constitutes grounds "to bring action against" Alice.

Goodwin cites anthropologist Max Gluckman's view that gossip can be used "to control aspiring individuals." Goodwin then notes that, in this instance, in real life, Alice is the same age as the other girls but has skipped a year in school. Betty, Carolyn, and Diane are all "annoyed at Alice for previewing everything that will happen to them in junior high school."

Goodwin found that while boys can resolve their disputes in "the present interaction," girls' "he-said-she-said disputes . . . may be extended over several days." Although boys can be verbally and physically aggressive, domineering, and cruel to each other, they can also end disputes quickly, ritualistically, and publicly. (This is precisely Margaret Mead and Robin Fox's point.) Girls do not react all at once. They first simmer behind closed doors, so to speak. They next embark upon a campaign to enlist others into their own private army of righteous indignation, by distorting or improving upon the truth and thus targeting another girl for exile or confrontation.

A number of studies in Finland, England, America, and Australia have in one way or another continued Goodwin's work. For example, in 1999, Australian psychologists Alan Russell and Laurence Owens confirmed that girls who ranged in age from seven to sixteen tended to use physical aggression against boys and verbal and relational aggression against other girls. The researchers conclude that "the targets of aggression appear to be important." Girls mainly target other girls for indirect aggression.

In their 1996 study on "bullying" behaviors among 573 twelve to thirteen-year-old Finnish schoolchildren, psychologists Christina Salmivalli, Kirsti Lagerspetz, Kaj Björkqvist and others found that the victims of bullying "scored low in social acceptance and high in social rejection." Thus, those targeted for bullying were seen as vulnerable, defenseless, without any allies who might retaliate on their behalf. This study confirmed that bullying is a group process that allows participants to feel less responsible for what happens.

Boys bully others more than girls do. Interestingly, boys who bully tend to have low status, but female bullies "formed an exceptional group: they scored above the mean in both social acceptance and social rejection." The authors theorize that, since girls use both verbal and indirect forms of aggression, female bullies may be "socially and verbally smart children who can choose their words and amuse the others by verbally— directly or indirectly—attacking their victims . . . Girls in the 'gang of bullies,' also rate high in terms of the current youth culture; they are 'tough girls' who know the newest fashions and the latest idols. It is possible that they are, even if frightening, also admired." Some girls—but more often, some boys—either take "empathic" stands with the victims of bullying or stand up to the bullies and stop the process. Mainly high-status boys take such stands, perhaps because they do not fear retaliation.

It is clear that girls who are trained in both real and false niceness not only bully others but allow such bullying to run its course. Salmivalli also found that, as the bullying continues, the unfortunate victim is increasingly perceived as "deviant, worthless . . . as deserving of being harassed." This is an important point, and we will return to it.

One wonders: How do nice girls justify gossiping against or bullying others? How do they justify winning, when winning inevitably involves hurting someone else?

In 1998, using a forced-choice, highly competitive game known as Foursquare, University of Delaware researcher Linda A. Hughes found that eleven-year-old girls rationalize winning by saying that they are not being *really* mean. According to Hughes, it was not possible to be "really nice" and still "play the game" of Foursquare. "In practice, almost anything players could do to 'be nice' to one person was by definition 'mean' to somebody else." If being "nice" (getting new people into the game) also meant being "mean" (in order to do so, players had to get rid of old players), then, by definition, "meanness was not 'really mean,' but something else entirely—in their own words, 'nice-mean.'"

Thus, girls were shown to be quite "capable of competition" and to "compete vigorously." They did not "fall apart in the face of conflict," nor did they "abandon the game." Instead, "nice" girls would verbally apologize to someone for "outing" someone, promise to "get them back in." Hughes notes that "It was also common for a player to turn to a 'friend' in line just before hitting a hard 'slam' past another player, and call, 'Sally, I'll get you in!' The message: this 'mean stuff' is really intended to 'be nice' to Sally, and not to 'be mean' to the player who must leave the game in order for this to occur."

In 2000, British psychologists Katy Tapper and Michael Boulton administered a questionnaire to 443 seven- to eleven-year-olds in the United Kingdom. They found that girls view aggression more negatively than boys do and thus tend to deny to themselves and others that they have *been* aggressive ("I am not *really* mean"). Citing an earlier (1996) study by other British psychologists, Tapper and Boulton note that "girls do not admit to themselves that they have carried out an act of (indirect) aggression and therefore do not respond with feelings . . . such as guilt and regret. As a result, the likelihood of them repeating such an act in the future is not reduced."

This is a good way of explaining why so many of my own interviewees, when asked, seemed to experience amnesia about whether they had ever hurt or betrayed another woman or whether they had participated in shunning anyone.

Girls view aggression more negatively than boys do. Therefore, according to Tapper and Boulton, girls have learned that "expressive terms are the most effective at lessening disapproval for their aggression, whereas boys may learn that by justifying their aggression . . . they avoid punishment and actually receive approval." "Expressive" statements include: "The worse thing about fighting is that it hurts the other person"; "If I hit someone and hurt them, I would probably feel bad about myself." "Instrumental" statements include: "If someone hit me I would be more likely to hit them back"; "The best thing about fighting is it makes the other person do what you want/it makes you feel better."

In a 1992 study, L. Rowell Huesman found that inner-city, mainly African-American children in Chicago as young as eight or nine expressed different views about aggression as a function of gender. Girls, more than boys, *said* that aggression is wrong. Believing that aggression is wrong is potentially a very positive social trait. But, if girls, not boys, are trained only to *say* that aggression is wrong, even while continuing to *act* in aggressive ways, then girls, even more than boys, may be learning to disassociate themselves from any negative thing they do and deny that they have done it, even to themselves. This disassociative capacity might prove quite resistant to the acknowledgment that is required before one can change one's own aggressive behavior.

In 2000, Australian educators and psychologists, Lawrence Owens, Rosalyn Shute, and Phillip Slee studied how fifteen-year-old girls set into motion indirect aggression: what exactly they do, whom they choose as targets, and what effect such aggression has on its target. An in-depth series of tests and interviews was done with twelve girls and their teachers.

Owens and his group found that girls persistently "spread rumors, break confidences, and criticize others' clothing, appearance, or personality." Sometimes, several girls "say nasty things, barely audible, about a girl who is sitting a few seats ahead." In addition, girls used "code names in plotting against others. The victim may suspect but she cannot prove that she is the target." Teachers, who were also interviewed, viewed these behaviors as "mean, deliberate, and often unprovoked."

Girls also engage in "exclusionary" behavior in which an entire clique, or an entire class will "ostracize" one female peer victim either for short or for very long periods of time—for up to three terms. Sometimes the ostracism is so severe that ostracized girls transfer to new schools. Sometimes, excluded girls contemplate suicide.

Girls also "harass" each other in other ways: by making prank phone calls, writing abusive anonymous notes, and enlisting the aid of adults or boys in hurting their peers. Girls also "huddle" together in order to be obvious about excluding others as they talk about parties and giggle loudly; girls stare at each other in order to threaten, intimidate, or demonstrate dislike. They make gestures and are sarcastic. Finally, girls call each other names: dyke, slut, tart, fat.

Why do girls harass and bully other girls? The Australian girls say that they "victimize" someone in order to "alleviate boredom/or create excitement." A teenage girl may consider herself important only if she holds exciting, cruel knowledge about someone else: she's "in"; the victim is "out." In a sense— and this is an unsettling idea—individual girls may be able to create a series of tribal-like dyads or small cliques only by excluding a series of enemies, who are, in some way, either different or merely vulnerable. Since girls yearn for emotional and social intimacy with their peers, such indirect aggression by their peers blocks them from having it.

When asked why one girl, and not another, is targeted, the girls' responses closely parallel those of boys who bully. The bullying girls blame the victims for having done something annoying, indiscreet, or aggravating, or for having started the conflict, thus bringing it on themselves. This is known as the *Provocative Victim* explanation. Some teachers thought that victims may come from homes in which they have not learned good social skills; most teachers believed that the victim had done nothing wrong and saw the perpetrators as aggressive bullies who deliberately victimized others.

The second explanation given was that of *vulnerability*. If a girl is a newcomer, has few or no friends, does not have the right friends, is unassertive, or is in any way different or geeky, she is vulnerable to victimization.

According to Owens and his colleagues, the effects of being excluded are serious and may last a lifetime. The victim of such indirect aggression will at first be confused. She will then try to deny what is happening, or she might vow not to let it get to her. Eventually, pain floods her consciousness, and she experiences hurt, fear, low self-esteem, high anxiety, reduced self confidence, and depression. Finally, the victim may leave the school or make some attempt at conflict resolution, especially one on one. Interestingly, bystanders also will experience fear and paranoia.

In an earlier, 1992 study, Polish educational researcher Adam Frączek found that, when questioned, girls more than boys referred to the fear of falling victim to aggression or attack (they responded to such items as "I often feel other people want to do me harm"). Girls, more than boys, also stated that they needed more self-confidence (they agreed with statements such as: "I am afraid to oppose others"); girls also "expressed approval" for "retaliation," (they agreed with the statement: "If somebody does me wrong, he/she will regret it"). Frączek viewed this "specific combination of anxiety and [the] tendency to aggressive counterattack" as describing or predicting "an anxious-retaliatory life orientation in social relations."

In the Salmivalli study, when asked about the bullying process, twenty-five percent of the "victims did not mention themselves, but someone else, as a victim"; an additional thirty percent of victims did not answer this particular question. The researchers believe that victims tend to deny or repress being victimized. This does not bode well for one's future capacity to recognize, name, avoid, or defend oneself against similar, or greater, bullying as one gets older.

As I've said before, many studies confirm that girls develop social intelligence sooner and are thus both more interpersonally sensitive and more interpersonally demanding than boys are; girls also excel in coding and decoding nonverbal, interpersonal, and social signals. One of my own sixteen-year-old interviewees eloquently reminds us of just how sensitive girls can be:

Girls look at their friends and try and see their
entire beings. We psychoanalyze each other and ourselves. The closer you get to another, the more intri-
cate her self becomes, and if you try to screw with
that by upsetting any of the many wires that make up
her personality, you'd trip and possibly bring her
down with you. Whatever happens, the friendship
would be changed and quite likely ruined. The
slightest mistake is monumental because "She
should have known me better, she should have
known how this would hurt me." And we recognize
this reaction in ourselves and so fear it in others.

Given the guiltless and brutal nature of boys' physical aggression, it is understandable that some might hope that sensitive
girls would be better peace negotiators. Indeed, in a 1997 study
on Conflict Resolution, Finnish psychologist Karin Österman
and cohorts studied "non-aggressive conflict resolution" among
eight-, eleven-, and fifteen-year-olds in four countries. They
found that girls of all three ages used "more constructive conflict resolution techniques" than boys did in Finland, Israel,
Italy, and Poland. (In some instances, national identity
"trumped" gender; that is, the Poles, of both sexes, used fewer
conflict-resolution behaviors; Finnish girls tended to withdraw
significantly more than others.) The authors hypothesize that
since girls develop social intelligence sooner than boys, this
allows them to apply nonviolent conflict-resolution techniques,
at least during adolescence.

In a subsequent 1999 study, Finnish psychologists Ari Kauki-ainen, Kaj Björkqvist, Kirsti Lagerspetz, and others found that empathy and social intelligence are correlated—but alas, not when it comes to indirect aggression. They note, correctly, that those who are indirectly aggressive have considerable social skills. What they say is reminiscent of Goodwin's 1990 study. Kaukiainen and his group write: "To use indirect aggression, the individual must be able to put his/her intentions to harm another person in a favorable light. At the same time, s(he) has to interpret the reaction of others and accommodate his/her behavior for the social manipulation not to backfire. These are all demanding skills." According to Björkqvist, girls may be better at indirect aggression because they command the kind of social networks required if gossip and shunning are to work.

These studies confirm that, although cultural differences do exist in general, girls in many different countries, more than boys, engage in indirect and intimate aggression, mainly toward other girls. It is not clear whether such cruelty is entirely gratuitous or whether it in some way maximizes (scarce) resources for one girl, while minimizing resources for another. Like boys, girls bully and torment others of their gender; boys also shun most girls, and, to some extent, torment and bully them as well. However, some boys also learn that it is manly to protect girls. Most girls do not learn this.

That these girls avoid use of physical violence in resolving conflicts, does not mean that these conflicts are resolved in meaningful and enduring ways. Girls may smile, give in, give up—and then continue the conflict behind their opponents' backs. Girls may also smile, give in, make fatal compromises, because their need to belong (or not to be excluded) is more important to them than sticking to their principles. Girls' greater social skills may escalate conflicts as well as resolve them.

It is possible, but unlikely, that girls, long used to employing indirect strategies of aggression, will behave very differently when they turn twenty-one. Girls who have been bullied, taunted, and shunned by other girls may not necessarily trust or think highly of girls—or of the women they have become. Having experienced patriarchal daughterhood and girlhood, a woman may expect less of other women than of men and may, wisely or unwisely, place her hopes in an alliance with a man or with a series of men. Of course, women will still continue to socialize mainly with other women out of a deep desire for intimate, dyadic or triadic union. According to Jill McLean Taylor, the central issue among girls at adolescence is trust:

> Something happens and the issue of trust suddenly becomes like a cliff—one false step and the fall is irrevocable. I think that the wish to continue a relational life . . . that really could move forward, comes into tension with a feeling that betrayal is inevitable—this is how it always goes, you always end up sort of disappointed. There's always an edge of bitterness around this giving up the wish or the hope for relationship.

One of my seventeen-year-old interviewees, Debbie, values her close female friendships and explains girlish "dishonesty" in another, more positive, way.

> The idea that women's strong attachments to each other are what make them so vulnerable is horrifying. I count my close friendships with a few girls that I know as one of the best things I have going for me right now. My love for them leaves me open to hurt, but . . . all love does, or at least that's the cliche. Perhaps girls and women do come to love each other too quickly, or once they are trapped into appearing as though they love one another, they don't want to back out of it. That is probably true. But a fear of confrontation in relationships is the downside. The ability to love easily is a positive.

What, exactly, do we know about female-female aggression among adults?

3.

WOMAN'S SEXISM

Women are often quick to believe the worst about another woman. Since, however, women are dependent upon each other for interpersonal intimacy, such negative information can be very threatening. Most women (men too) have experienced women as more interpersonally "present" than men. Research suggests that both men and women are attracted to women who score high on warmth and positive emotions.

As a group, women do excel in certain interpersonal skills. They tend to listen well, smile, nod, and hear what others are saying. Women rate other women as skillful communicators and as listeners. Both men and women think that women exhibit high levels of conversational smiling and gazing, which are experienced as interpersonal closeness.

Women, not men, are also the caretakers of dependent children, the elderly, and the ill, and are trusted to remain even-tempered while performing the tedious, demanding, devalued, and financially unrewarding tasks that are required for such care. Of course, this does not mean that all caretakers are generous or kind; some of them are vicious and abusive.

According to Purdue University psychologists Alice Eagly and Steven Karau, women's contributions to a group seem to be "social emotional" in nature and to consist of "showing solidarity and expressing agreement." University of California psychologist Campbell Leaper finds that white college women use "active understanding responses" with female friends, but not with male friends, with whom, instead, they use "clarification requests." According to MIT linguist Lynette Hirschman, although female speakers interrupt each other often, they also tend to "elaborate on each other's statements, while the males tended to argue." Research has shown that female-female dyads are more verbally affectionate than male-male dyads are.

Dr. Edgar Kenton conducted a study at the Indiana University School of Medicine which showed that, when women listened to the tape of a novel, they listened with both their "left and right temporal lobes," whereas men listened only with their "left temporal lobe." (Listening was measured in terms of increased blood flow to various parts of the brain.)

Such studies confirm that women attract others in positive ways that tend to inspire trust. But, as we have seen, studies also demonstrate that the same interpersonally skillful women may be aggressive and cruel—mainly toward other women.

It is psychologically difficult to accept the fact that one's mother, sister, best friend, or female co-worker, who can be comforting and understanding at one moment, can, in the next moment, turn cold and rejecting. People often deal with this by "splitting" women in half: the Good Fairy Godmother and the Evil Queen Stepmother—who may in reality be the same woman, compartmentalized.

Class and race differences exist. As we have seen, daughters of poverty and victims of racial discrimination are more directly aggressive than more privileged women, and they expect other women to behave similarly. Middle-class and white women do not like to admit that they are competitive or aggressive or that they are afraid to stand up for women who have been targeted for ostracism by other women.

As girls, most women have learned how to express aggression in indirect ways, behind someone's back. And they have learned how to pretend, even to themselves, that they have *not* been aggressive, especially when they have been; or that they didn't really mean it and, therefore, it doesn't count, or that no serious harm resulted from what they didn't "really" do.

Women expect other women to conform to this code of indirect aggression. Some recent research, however, supports two opposing views. On the one hand, according to Simon Fraser University psychologists Marc A. Johnston and Charles B. Crawford, "aggressive women or women in positions of authority are generally disliked and shunned by other women. Therefore, a woman attempting to cooperate with other women is likely to downplay her aggressive tendencies in order to be accepted within a female group." On the other hand, according to experiments conducted by a team of Dutch researchers headed by social psychologists Charles Goldenbeld and Jacob M. Rabbie, women are more aggressive in groups than when they are alone and are more easily influenced than men are to punish an opponent who has been programmed to violate a group norm.

As I have noted, both historically and cross-culturally, women have been very aggressive toward other women. According to University of California anthropologist Victoria Burbank, women mainly target other women for aggression. They did so in ninety-one percent of the 137 societies Burbank surveyed; men were victims of women's aggression in fifty-four percent of the societies studied.

Historically, in ancient China, Japan, and India and on other continents as well, mothers-in-law have wielded great power over their daughters-in-law, whom they have physically and psychologically abused and overworked. Female servants, slaves, adopted daughters, and even biological daughters often fared equally poorly at female hands. Rivalries between co-wives and between wives and "other women," have always been—and remain—intense and painful.

In the Mother-Daughter section (which begins with the next chapter), we will find psychological themes coming into play, such as envy and competition, fear of merging, fear of abandonment, and a terror of "difference" as persecutory. Such themes often accompany otherwise "good enough" contemporary mother-daughter relationships.

Women, as noted, aggressively compete against each other, sexually, for men and for the resources men have. Poor women have tried to use their youthful beauty in order to marry "up." Of course, most can't; there aren't enough Princes to go around. And, poor women face formidable opposition from more educated and wealthier women, who are also young and sexually alluring.

In the United States, according to anthropologist John Townsend, of Syracuse University, one way to compete sexually is either to make oneself look more attractive or to make one's competition look less attractive. In a review of the literature, Townsend writes:

> A common method of making someone appear less attractive is to derogate, slight, and insult them . . . women criticized other women's physical appearance, and implied either that they were promiscuous or that they were sexual teases.

Thus, one way in which women compete with one another is by calling into question whether men can trust a particular woman's capacity to be sexually monogamous.

Townsend conducted a study in which female medical students described their female competition as less intelligent than themselves. According to Townsend, one reason "professional women might derogate a competitor's intelligence is that their own criteria for attractiveness—which are largely socio-economic and include intelligence—seem natural and right." Men's preference for female youth and beauty rather than for female brains or accomplishment seemed "foreign, incomprehensible" to Townsend's female medical students.

> Numerous women in the study deprecated female competitors with lower Social Economic Status (SES) by calling them bimbos, airheads, and dinga-lings. These women also derogated male peers who dated women with lower SES, particularly if those women were younger.

Townsend's study confirms that a woman's educational and professional achievements do not always eradicate her need to compete with other women in more traditional ways as well. Interestingly, Townsend implies that feminist "protective" regulations about sexual harassment on the job might be designed for the benefit of higher-status women as against lower-status women. According to Townsend,

> organizational limitations on dating between men and their status inferiors may serve the ostensible function of protecting against sexual harassment, but they also tend to limit the ability of lower-status women [who are often younger and therefore more

sexually attractive to men] to compete with higher-status women for higher-status men.

Florida anthropologists Nicole Hines and Douglas P. Fry found that Argentinian women were "very competitive, envious, and jealous" of each other; they competed for men and sex by competitive dressing and self-adornment. Hines and Fry's male and female interviewees said that women lied about other women more than men lied about either men or women, spread rumors, interrupted, judged, and excluded others from social events.

Finnish psychologists Kaj Björkqvist, Karin Österman, and their colleagues report that, although both sexes engage in competitor derogation, women are more likely than men to use subtle forms of aggression such as starting and perpetuating rumors, talking behind someone's back, or manipulating who's "in" and who's "out" socially.[1] Women told Björkqvist and Österman that women use indirect aggression as a means of workplace aggression. The researchers found that women in the workplace will, more than men, spread false rumors and refuse to speak to someone, usually another woman.

When Finnish male university employees were (experimentally) interrupted, forced to experience reduced opportunities to express themselves, had their work judged unjustly, were criticized, or had their judgement questioned, the men responded with aggressive strategies, which they justified as "rational." Finnish female university employees, instead, used social manipulation strategies. These include: insulting comments about one's private life, insinuative negative glances, backbiting, the spreading of false rumors, insinuations without direct accusation, and "not being spoken to," and "do-not-speak-to-me" behavior.

Such behavior on the job is not unique to Scandinavia or to Europe. For example, in their study of Argentinian women, Hines and Fry similarly note that female university employees tend to employ a "direct-yet-indirect" kind of aggression. In one instance, when students arrived late for meals, a female university food-server expressed her annoyance by roughly slopping the food onto the tray, giving the students less desirable food, and ignoring their food requests. If challenged, such *direct-yet-indirect* behavior can be readily disavowed as an accident or as a misperception by the recipient. The food-server does not have to acknowledge that she has been aggressive. (Nor do overcritical mothers have to acknowledge that their constant criticism of a daughter is aggressive or hostile. When challenged, such mothers usually insist that they love their daughters and mean no harm; often, their daughters concur.)

Columbia University's professor of Public Affairs Robin Ely found that professional women were reluctant to describe themselves as competitive, but they had no trouble attributing competitive behavior to other women. Ely's subjects tended to under-report their own competitive behavior, despite having "described a number of [such] experiences in their interviews." Ely suggests two reasons for this. Competition is taboo among women. And, if a woman had even one supportive relationship with another woman and an ideological commitment to solidarity among women, she tended to "give higher ratings on the (female-female) supportiveness dimension of [Ely's] questionnaire."

Women are adept at masking anger and aggression. However, a woman's intense stare can turn another woman to stone. The stare signifies hatred. According to psychology professor Dana Crowley Jack, in *Behind the Mask: Destruction and Creativity in Women's Aggression*:

> Certain types of looks—steely-eyed hatred, cold disdain—are ways of delivering aggression indirectly. Eyes can express powerful emotions and intentions, such as a determination to hurt or destroy another. One can always deny the intent or feeling behind a malignant stare, and this makes it a relatively safe means to deliver hostility . . . Verbal expressions reveal the persisting belief that the eye carries malevolent power: "if looks could kill, he would be dead." Eyes "burn holes" in others, people "look daggers," glances are sharp, penetrating, keen, deadly. The fear that the eye has the power to injure or to alter reality is captured in "evil eye" superstitions. Women tried as witches were often accused of looking at others in a harmful way. Cross-culturally, people share the idea that the human eye penetrates or pierces, and that it can invade personal space.

Of course, men stare at other men and at women too; the male stare also asserts and exerts power. Jack notes:

> While not reserved for women's use alone, the powerful, paralyzing look has been emblematized in the female personage of Medusa. Her power is both destructive and creative; it becomes ambiguous as it symbolizes both . . . the women I interviewed gave striking descriptions of "the look" that paralyzes. They recall receiving this look from other women; they also speak of becoming Medusa themselves, by gathering up their forceful anger and focusing it on someone else in a laser-sharp stare.

One Argentinian woman informant explained to anthropologists Hines and Fry that women are "quicker to anger than are men." She and other interviewees strongly (and incorrectly) believed that "the jealous, impassioned woman is equally capable of murder as her male counterpart." In reality, Buenos Aires homicide statistics showed that men were almost nine times more likely to commit murder than women were.

One must always remember to take people's (unconscious) sexist perceptions with a large grain of feminist salt. To what extent have social scientists been able to measure conscious and unconscious bias? After the Second World War, scientists began to measure racism—no doubt, in the hope that its study might lead to its abolition. With the advent of the Second Wave of feminism in the late 1960s, psychologists developed measures of sexist as well as racist bias. Such scales include the Attitudes Toward Women Scale (AWS), which was pioneered in the early 1970s; the Sex-Role Egalitarianism Scale (SRES); and the Hostility Toward Women Scale (HTW) first developed in the mid-1980s as a measure of *male-only* sexism and later adapted to measure women's sexism in the late 1990s; the Modern Sexism Scale (MS), the Neo-Sexism Scale (NS), and the Ambivalent Sexism Inventory (ASI), which were all pioneered in the mid-to-late 1990s. These scales measure both overt and covert "hostile" and "benevolent" stereotyped views of the genders.

In 1968, in an article in the journal *Transaction*, P. Goldberg asked subjects to judge an essay attributed to either a male or a female author. The subjects rated the same essay as more competent if they thought it was written by a male author. Goldberg viewed this as an example of unconscious sexist bias, since the subjects did not consciously know that gender was at issue. Over the years, Goldberg's findings were widely publicized in textbooks.[2]

Socio-linguist Deborah Tannen found that women dislike female leaders who employ an authoritarian leadership style: "Woman managers do best if they avoid behaving like 'authority figures.'" Initially, Indiana's Purdue University psychologist Alice Eagly and her colleagues found that, no matter what leadership style was employed, "female leaders tend to be devalued by female subordinates." University of Delaware psychologists Dore Butler and Florence L. Geis showed that both men and women rated female and male leaders similarly, but that "nonverbal behaviors" toward female leaders were more negative than toward male leaders. Butler and Geis's subjects were unaware that they were biased.

Yale University's Mahzarin R. Banaji and the University of Washington's Anthony G. Greenwald believe that biases are usually "implicit," "subtle," "unintentional," and "outside of the stereotyper's awareness." Therefore, rather than ask people about their attitudes toward race or gender, Banaji and Greenwald measured experimentally the unconscious way in which bias operates. In one study both male and female subjects were found to be able to remember male names more easily than female names. In a second study Banaji and Greenwald found that both male and female subjects could be influenced to regard women as "more dependent" than men who behaved in exactly the same way. In a sense, this latter study is similar to one done by H.A. Sagar and J.W. Schoenfeld, who found that (white) children viewed the very same behavior as "more aggressive" when performed by black people than when it was performed by whites. These subjects were not told that race or gender was at issue.

Sexism is both similar to and different from racism. Both are complex prejudices. Neither sexists nor racists hate The Other. A toxic ambivalence reigns. White racists like or depend upon those Blacks/Hispanics/Asians/Jews/Arabs who "know their place," or who have, themselves, internalized racism and share its prejudices. Racists may depend upon the labor of The Other, but they do not have to marry those whom they dislike, distrust, or despise. On the other hand, most heterosexual male sexists still have to marry or live with women in order to have families and children. Women do not.

What else do we know about women's "sexism"?

In a series of studies, Alice Eagly and her colleagues found that, among white college students, men emerged as leaders, but not because men were preferred to women. Eagly found that "the tendency to choose men may instead reflect a tendency to (instantly) define leadership in terms of task-oriented contributions . . . Women apparently have more chance of achieving leadership (when) socially complex tasks (are required)."

In subsequent studies, Eagly and her colleagues found that male and female white Midwestern college students actually rated women more positively than they rated men. Eagly's subjects also rated Republicans more positively than they rated Democrats. (Remember: Women are "warm," and excellent communicators.) Although positive toward women, Eagly's female respondents were also significantly more favorable emotionally toward men.

Perhaps Eagly and her group were measuring heterosexuality; perhaps, as I suspect, they may have been tapping into male and female approval for traditional women—hence, their subjects' approval for Republicans over Democrats.

In 1996, psychologists Peter Glick, of Wisconsin's Lawrence University, and Susan T. Fiske, of New Jersey's Princeton University, confirmed that hostility toward women may coexist with positive feelings toward those women who know their place and who support traditional gender inequality. They call this *ambivalent sexism*. Two thousand white college students who scored high on this inventory were found to love, admire, romanticize, and idealize certain women (homemakers; attractive, sexually available women) and to fear and despise other women (career women, feminists, sexual teases, unattractive women). According to the authors, such ambivalent sexism helps maintain traditional and unequal gender roles and serves as a

> balm for the conscience of the dominant group members ("We aren't exploiting anyone; they couldn't get along without us telling them what to do and taking care of them"), as well as a more effective and pleasant means of coercing cooperation from the subordinate group, whose members receive various perks and even affection in return for "knowing their place."[3]

Interestingly, Glick and Fiske found that men have positive affect toward women who are homemakers or who are attractive and sexually available. Women, who themselves may approve of such traditional roles for women, nevertheless also see themselves as competitors with other woman and do not display positive affect toward other (traditional) women. In the authors' own words: "Female sexists are not so much ambivalent as hostile toward women." This finding is not surprising.

Men probably receive more warmth from women, both at home and at the office, than women do. Remember: Women are aggressive mainly toward other women, not toward men.

In a subsequent study, Peter Glick and others were able to differentiate between sexist and non-sexist men and women. Sexist men thought about women in highly eroticized ways. That is, women either were "attractive" and "sexy" or they were "whores, sluts, dykes." Both sexist and non-sexist men rated traditional women positively. Sexist men described them as "decent," "religious," "caring, warm, loving, giving, patient, innocent." Non-sexist men saw traditional women in this way too—but they also saw them as "Daddy's Girls," "quiet," "passive," "airhead(s)," "ditzes," and "simple." Sexist men described non-traditional women negatively: they called them "know-it-alls," "jocks," "manlike," "aggressive," "feminazis." Non-sexist men sometimes described non-traditional women in this way too, but they also described them as "independent," "able-minded," "tomboys," "women who don't take crap from anyone."

Women viewed homemakers more positively than they viewed career women. (Glick's female subjects were themselves college students. So much for higher education!)

In this study, men viewed career women as "intelligent, hard working, and professional." Sexist men, however, also viewed career women as "aggressive, selfish, greedy, and cold" and stated that they "feared, envied, were intimidated by, or felt competitive with" career women. Non-sexist men viewed career women as "confident and honest." They did not mention feeling intimidated, and often stated that they admired such women. Once again, men had a wealth of positive feelings toward homemakers.

Female sexists, as compared with non-sexists, generally rated career women less favorably and reported more "positive affect" toward homemakers. However, although sexist women approved of women who are homemakers, such women, unlike men, manifested no consciously benevolent feelings toward homemakers.

Having developed and tested their measures in the United States, Glick and Fiske undertook to measure sexism across cultures—no small undertaking; actually a rather breathtaking one. Glick, Fiske, and twenty-nine other researchers administered the Ambivalent Sexism Scales to more than 15,000 male and female respondents, who live in nineteen countries including the United States.

Researchers on five continents participated in this work: Africa (Nigeria, Botswana, South Africa), South America (Columbia, Chile, Brazil, Cuba), Europe (England, Spain, Holland, Germany, Italy, Belgium, Portugal), Asia (South Korea, Turkey, Japan, Australia), and North America (the United States). The United States study used college students. Participants were more wide-ranging in other countries.

Dr. Glick notes that "whereas women as a group scored lower than men on hostile sexism in every nation studied, their scores on benevolent sexism were often no different than or sometimes significantly higher than men's."

This makes sense. Although one might expect hostile sexism (HS) to elicit female outrage, in fact what happens is that "particularly virulent" sexism (as measured both by United Nations indices of gender inequality and male HS scores) seems to evoke extreme benevolent sexism (BS) among women. According to the authors, "the idealization" of traditional women is a "crucial complement to the demonization of those who defy male power and authority." In the authors' view, "hostile sexism" (HS) and "benevolent sexism" (BS) "work together" to "elicit women's cooperation in their own subordination."

The authors observe that "the more sexist the nation, the more women, relative to men, accepted benevolent sexism, even to the point, in the four nations with the highest mean sexism scores (Botswana, Cuba, Nigeria, South Africa), of endorsing benevolent sexism significantly more than men did." The authors conclude that "members of subordinate groups find ostensibly benevolent prejudice more acceptable than hostile prejudice toward their group."

Many men do protect some—if not all—women from more hostile forms of sexism. This is precisely what allows both men and women to view men as protectors and not just as hostile dominators. In Glick's view, "benevolent sexism" may "undermine" attempts by women to achieve equality by "rewarding them for enacting conventional gender roles and by deflating the resentment they feel about men's greater power (as one is less likely to resent another's power if that power is used to protect oneself)." As men's sexism increased, so did women's acceptance of sexist ideologies. However, women's acceptance of hostile sexism had its limits, and began to decrease as men's hostile-sexism scores became extreme. Commendably, Glick's group insists on viewing these data in an optimistic light. They suggest that reducing "men's hostile sexism may free women to reject benevolent sexism as well as hostile sexism."

If women hold sexist views, what might that mean in the real (as opposed to the laboratory) world? Some feminists say that women have so little power that, even if they *do* hold sexist views, such views are not as consequential as male sexist views.

I disagree. For example, consider how important it is for a female rape victim to have access to a sympathetic—or at least objective—woman police officer, mental health professional, physician, and emergency room nurse. (I do not mean to minimize the importance of sympathetic or objective men, but a minority of good or non-sexist men cannot hold up the sky alone.) Like men, women sit on juries. An increasing number of judges and lawyers *are* women. What attitudes toward women do they hold?

For a moment, let's step back in time to 1976. In that year, Australian researchers studied women's attitudes toward female crime victims. They found that female college students believed that married women, virgins, and unmarried non-virgins were victims in cases of rape, but "divorcees and prostitutes *in identical circumstances* were seen as responsible for the act, so were ruled out of being victims of the crime." Clearly, these college students did not identify with divorcees or prostitutes.

In the 1970s, an experienced defense lawyer told beginning lawyers that, if an alleged rapist was "handsome" and if his accuser was a woman, they should choose women as jurors. "Women will be sympathetic" to a handsome man accused of rape, said the lawyer, and are also "somewhat distrustful of other women." A second trial lawyer agreed and stated that "biases against women may . . . be held by women jurors: the trial attorney must be as concerned about the hostilities of women jurors as about those of men."

Such views have changed—but not enough. In 1991, fifteen years later and thousands of miles away, a female juror, Lea Haller, sat on the Florida panel that acquitted William Kennedy Smith of rape. Haller told New York journalist Amy Pagnozzi that "I think (Smith is) too charming and too good looking to have to resort to violence for a night out."

In 1991, Law professor Anita Hill was forced to publicly confront Clarence Thomas, her former boss at the Equal Employment Opportunities Commission, as her sexual harasser. I was quite disconcerted by the large number of women who, with great feeling, insisted that Anita Hill was a liar—as if their own lives depended upon it. I am referring not only to the handful of women who publicly testified against Hill, but to those women *who did not know her.* Of course, large numbers of feminist and other women also believed and supported Hill.

In 1991, Desiree Washington, a beauty-contest winner, accused boxer Mike Tyson of having raped her in her hotel room. I interviewed several African-American women about

their attitudes toward Hill and Washington. One woman, a professor of African-American Studies, described her own frustration when many of her friends refused to believe Washington,
but in fact, blamed her for "airing that dirty laundry in public."
The professor's friends also blamed Washington for entering
Mike Tyson's room at three o'clock in the morning and for
failing to scream and call the police immediately afterwards.
My interviewee said:

> I brought this up in a small group. I said it's not the
> woman's fault. At her age, if some cute guy (not Mike
> Tyson) said "Hey let's go hang out, I've got a car and
> driver," I'd do it. If he said, "I gotta go back to the
> hotel and get something," I'd say—okay. And if he
> said: 'Do you want to wait in the limo?' I'd say no,
> because I'd be thinking I don't know the limo driver.
> And I wouldn't wait in the hotel lobby because I'd
> feel slutty sitting in a hotel lobby. I probably would
> have gone up to his room and guess what? I might
> have started fooling around and guess what? At some
> point I would have said Stop. I would have made
> every single choice that Desiree made. There but for
> the grace of God, I have not been date-raped.

When I asked how the group responded to her, she said: "Respond?
They said nothing. They just stared at me but said nothing. Afterwards, I heard that some women said I was 'crazy.' "

The silent stare. The silent treatment. Silence among women often means disapproval. No happy little hum and buzz. Women express disapproval by disconnecting, both verbally and energetically. Silence, whether temporary or permanent, is often what two or more women do to a third woman whose words, ideas, physical appearance, sexuality, threaten and challenge them. Sometimes, women fall silent as a way of punishing any woman who expresses herself directly, openly, regardless of what view she expresses. The directness itself seems to challenge women's enforced/preferred style of indirect expression and indirect "backtalk."

My second informant, an African-American lawyer, had a similar series of conversations with her friends. In her view, "three o'clock in the morning is not that late." My lawyer-informant also pointed out that even if "black people refuse to trust the criminal justice system" where black men are concerned, Tyson had consistently been in trouble with the law.

According to his ex-wife, Robin Givens, Mike Tyson beat her up. We know he used to knock over little old ladies for their purses. He's a *prizefighter,* and here's this little girl from the Midwest, a suburban girl, a farm girl, trying to become a Black Beauty Queen. C'mon, if you judge them on character alone, you have to think it probably happened the way Washington said it did.

Karen Jo Koonan and Terri Waller of the National Jury Project in Oakland, California found that, when a battered woman kills in self-defense, the most sympathetic juror for the defense is not necessarily another woman or another *battered* woman. Koonan and Waller came to the aid of a battered woman who had been found guilty of killing her batterer. A jury composed of nine women and three men found Sally Blackwell, a battered woman who had killed her husband in self-defense, guilty. Koonan and Waller report:

> "During the voir dire in the first trial, one of the jurors denied having any experience with domestic or spousal violence and also denied having any "preconceived position" about battering or abuse. Following the defendant's conviction of second degree murder. It was revealed that that juror had in fact been the victim of an abusive spouse and in evaluating this case, had compared the defendant's experience to her own. The conviction was reversed by the First District Court of Appeal, which held that a juror's failure to reveal her personal experience with domestic violence constituted juror misconduct.

The juror who had concealed her own battery had not been sympathetic to the defendant who had murdered her abuser. Koonan and Waller concluded that "similarity in experience does not necessarily make a juror sympathetic . . . [but] may lead to less objective and more harsh responses." Based on their analysis of the first jury Koonan and Waller conducted a voir dire of a new jury pool. A number of potential jurors who had experience woth domestic violence in their own lives were peremptorily challeneged by the defense, as well as by the prosecution. In the second trial, Koonan and Waller eliminated six women. The second jury consisted of ten men and two women. After about seven hours of deliberation the jury came back with a verdict of not guilty.[4]

In 1993, a legal researcher, Lynn Hecht Schafran, reviewed the previous decade's studies on the attitudes of the public, mock jurors, and actual jurors, toward rape. In her view, the studies "revealed significant adherence" by men and women to certain sexist myths, such as:

> only 'bad girls' are raped; women provoke rape by their appearance and behavior; women enjoy rape; women charge rape out of vindictiveness; black women are more sexually experienced than white women and thus less harmed by an assault; rapists are abnormal men without access to consensual sex.

According to Schafran, many women, including women judges and jurors, "avoid acknowledging their own vulnerability by blaming the victim. This distancing mechanism operates particularly in non-stranger rape cases, because it is in acknowledging the likelihood of these crimes that women jurors feel most at risk."

Schafran's legal research has been confirmed and expanded upon by a number of psychologists. In a study of college students, University of Illinois psychologists Kimberly A. Lonsway and Louise F. Fitzgerald found that respondents with high scores on the Hostility Toward Women Scale blamed women for being raped. This finding was twice as true for men as for women. (Glick's group might consider this a measure of Hostile Sexism.)

Pennsylvania State University psychologists Janet K. Swim and Laurie L. Cohen found that those who score high on the Modern Sexism Scale will, in real-life situations, tend to minimize economic discrimination, sexual harassment, and hostile workplace environments, and will tend to disbelieve women who allege sexual violence.

In their first study, Swim and Cohen asked white college students to assume that they were personnel managers; embedded in ten personnel problems were three cases of sexual harassment with a male harasser and a female victim. Participants were asked to indicate to what extent they believed that the harasser had behaved "inappropriately" and to what extent the woman had "elicited the treatment." In the second study, psychology students read a summary of an actual sexual harassment court case in which both the prosecution and the defense had expert witnesses. Participants were asked to decide to what extent they believed that the (male) defendant's behavior was "intimidating, disgusting, interfered with the woman's performance, and was done with the intent to harm." They also rated the extent to which they believed that the female plaintiff should be "flattered by the men's attention and was overreacting."

The authors found a predictive correlation between how both men and women scored on the Modern Sexism Scale and their views on sexual harassment. In other words, if either a man or a woman is hostile toward or unconsciously biased against women, this attitude may well affect that person's real-life behavior.

In 2001, the Executive Director of a state-wide Sexual Assault Program in the Mid-West answered a lawyer's query about whether to choose women or men for a rape jury this way:

> After ten years in the field, I have had many prosecutors tell me that they prefer to not have women on their juries because women will not identify with the woman survivor, as a psychological means of reassuring themselves that nothing so horrendous could ever happen to them. Women either believe that the raped woman did something wrong that "allowed" the rape to happen—or that what happened was not rape. Either way, they themselves remain out of the Possible Victim category in their minds.

In 2000 California State University psychologist Gloria Cowan surveyed 155 American college women to determine how "hostile" they were toward other women and how willing they were to blame the (female) victim of sexual violence.

Cowan's population consisted of working and middle-class white, Hispanic-American, African-American, Asian-American, and Native-American college students, and ranged in age from eighteen to fifty-five. Cowan found that women did have significant "hostility toward other women" and that such "hostility" was "positively associated with their beliefs in victim precipitation myths in the area of both rape and sexual harassment." Her subjects believed that women "provoked" or somehow deserved to be raped or harassed. Women's "hostility" to women and their consequent victim-blaming was more prevalent among younger than among older women.

According to Cowan, women who tend to victim-blame also tend to "dislike and distrust women." Such hostility has, in previous studies, been correlated, in women, with "low self-esteem, both personally and collectively," with "emotional dependence on men," less happiness and satisfaction in their own lives, and with resistance to labeling oneself a "feminist." In addition, in a private communication, Cowan wrote:

> I have found women's hostility toward women to be related also to lower self-efficacy, lower optimism, lower sense of internal control, higher belief in external control, higher objectification of body, higher loss of self, less intimate relationships with women and with their male partners, less willingness to work with women, more competition with women, and on the violence end: more acceptance

of rape myths, acceptance of interpersonal violence, and sexual harassment myths (that women ask for harassment). What I have found, and am disappointed by, is that women's hostility toward women is unrelated to their self-labeling as a feminist or to a feminism scale.

What Cowan is saying is that feminist ideology alone does not necessarily help a woman to overcome her hostility toward women.

A National Family Health survey of 90,000 women in India confirms Glick's 2000 cross-cultural findings, as well as Cowan's American findings. The survey, done in 2000, found that more than fifty percent of the women believed that "wife-beating can be justified under certain circumstances." Forty percent viewed wife-beating as "justified" if a woman "neglected the house or children"; thirty-seven percent felt that "going out without informing their husbands constituted a valid reason." A third of the women surveyed thought that "disrespect to in-laws" and a husband's "suspicion of infidelity" were "acceptable grounds" for wife-beating. In addition, some women viewed "improper cooking" and an "inadequate dowry" as grounds for a beating.

As Cowan might have predicted, rural and less educated Indian women held views that were more "hostile" to women than those of urban, better educated women. In Cowan's view, "women's hostility toward women can be thought of as internalized oppression or as false consciousness—'the holding of beliefs that are contrary to one's personal or group interest.'" Women who are "hostile" toward women will continue to "collaborate in maintaining a misogynist culture" and will also "resist bonding in feminist ways to oppose it."

In daily life, hostile attitudes toward a woman or to women in general are powerfully conveyed through gossip. We have seen earlier that girls taunted and shunned other vulnerable girls. Grown women also target and shun other women, most often for violating patriarchal group norms. This seems to be universally true.

For example, in the Hines and Fry study of Argentinian women, women viewed all-male offices as having few or "no problems." In their opinion, if office workers "are all women, at any moment problems will arise due to gossip . . . we women are the ones who start things." A male interviewee suggested that since women "value relationships more than men do, exclusion (of women by women), is a crucial form of (female) aggression." Hines and Fry agree, and suggest that exclusion "increases the pain of the (female) victim."

It is one thing to study laboratory-induced behavior or to analyze responses to questionnaires on the assumption that people respond to such questionnaires honestly and accurately. But one must also observe behavior in the real world. Luckily, anthropologists have done so for the last seventy-five years. I think their work is both elegant and relevant to our subject.

What is "gossip?" According to Roland Barthes, gossip is

"death by language." Australian anthropologist John Beard Haviland describes gossip this way: "Bad words are like physical blows: they violate personal space, and their heated exchange leads to colder but harder legal and social repercussions." The word "trivia" comes from the Latin "tre via" (three roads, or crossroads) where gossip was exchanged by travelers. According to the sociologist Alexander Rysman, the word *gossip* was once a positive term which meant "god parent" or "family friend" and applied to both sexes. By the sixteenth century, *gossip* referred to women who gathered at home births and to (male) "drinking companions." In the nineteenth century, *gossip* became a "derogatory term applied to women and to their 'idle' talk."

Is gossip "idle," or does it have a purpose?

In a study of rural Haitians, anthropologist Melville J. Herskovits found that "gossip functioned as a way of maintaining morals and (patriarchal) group solidarity." In a study of a small Midwestern town in the United States, anthropologist James West found that the "religious control of morals operates mainly through gossip and the fear of gossip. People (learn to) behave carefully to avoid being caught in any trifling missteps of their own." In a study of a rural village in Trinidad, Herskovits found that gossip actually functioned in multiple and opposite ways. While gossip upholds group morality, it may also function to "protest injustice."

Elizabeth Colson and Max Gluckman (both anthropologists) studied the "much diminished" Makah Indian tribe, who live opposite Vancouver Island. According to Gluckman, although "hostile to Whites," the Makah are also "torn by dissension . . . and struggles for status. They constantly use the tongue of scandal to keep each other in (their) proper place." The Makah verbally denigrate each other, partly to make sure that no one Makah gets ahead of any other Makah; strangely, this also functions as a way of solidifying Makah group identity. In Gluckman's view,

> gossip is what keeps a group together and allows it to exclude others . . . gossiping is a duty of membership of the group. That is why it is good manners to gossip and scandalize about your dearest friends with those who belong . . . but it is bad manners . . . to tell unpleasant stories about your friends to strangers.

Thus, according to Gluckman, gossip or scandal is "virtuous" when it demonstrates "social unity." But not otherwise.

According to Gluckman, women's friendships have been frowned upon because "friendship leads to gossip," which might create an opening for "sorcery by a member of the opposing group." Gossip is a form of indirect verbal aggression whose object, according to anthropologist David D. Gilmore, is to "damage the subject." The "moral poses" and the exchange of useful information are merely rationalizations or side benefits. As Jeanne Favret-Saada says, The "bad word is the linguistic equivalent of witchcraft . . . a covert magical pin in the heart of the victim."

Thus, gossip reinforces traditional morality, solidifies group identity, excludes "outsiders," and serves as a warning that one may become the focus of gossip if one behaves anti-normatively. Gossip reinforces patriarchal ethnic and class solidarity. The prohibition against female gossip serves also as a prohibition against female solidarity.

In her book, *Between Sisters: Secret Rivals, Intimate Friends*, journalist Barbara Mathias suggests that girls gossip not only to criticize "peers who stand out or appear better than others" but also as a way of covertly criticizing their biological sisters. She writes:

> For girls in grade school and high school, the desire or need to gossip often facilitates the need to commiserate about or criticize their (biological) sisters. It was not uncommon for women in the survey to recall how they would complain about their sisters to their closest friends. Or, how they "couldn't believe" how their wonderful friends could have such "horrible" sisters.

According to Literature professor and psychotherapist Laura Tracy, author of *The Secret between Us: Competition among Women*, women "have friends, most adult men do not." Good friends "tell stories," which our society calls "gossip."

But women who are good friends know that all gossip is not equal . . . When good friends tell each other stories about friends who are absent, they do so in order to continue the web of relationships in which they participate. They do so in order to create that web. Those stories, filled with the same details as more malicious gossip, are dominated by loving concern.

But when women tell stories about other women who are not their friends, whom they envy, with whom they cannot identify, they seek to destroy. As all women know, gossip can be destructive and terrible. Because we have been forced to separate our aggressive and our erotic drives in relation to men, we locate our aggression in our relations with other women.

According to Alexander Rysman, traditional societies view gossip as a "sin" because women who gossip might "develop social ties outside the institutions of male dominance." Sadly, most female gossips do not do this.

According to John Beard Haviland, in a study of the Mexican Zincantan, "A new bride, introduced into her husband's household, represents a serious potential breach of confidentiality; her in-laws begrudge her even occasional visits to her own mother, where she can leak out family secrets and gossip about her new household to an outsider."

This is an entirely new explanation of why brides are sequestered, viewed with suspicion, and harshly controlled by mothers-in-law. According to anthropologist Douglas P. Fry, Zapotec women in Mexico are viewed as very aggressive (indirectly) through their use of "gossip and witchcraft." Fry, writing in 1992, quotes from the fieldnotes gathered by another anthropologist, one of whose informants said that "when people engage in malicious gossip, 'all sorts of heavy things float to the surface, things which should remain at the bottom . . . it's like a can of lard, if you tip it over, it will spread, slowly, but it will spread and spread.'" According to Margaret L. Sumner's fieldnotes, both men and women believed that women gossiped more than men. "Women emphatically nominated their own sex as gossiping more than men. One woman from La Paz explained, 'The women gossip more. When a woman comes by, soon the whole town knows!'"

The Zapotec have a phrase for someone who is more "evil-hearted" than a witch; it is the "wana bieha," who is a "tale-bearer about sexual infidelities" and whose "evil gossip creates conflict and undermines social relationships."

Gossip can break one's heart and spirit. Gossip can also lead to "social" death and, sometimes, even to physical death. In a book on Andalusian culture in Spain, the anthropologist David D. Gilmore tells Conchita's story:

> Gossip, it seems, had ruined her forthcoming wedding. As a girl, Conchita already had somewhat of a

reputation in town for her headstrong manner, high
spirits, and for occasionally flouting convention . . .
Thus, Conchita was the object of much envy among
her peers.

Still, Conchita had close female friends. One, whose name was
Maria, was neither as "beautiful" nor as "spirited" as Conchita. As
the village girls matured, "forwardness" and "curiosity" became
synonymous with "promiscuity." As a group, the girls became
"shamed," "circumspect," "alert," and "suspicious." "Bested at
every turn by the fortunate Conchita, Maria's envy grew. Especially galling was Conchita's open love for [her fiancé] Eloy,
which was so obviously reciprocated."

   Maria also had a fiancé, but, because Maria "felt overshad-
owed by her radiant friend," she resolved to "put an end to her
rival's happiness." Maria observed Conchita and Eloy "necking
in a darkened alley." This emboldened Maria to try to destroy
Conchita through secret "character assassination, the vengeance
of the envious." Maria would "enlist the envy of the town in her
secret campaign." Maria let it be known that Conchita was
pregnant, that Eloy did not really want to marry her, and that
it was a shotgun wedding. This was a great, bold lie. Still, old
women who had seen Conchita grow up now literally hissed at
her when she walked by. The gossip had

   taken its course, flaring up and spreading through
   the dry wood of Conchita's capricious character . . .

Conchita was chastened. And subsequently, she was marked by a certain resigned sadness . . . The town, galvanized into moral condemnation by the hostility of one sour girl, arose as one to punish its wayward beauty.

In Gilmore's view, the fear of just such gossip "discourages non-conformity" and is the "strongest force of conventionality, blandness, and anonymity." Some people insist that "gossip" is really "harmless," that it causes only "minor" harm. I disagree. The ways in which women use gossip can—and does—result in other women's shame and "social death." It can also cause the physical death of other women.

An American novel written in the early twentieth century about very wealthy women, and an anthropological study of gossip among very poor Arab women in the latter part of the same century, are instructive.

Women's envy and gossip lead to rumors against the too beautiful and too socially vivacious Lily Bart—Edith Wharton's heroine, in the novel, *House of Mirth*. The rumors lead to Lily's ostracism and, ultimately, to her suicide. As a daughter of wealth, Lily has been trained to a life of idleness, filled with incessant socializing, material acquisition, travel, snobbery, the American cultivation of European royalty, the non-stop display of outward beauty. Still, Lily also embodies an old-fashioned honor. Unlike many of her companions, Lily is neither cruel nor crass; she cannot "clinch" commercial deals; she is, essentially, gracious and kind and entirely without guile. Lily is an orphan, completely dependent upon her very wealthy aunt, Mrs. Peniston, with whom she lives. She is expected both to inherit a fortune and to marry, but she has turned away every suitor.

Bertha Dorset, a society matron, is Lily's friend. Bertha is an inveterate adulteress who often invites Lily along to distract her husband, George Dorset. On a fateful cruise to Monte Carlo on the Dorset's yacht, Bertha disappears, overnight, with her latest paramour. To cover this up, Bertha, the next day, publicly accuses Lily of having spent the night alone with George. Humiliated, Lily still refuses to tell George Dorset the truth about his wife or to protect herself from Bertha by threatening to do so. From this moment on, high society cuts Lily dead. Lily retreats "like some deposed princess, moving tranquilly to exile."

(Untrue) rumors about Lily abound. When her aunt learns of them, she disinherits Lily, who is thus immediately impoverished. Lily's distant cousin, Grace Stepney, who inherits everything in Lily's place, turns Lily out. Lily has to work for a living, first as a social secretary, then as a milliner's assistant, and she keeps failing at the task. Once, she floated from palace to palace; now, she can't afford anything but the meanest of rooms in a boarding house. Lily's astute explanation is as follows:

> It's a great deal easier to believe Bertha Dorset's
> story than mine, because she has a big house and an

opera box, and it's convenient to be on good terms with her . . . You asked me just now for the truth— well the truth about any girl is that once she's talked about she's done for; and the more she explains her case the worse it looks.

Pride, passivity, character, fate; Lily will not stoop to conquer, she is no blackmailer. The constant worry about survival money and the social ostracism begin to weigh heavily upon her. "If one were not part of the season's fixed routine, one swung unsphered in a void of social non-existence. Lily, for all her dissatisfied dreaming, had never really conceived of the possibility of revolving around a different centre." Lily explains:

> I have tried hard—but life is difficult, and I am a very useless person. I can hardly be said to have an independent existence. I was just a screw or a cog in the great machine I called life, and when I dropped out of it I found I was no use anywhere else. What can one do when one finds that one only fits into one hole? One must get back to it or be thrown out into the rubbish heap—and you don't know what it's like in the rubbish heap!

Lily does; she prefers death, and so she kills herself.

In 1994 the anthropologists Ilsa M. Glazer and Wahiba Abu

Ras studied the relationship between women's gossip and the family, or "honor" killings of women in the Arab world. In their view, "gossip is a mean spirited act of verbal aggression." It is also the most powerful way in which utterly subordinated women enforce their own subordination and also improve their own positions in the all-female hierarchy of subordinated women.

Interestingly, Glazer first became interested in women's aggression toward each other when she tried to understand why the women political leaders in Zambia "scapegoated rather than supported young educated women." Later, in Israel, Glazer found the concept of "inter-female aggression" useful in understanding how female kibbutz members "facilitated" the maintenance of their own "inferior status." Glazer and Abu Ras tested the hypothesis first proposed by the anthropologist J. Ginat: that "the public accusation which leads to murder for family honor is by a member of the woman's patrilineal group, often a woman." They conclude that: "Women's gossip creates the climate in which the [honor killing] of a young woman is inevitable."

Glazer and Abu Ras, who grew up in a small village in the Galilee, offer a careful and complex analysis of the murder of one young Arab Muslim Israeli woman named Jamila. The story is complicated because there are many half-siblings involved, as well as people who are related in multiple ways, both by marriage and by blood. The murder took place in a small village, Masdar El-Nabea (the source of a fresh water spring), with a population of 2200 inhabitants who belong to seventeen patrilineages. When the men are away at work, "women monitor each other's daily behavior."

Jamila was a young, "secluded," uneducated, unemployed, and unmarried girl who lived with her impoverished, widowed mother. Jamila was totally innocent and completely naive. At first glance, her murder does not support Ginat's theory. Jamila was not "publicly" but "privately" denounced by her new husband, who spoke only to Jamila's brothers. Within hours, Jamila had been murdered by these brothers. Nevertheless, "women's gossip played a critical role" in this tragedy. First, Jamila, who was illiterate, asked a literate, young, female neighbor, Aisha, to read a love letter written to her by a boy named Saied. Jamila is "socially vulnerable" and can be approached by higher-status boys. Aisha scolded Jamila and, with the help of another young girl, Khaula, who worked in the post office, returned the "trinkets" that Saied had sent to Jamila. Both Aisha and Khaula "talked" about this to others.

Then Jamila was observed by Nasrah, the village herbalist, as Jamila "held hands with Younis." The herbalist, a woman who travels from home to home, "talked." Then Lila, Jamila's younger sister, reported to their mother that she had seen Jamila "having sex" with Younis. Lila also "talked." When confronted by her brothers, privately, Jamila told them that "Younis (like Saied, also a higher status boy) gave her sleeping pills and took her virginity." Younis ran away. The village elders got involved, which "made public the family's shame." This shame was "further heightened" by a forced and "disrespectful" marriage ceremony between Jamila and Younis, in which no gifts were exchanged and no marriage certificate issued.

Jamila's new mother-in-law would not allow the newlyweds to live with her because of the gossip against Jamila. In addition, ongoing jealousies between Jamila's and Younis's extended families fueled a fight between two women, one from each family; each accused the other of having "suspect morals" or of harboring a sister with "suspect morality." The fateful, final accusation against Jamila was leveled by Jamila's unmarried sister-in-law, who was, herself, suspected of not being a virgin.

In the authors' opinion, the very swiftness with which her brothers killed her confirms that Jamila had first been "encircled" and rendered "vulnerable" by the gossip of at least six village girls and women. (Aisha, Khaula, Nasrah, and by three women of Younis' family including Jamila's mother-in-law). Their gossip functioned to uphold the patriarchal mores that subordinated them, but also bestowed upon Younis and his mother both the riches and the prestige of a higher-status bride/daughter-in-law. In fact, after Jamila's murder, Younis married a "higher-status" woman.

According to Glazer and Abu Ras's anthropological postmortem, Younis kept Jamila locked up for the fifteen days of their marriage. He allowed no one to see her, nor did he allow

Jamila to go out. Younis beat Jamila, anally raped her, and starved her. He (and his family) wanted to be rid of her; because she was a very poor girl, the marriage brought them no "enhanced" social status. When Jamila's brothers finally inquired about their sister, whom no one had seen, Younis, for the first time, complained that he had not married a virgin. (He had, of course, raped the virgin Jamila before he was forced to marry her; hence, technically, Younis had indeed not married a virgin.) Within hours of Younis's accusation, one of Jamila's brothers had knifed her to death.

Glazer and Abu Ras report that Jamila's mother did not mourn her daughter. When she wept, she said, "Why did (my) daughter behave in a manner which made her death necessary?'"

The authors conclude that "aggressive gossip which supports the cohesion of a subordinate group is not in itself a 'social good.'" The internal rankings within the subordinate group mean that "women have an interest in keeping those beneath themselves in their place."

In 1991, editors of an Arab Israeli newsletter published an article, "The Role of Rumours and Gossip in the Oppression of Women." The article describes the women who actively participate in this "rumor system" as "faithful collaborators (who uphold) the oppressive traditions of the patriarchal regime which are directed against them." The Israeli-Palestinian feminist organization Al-Fanar has organized public demonstrations when they hear of a "family honor murder"; they also offer a support network for those trying to flee such circumstances.

In 2001, Nadera Shalhoub-Kevorkian, a Palestinian therapist and activist, redefined "honor killings" as femicide. She writes about an incident in which a fourteen-year-old girl, Laila, was raped by her thirty-five-year-old cousin. Laila's father immediately intended to kill her. But Laila's cousin offered to marry her. Laila's father says:

> I still might end up losing my mind and killing her. The whole village learned about the rape and the cousin—the rapist—was kind to us. He was kind to us and agreed to marry her. This is the best way of coping with this catastrophe that she brought to this family.

Laila's mother said:

> It is such a shameful thing, something that people in this village never forget and they will never forgive this family. It has brought so much pain to the whole family. I wish she had died rather than putting us in such a shameful state.[5]

Do mothers, world-wide, want to keep their daughters "in their (patriarchal) place?" How does this conflict with a mother's desire to protect and empower her daughter? To what extent do mothers (as opposed to mothers-in-law and stepmothers) force patriarchal group norms upon their daughters? To answer these questions, we will now turn to fairy tales, myths, and psychoanalytic theories.

4.

THE MOTHER-DAUGHTER RELATIONSHIP IN FAIRY TALE, MYTH, AND GREEK TRAGEDY

F airy tales have functioned as a secret history of embattled female relationships—a history that we repress only at our own peril. According to the scholar Marina Warner, fairy tales "vibrate" with the

> insecurity, jealousy, and rage of both mothers-in-law against their daughters-in-law and vice versa, as well as the vulnerability of children from different marriages . . . the experiences these stories recount are remembered, lived experiences of women.

Warner points out that much of the competition between women is due to their economic and social dependence upon "the male hero," who

often cause(s) the fatal rivalry in the first place . . .
the position of the man as savior and provider in
these testimonies of female conflict has continued to
flourish in the most popular and accessible and conventional media, like Disney cartoons.

Fairy tales depict older women as witches, monsters, and
wicked stepmothers. *Cinderella, Rapunzel, Sleeping Beauty, Snow
White,* and *Hansel and Gretel* all come to mind, but there are
many more such stories.

Historically, many mothers have died in childbirth and many
children have been reared by stepmothers, as well as by wet
nurses and governesses. Although stepmothers may not all be
evil, neither are they all saints. According to Princeton University researcher, Ann Case, in a series of studies released in the
year 2000, children raised in modern families with stepmothers
are likely to have less health care, less education, and less
money spent on their food than children raised by their biological mothers. The studies conclude that "for complex reasons" stepmothers do invest less in children than biological
mothers do, with fathers, to a large extent, leaving child care to
the women.

In polygamous societies, older and younger co-wives are
forced into unrelenting rivalries. Thus, the evil queen or stepmother might also be a first or second co-wife, a co-concubine,
a sister-in-law, or a mother-in-law, for whom the arrival of a
younger woman may spell serious—or even fatal—hardship.

Such fairy-tale themes still resonate today. I personally have counseled and testified for women whose husbands left them for younger women. For example, thirty-eight-year-old Lucy is facing a gut-wrenching divorce and custody battle for her three young children. She tells me:

> My husband decided to leave me for our young babysitter. For ten years I was the stay-at-home, full-time mother of three young children. I was no longer independent economically. Now, my husband is arguing that, since the babysitter knows the children almost from the time they were born, he and she should have custody. He says I'm not entitled to alimony or child support. He wants me to work at Burger King.

Today, although some mothers-in-law and daughters-in-law forge loving and supportive relationships, many do not. For example, thirty-year-old Simone was never accepted by her then future mother-in-law. At first, Simone tried to be polite. She says:

> This woman refused to talk to me. When she did, she attacked me. Vito, my fiance, never told her to stop. Vito was her eldest son and he'd been her surrogate husband and the "father" to his younger sisters for years, after his father died. True, we weren't married yet, but I'd been engaged to Vito for two years.

One year, Simone celebrated Christmas with Vito's family. Ebullient, she invited everyone to her mother's house for the following Christmas. It was a turning point. "Vito's mother looked at me with daggers in her eyes and said: 'He's my son. I don't have to share him with you. Not yet. Maybe not ever. I don't see a ring on your finger.'" Simone broke off the engagement.

Most mothers-in-law are unaware that they are jealous of their daughters-in-law. They may not want to admit that any woman has "replaced" them as a son's primary woman. Some mothers-in-law wage all-out campaigns against their daughters-in-law/replacements/rivals. Twenty-nine-year-old Brenda is the mother of a five-year-old boy. She says:

> When my mother-in-law first met me, her son was divorcing his first wife. She told him I was wonderful, why couldn't he have married somebody like me? But, as soon as we married, she suddenly loathed me and set out to destroy me. I believe she is mentally unbalanced. She expected me to treat her like a queen. She treated me like her servant. She once screamed at me: "You are not that boy's mother. I'm his mother." She literally used to call me in the middle of the night and say, "We know that you have men over while my son is out of town."

A younger woman/daughter-in-law, both in fairy tales and in real life, poses a threat of her own. Time is on her side. If she is fertile, doesn't die in childbirth, and produces sons and heirs, her children will eventually inherit the keys to the castle. And, as a mother-in-law ages or becomes ill, a daughter-in-law may persuade her husband to send his mother away, to die alone, elsewhere. The queen is dead; long live the queen.

Lottie is eighty-three years old. She lives in a retirement home in Miami and has not seen her only son in more than a year. She blames her daughter-in-law, but not her son, for this. Lottie says, "she has him wrapped around her finger." She explains,

> He never calls me himself. He has her do it. She doesn't let him see me alone. She always has to be there. He won't make a date with his own mother without checking with her first. I know she resents me because he sends me money.

Lottie blames her daughter-in-law, but not her son, for this behavior.

The fairy tales that we know and love are not only more gruesome than we allow ourselves to believe—they are actually highly sanitized versions of darker, even more diabolical stories. According to Amherst's Emeritus Professor of Psychology, Sheldon Cashdan, an early, Italian version of "The Sleeping Beauty" also exists. In that version, a married prince rapes and impregnates a comatose woman who then gives birth to twins. When the prince's wife learns of his adultery, she invites the beauty and her twins to the castle and orders her servants to kill, cook, and serve the twins to their father. The wife also plans to have her rival burned to death. However, the cook spares the twins. The prince, convinced that his children have been murdered, throws his first wife into the fire and marries the sleeping beauty. By the time the Grimm Brothers rewrite this, their valiant prince has become an unmarried hero who merely kisses the spellbound beauty awake.

In a sense, daughters (and younger women) "replace" their mothers (and older women) as sexual, fertile, pregnant, and lactating beings. Children are meant to outlive their parents; this is nature's way of being kind. However, not all younger women are one's own daughters, and the loss of one's husband, job, best friend, and entire social circle to a younger or just another woman can have devastating consequences. In addition, the overemphasis on female appearance, the early age at which female children are eroticized, the aging male's preference for ever-younger women, and the consequent female terror of aging, together lead to a non-stop, all-female competition for the "fairest of them all" prize. It is hard to grow old gracefully under such circumstances. What complicates the aging process is a woman's life-long experience of all other women as rivals and potential replacements.

Another example is the Grimm Brothers' "The Goose Girl"—a chilling tale in which the princess's female servant replaces the princess and marries the prince in her stead. The princess is condemned to work as a "goose girl." The forlorn princess says: "Here I sit forsaken . . . I am a king's daughter. A wicked waiting-woman forced me to give up my royal garments and my place at my bridegroom's side, and I am made a goose girl and have to do mean service." Eventually, a dead mother-queen's magic and a discerning royal father-in-law-to-be combine to resurrect the class structure.

I have a "replacement" story of my own. I had already published two books and knew many other successful writers when Kitty moved to New York. Kitty had been published, but not as successfully as she wanted to be. She knew my work, and came to see me. Then—there is no other word for what she did—she began to "court" me and to seduce me with maternal warmth, adoration, and attention. Whenever I did a public reading, she was rapt, super-attentive. She would leave little messages on my answering machine. "What a wonderful reading you gave. I will treasure it always." She started reviewing my work in journals. I had never experienced anything like this before, and it felt so good. I never asked myself, "Why is she doing this?" Of course, Kitty wanted to meet every important person I knew; in due course, I arranged for her to meet them all. However, she did not want to join me in my circles; in Kitty's mind, she would always be "second" to me. She therefore needed to replace me. To an extent, she did just that. This was an eerie and haunting experience.

Women are always replacing other women. Often, women tend to identify sympathetically with the replacers. As daughters, we have replaced or are merely different from our mothers. Psychologically, daughters are unconsciously guilty about both facts. Perhaps this is why so many women are drawn to Gothic romances. Women might turn to brooding, enigmatic fantasy princes so as to be rescued from the cruel and arbitrary rule of an all-female world in which women replace—and are themselves replaced by—other women.

Daphne du Maurier's ever-popular Gothic novel *Rebecca* tells the story of a dead first wife (Rebecca) and a new, young wife (the narrator). Mrs. Danvers, the housekeeper, is an older, fairy-tale-like, evil woman who remains devoted to her dead mistress. Danvers persecutes the young narrator-bride, who cannot understand why Danvers hates her. "You tried to take Mrs. De Winter's place," is Danvers' answer. The reader is meant to hate Danvers for her almost criminal loyalty to a dead, older woman, Rebecca—whom her husband has murdered because she was cruel to him. Danvers suggests that the bride kill herself:

> "Don't be afraid," says Mrs. Danvers. "I won't push you . . . you can jump of your own accord . . . you're not happy. Mr. De Winter doesn't love you . . . Why don't you jump now and have done with it? Then you won't be unhappy anymore."

This is fairly hair-raising stuff. Most women are not put off by it.

Often, we are able to criticize "the other" for what we cannot see in ourselves or in our own familiar culture. Most people tend to deny—or fail to consciously acknowledge—their own dark side and the shadow side of fairy tales, movies, and plays. I am as guilty as everyone else. For example, for years I would find myself humming songs from *The King and I*. What a charming, harmless despot that Yul Brynner was; what a romantic Victorian Gertrude Lawrence's British governess was! How wrong I was. Anna H. Leonowens, the real governess upon whose life the musical was based, wrote a book entitled *Siamese Harem Life*, which she published in 1873. It is a heartbreaking and noble book, one in which she recounts the lives of female slaves, prisoners, and royal princesses in nineteenth-century Thailand. Leonowens writes:

> Every harem is a little world in itself, composed entirely of women—some who rule, others who obey, and those who serve. Each one is for herself. They are nearly all young women, but they have the appearance of being slightly blighted. Nobody is too much in earnest, or too much alive, or too happy. The general atmosphere is that of depression . . . most girls, as soon as they have overcome the horror which such a life must naturally inspire in the young and enthusiastic, begin to calculate on their chances of promotion to the highest place in the harem.

Leonowens is a great storyteller. One tale haunts me still.

Once, a female slave tried to buy her freedom. As punishment, her royal mistress had her "chained (to a stake) like a wild beast by one leg, (and kept half-naked) in a public square for more than five years without the least shelter under that burning sky." Finally (but only because Leonowens intervenes), the princess allows a female judge to hear the case. The princess insists that, even if she accepts the slave woman's money, the slave's son still belongs to the princess, not to his mother. As the slave woman prostrates herself, sobbing and pleading, the royal ladies look into "jeweled hand-mirrors and cream their lips with the most sublime air of indifference."

Today, Thailand remains an impoverished country in which female children are routinely sold, kidnapped, or tricked into prostitution. They no longer belong to a single ruler, but to any and all bidders in the global harem.

Harsh fairy-tale-like female rivalries still exist in countries where husband-based extended families, child-marriage, child-prostitution, arranged marriages, polygamy, concubinage, and intractable poverty once existed or still do.

In *Wild Swans: Three Daughters of China*, Jung Chang explores three generations of her female ancestors. She describes an early twentieth-century Chinese family, consisting of a man, his two concubines, his wife, and their son. Barren and socially inferior, the concubines are wild with envy. They drug both the wife and a male servant, put them in bed together, and tell the man that his wife is having an affair. Although "he had a sneaking suspicion that the whole thing might have been a plot by his concubines," the husband nevertheless imprisons his wife in a small room and forbids her ever to see her son. The concubines raise the child.

Women's jealousies over fertility exist today in the contemporary western world. Laura, a forty-one-year-old university professor whom I interviewed, says: "I had no idea how much infertile women envied fertile women until I got pregnant for the first time." Laura had a friend who had been trying to get pregnant for years. "As I walked down the street," Laura continues,

> She did not say hello. She physically stopped me, and in a hostile, menacing tone said: "What did you *do* to get pregnant? Why was this so easy for you, and so hard for me?" Then, she walked off. We never spoke again.

An anonymous Korean poet, quoted in *Fragments of a Lost Diary*, eloquently argues the daughter-in-law's case. The mother-in-law is "skinny and wrinkled," the father-in-law is "tough and rank," the sister-in-law is "sharp as a gimlet," and the son-husband is a "weed," and "miserable." The poet writes: "Mother-in-law, don't fume in the kitchen/and swear at your daughter-in-law./Did you get her in payment of a debt? . . . How can you criticize a daughter-in-law/who's like a morning glory/blooming in loamy soil?"

In "Imem," a short story, the Indonesian political prisoner and novelist Pramoedya Ananta Toer describes the mid-twentieth century plight of an eight-year-old girl whose parents have sold her to an adult rapist and batterer. The child's mother is a live-in servant to a wealthy woman who will not allow the runaway child-wife to return to her household. The wealthy woman tells the eight-year-old that she must return to her husband even though he beats her and forces her to "wrestle" at night. The child cannot bear it and becomes a divorcee at nine.

> And thereafter . . . since she was nothing but a burden to her family, [she was] beaten by anyone who wanted to: her mother, her brothers, her uncles, her neighbors, her aunts. Her screams of pain were often heard. When she moaned, I covered my ears with my hands. And [the narrator's] Mother continued to uphold the respectability of her home.

As I read fairy tales and listen to my interviewees, I begin to understand the popularity of Laura Esquivel's novel, *Like Water for Chocolate*. Esquivel's fictional mother, the widow Mama Elena, is a turn-of-the-century Mexican mother, but one who resembles an evil, fairy-tale stepmother. Mama Elena verbally and physically abuses her female servants and demands absolute obedience from her three daughters.

> When it came to wringing the necks of quail, turkeys, chickens, capons, Mama Elena was merci-less, killing with a single blow. But then, not always.

For Tita (her youngest daughter) she had made an exception; she had been killing her a little at a time since she was a child, and she still hadn't quite finished her off.

Tita is Mama Elena's sixteen-year-old body-servant, responsible for preparing her mother's bath, washing her mother's body, shampooing her hair, ironing her clothes; her mother criticizes her non-stop. ("Mama Elena's genius was for finding fault.") Mama Elena is a sadist. Knowing that Tita loves Pedro and that Pedro loves only Tita, Mama Elena insists that Pedro marry Rosaura, another of her daughters, thus condemning one daughter to a loveless marriage, the other to a life without marriage or biological children.

Eventually, Mama Elena's ceaseless cruelty toward Tita, which includes solitary confinements, causes Tita to have a nervous breakdown. Mama Elena immediately moves to have her institutionalized. She forbids her family, the servants too, from ever visiting or mentioning Tita. Mama Elena's third daughter, Gertrudis, runs away to become a revolutionary bandit and is also rumored to be working in a brothel. "Mama Elena burned Gertrudis' birth certificate and all of her pictures and said she didn't want to hear her name mentioned ever again."

Mama Elena is precisely the kind of mother who would defend a criminal son with passion, money, forged documents, her own life.

Esquivel suggests that Donna Elena became a tyrant because

she once had a love that was "frustrated." I agree. In my view, a woman who is not permitted to love herself will, in turn, refuse to allow her daughters to have what she herself has been denied.

I recognize Mama Elena's style of tyranny; I know Mama Elena as my very own. My mother never *asked* me to do anything. She demanded, ordered, accused, threatened, punished, screamed. Slapped. Pulled hair. By the time I was five or six, I had learned that I could not count on my mother to be kind or fair and that I could not count on my father to rescue me from her.

Thus, I lived in a fairy tale. For a long time I believed that I had been adopted or stolen and that my real parents were a King and a Queen who loved me and who were searching for me day and night. Before I was seven I had learned that other people—relatives, neighbors, teachers—never interfere with a mother or a father's right to terrify or deprive their own child. I learned to trust no one—but I also learned to trust strangers more than relatives.

When I was a child I read all the time. I preferred books to reality. Perhaps I still do. I read fairy tales, but I also read Greek and Roman myths that depicted biological mothers like the goddess Demeter—as powerful goddesses who loved and protected their daughters. Unlike fairy tales, pagan myths also depicted such deadly rivalries between mothers and biological daughters as that between Queen Clytemnestra and her daughter Electra. Like fairy tales, myths allow us to "see" or vicariously experience such forbidden realities.

For example, women may want—but may also fear—a relationship with a powerful, protecting mother. Such desire and terror recall the myth of the goddess Demeter and her daughter Persephone, who remains merged with her mother.

When Demeter's daughter is kidnapped by Hades, god of the Underworld, Demeter threatens to destroy the world. Ultimately, Demeter negotiates Persephone's return to her for half of every year. Persephone will sojourn Underground for the other half-year. According to British psychoanalyst Nini Herman, the loyalty of the maiden Persephone is henceforth divided between her husband and her mother. The reunion of Demeter and Persephone requires a transformation in both mother and daughter: Demeter must overcome her rage and grief; Persephone must return—different, but still the same.[1]

According to the scholar Carl Kerényi, Persephone "descends to the underworld." She dies, but she is "reborn." She is the ancient world's version of the Christ. Demeter and Persephone, mother and daughter, are one Goddess; they are both separate and reunited; each woman has a "doubled" presence.

As psychologist Paula Caplan has documented so well, psychiatric experts continue to blame mothers, wrongfully, misogynistically, for anything that goes wrong. Lay people also scapegoat mothers for the harm caused either by fathers or by an unjust society. In addition, we have excessively high expectations for mothers and little compassion for mothers who fail at even one of many tasks. Real women are doomed to fall short of our ideals for mothers.

Nevertheless, most daughters continue to long for their mothers' love, approval, support, wisdom, and protection. Maternal absence is suffered far more than maternal abuse. According to Nini Herman, a mother remains the object of her daughter's "deepest passion." According to the Argentinian-American psychiatrist and author Teresa Bernardez,

> In every woman the image of the idealized mother lies barely beneath the surface . . . the desire for mother's special attention, for being valued and for being taken seriously, for being regarded with joy . . . persist and appear in the transference reactions of women patients to female therapists. The "identificatory hunger" with female role models and supervisors that has been observed in female therapists . . . attests to these absences in their background.

Laura Tracy, the author of *The Secret between Us: Competition among Women,* notes astutely that what Cinderella and her sisters really compete for is the love and protection of a fairy godmother:

> With her help, Cinderella wins the prince. Without her, the stepsisters, whatever they may do, remain ugly. Like Cinderella and her stepsisters, when real sisters compete for their mother, they compete for a

magical, idealized mother, like Cinderella's fairy godmother.

Some writer-daughters describe romantic fairy-tale-like relationships with their real mothers. In *Cravings: A Sensual Memoir*, Jyl Lyn Felman's description of her deceased mother, Edith, is passionate, obsessive, poignant, and heartbreaking. Felman remembers the taste of her mother's cooking, the color and style of her clothes, the smell of her perfume. Felman writes:

> I am sleeping when my mother comes to me in a dream more vivid than when she was alive . . . she hovers over my bed. With her arms outstretched, she reaches for me . . . I am floating in the water. You're adoring me, the way we used to be, soaking in the tub . . . I am soaking in your love of me.

In *Where She Came from: A Daughter's Search for Her Mother's History*, the writer, Helen Epstein, describes her mother, Frances (Franci), a fashion designer and dressmaker, who survived Bergen-Belsen. Epstein writes that her

> relation to (Franci) was the most passionate and complicated of all. So intense was our bond that I was never sure what belonged to whom, where I ended, and she began . . . I had always viewed her as

a heroine more compelling than any in the Bible,
any novel or myth.

Epstein does not break with her mother in adolescence. "She
was the engine behind my energy, my defender when I needed
one, my solace."

Psychoanalyst Anna Aragno interviewed a diverse group of
New York City area mothers. She writes: "virtually every mother
I spoke with recalled nostalgically, and with deep joy, a lengthy
period of harmonic bliss with her little girl, a sort of prolonged
psychical union . . . my daughter was 'enchanting,' 'blessed,'
'affectionate,' 'easy-going.'" Aragno herself has only "glowing
memories of (her) enchanted daughters in whose childhoods
(she) thoroughly delighted."

There is a downside to all this rapture. As Charlotte Watson
Sherman notes:

> The reality is that many (black women) spend a
> good portion of our lives trying to learn to live as
> independent-spirited grown women in spite of strug-
> gling with the fierce controlling love of our mothers.

Daughters often flee their mothers' traditional lives, only to
discover how much they still have in common. In *A Good
Enough Daughter*, the writer Alix Kates Shulman realizes that
Dorothy, her mother, had also been a serious art collector and
a writer of short stories, one-act plays, historical essays, "even

chapters of a family novel penned on Dad's obsolete stationery in a hand so like my own."

> Confronted by such incontestable evidence of Mom's serious literary aspirations going all the way back to my early childhood, I had to ask myself why it had never occurred to me to attribute my ambition to hers, rather than hers to mine.

Ah, yes.

And so we begin to understand that, as the writer Judith Arcana concluded, the "blood bond *is* the love bond"; that although many mother-daughter relationships are embattled, ambivalent, painful, and require long periods of separation, many are "sisterly," loving, empowering, and harmonious. Although some daughters have to flee home, many do so only in order to return.

The writer Vivian Gornick describes her "fierce attachment" to her mother in a book of the same name. Mother Gornick remains focused on her own lost romantic love—so much so that she fails to focus on her daughter's separate life and achievements. They are well-matched combatants. Daughter Gornick flies into a rage: "What *are* you talking about? Again love? Does my life mean nothing to you? Absolutely nothing?" Mother Gornick reverts to Yiddish,

> You'll write down here on my tombstone: From the

beginning it was all water under the bridge. Why don't you go already? Why don't you walk away from my life? I'm not stopping you.

To which daughter Gornick can only reply: "I know you're not, Ma."

According to classical scholar Erich Neumann, "The Eternal Feminine" never lets anything go—in his words, it "tends to hold fast to everything that springs from it and to surround it like an eternal substance." Thus, the union and reunion of mother and daughter are fraught with peril and require enormous psychological growth in each woman.

Nini Herman believes that a "secure" and "fulfilled" mother can let her daughter grow, both intellectually and sexually. But, if she envies this "young competitor," her daughter may

> linger at the stage where she has a need to please, in order to obtain reassurance that her destructive phantasies and her hostile impulses have not caused lasting harm [to her mother]. Then she may turn out to be excessively preoccupied with making herself beautiful, because a beautiful body is felt to serve as evidence that all is well inside too.

In Nini Herman's view, a "truly disturbed mother" makes it almost impossible for her infant, young child, or grown daughter to assert "any needs at all."

The repetition of the maternal destiny is what terrifies many contemporary women who *also* want to enact paternal-heroic destinies. A daughter needs to differentiate herself from her mother, but the smallest difference is often experienced by both mother and daughter as the most profound betrayal. Daughters want to be "themselves"; they want their mothers to celebrate them as "different." Mother-daughter differences are maddening, but so are the similarities.

Some Demetrian mothers refuse to let their daughters go. They bind them with maternal envy, disapproval, anger, insecurity, depression; they remain merged together in embattled relationships.

On the one hand, it is important not to demonize mothers. On the other hand, it is equally important not to deny the realities of maternal abuse. A mother can "kill" her daughter in many ways. The fictional Sethe, in Toni Morrison's novel *Beloved*, kills her daughter so that her daughter will not have to grow up as a slave. Either Sethe has committed a terrifying act of love or Sethe has been driven murderously "crazy." Most normal mothers do not kill their daughters, but neither do they teach them how to resist slavery.

A mother may keep her daughter at home by bullying her— or by needing her. B. D. Hyman, Bette Davis's daughter, and the academic Jill Ker Conway both describe "raging" mothers. Ker Conway's mother, who was descending into paranoia, would not stop her tirades until Ker Conway agreed that her mother's (mis)perceptions and monstrously destructive actions had been warranted. When B. D. Hyman stood up to her mother, who often physically attacked B. D.'s live-in maternal aunt, the actress would burst into tears and plead: "Don't do this to me B. D. Not tonight. You know I'm dead. You can't do this to me." Although such mothers have periods of lucidity or can otherwise pass for sane, while they are raging they are absolutely unreachable.

Christina Crawford, in *Mommie Dearest*, describes a rigid, sadistic, controlling mother who programmed every minute of the day and locked Christina in the linen closet with the lights off because she knew that Christina was afraid of the dark. In *Understanding the Borderline Mother: Helping Her Children Transcend the Intense, Unpredictable, Volatile Relationship*, Indianapolis clinical social worker, Christine Ann Lawson, writes:

> In a starkly candid interview, Joan Crawford revealed her draconian philosophy of disciplining eight-year-old Christina: "It is not easy to discipline her, but I am forced to, when she insists on doing things her own way. I find punishing her by hurting her dignity is very effective" . . . borderline mothers may use denigration as a method of discipline without being aware of its destructiveness.

The writers Sylvia Plath, Doris Lessing, Signe Hammer, and Linda Grey Sexton all describe psychotic or abusive mothers. It makes no difference to a helpless and dependent child that her mother may be "mad" or culturally oppressed or trapped in a hellish marriage with no exit. The mother applies her full Demetrian body-weight against her young daughter.

Those of us who love Plath's poetry and who have read what Plath has written about her relationship to her mother and about her psychiatric hospitalization tend to view Plath sympathetically. Many have viewed her as a feminist martyr, trapped in the 1950s, cruelly abandoned by a philandering husband. There is, however, another side to Plath, one best known to her intimates. Biographer Anne Stevenson, in *Bitter Fame: A Life of Sylvia Plath*, described Plath as

> first the bright and smiling mask that she presented to everyone, and then, through that, the determined, insistent, obsessive, impatient person who snapped if things did not go her way, and (who) flew into sudden rages. Plath wrote that "if anyone ever disarranged my things I'd feel as if I had been raped intellectually." Indeed, when a friend penciled some passages in a book she had borrowed from Plath, "she brought down the wrath of the avenging angel."

According to Lawson, Plath—and other "borderline hermit mothers"—might view suicide as an "accomplishment," a "last act of free will." Such a mother "must have control of her death as well as her life, and may leave treatment just as she begins to trust her therapist. Trust is dangerous." Lawson, quoting from the Stevenson, Hughes, and McCullough biographies of Plath, suggests that Plath was cold, secretive, asocial, "guarded her lesson plans as though they contained classified information," and was "intensely jealous." According to Lawson, long before her husband, the poet Ted Hughes, had been unfaithful to her, Plath assumed that he had. Once, while Hughes was at a business meeting, Plath

> . . . became hysterical and destroyed his manuscripts, as well as his favorite book, *The Complete Works of Shakespeare*, in a vicious display of unbridled rage, irrational jealousy, and paranoia. Hughes later confided in a friend that the incident was a turning point in their marriage.

Few feminist supporters—myself included—ever paused to acknowledge that Plath, the victim, could also be Plath, the victimizer. Indeed, this is precisely how intergenerational patterns of pathology tend to work. In Plath's view, *her* mother, Aurelia, dominated her children through martyrdom.

> The Children were her salvation. She put them First. Herself bound to the track naked and the train called Life coming with a frown and a choo-choo around the bend. The burden upon Redeeming children is too great, unfair. What to do with her, with the hostility, undying, which I feel for her?. . .

She's a killer. Watch out. She's deadly.
WHY HAVE I PERSISTED IN THE DELUSION THAT I COULD
WIN HER LOVE (APPROVAL) TILL SUCH A LATE DATE?
NOTHING I DO WILL CHANGE HER. DO I GRIEVE BECAUSE I
REALIZE THE IMPOSSIBILITY OF THIS?

By committing suicide, Plath continues to compete with her
mother. One might, in fact, argue that Plath has continued
"talking" to no one *but* her mother. If Aurelia has been abusive,
then Plath means to one-up Aurelia: Plath will absent herself
entirely from the lives of her two small children. Plath's children are "lucky." They are to have no mother—an option that
Plath herself did not have. Perhaps Plath wishes to save her
children (herself) from Aurelia by depriving them of a poisoned mother/daughter. Perhaps Plath also experiences her
children as making Aurelia-like demands upon her, demands
she could not, would not, meet.

Doris Lessing exorcises her mother-demon over and over
again in her novels. She enters psychoanalysis to accomplish
this same goal. Lessing's mother arrives in London "full of
emotional blackmail." She wants to be her daughter's secretary.
According to art historian and writer Claudia Roth Pierpont,

> Lessing went into treatment even before her mother
> arrived; just the letter announcing her intentions
> proved incapacitating. Lessing credits her psychia-
> trist, a Jungian who encouraged her to enter the

minds of such un-swayable role models as Electra, Antigone, and Medea, with giving her the strength to resist all the appeals and to send her mother [away]. In her memoirs, Lessing notes that her mother died not long afterward at the age of seventy-three: "She could have lived another ten years, if anyone had needed her." As for herself, Lessing believed that she had been narrowly "saved."

The writer Signe Hamner cannot forgive her mother for committing suicide, and she cannot forgive herself. The daughter writes: "Suicide takes place in another dimension. The dimension in which Clytemnestra operated, and Medea." Hamner interprets her mother's suicide not only as the desperate act of a deeply unhappy, trapped wife, but as that of an enraged mother who was "driven to fury" by her daughter's normal "impulses and desires."

It was as if, in the face of my two-year-old needs, her fragile, hard-won sense of selfhood . . . broke down, and she was overwhelmed by an avatar of her helpless infant self.[2]

New York psychoanalyst Arlene Kramer Richards discusses the poet Anne Sexton as an abused child, an abusive mother, and a great poet. Richards uses Sexton's poems, as well as the autobiographical writing of Sexton's daughter, Linda Grey

Sexton. The mother-poet is exquisitely, painfully, aware that she has failed her daughter and that her daughter knows it. In "Poem Entitled: Pain for a Daughter," Sexton writes:

> "I stand at the door, eyes locked
> On the ceiling, eyes of a stranger
> and then she cries . . .
> Oh, my God, help me!
> Where a child would have cried Mama!
> Where a child would have believed Mama!
> She bit the towel and called on God
> And I saw her life stretched out . . .
> I saw her torn in childbirth,
> And I saw her, at that moment,
> In her own death and I knew that she
> Knew."

The poet Sexton's biographer, Diane Middlebrook, posits that Sexton was sexually abused by her alcoholic father and that no female blood relative rescued her. According to Richards,

> From her biography we know that Sexton was ashamed of her relationship with her daughters. She was a stranger to them in their earliest years. When she became psychotically depressed, after each of their births, the babies were sent [away] . . . barely

able to tolerate them as little children, she was unable to feel pleasure in loving or nurturing them. Later, when they were adolescents, she was preoccupied with love affairs, poetry, her failing marriage, her own quest for parental nurturance . . . from her poetry we can see that she was consumed with horrific images of her own childhood and her own victimization.

In her 1994 memoir, *Looking for Mercy Street,* Linda Grey Sexton describes how her alcoholic mother raged, slapped, tried to choke, sexually molested, and blamed her own illness on her three-year-old child.

> Naked from the waist down, she is making noises and her fingers curl through her crisp black pubic hair. She pushes her long clitoris back and forth against the dark lips of her vagina. I drop my eyes, ashamed. She does not stop even though I am in the room. Her eyes don't seem to see me or know I am here. I am scared. Maybe she is having some kind of a fit? Maybe they will take her away to the hospital again?
>
> I close my eyes on this scene and try hard not to see it, though it happens again other times, once in the bathtub, more times on the bed.
>
> The basic theme . . . consisted of this: I had over-

whelmed my mother, the needs too intense for this fragile, dependent, twenty-eight-year-old woman. I had been, Mother later said, an impossible three-year-old. "You cried all the time," she explained, "You whined. You were a difficult, annoying child."

Typically, Grey Sexton does not expect her father to rescue her, and she does not blame him when he fails to do so. She reserves all her scorn for her mad mother, for her cold grandmother, and for the inadequate, battered, maternal aunt who takes her in.

What makes Sexton both unique and useful is that she was also a writer—and that her daughter became a writer too. They have left a record of their relationship. Richards notes that the same sexual abuse and violence that wounded Anne Sexton was repeated in the life of her daughter.

A mother so damaged, so scarred, turns her hurt against her daughters and creates another generation of mothers who, unless they are helped and supported, go on to abuse their children also.

The Demetrian Mother may be "maddened" by pregnancy and labor, by the unending demands of an infant, who at every moment, is growing away from her mother. A woman so "maddened" may seek to keep her daughter with her forever by damaging her.

For example, some mothers are sadists who physically and sexually invade their daughters. The patient known as Sybil had a mother, Hattie, who penetrated her orifices with kitchen utensils and induced ejaculation with enemas. This early and prolonged sadism led Sybil to develop "multiple" personalities. Medical records indicate that Sybil was also beaten, burned, and semi-suffocated. Sybil manifested other disorders of incest, including an eating disorder and time and memory losses that we now associate with Multiple Personality Disorder.

Psychologist Lee Fitzroy theorizes that, when an incestuous mother sexually violates a daughter, the mother may be "enacting a form of self-mutilation . . . (which is) a manifestation of self-hate or internalized misogyny." On the other hand, such a mother may also be exerting power in the only way she can—and in a way that she once experienced as a child herself. Fitzroy suggests that the sexual abuse of "self/other" could also be "an attempt to create an adult 'self,' and to exert power and control." A victim/offender may be able to feel powerful only when she is abusing an Other.

> Therefore, the one who penetrates, invades the body of the 'other,' is constructed as powerful in our social order. The victim is annihilated and therefore denied a separate identity. For some women, the 'other' is themselves or a bodily extension of themselves—their daughter.

"Mad" mothers also invade their daughters, psychologically. Daughters may resist, but most are relatively helpless before the onslaught. Few daughters kill their mothers in self-defense.

In *Perfidia*, the writer Judith Rossner creates a fictional matricide. Anita is an alcoholic mother who isolates, neglects, abuses, and torments her daughter, Maddy. Anita is a feral, secretive, vital, violent, promiscuous woman with no female friends and no known past. Anita dotes on her younger son Billy (she neglects him too), but she screams at, hits, overburdens, and emotionally starves Maddy—that is, when she isn't confiding in Maddy as if they were best girlfriends. Finally, Anita throws the sixteen-year-old Maddy out of the house. When Maddy attempts to return, a drunken Anita attacks her with a jagged, broken bottle. At first, Maddy defends herself, but then she "goes crazy," and keeps slashing Anita, long after Anita is dead. By the end of the novel, Maddy is eighteen and just released from prison. She becomes pregnant almost immediately. Maddy is well on her way to becoming her mother. It is what daughters most fear and desire. Maddy is merged with Anita. She says:

> Long before my brother was born, my mother had spoiled me for everybody else . . . Her intensity, happy or unhappy, spoiled me for other humans.

Maddy understands that she's killed her mother "out of weakness, not strength"; she views herself as guilty because she could not let go of Anita—not until Anita had either moth-ered/retained the connection with Maddy or died for refusing to do so.

Such a "maddened" Demetrian mother represents a psycho-logical extreme. To escape both her abuse and the danger of being incorporated by her forever, a daughter might have to kill her. The loyally embryonic Persephone does not kill Demeter as the only way to "become" her. This is what the mythic Clytemnestra's daughter, Electra, does. To escape being swallowed alive by one's mother, many women psychologically enact the mythic Electra role: we psychologically murder our Queen mother Clytemnestra in order to replace her. These primal psychological dramas take place in the theater of the unconscious. Electra is not, as Freud's followers would have it, merely competing with her mother for the same man: her father; she is also competing with her father/brother/sisters/ mother's male lover, for the same woman, her mother.

Theater functions as both ritual and spectacle; it allows us to exorcise certain psychological demons. In this case, since women continue to live in both a Demetrian and Clytemnestrian world, the re-enactment of matricide might allow women to share in the public ritual undoing of dictatorial mothers, while remaining safely merged Persephones in their private lives. Such a re-enactment might legitimize a daughter's own rebellion against her mother and against the authority of older women.

Just as women are all Persephone, merged, they are also all Electra, defiant and murderous; certainly, women are all

Persephone/Electra's daughters. They, and their mothers before them, have all been merged with and have conspired in Clytemnestra's downfall. Like Electra, women are not necessarily haunted by the Furies afterwards.

Aeschylus, Euripides, and Sophocles all wrote plays about the mythic Electra; so did the great modern playwright Eugene O'Neill. The composer Richard Strauss wrote an opera about Electra.

According to Greek myth and drama, Queen Clytemnestra is the mother of three children: Iphigenia, Electra, and Orestes. She is also the wife of Agamemnon and the sister of Helen of Troy, who is married to Agamemnon's brother, Menelaus. (This is a story about two brothers who are married to a pair of sisters.) Helen runs off with Paris, a prince of Troy. The two brothers mount an expedition, ostensibly to win Helen back, but also to win the riches of Troy. For more than a decade, the warrior-brothers lay siege to Troy, which was, some say, an earlier, matriarchal civilization.

Agamemnon tricks Clytemnestra into sending their daughter Iphigenia to visit him, presumably to betroth her to a great prince. Instead, her father ritually sacrifices her in full view of his troops as an offering to the Gods. Agamemnon captures and destroys Troy, kills and enslaves its people and sets sail for home. He brings his slave mistress, the Trojan visionary and princess, Cassandra, back with him. His abandoned queen, Clytemnestra, has taken a lover, Aegisthus, who stabs Agamemnon to death.

Clytemnestra's daughter, Electra, conspires to kill her mother for having murdered Agamemnon. Electra plans her mother's murder; Orestes commits the matricide. Electra kills her mother "indirectly"; technically, her hands remain clean. Orestes is haunted and pursued by the (female) Furies. The tormented Orestes demands and receives a divine jury. The Gods are deadlocked. Athena, a male- and father-identified goddess, casts the deciding vote in Orestes' favor. Henceforth, husband-murder is viewed as a more serious crime than matricide. The Furies do not pursue Electra. Her post-matricidal torment, if any, remains unknown to us.

What is amiss between Electra and Clytemnestra is what they already symbolize: The Fall, the end of (childhood's) mother-rule. Nini Herman writes:

> About twenty-five centuries ago, Demeter and Persephone underwent the ordeal of being wrenched apart by a growing consciousness of the Law of the Father.

Electra is wild with rage and grief. In her view, her mother has cheated her of everything: a father, a royal marriage, respectability. Clytemnestra insists, cruelly, on remaining the only sexual woman; Electra feels doomed to eternal chastity and childlessness. Clytemnestra refuses to yield to her daughter's inevitable sexual ascent.

Electra is one of our earliest, patriarchal heroines. She is a daughter who does not identify with her mother; she hates her mother. Electra is a quintessential "Daddy's Girl." Aeschylus' Electra sees herself as a slave and an outcast. Of Clytemnestra, she says: "She is no mother in her heart . . . (she) hates her children." Here, Electra means herself. Eugene O'Neill's Electra is "square shouldered, with military bearing." She is not comfortable in her woman's body. O'Neill's Electra is a grim goody-two-shoes; her brother calls her the "fuss-buzzer."

Strauss's operatic Electra intends to kill her mother with her father's mighty, bloody axe. Musically, Strauss's opera opens on a note of high-pitched terror. Tension mounts; there is no relief. Strauss's Electra is untamed, creepy, with the physical strength of a madwoman. Strauss's Electra "hisses at us like a cat"; his Clytemnestra says: "Electra can kill me with her looks." (How many mothers of teen-aged daughters say this very thing!)

Sophocles' Electra is the "screaming" Electra whom Strauss set to music. This Electra vows, prophetically, that "I shall cry out my sorrow for all the world to hear." So she has; we can still hear her screams. Electra yearns for freedom from The House of Persephone; she does not want to remain mother-merged. This Electra wears "ugly rags" and "stand(s) at a scanty table." She is "dishonored," like a "foreigner." Her father is dead, her mother is "that Enemy Woman."

Sophocles' Electra accuses her mother: "You let me say what I please, and then you are outraged. You do not know how to listen." Electra wants her mother to listen to her, to focus on her, not on a male lover, to take her daughter seriously.

Sophocles' Clytemnestra mocks Electra for her extreme histrionics. "Are you the only one whose father is dead?" "Your father, yes, always your father . . . Nothing else is your pretext."

From Clytemnestra's point of view, Electra's lack of compassion toward her amounts to a form of extreme cruelty. Clytemnestra can do no right; Agamemnon can do no wrong. Perhaps Clytemnestra is jealous of Electra's irrational love for her long-absent father. While Electra finds fault with everything Clytemnestra does, she continues to idealize the father who abandoned his family for a decade, slaughtered Electra's sister, Iphegenia, but spared the faithless Helen's daughter. Electra remains indifferent to her sister's murder. For both mother and daughter, sisterly rivalry (Clytemnestra and Helen, Electra and Iphigenia) may also have a determining, though unexamined, role here.

According to Euripides' Clytemnestra, Electra has no pity for her mother. Agamemnon has returned home with a slave-mistress; "two brides stabled in one stall" is how Clytemnestra puts it. Also, Electra has stolen Clytemnestra's son, Orestes, and has competed with her mother in all things. O'Neill's Clytemnestra says:

> I know you [Electra]! I've watched you ever since you were little, trying to do exactly what you're doing now! You've tried to become the wife of your father [and your brother's] mother. You've always schemed to steal my place.

Euripides paints a more compassionate picture of Clytemnestra, who notes that "When a woman gets an evil reputation she finds a bitter twist to her words." Clytemnestra understands that, once "dirty gossip" finds a woman, "the guilty ones, the men, are never blamed at all." This Clytemnestra "though savage in soul . . . saves (Electra) from Aegisthus' blow."

Electra has been married off to a common farmer who, nobly, does not consummate the marriage. Electra vows: "I will be the one to plan my mother's death. She will come, she will be killed. All that is clear." Electra lures her mother with false news that a grandson has been born. Clytemnestra/Demeter rushes to her daughter's side to perform the necessary sacrificial rites; Electra incites Orestes to kill their mother. She mocks Orestes for hesitating. "Don't tell me that pity catches you at the sight of her."

Electra is judged by the Dioscuri, the twin sons of Zeus. They tell Orestes that "the dreadful beast-faced goddesses of destiny will roll you like a wheel through maddened wandering," after which, you will be "released from distress." And they pronounce Electra guilty of matricide too, and banish her from Argos, her homeland. They state: "You shared in the act, you share in the fate: both children, a single curse."

Psychologically, however, things are more complicated for Electra than for Orestes. Electra feels cheated of her mother's love; she has been displaced not only by a father and a brother, but also by a slaughtered sister and by a male lover. Euripides' Electra says, "Women save all their love for lovers, not for children." Electra describes her mother as "the one I loved and could not love." Did Electra kidnap Orestes in order to save his life—or, in order to cheat her mother of a son, in order to have her mother all to herself? Perhaps Electra expected to occupy center stage in her mother's affections—and then along came Aegisthus.

Perhaps Electra is "maddened" by her need to break with her mother and terrified of becoming a sexual woman. Eugene O'Neill understood this and, in his *Mourning Becomes Electra,* states that this is a drama about "soul-snatching": the daughter steals her mother's soul; the dead steal the souls of the living. O'Neill's Electra accuses her mother, outright, of having "pushed her away," of loving only her son. She tells her mother: "You stole all love from me when I was born! . . . Oh Mother! Why have you done this to me? What harm had I done you?"

Once O'Neill's Clytemnestra is dead, his Electra undergoes a transformation. His Orestes notes this: "Little by little, (Electra's soul) grew like Mother's soul—as if you were stealing her, as if her death had set you free to become her!" Now, the formerly stiff Electra, who always dressed in black, starts wearing colors. Orestes descends into madness after his mother's death; Electra becomes a sexual woman only after her mother is dead.

Like mother, like daughter. In different ways, both women prefer men, not women. This is precisely what they most hold against each other.

These pagan myths depict unconscious psychological possibilities. Demented Demeters, ghostly, embryonic Persephones, arrogant Clytemnestras, murderous Electras exist in all women; however, only "mad" women (and actresses) act it out.

I have turned to these myths for four reasons. First, because they embody tabooed, unconscious, psychological processes that are, nevertheless, normal. Second, because I needed to find a way to pierce the amnesia that accompanies many female conversations about the "shadow side" of relationships between mothers and daughters and among women in general. Among my interviewees, the amnesia (or the silence) was almost total. Third, I wanted to offset the pathologizing of behavior that wrongfully accompanies insights gained from modern psychoanalytic theory—which the use of myths and drama allows us to do. Nini Herman believes that the unresolved issues "which are active at the core of the mother-daughter dyad" are, to some extent, what psychologically holds women back and accounts for women's unconscious collusion with patriarchal edicts. I agree. Nini Herman believes that the unexamined mother-daughter relationship is precisely where women are "obstinately marking time" rather than moving toward freedom.

5.

SOME PSYCHOANALYTIC VIEWS OF THE MOTHER-DAUGHTER RELATIONSHIP

In 1931 Freud admitted that he did not really understand the mother-daughter relationship. He wrote that a daughter's "pre-Oedipal attachment" to her mother is "so difficult to grasp in analysis—[it is] grey with age and shadowy and almost impossible to revivify—that it was as if it had succumbed to an especially inexorable repression." This insight "came to [him] as a surprise, like the discovery, in another field, of the Minoan-Mycenaean civilization behind the civilization of Greece." Actually, Freud understood quite a lot, namely, that girls are as attached to their mothers as they are to their fathers and that, in certain circumstances, they might even "retire from the field of heterosexuality" in order to placate or please their mothers.

Freud made this admission in a case history published in 1920. A sexually inactive eighteen-year-old Viennese girl had been sent by her parents into treatment with Freud when she suddenly—and quite openly—fell in love with an older woman, a "cocotte." Freud learned that the girl's mother was "harsh" toward her daughter while she "overly indulged her three sons." Nevertheless, in analysis, the girl did not criticize her mother; she raged only against her father. Freud writes:

> The analysis revealed beyond all shadow of doubt that the ladylove was a substitute for—her mother . . . The first objects of her affection after the (recent) birth of her youngest brother were really mothers, women between thirty and thirty-five . . . Her latest choice combined satisfaction of the homosexual tendency with that of the heterosexual one . . . The girl we are considering had in any case altogether little cause to feel affection for her mother. The latter, still youthful herself, saw in her rapidly developing daughter an inconvenient competitor; she favored sons at her expense, limited her independence as much as possible, and kept an especially strict watch against any close relation between the girl and her father . . . Since there was little to be done with the real mother, there arose from this transformation of feeling the search for a substitute mother to whom she could become passionately attached. There was, in addition, a practical motive for this change, derived from her real relations with her mother . . . The mother herself still attached great value to the attentions and the

admiration of men. If, then, the girl became homo-
sexual and left men to her mother (in other words,
"retired in favour of" her mother), she removed
something that had hereto been partly responsible
for her mother's disfavor.[1]

Standing on Freud's shoulders, many other theorists (but
especially Melanie Klein) observed that girls engage in an even
more smouldering rivalry for their mother's affection and
attention than boys do. Like boys, girls may come to despise or
even hate women and to prefer and respect only men. Karen
Horney referred to this as a "flight from womanhood" on the
part of both sexes. Although both girls and boys may become
"matrophobic," a child's fear of maternal power—and of
maternal powerlessness—is experienced differently as a function of gender.

Psychologically, boys do not "kill" their fathers. For a
number of reasons (fear of castration/loss of social power),
boys instead "give up" their mothers and try to become like
their fathers. Psychoanalytically speaking, heterosexual male
identity is based upon a boy's willingness *not* to identify with his
mother, in return for his father's benevolent protection and in
the hope that someday he, too, will have a mother/wife of his
own. A boy does not have to compete with his mother in order
to "become" her; so he does not have to reject her, within himself, in the same way that a girl does.

On a psychologically superficial level, a girl tries to kill her mother in order to escape her mother's powerless fate; on a deeper level, she may do so in order to retaliate for the loss of her mother to a brother or to a husband. The girl wants her mother's love all to herself. As we have seen, it is not only Demeter who experiences merging as ecstatic union; Persephone does too. Whether a girl once had and then lost her mother or whether she never had her mother in a perfect-enough way, what the girl wants is nothing less than union with the Feminine Eternal; she cannot accept its loss or its ongoing absence in her life. The psychoanalytic theorist Nancy Chodorow suggests that women become mothers in order to *be* mothered, as a way of revisiting or repairing the imperfect union with their own mothers.[2]

Human beings tend to forget what is painful or dangerous. Like sons, daughters were once completely dependent on a female caretaker. Perhaps remembering *any* conflict with another woman might remind a woman of a primary dependence so total that to have even once contemplated losing it was to contemplate death. Perhaps an infant or a child imagines—or has actually experienced—terror and deprivation at female hands. Perhaps one's mother or female caregiver was largely absent or malevolently present, over-critical, subject to rages. According to some psychoanalytic theorists, daughters, perhaps even more than sons, respond to perceived and real maternal anger with "guilt."

Why *guilt?* According to psychoanalyst Melanie Klein, envy (in women) is a form of "infantile aggression" directed toward the "riches" of the maternal body. In Klein's view, an infant is insatiable and utterly dependent upon a breast-feeding or care-taking mother. The infant may fear that her insatiability can hurt or devour her mother—or has already done so. She might fear maternal retaliation for this fantasized "sadistic" devouring and dependence. The Kleinian infant feels profoundly guilty about this, terrified of her own enormous desires, resentful and envious of her mother upon whose bountiful resources she depends, jealous of all others who might deplete that maternal resource, guilty herself for having done so or for *believing* that she has. She is also terrified of maternal retaliation.

In my view, when the infant is grown, this primal and totally unconscious guilt may be aroused by any situation in which one woman is dependent upon another for love and sustenance in any sense—physically, psychologically, economically, socially, or sexually.

On the one hand, the Empress-Infant wants her mother to serve and provide for her every need—and she is insatiable; on the other hand, the Empress-Toddler may fear that by satisfying her own insatiable desires she may have weakened or even destroyed her mother. A girl may be guilty of desiring her mother excessively and also outraged if that desire is not recip-rocated. The five-year-old girl may begin to understand that she, too, is fated to become a depletable natural resource, that is, a mother, and that the most powerful person she knows—her mother—has relatively little worldly power, except for that derived from her connection to men. To the four- or five-year-old girl, her mother may appear to flaunt her male-preference just as the mythic Queen Clytemnestra does. Whether the girl begins likewise to prefer men or refuses to do so, neither method will get her what she wants: union with her Mother.[3]

Psychoanalysts Judith Lewis Herman and her mother, Helen Block Lewis, have written about anger in the mother-daughter relationship. They write: The daughter's pride "is deeply wounded by the discovery that even her mother prefers males to females" and places her husband and her sons "above her daughter." A daughter experiences her mother's male-preference "as a rejection [and] as a betrayal . . . Not only does her esteem for her mother suffer, but her own self-esteem is endangered by the thought that she might share in her mother's inferior status."[4]

Psychiatrist Teresa Bernardez notes that women often "resent" their mothers for "depriving them of love and self-esteem." Daughters are disappointed in their mothers' acceptance of their own second-class status.

> Many women criticize their mothers without recognition of the subordinate role and limited choices their mothers had. The mother is perceived as the person responsible for the second-class status of the girl and for the indoctrination into obedience and compliance in the role of woman. This aspect of the conflict may lead to defensive identifications with men . . . Since she is forbidden to take cognizance of

her subordinate position in the social world, her complaints about her mother and maternal objects become the focus of the resentment.

Literature professor Nancy K. Miller, the author of *Bequest and Betrayal: Memoirs of a Parent's Death*, writes that there is a "composite" mother whom daughters of all classes and races wish *not* to become. She is

> The mother we think didn't love us, the mother we don't think we loved. This is the mother who betrayed us, for whom one daughter should have been enough. This is the mother whose recognition we seek ceaselessly, uselessly . . . This is the mother who keeps us imagining—and longing for—the Good Mother.

In 1972, in *Women and Madness*, I first suggested that most women are "motherless daughters." What I meant was that daughters were not "mothered" into heroism nor did they inherit matrilineal control over the means of production and reproduction. Both Demetrian mother-daughter merging and a daughter's flight from that merging were routinely viewed and experienced as "madness." I called on women to cultivate the capacity not only to tolerate, but to celebrate "difference."[5]

In 1976, Adrienne Rich published *Of Woman Born: Mother-*

hood as Experience and Institution, in which she further refined my analysis of patriarchal motherhood and introduced the concept of *matrophobia,* which she defined as a "desire to be purged once and for all of our mother's bondage, to become individuated and free." According to Rich, daughters experience their mothers as "unfree victims and martyrs. A daughter fears she is fated to inherit her mother's 'condition,' as well as her mother's individual character."

Literary critic Marianne Hirsch describes how difficult it is for a group of feminist women who are themselves mothers to identify sympathetically with their own mothers. She writes, "When we spoke *as mothers,* [our] group's members were respectful, awed, helpful . . . when we spoke *as daughters* . . . we [giggled knowingly about our] shared problem—our 'impossible mothers.'" As daughters, Hirsch's women cannot "hear" their mothers' stories. In her view, this reveals the "depth and the extent of [our] 'matrophobia,' which exists not only in the culture at large, but also within feminism, and within women who are mothers."

According to the literary critic Judith Kegan Gardiner, "In the Oedipus myth, the son murders his father in order to replace him. Contrastingly, in the new woman's myth, the daughter 'kills' her mother in order not to have to take her place." A matrophobic daughter wishes to free herself both from a mother's powerless fate and from her own (imagined) complicity in that fate.

Love, hate, ambivalence, and devouring greed on the part of

both mothers and daughters are examined by psychoanalytic theorist Jane Flax. On the one hand, women who enter therapy with her often feel as if they must "rescue" their mothers, but they also feel "guilty (about) betraying their mothers" simply because, as daughters, they have tried to "resolve and terminate (this) symbiotic tie." In Flax's experience, daughter-patients are both obsessed with "getting enough" unconditional love and "terrified of their deep, 'greedy' need for it."

A daughter "will dread retaliation from her (mother) for attacks that she has launched in the realm of phantasy, out of envy and hatred generated by frustration," writes British psychotherapist Nini Herman.

Molly Walsh Donovan, a psychoanalyst, refers to a "reverberating cycle of envy and rejection in the troubled mother-daughter relationship." Each experiences "differentiation" as "rejection":

> The mother's envy of her daughter's potential and freedom, and her feeling of rejection as her daughter appropriately moves away from her, can be communicated to the daughter in many, often unconscious ways. This can lead to the daughter's inhibiting herself or to guilt about surpassing her mother. From the other side, the daughter's envy and resentment of mother's power, her attachment to and dependency on mother, and her need to

define herself can lead to angry rejection of the mother, perhaps alternating with attempts to reconcile by renouncing her differentness. In this scenario neither mother nor daughter can flourish.

Teresa Bernardez describes how women in group therapy often "relive" their "perceived abandonment of their mothers who relied on their daughters for their emotional survival."

Some women recall cruelty or sexual abuse at their mother's hands, but more often the mother is perceived as vulnerable, or weak or ill, and ineffective in protecting the daughter from abuse or in helping her and encouraging her to be persistently ambitious and self-confident. The self-absorption or depression of the mother in circumstances that required her lively interest and commitment to the daughter are painfully recalled with such frequency that it alerts us to the social conditions under which women—particularly women of the two preceding generations—have had to rear children, without support and often in emotionally hostile and socially deprived circumstances.

Marilyn Meyers, a psychoanalyst, describes a female patient, Ms. K, who announces that she "can't have children, I would be too envious of a baby and I would be dangerous." Meyers understands that, like many other women, Ms. K is "loath to repeat" certain early mother-daughter dynamics.

> The danger that Ms. K perceives, and knows all too well, lies in the aftermath of an early mother-infant relationship that is tinged with a particular type of envy: envy that the mother feels toward the child whose dependency needs she is meeting. Such envy occurs within a dyad where one individual envies the other for some possession or quality and wants to spoil or destroy what the other has . . . At its worst, attacks of envy exceed the mother's capacity to love and the result is thwarted development of the daughter's capacity to love.
>
> The mother, herself a daughter, views the child ambivalently . . . at the core of this early object relation is a reversal around giving and receiving between mother and child wherein the child is called upon to fulfill the unmet dependency needs in the mother.

A woman's need to escape or repair her relationship with her mother may often lead her to follow blindly any woman who offers her the slightest maternal warmth—or to attack, reject, and disconnect from any other woman whom she later views as either too (maternally) powerful or too powerless.

Although many women seem to experience any competition with other women as something of a life-and-death matter, as I have noted, women also tend to have an Electra-like amnesia about what they themselves might have done to hurt other women. In the first round of interviews for this book, women would tell me precisely how *other* women had hurt them. Just that, nothing more. I'd ask them whether they had ever said or done anything to hurt another woman. Most said no.

The above, mainly unconscious, mother-daughter dynamics profoundly influences how adult women treat each other. Psychologically, no matter how old they are, most women continue to (unconsciously) experience themselves as daughters and all other women as potentially benevolent, withholding, or threatening mothers.

For example, I once hired a forty-year-old gardener, whom I shall call Sallie. She told me that she had endured years of savage abuse (beatings, solitary confinements, neglected medical needs) at the hands of a sadistic mother. Sallie said that she had "systematically planned an escape" and then "totally disconnected." She had not seen or talked to her mother for more than twenty years. Sallie was familiar with my work; perhaps she assumed I'd be the Good Mother she never had. She was quickly disappointed. In my garden there were only weeds to pull, flowers to plant, nothing else. Sallie soon became depressed, made serious mistakes, entered "fugue" states on the job. I was sympathetic, but I was also frustrated. My criticism, coupled with my unspoken frustration, constituted for Sallie a life-threatening situation. She must have experienced me as an avenging maternal ghost, because, true to form, Sallie left my employ just as she had left her mother's house: she planned it and then "disappeared," with no advance notice and no forwarding address.

Thus, mother-daughter dynamics often continue to "shadow" relationships between adult women at work. For example, Natalie is a forty-eight-year-old New York City magazine editor-in-chief. She loves working with women only; she has many protégés and a large circle of colleagues. Natalie surprised me when she said that, for her, working in an all-female space is even more "dangerous" than working among men. She explains: "The competition is unleashed. Someone has to win and it's gonna be a woman but it may not be you." In Natalie's view, every woman at work is, potentially, your "deadliest rival." More important: One minute, a woman can be "your best friend, all warm and seductive," but she can turn into your "worst nightmare in a flash." Natalie describes how a colleague can say the most awful things to you:

> You can hardly breathe, you think you're going to pass out, you want to die, and then, it's as if it never happened. But it did happen. It changes things. The air remains thick with it. It's like being in the house with your mother and you've just had a fight. I can't change who my mother is, but someone who isn't my mother has no right to treat me that way.

Novelist Daphne Merkin writes about a protagonist's tormented relationship with her mother: "Desires that aren't met don't go away, they just get twisted." The African-American writer Audre Lorde credits her "light-skinned mother" for having kept her "alive within an environment where my life was not a high priority." However, Lorde's mother also viewed Lorde as "full of the devil" and preferred her "good-looking" (lighter skinned) and well-behaved daughters. Lorde writes:

> I was dark. Bad, mischievous, a born trouble maker if ever there was one. [My anger] attach[ed] itself in the strangest of places. Upon those as powerless as I. My first friend asking "Why do you go around hitting all the time? Is that the only way you know how to be friends?"

Like many women, Lorde visits her daughterly frustrations upon her friends. As we have seen, many girls also re-enact their relationship with their mothers by developing a series of best friends, each of whom helps her friend to become more independent of her mother. Ultimately, nothing "works." We never quite "get over" or "give up" our need for a Perfect Mother—some might say, for a loving God.

"Strong" women (mothers, older women) are often hard to mother. They don't let their weaknesses show (women are afraid to see them); "strong women" don't seem to behave in "girlish" ways. As a group, women tend to "protect" weak women and punish "strong," expressive, direct, risk-taking, or "original" women. This is what a Mother is: a point of origin, a passage through, from non-being into being. Pure power. In an interview, the writer Joanna Russ told me:

> Women will try and kill you if you're strong and your work is known. If a woman is effective and visible, to other women, she is expected to be also Santa Claus and Wonder Woman and God combined and *therefore* anything can be done to her because she's so strong and they're so weak.

I knew what it felt like to be a daughter. I began to understand what it might feel like to *mother* a daughter only when I became an intellectual mother.

Other women have often perceived me as a "supernaturally" powerful woman. Some students, readers, patients, colleagues, and lecture audiences have treated me as if I were a Fairy Godmother, or they resented and felt intimidated by my Evil Stepmother accomplishments. My intellectual daughters did not merely challenge my views; they challenged my character, my authority, my (maternal) right to "exist." My intellectual daughters assumed that I was all-powerful and could never be hurt by anything they did or failed to do. I came to understand that when my daughters attacked my right to "be," their attacks felt just like my *mother's* attacks on my right to "be." And so I tended either to deny and minimize such attacks—or to overreact to them. This reaction parallels some real-life experiences of motherhood.

For example, Cybele, whom I interviewed, is a forty-five-year-old Innkeeper. She said: "My mother's mother had seven boys and two girls. The girls were expected to help their mother take care of nine men: their father, brothers, and an uncle who lived with us. All the children were brought up to be very obedient, the girls even more so." Cybele fought with her mother, whom she describes as "very oppressive." Cybele began to understand things differently only after her mother died. She found her mother's diary. "I felt terrible. For her, and for our past relationship. My mother could not rebel against her mother. But she expected me to be the rebel for both of us." That allowed Cybele's mother to stand with *her* mother (Cybele's grandmother) and oppose Cybele for being too rebellious and selfish. "My mother accepted her fate. She thought she had no choice. Her acceptance killed her." Cybele now finds herself caught up in the same dynamic with her three teenage daughters. "When they fight with me, or contradict me, I feel like they're betraying me. I need them to side with me, to support me emotionally." Cybele also experiences her daughters as if they were her mother. "When they beat up on me, and that's what it feels like, I forget all about why it's important for daughters to rebel. I only feel they're about to destroy me. Like my mother tried to do."

I recall a woman academic, Bianca, for whom I worked in the early 1960s. She was both beautiful and brilliant, but she was going through a devastating divorce. Bianca started coming to work late, leaving early. Sometimes she cried, or forgot what she was about to say. Once, Bianca summoned me to her bedside at home. I was extremely uncomfortable. Disdainful, perhaps. Disgusted. (Youth really has no mercy.) I had no way of understanding what she was going through. Here lay my powerful woman employer—defeated. Although I had not caused this, it was still too threatening for me to see an older woman undone—or simply in need of sympathy. I gave her none.

A decade ago, nineteen-year-old Jennie found her way to my doorstep, where she stood, giggling. I had admired an article she wrote and I'd tracked her down to congratulate her. She exclaimed over and over again: "This is awesome! The real Phyllis Chesler is on my line!" Within days, she was on a plane. ("I was moving into your neighborhood anyway. What karma.") I hired her to do research on the subject of her article. But within forty-eight hours it became clear that Jennie was not capable of working for me. She stared into space. Ran in and out for coffee. She said she needed ever-more clarifications from me, given our "mis-communication." (What mis-communication?) At the time I was ill with Lyme's Disease, as yet undiagnosed. Perhaps I was not administering this project effectively enough. Perhaps I needed a more mature and independent assistant. Perhaps Jennie was terrified that the Amazon was a disabled woman. Within a week, I let Jennie go.

Years later, in a book, Jennie addressed a letter to me about how "abusive" feminist employers are. She said her friends had encountered similarly disappointing feminist employers. Ah, Jennie, some young women, feminists included, are too unsure of themselves, ambivalent, perhaps, about working with any (female) authority figure—not to mention a Major Mentor. They may need to strike out on their own. Misguidedly, they may strike out, first, at their chosen feminist mentors.

After I completed a first draft of this book I re-read Jennie's letter to me. It was not really about *me*, but about relationships between feminist employers and employees in general. But, I had initially experienced it as devastating because I had wanted Jennie to like my work (as I'd liked hers), and to assist me in doing that work. Clearly her inability to do so was neither personal nor malevolent. Perhaps, because I was disabled, I was very diappointed that it hadn't worked out. I wanted Jennie to say only "nice" things about me and my cohort. Thus, I suffered Jennie's challenging me in public as an affront, a betrayal. It was no such thing.

Bianca, now, too late, I begin to understand . . .

Psychoanalyst Anna Aragno describes her own painful experiences as the mother of two adolescent daughters. She notes that her role now demands that she "endure insult," as her daughters find the "weakest spot." Overnight, Aragno is "transformed into a mortal enemy."

> Unwittingly and unwillingly we are dragged along to participate in a scenario and perform a role we vigorously resist, to serve a function for our daughters' development from which we recoil with all our might. The function is that of a trampoline—that from which to rebound. Separation, after all, entails

separating from something. As one daughter put it, "mother is the biggest part of what you say 'no' to." yet mother must also never be too far away.

With two years separating them, when my first slid silently into puberty and drastically distanced herself from me, I felt I had lost a daughter. When my second, a far quieter and stuck-to-mommy child, approached the same age, however, I was not prepared for what was in store. "Die so that I may live!" she screamed at me, flinging herself on the floor of our hallway. And with this resounding battle cry she announced her entrance into a long, drawn-out struggle to disengage from me while never straying too far, a struggle from which it was impossible that I emerge unscathed.

In the face of feeling betrayed, discarded, devalued, and provoked to boot, the mother must be able to tolerate an increasing sense of loss while standing still witnessing her daughter's petulant disengagement, realizing that this is the only way for her to establish an identity that is truly distinct and uniquely hers.

Does thinking psychoanalytically shed light on my experiences as an intellectual mother? It does. For example, some of my intellectual daughters routinely "borrowed" my published ideas without acknowledging the source. This sort of thing happens all the time, among men as well as women. However, if this "borrowing," or incorporation process has no deeper psychological significance, one would expect no emotional fallout to follow. But fallout there is. For example, the woman who uses, borrows, or steals published ideas from another woman tends, afterwards, to distance herself from her rival, or foremother. Perhaps, à la Klein, she feels guilty and wants to avoid any contact with someone who might remind her of a more primal, imagined "theft" which in turn, might provoke a more primal guilt and terror.

In addition to creating distance, a handful of my intellectual daughter-borrowers have, afterwards, been outraged when I dared point out that they had taken something valuable without saying "thank you." (Intellectual "thank yous" are accomplished merely by citing the creator's work; it's no big deal.)

The first time I remember that a woman borrowed an original idea of mine without saying thank you, I told her so. I was completely unprepared for the two long, single-spaced letters I received, one from her, one from her husband. They both denied any borrowing—and they took ten pages to say so. This woman refused to talk to me for more than a year. Once, she left a party when she heard I was there. More often, my beloved borrowers have, unilaterally, disappeared from my life.

One of my very earliest woman students later co-authored a book about the university program I had pioneered; in that book she remembers her own contributions, but no one else's. For her, my contributions did not, could not exist. Another early student—we had been very close—once confronted me in the school cafeteria. She yelled. She wept. She repeated over and over: "And I loved you!" She demanded that I prove myself worthy of her love by publishing my first book "anonymously" because "all women are equal, aren't they? So, there's no need to push yourself forward, is there?" Perhaps she feared that my publishing a book meant that I'd abandon her. She went on to co-found a feminist organization, but she never spoke to me again. Other than this one emotional confrontation, we had never fought; there was no objective or rational reason for us to stop talking. Perhaps she felt diminished, engulfed by my looming, maternal presence. Perhaps she felt that she could not become her own hero and, simultaneously, remain connected to her point of intellectual origin—without guilt or obligation.[6]

I am the mother of a biological son; I have no such biological or social relation to a daughter. However, as a feminist intellectual and activist, I do have a relationship to "daughters." Often, painfully, it is like Clytemnestra's relation to Electra.

I created a bibliography for my book, *Letters to a Young Feminist*. In response, two highly successful feminist writers each yelled at me because I had not listed all, but only some, of their many books. Am I their mother or their therapist, obliged to bear witness to their enormous creativity? Do I have similar expectations of other feminist intellectuals? So many feminists (like mothers? like daughters?) feel unappreciated, not fully credited by each other. Is our hunger for omnipotent mothering and for dutiful daughtering so great that we expect and demand it from every other woman at all times? Why are we so ready to punish each other for failing to live up to such demonic ideals?

Why do feminists (like other ideologues) often recognize our intellectual foremothers so selectively? Why do we write women we don't like out of our history even as we are making it? Why is it easier for a feminist to remember a dead foremother than a living one; a minor rather than a major one? Why such amnesia—if not in the service of psychological matricide?

Until now, I had "forgotten" these questions. Writing has opened Memory's floodgates. Suddenly I also remember Kathy, my best student, and a most dedicated research assistant. Kathy became pregnant, the result of a love affair with one of my male colleagues. (Back then, neither I nor anyone I knew of thought that having sex with one's students was unethical or actionable. Kathy certainly did not think so, she said she loved the guy.) Kathy had a miscarriage. She required emergency surgery. I visited her every day; my male colleague never once turned up. "He has a thing about hospitals and death, he can't face them," Kathy explained. Since her family lived 2000 miles away, I allowed Kathy to move in with me while she convalesced. She was bed-ridden. I arranged for her care while I was teaching. Then, one evening, I came home to find Kathy up, dressed, and cooking. "He's agreed to come over," she told me. "I'm cooking my best dish for him." The table was set for two, not three. I was hurt, outraged. I said: "Why not cook for me?

I'm the professor who lost her research assistant and gained a patient." I told Kathy that she would have to move out.

Thirty years later I can still taste my disappointment. I miss the phantom bond between us that died right then and there, stillborn. Kathy did once write to me to tell me about how moved she was by something I had written and about her own intellectual accomplishments. (Kathy, if you're reading this, you know who you are: Call home.) Obviously, intellectual mothers enjoy certain luxuries that real mothers do not enjoy. For example, most mothers would not throw a daughter out because that daughter preferred her absent, dazzling, father to her grumbling, servant-mother.

In 2001, a reviewer begins her positive review of Katha Pollitt's work in this way: "Is there a feminist who hasn't wished, at one time or another, that she could be Katha Pollitt?" Is there a male intellectual in the world who would phrase things in quite this way? I think not. When a woman admires a woman who is different from herself, she may also envy her—as a way of remaining connected to her. Laura Tracy is enlightening on this. She writes:

> When women compete with each other, we are trying to differentiate ourselves. But since knowing we are different from other women frightens us and makes us feel that we will be abandoned and alone, most of us have learned to disguise our competitiveness. Instead, we feel envy. We feel envious of the

women with whom we compete, far more consistently than men envy the other men they come up against.

Envy can be understood as a form of thwarted identification. Envy indicates our desire for sameness, not for difference. Unlike jealousy, which indicates we are perceiving a loss, envy implies desire—the desire for a connection we feel is disrupted by difference. We experience envy when we meet someone who is different from us and, we think, better than we are. We covet what that person possesses because her possessions, whether material, physical, or intellectual, disconnect her from us.

Recently, two young feminists interviewed me for their book. Afterwards, one of the authors sent me a letter in which she assured me that they had not "targeted" me for criticism. I found the letter strange, thought no more about it, saw both authors at a variety of events, returned each woman's smooth smile. When reviews of their book, which I had not read, appeared, reviewers insisted that I had indeed been targeted. The authors did not attack my ideas or actions. Instead, they related a personal incident gleefully, as if it were gossip, and they mocked the maternal tone of voice I'd used in my book *Letters to a Young Feminist.* (I had adopted a maternal persona mindfully, in order to speak as an intimate to those who were young enough to be my children and grandchildren.) I approached one of these authors' mentors and told her that, although I was mystified, and surprised by what felt like a sneak attack, the authors and I need not be enemies. "Please have them call me, so we can work this out," I said. Neither feminist responded. And I did not call them. A year later, I met one of them at a reading. She said: "Maybe we did single you out. It's probably a mother-daughter thing. What do you think?"

I think it might be.[7]

A number of intellectual mothers and daughters have left a record of the ways in which they have engaged in the forced competition for the token "only great woman" spot. Intellectual mothers have not always mentored their female replacements; like their male counterparts, they have, instead, often beaten them back for as long as possible. Intellectual daughters have wished not only to join, but to replace their intellectual mothers. For example, according to Princeton University Professor of Literature Elaine Showalter, only one "dark lady of American letters" could exist at any given time:

> That role [according to Norman Podhoretz] had been "carved out" by Mary McCarthy; but since McCarthy was now too old for the role, "a public existed when [Susan] Sontag arrived on the scene which was searching for a new dark lady, and she was so obviously right that a spontaneous decision was made on all sides to cast her for the role." When Sontag met Mary McCarthy in the late 1960s, McCarthy declared, "Oh, you're the imitation me."

According to Showalter, nearly thirty years later, Camille Paglia applied for this token position. Paglia expected Sontag to anoint Paglia. If not, Paglia would take the position by any means possible.

> But whereas Sontag had dismissed the cult of the dark lady as "grotesque" and renounced its assumptions of tokenism and competition among women, Paglia accepted them fully. In the terms of her childhood belligerence, and her zero-sum game of feminist combat there could be only one dark lady at a time. According to this model, she should have been next in line for the job. When she managed a private meeting with Sontag, Paglia was bitterly disappointed by Sontag's refusal to see their encounter as a passing of the torch . . . Finally, Sontag asked, "What is it you want from me?" [Paglia] stammered, "I just want to talk to you." But that was wrong. I wanted to say, "I'm your successor, dammit, and you don't have the wit to realize it." It was all about Eve, and Sontag was Margo Channing stalked by the new girl." But Sontag did not play her part in this Hollywood cultural script, and Paglia never forgave her. By the time *Sexual Personae* appeared in 1990, Paglia "viewed Sontag and her coterie as fossilized petty tyrants." . . . In *Vanity Fair*, Paglia chortled triumphantly, "I've been chasing that bitch for twenty-five years and I've finally passed her!" Sontag's

maddening refusal to take any notice of [Paglia's] presence at all was an additional insult. "She could scarcely retain her claim to intellectual preeminence," Paglia fumed, "while not having heard of a controversial woman thinker of my prominence."

Intellectually accomplished women are no more exempt from such rivalries than are intellectual men (or non-intellectual) women and men. My point: no matter how accomplished or powerful the designated mother figure may be (e.g., Mary McCarthy), she may still experience routine intellectual competition in gender-stereotypical ways. (There can be only one queen, one Miss America, one wife, etc.) The self-designated daughter figure may feel, à la Paglia, that excessive force is necessary against so formidable a (maternal) rival. Such contenders, who experience themselves as daughter-rivals or daughter-successors, can sometimes assault their maternal rivals, full force, without fully understanding the harm they do.

I too am a disobedient daughter, one who did not respect or admire her mother. Even here, I am ready to yield up my mother's secrets, bare her shame for all the world to see. They say: pity the mother of daughters; I say, pity the mother of a daughter who writes.

I fought with my mother every day of my life, from the time I was five years old. I never volunteered to help my mother serve a meal, never learned how to sew or shop, and refused to do the dishes. I never kept her company as she cooked or ironed or mended. I escaped into a book, without (I can hear her saying this) "a backward glance."

I continued to want *her* love and approval, while withholding mine from her. I was never able to accept her as she was: a fierce, rigid, cold, controlling woman, from whom I could expect little in the way of warmth or approval, but everything in terms of what I needed to survive and grow, at least intellectually. From her point of view, I was the failure, not she. She had delivered in every sense of the word—I was the living proof. In return, I was supposed to remain an Orthodox Jew, marry young, live near my mother, be the schoolteacher of young children, and do for my mother what she had done for her parents. No more, no less. My failure to live up to this precise expectation outraged and embittered her and probably broke her heart.

I have repeatedly asked friends who knew my mother and who had seen us together whether I had ever been cruel to her. Was I exaggerating her cruelty to me? Reluctantly, one friend said: "You kept trying to please her and she kept rejecting you. She even talked against you to me, behind your back." Another friend of thirty-five years said: "I never heard her say a kind word to you."

Like most daughters, I still keep trying to prove that she loved me—or prove that, if she did not, it was because I had failed her too.

I am only one woman, one intellectual mother, but my experiences are hardly unique. I belonged to a feminist generation that pioneered the idea that female role models are important, but who, nevertheless, acknowledged no mothers. Psychologically, my generation arose one morning, or so it seemed, like the goddess Athena, newly hatched from her father Zeus's brow. We experienced ourselves as motherless daughters. We were a sibling horde of sisters. Although we were of many different ages, psychologically we acted as if we lived in a universe of same-age peers. Perhaps we knew of no other way to break with the maternal past. Despite the fact that some of us were mothers, and even loved our real mothers, when we stepped out onto the stage of history we did so primarily as motherless daughters/sisters/sibling rivals.

Psychologically, like Electra, we had to commit matricide. Like Electra, we needed to have no memory about the real (or imagined) role we might have played in our mothers' downfall. If our mothers had been "defeated," we did not want to consider consciously, collectively, the possibility that something similar might happen to us too. Betty Friedan and Jill Ker Conway are two heroic, mainstream feminists, both many years older than I am, but certainly members of my *feminist* generation. Here is what they have written about their own mothers:

> Betty Friedan: There was my mother and her discontent . . . I didn't want to be like my mother . . . nothing we did ever seemed to satisfy her. I know now that I have fought for women because I did not find it good

being a woman, and I wanted to. I knew my mother didn't like being a woman, and had good reason not to. [In my] determination not to be like her, I embraced the feminine mystique for awhile . . . Reacting against her, I would have forgone the use of my own abilities in society and sunk deeper into that vicious cycle of "resentment." [As feminists], we found our strength by confronting the conditions that made us what we were as women, and by acting together to change them.

Jill Ker Conway: [My mother's] anger shook me. Her complaints were never-ending . . . How could I tell this woman who lived for me that I did not want to live for her? I began having trouble sleeping . . . [she] jeered at psychiatry and mocked the clergy, so there was no way to seek healing for her sick spirit, and hers was very sick . . . It was hard to think of such a strong-willed woman as a victim. So much of her deterioration seemed self-imposed . . . I had tried to rescue her . . . I'd been a dismal failure. The only way I could pay her respect now would be through some sublimated expression of my guilt, generalized towards caring for all frustrated and angry older women. I'd have to understand the history of woman's situation in modern society better.

Conway's choice of a feminist path (Friedan's too), might also be one way to remain connected to women when one needs at the same time to disconnect from one's own mother. I may have done the same thing. Perhaps, for some, feminism is a daughter's fantasy of rescuing her mother and a form of atonement; a flight from bad (normal) mothering, a search for good (ideal) mothering. Ker Conway decides to leave her mother's home and Australia forever. She writes:

> I wasn't nearly tough enough to stay around in an emotional climate more desolate than any drought I'd ever seen. I wasn't going to fight anymore. I was going to admit defeat; turn tail; run for cover.

Many women have felt it necessary to flee from their own mothers (or from a feared maternal destiny). My feminist generation all did so at the same moment in history; thus, we exulted in feelings of liberation. If we felt guilty about leaving our mothers behind, we did not say so; if we had good reasons to flee without looking back, we kept those reasons to ourselves.

Having a domineering and unhappy mother does not guarantee that a daughter will either escape or become a feminist. Most don't; most daughters stay. For example, when she was twenty-two years old, the writer Eudora Welty was imperiously summoned home by her newly widowed mother and remained at home for the next twenty-five years. Welty neither complained nor rebelled—nor did she become "political." Welty did, however, write a short story, "June Recital," which she described as "her most personally meaningful" story. Claudia Roth Pierpont tells us that this story is about an "old-maid piano teacher who is slowly driven insane; rumored to have murdered her overbearing mother, she is led away after trying to burn down their house."

What if a woman has no mother to flee? What if she (unconsciously) believes that she—her very birth—has fatally weakened or even killed her mother? Such a daughter might idealize her dead mother forever. She might also become a misogynist.

An example is Eliza Linton (1822-1898), the prolific British novelist and essayist, who was a virulent misogynist. According to her biographer, Elizabeth Fix Anderson, Linton wrote: "I hate women as a race. I think we are demons. Individually, we are all right, but as a race we are monkeyish, cruel, irresponsible, superficial." Paradoxically, Linton "deeply valued female friendships" and was "protective toward more feminine women." Anderson provides biographical information that might explain this apparently contradictory behavior. After bearing twelve children before she was thirty-nine, Linton's mother, Charlotte Alicia, died when Linton was five months old. Linton came to idealize her mother, but she had strong views against sex. Although she married, she had no children. According to Anderson, Linton "unconsciously felt responsible for killing her mother, a daughter's primal rival." Matricide and Oedipal fantasies recur in Linton's novels and short stories. In one novel, a female hero poisons her stepmother and dies as atonement; in a short story, another female hero is blamed for causing her mother's death. A "clergyman blames her: 'see what your unruly appetite, your selfishness and greediness, have done! . . . You have killed your mother.' "

Thus, the fear that one has destroyed, weakened, even killed one's own mother may lead a daughter either toward—or away from—feminism and an intellectual life.

6.

THE "GOOD ENOUGH" MOTHER AND HER PERSECUTION OF THE "GOOD ENOUGH" DAUGHTER

We expect mothers to be good; they are all that stands between us and death in a cruel or indifferent world. So we are terrified and outraged when a mother is not only imperfect, but abusive. Most people, women as well as men, overlook a father's absence and forgive his non-rescue of a child from a cruel mother. Such paternal behavior is a given. (Read fairy tales—this theme is omnipresent.) But comparable maternal behavior cannot be overlooked. It is dangerous to deny or minimize the harm that some mothers do, for fear of playing into misogynist hands.

Daughters are ambivalent about uncovering our mothers' nakedness. We fear their (imagined) retaliation; we (unconsciously) fear that we, too, might suffer a similar fate. We remain steadfast in connection. What many daughters do, therefore, is to challenge our mothers psychologically, over and over again—but at a safe remove. We do so also in our relationships with other (older) women whom we experience first as promising and then as failed mothers. As we have seen, pre-adolescent and adolescent girls practice this leaving/cleaving to their mothers in their relationships with a series of best friends.

Most mothers do not abandon their children. They sacrifice a great deal—in fact everything—in order to rear their broods. However, whether a mother remains at home as a full-time caretaker or works three jobs to feed her family, neither arrangement guarantees ideal mothering. We may unfairly and misogynistically blame mothers for everything, but we also allow mothers a great deal of latitude. We rarely focus on how "good enough" mothers actually treat their daughters.

A *good enough* mother may routinely treat her daughter in ways that are acceptable yet horrendous. For example, a good enough mother may despise and envy women, including her own daughter. She may be a "rage-aholic," given to wild mood swings, which she may not remember. She may also engage in any of the following behaviors: constant criticism, especially of a daughter's appearance; pathologizing of a healthy daughter (e.g., incessant visits to physicians and emergency rooms, daily administering of enemas); physical beatings; obsessive sexual surveillance and repression; collaboration in the physical or sexual abuse of a daughter by an adult male. In addition, a good enough mother may be extremely cold. She may withhold affection and praise; she may repress and punish intellectual and psychological growth and independence. She may prefer sons to daughters.

Whether a daughter remains close to such a mother or flees from her, she will probably feel unmothered and unnourished. She will look for perfect mothers everywhere, especially in the man she marries. She may have a hard time trusting another woman again.

Constant Criticism of Appearance

Jill, a sixteen-year-old interviewee, told me that her "mom is always after her" about her clothes being too tight. "She never likes my color lipstick or nail-polish. She hates my hair. 'Can't you do something with it for God's sake?' " Jill shaved it all off. "But that made her even crazier. I know she loves me, but this has got to stop."

According to the psychoanalyst Rozsika Parker, author of *Mother Love/Mother Hate: The Power of Maternal Ambivalence*, some mothers experience any daughterly deviation from what her mother desires as "an almost physical wound." Parker describes one mother who claims to "feel ill" whenever her daughter wears "unflattering shapes, clashing colors and horrid fabrics." This mother started fighting with her daughter about clothes when the girl was five years old. While the mother concedes that her daughter's body belongs to her daughter, she also says that "just as I struggled to control and improve my appearance, I feel compelled to control hers." Parker comments: "This mother experiences her daughter's body as if it were hers. After all, it was once part of her body."

This is Demetrian psychology at work. Demeter's daughter Persephone is supposed to remain merged with her mother or to resemble her in every detail.

Many of my interviewees described mothers who continued to criticize their appearance long after they became adults. One of them, Celia, a thirty-eight-year-old legal secretary, says: "I've been married for twenty years. Once, before my mother arrived, my husband bet me that she couldn't be there for more than ten minutes without beginning to criticize me." Celia's husband was wrong. As usual, Celia's mother did start criticizing her complexion, hair cut, posture, clothes, "but she waited a full fifteen minutes before she started!" Celia's husband asked his mother-in-law: "What have you got against your daughter? Why do you always criticize her?" Celia's mother said: "What are you talking about? I love my daughter. I only have her best interests at heart."

Mothers have traditionally discouraged vanity in their daughters. The journalist and feminist Charlotte Perkins Gilman (1860-1935), writes: "If I were a pretty child, no hint of it was allowed to enter my mind." Gilman's mother cut off her "fat little brown curls at an early age—lest I should be vain." Jill Ker Conway writes that her mother has never complimented her on her appearance. Rather, "my mother's comments about my swollen ankles were tactless; her comments about some of my other personal defects were downright depressing."

Constant Generalized Criticism

Good enough mothers may also criticize and demean their daughters in general, not just in relation to appearance. According to therapists Karen Fite and Nikola Trumbo, "We experienced an ongoing critical, belittling, undermining behavior from our mothers. Nothing we did was quite right, and the way we looked was never good enough." Summarizing an interview study they conducted, Fite and Trumbo write:

> We experienced confusion about what kinds of behaviors would be approved of by our mothers and remember that sometimes strength and autonomy were approved of and sometimes they were disapproved of. Sometimes intelligence and success were rewarded and sometimes frowned upon. We felt we got a kind of random reinforcement from our mothers, the kind of reinforcement that was so unpredictable as to rob us of a sense of power over our world, to leave us forever dependent upon the approval of others, starting with our mothers. Since we didn't know which actions would bring approval, which disapproval, we could not make the choice of consequences for ourselves.

Professor and author Nancy K. Miller writes that her mother says things that "hurt" her all the time. Nevertheless, her mother asks: "How can you think I would say something to hurt you?" When Miller tries to explain the concept of the unconscious, her mother's voice "would harden, since to invoke the unconscious is to blame her. My mother, after all, is the one who, when I began therapy, insisted on her right to see the therapist in order to tell him what really had happened in my childhood, and why I was wrong."

The writer, Laurie Stone, describes her mother.

> Toby is not an easy anything. She bullies waiters and salespeople . . . The waiters move around as if they are in occupied France and we are the Germans. They want us dead, and I'm on their side. . . I hadn't seen much of Toby in the preceding year, though we live only two miles apart. I'd grown tired of being called poison and told I should die. Call me touchy.
>
> She doesn't ask about my life. When I mention that I published two books in the intervening time, she doesn't ask what they are about, instead says, "Did you make any money?"

My own mother never had a kind word to say to me. If I received a grade of 95 on a test, she would say: "Big deal, that only proves you could have got 100 if you'd really tried." By the time I was ten years old, my mother had convinced me that I was both ugly and stupid. "You only have book knowledge," she would jeer. "See how far that will get you." When my father dared to compliment me, she'd turn on him. "You don't see through her the way I do. She'll make a fool of you." My mother taught me how to succeed against the odds with absolutely no support—a very valuable lesson.

Most daughters minimize the harm that such constant maternal criticism does on the grounds that the harm is unintended. "I'm used to it," says Casey, a twenty-nine-year-old housewife and mother. "My mom criticizes my mothering constantly, but I know she really loves me. It's just her way." Most mothers who verbally denigrate their daughters are still considered loving by their daughters.

Such constant, maternal criticism maims the spirit. It also teaches women to deny what is being done to them—and what they, in turn, do to other women. ("I didn't say that, but even if I did, I didn't *mean* anything by it.") Being shamed becomes confused with being loved. A constantly critical mother is not teaching her daughter how to establish interpersonal integrity within an intimate space. Rather, she is accustoming her daughter to humiliation at the hands of another woman. Girls soon become deadened to this—and hooked on it as well.

Fite and Trumbo note that many of their interviewees experienced mothers who were strangely jealous of their daughters' female friends and who constantly sought to separate their daughters from their girlfriends:

Sometimes they belittled us in front of our friends, sometimes they belittled or criticized our friends, sometimes they attempted to intrude into these relationships. One woman told us that she experienced her mother's reaction to her first lover not only as disgust and outrage but also as a kind of jealousy that her daughter had chosen another woman, as though this was a rejection of her.

Women also told us that they experienced maternal discouragement of close friendships with other girls beginning in adolescence. Some experienced their mothers as supporting their father's homophobia and carrying out the programming to separate them from their girlfriends, and others experienced their mothers as failing to support the legitimacy of their ties to other girls in the face of the of the fathers' disapproval. In either case they felt betrayed.

Coldness and Silence

Rosa, a forty-year-old math teacher, says: "My mother comes from a family that fights when they eat, and then they don't speak to each other for years on end. At least she keeps talking to me." As previously noted, if you are a woman, to be "cut off" is worse than being verbally abused; it is experienced as psychic death, not autonomy. Therefore, mothers who are excessively or routinely cold, cutting (cut off from their own feelings), have the power to wound their daughters very deeply.

California writer and therapist Kim Chernin describes her mother's punitive withdrawals as even more painful than her angry maternal outbursts. Chernin remembers that when she had done something wrong her mother "could fall silent, completely silent, and not address me for days on end, until I could not stand it anymore. There was no limit to what she could stand of her own coldness, and the complete cutting me off." Only Chernin's abject apologies for real or imagined sins ended this silent treatment.

Novelist Daphne Merkin describes a similarly cold mother, who "straddles (her) childhood like a colossus." Merkin's protagonist, Hannah, is reduced to tears by her mother's cruelty. "Your tears don't move me," her mother says. Hannah tells her mother to "shut up"—and her mother does not speak to her for ten days. The painful, prolonged silence ends only when Hannah profusely apologizes.

Christine Ann Lawson notes that in 1978 Christina Crawford won a part as a guest star on a television program. She telephoned her mother, Joan Crawford, to share the good news.

> Her mother hung up on her in the middle of their conversation . . . shortly thereafter Christina became convinced that her mother could never allow her to enjoy her own success.

Lawson also notes that many daughters of borderline mothers remember turning to their mothers for comfort and "feeling worse afterwards." One does not have to be a celebrity—or the daughter of one—to experience similar harrowing cruelties.

Barbara Mathias, the journalist and author of *Between Sisters: Secret Rivals, Intimate Friends,* describes, for example, a mother who does not call her daughter, Gretchen, to acknowledge the death of Gretchen's twelve-year-old daughter (her own grand-daughter) "until three months later." When Gretchen loses her husband a year after that this same mother "took six months to call." Typically, Gretchen still calls her mother regularly, to "check in" and to "attempt forgiveness." Mathias also describes a daughter, Betty, who "worked hard at gaining her (elderly) mother's favor." Her mother preferred Nan, another daughter. Nevertheless, once a week, every week, Betty would drive a long distance to take care of her mother for one full day.

And each Thursday night she would return exhausted, and disappointed that her mother never reached out except to criticize that she wasn't doing things right or as well as Nan. Betty's husband would always ask, "why do you go?" "She's my mother," Betty would insist, "and you have to be respectful."

"If you want to know how cold my mother really was," says Betty, "she told me on her deathbed, 'I want you to get away from me.'"

"I wasn't hurt," Betty says cavalierly. "I did get away from her. My youngest brother was in the room and he heard her say it. He was her darling. I just let it roll off my back . . . But you don't say that to a child, 'get away from me.'"

My mother was also cold. She took pride in the fact that she was not physically affectionate. "To you, kisses are the most important thing, but you're wrong," she would tell me. "You have a roof over your head and a full stomach. You have nothing to complain about." When I was a child, my mother never hugged or kissed me; this did not change when I became an adult. (I can hear her comments: "Are you still on this subject? Will you never grow up?" Of course, she is right—but so am I.) Years later, when she was in her late seventies, she made a serious effort to hold still for my kisses. She even began to peck my cheek too, but quickly, as if it were an act of defiance, as if she felt guilty about doing so.

My mother was suspicious, secretive. It was hard for me to get her to tell me about her life. Once, I took her away to a hotel. First, we fought—that always happened when I tried to defend myself against her barrage of non-stop criticism—but then we talked. Or rather, I listened. In passing, very casually, but for the first time, my mother mentioned that she had slept in the same bed with her father until she was sixteen. My face probably fell open, for she quickly said: "Don't make a big deal about it. Back then, it didn't mean anything. My mother was sickly, she needed her bed to herself." I draw no obvious conclusions. I wonder: Is this where she learned to mistrust kisses, and to hold herself rigid, unmoving, when another body brushed hers? Did I fail her by failing to understand that she may have had good reasons to be physically aloof?

A Mother's Preference for a Sick Child

Like so many mothers of her time (of all times perhaps), my mother was at her best when a child was ill and required care. I had almost forgotten how much certain mothers feel needed—and therefore powerful—when they have a "sick" child.

For example, Molly, a thirty-two-year-old kindergarten teacher, says: "My mother prefers my mentally ill sister to me. I'm too healthy for her to control. I'm not needy and dependent." Still, Molly is hurt every time her mother signs her sister out of the hospital—to attend the very family event that she'll "forget" to tell Molly about. A number of interviewees described mothers who denigrated them as "mentally ill" or who pathologized and infantilized them by diagnosing imaginary physical illnesses.

In an extraordinary and horrifying book about her psychoanalytic treatment, the Algerian-French writer Marie Cardinal describes a mother who resented, humiliated, deprived, and manipulated her. According to Nini Herman, Cardinal's mother was considered "an angel of righteousness and a savior of Algeria's poor." But she "was not interested in a healthy child." Only when Marie was sick "could she be the subject of [any maternal] attention."

Christine Ann Lawson notes that "borderline witch mothers" tend to seek treatment for their children, but not for themselves:

Borderline mothers may subtly imply or blatantly accuse their children of being crazy, with statements like "there is something wrong with your head," or "you are out of your mind," or "you're crazy!" They project their own disorganized thinking onto their children . . . witch mothers . . . denigrate the mental health profession because they fear its power. The witch's greatest fear is of having no control, of being locked up . . . A witch mother who brought her son for treatment registered a complaint with the therapist's professional organization demanding that the therapist's license be revoked after the therapist recommended that the mother seek treatment . . . witch mothers . . . project their own pathology onto their child, and often expect the child to be institutionalized.

Mentally ill mothers can also make their children psychologically ill. Marie Cardinal's mother, Solange, tried to abort Marie when Solange was twenty-seven. Every measure (excessive horseback riding, quinine) failed. When Solange's daughter Marie turned twenty-seven, she started to bleed continuously. Marie calls this "the thing" and it lasts for years. Because of it, "days are spent on the bidet, or curled up on the bathroom floor." Her husband leaves her, and Marie cannot care for her children. Nini Herman notes:

When Marie was twenty-seven, her symptoms took hold. She would finally submit and accomplish [Solange's failed] abortion . . . as a dutiful daughter: as the one who really loved mama.

Ultimately, in analysis, Marie is also able to acknowledge—and experience—her love for her cruel, sick (now deceased) mother who was once, Marie intuits, a hopeful, dazzling, beautiful woman. Marie writes:

How good it was finally to love her in the light, in the springtime, in the open, after the terrible battle from which we were delivered. Two blind people armed to the teeth, claws exposed . . . what blows she had struck me, what venom I had distilled! What savagery, what butchery!

Pathologizing a Healthy Daughter

A woman I shall call Kara was forty-two years old and the manager of an international chain of hotels; she consulted me when previously well-contained phobias began to interfere with her business life. Kara described her mother as having "administered an enema a day," in addition to routinely "scrubbing and cleaning out" her vagina. Kara's childhood was filled with after-school appointments with pediatricians, gastroenterologists, dentists, optometrists, podiatrists. (This took place decades before the diagnosis of Munchausen's Syndrome by Proxy became fashionable.) Perhaps Kara's mother experienced her own bodily functions as dirty and sick; so anything (like Kara) that came from her body was, by definition, also dirty and sick, and in need of detoxification rituals. Such behavior is abusive. The abuse is magnified when people refuse to discuss it.

Stephanie, a forty-year-old clothing store owner, described how her mother had subjected her to a series of invasive medical treatments, including surgery for imaginary illnesses. In Stephanie's case, her mother was "covering up" paternal physical and sexual abuse. She says: "A blackened jaw got treated as an abscessed tooth." Today, Stephanie feels as if she is "committing a mortal feminist sin when she talks about mothers' being responsible for abuse." When feminists demanded that she blame her father, but not her mother, Stephanie responded this way:

> Is my father somehow more responsible for the abuse that he inflicted because he had more economic and social resources than my mother? Does a lack of resources make my mother less responsible? I don't think so.

The night my own father died, my mother demanded that I sleep with her—not just in her bedroom, but in her single bed.

I was horrified. How could I go from a lifetime of practically no physical contact to a night together in the same bed? I wanted to comfort her. I could not sleep with her. In asking me to take my father's place in her bed, she wanted to use my body as a "thing." I felt as if she were "killing" me. My mother kept insisting, I kept refusing. Maybe her request was a common nineteenth-century European practice; maybe, if she'd shown me the slightest physical affection, this request might not have seemed so strange, almost murderous. I fled the house that very night.

Who else could the poor woman turn to, if not to her only daughter? In the most primal of ways, I was not there for her. As I write this I regret—but coldly, without emotion—that I withheld my body from her at that time. Perhaps I was treating my mother just as she'd treated me. I was her star pupil and thus, her star betrayer. (Do I merit a grade of 100 now, my dead, dear, mother?)

The Mother's Body, The Daughter's Body—how hard it is for us to stay safely connected, safely separated. Both connection and separation feel extreme, dangerous. Terrified, we merge—and then we abandon each other. Again and again.

Beating and Whipping

In many nineteenth-century families, mothers, even more than fathers, disciplined children, daughters especially. We have a record of this in the writings of daughters. For example, South-

African novelist Olive Schreiner (1855-1920) is quoted by Claudia Roth Pierpont as reporting that her "most searing early memory was of a beating—fifty strokes with a bundle of quince rods"—that she received from her mother when Schreiner was five. Both the revolutionary Agnes Smedley (1894-1950), a daughter of Missouri frontier poverty, and feminist writer Charlotte Perkins Gilman (1860-1935), a daughter of New England privilege, were whipped by their mothers. Both girls accepted this as "normal." If Smedley dared to cry, her mother would "order (her) to stop or she would threaten to 'stomp (her) into the ground.'" In her autobiography, Gilman writes that once, after doing something wrong, she immediately "humbled (her) proud spirit and confessed, and beg(ged) her mother to forgive her." Gilman's mother agreed to do so—but then whipped her anyway.

Although it is true that fathers (and society) expected mothers to "whip their daughters into obedience" and therefore shared responsibility for the whippings, nevertheless, because those whippings were actually administered by mothers, the psychological effect was female-specific and had long-range psychological consequences. For example, ever after, Gilman had trouble with people who claimed to believe in "forgiveness" but who, like her mother, believed in punishing you anyway. Smedley, whose father was a Cherokee Indian, writes that her mother beat her *more* frequently and *more* savagely as time passed. When Smedley tried to "tell," her mother called her a liar. Smedley writes: "It has been one of the greatest struggles of my life to learn to tell the truth . . . in pain and in tears I have had to unlearn all that my mother beat into my unformed mind."

We now understand that an abused child or adult hostage may cling to her abusive parent or captor; we call this the "Stockholm Syndrome." In a study of slave narratives, Brenda Stevenson confirms (and so does the anti-lynching crusader Ida Wells) that very young and mother-orphaned African-American slave girls often became attached to very cruel masters and mistresses. For example, a Reverend and Mrs. Hunter refused to free one such girl, Armaci Adams, for six years after the end of the Civil War.

> Skillfully employing well-honed techniques of psychological and physical intimidation, they were able to gain and maintain control of Armaci. They developed an emotional hold over her even though they treated her harshly . . . over the years, (Armaci's) emotional dependency became acute . . . Mrs. Hunter told the child (false) stories about her stepmother, and Armaci was afraid to leave with her father.

Agnes Smedley writes: "It was difficult for (my mother) to beat my need of her love out of me. It took years, for with the

least return of kindness in her, my love swept back." Una Stannard, the writer, agrees with that assessment. In an interview,
she notes:

> Some mothers give their babies non-possessive love,
> but a huge number of mothers nurture their babies
> on the opposite of possessive love—hate. And yet,
> strangely, babies who are hated are just as attached
> to their mothers. If a mother is a rejecting, hating
> mother, babies treat the hate and rejection as love.

Slave mothers also whipped their children—some say, in imi-
tation of white slave-owner whippings, but also in an effort to
exert some control over their children. Sojourner (Isabella)
Truth (1790-1883), the iconic orator and abolitionist, was born
into slavery in New York. Her earliest memories include the
sight of her parents grieving for children who were sold away.
According to her biographer, Nell Irvin Painter, Truth grew up
with "chronically depressed parents and her own guilt as a survivor." When Truth was nine years old, she also was sold away
from her parents. Her first masters (and parental surrogates)
whipped her—she bore lifetime scars on her back. Within a
year, Truth was sold again. Her second masters (and parental
surrogates) physically and sexually abused her; her sexual
abuser was a woman. While Truth clung to her physically abusive master, she came to despise her sexually abusive mistress.

In this century, the African-American writer bell hooks was "whipped and told that the punishment was 'for (her) own good.'" hooks describes a family in which "aggressive shaming and verbal humiliation co-existed with lots of affection and care." She remembers being "encouraged" for being a "smart girl" and then "within hours" told that because she was smart she was "likely to go crazy" and be psychiatrically hospitalized, and that "no one would visit (her)." hooks did not "feel loved," but she did "feel cared for . . . (my parents) gave me what they had been given—care." However, in her view, she did not receive affection, love, or kindness. Thus, for the rest of her life, hooks became used to settling for "care . . . mingled with a degree of unkindness, neglect . . . (and) outright cruelty."

Bertha Harris, a Professor of Literature and writer, relates:

> I was myself so ashamed of being my mother's victim, and of my helplessness in her power, I made every attempt to conceal the facts of my early life from intimates, even from myself: I had, for example, spent most of the first four years of my life in a crib which was, in effect, a cage; my mother had ordered a sixth side carpentered for it, a hinged "lid" that locked me inside for most of the day and all the nights. One day my father was moved to take me out of the cage and destroy it.
>
> My mother's chief contribution to my upbringing

had been to beat my legs and back with a walking cane every time she thought that I was, in her words, "showing off " or giving the appearance of believing that I was better than other people." My mother told me that because of me, she'd been cheated of everything she ever wanted. I am, to this day, very careful never to compete with other women; I will go to any amount of trouble to help a woman get what she says she wants; if I must sacrifice something I want in the process, so much the better. Sometimes this behavior is mistaken for feminism; it is penance.

A Mother's Preference for a Son

Sylvia Plath describes how, as a three-year-old, she "sulked" when her mother left home to give birth. Plath's mother, Aurelia, was gone for three weeks; she returned with a baby boy. Plath writes:

> Her desertion punched a smouldering hole in my sky. How could she, so loving and faithful, so easily leave me . . . I who for two and half years had been the centre of a tender universe felt the axis wrench and a polar chill immobilize my bones. I would be a bystander . . . Hugging my grudge, ugly and prickly, a sad sea-urchin, I trudged off on my own. My beautiful fusion with the things of this world was over.

When Doris Lessing was born, her parents had decided only on a boy's name: Peter John. At a loss, they allowed a nurse to name their newborn "Doris." African-American poet and essayist, Toi Derricotte, writes that, although her mother had nearly died in giving birth to her, within two years Dericotte's mother had become pregnant again "with a child (her parents) hoped would be (her father's) boy." Derricotte's mother "had to try again. All the women were obligated to try a second time if they hadn't gotten it right the first."[1]

Going through my mother's papers, I found some correspondence from 1940, the year I was born. A friend of my mother commiserated with her because I had turned out to be a girl, not the expected boy. My mother psychologically abandoned me when she gave birth to *her* second child, a son. No three-and-a-half-year-old—especially a girl—could ever compete with a newborn, especially a boy. Perhaps, if my mother had been one ounce warmer, if she had invited me to join her in her mothering tasks, things might have been different; not better, only different. Alas, she jealously guarded her importance as the only mother in the house. She spared me from becoming her "little helper" and left me to my books.

Have I no pity, no desire to protect my own mother, even now, after she is dead? I am a writer, a cruel and canny Electra. I write to avenge the loss of my mother's love, her preference for sons; vengeance is mine. As Sophocles' Electra says: "I will never cease my dirges and sorrowful laments . . . I will cry out my sorrow for all the world to hear." My mother was as haughty as Clytemnestra, and she loved her first-born son with an unnatural passion. I have a photograph in which the two of them are kissing on the lips, in a profound embrace. It was taken when my brother was in his thirties. I stare at it. I hide it. This photo, which I came across after she died, still has the power to shock me.

In a way, my mother was a hero. She was determined to be a "modern" mother. In 1940, this meant listening to what the male medical experts told you to do. Thus, in order to minimize the risk of germs, she wore a surgical mask whenever she came near me when I was a baby. I have photos of my mother (the masked stranger) holding me in my bedroom. My mother did not breast-feed me; she did as her American generation was ordered to do: bottle-feed at rigid intervals. Otherwise, let the infant cry. Do not pick her up or feed her. Truly, I am the daughter of male experts, I am not my mother's daughter.

I try to imagine my mother as a young girl; to do so requires all the courage I have. What if my heart begins to break for her, what if I am among those who used her but did not love her? I close my eyes and summon her up. There she is, a young, pale, thin girl, the only one in her family who is born in America, whose birth, seventeen years after her oldest sister, may have destroyed her mother's already fragile health. Perhaps, after four daughters, only two of whom had survived, my grandparents had hoped for a boy and viewed my mother's sex as a bitter disappointment. The way she treated me may have been a re-enactment of—or an improvement upon—how she herself had been treated.

There she is, the only one who can read and write English, the family translator, the only girl with a "future" to end, and stifle it they did. Her parents and her older married sisters used her as their servant. She was the onion peeler, pot-stirrer, babysitter, errand girl, letter-writer, and nurse, for three households. As the youngest daughter, my mother was also obliged to financially support and nurse her parents—even if doing so meant dropping out of college in her first year, which she did, and living with them until they died, which she did, and even if the cramped living arrangements once caused my father to tear the phone out of the wall and threaten to leave or kill her or kill himself.

In her world, a girl did what she was ordered to do—and she idealized those who issued the orders. She spoke of her parents in a hushed, adoring, obedient, slightly frightened, rather awe-struck tone. "Ma," I would ask, "how could you stand it that they didn't let you go back to college?" "What do you know," she'd say, "they need you, you don't ask questions, you just help out."

She must have thought that becoming a mother entitled her to tyrannize me the way she had been tyrannized or, at least, entitled her to a mother's "helper." Poor woman. What she got instead was as fierce a rebel as any mother has ever encountered. From her point of view I was unnatural. I behaved as if I were entitled to be waited on by her, not the other way round.

My mother was my Chief Criticizer, Threatener, Belittler, Screamer, Pincher, Hair-Puller, and Twisted-Red-Face Terrifyer. "I'm telling your father what you did. He'll take care of you." She did not administer the serious beatings; she forced my father to do that—beatings so serious that I had to be ordered to lie in school the next day about my black eye or swollen lip. I remember only one such beating very clearly. Perhaps there was only one; perhaps there were so many that I have "forgotten" them all. Like Agnes Smedley's mother, my father would yell that if I cried or made one sound he would beat me harder. I learned how to be quiet while I was being beaten. I was terrified of these beatings, not only because they hurt, but because my father would lose control the longer or harder he hit me with his belt or with his fist. This frightened me, because the beatings had something dreadfully mysterious (sexual) about them and because, to a child, an out-of-control parent means that the whole world is out of control.

As she got older, my mother would remember her father more clearly. She would smile, with obvious pride and nostalgia, when she said: "Oy, did he have a bad temper! He always had to arrive first to a wedding. We had to jump when he snapped his finger! Would he yell!" Once, a kindergarten classmate of mine came to school with a chunk of hair missing. Her mother, my mother's friend, had pulled it out in a rage. My mother must have admired this (because she kept referring to it with an odd mixture of approval and excitement), or perhaps she wanted me to understand that here was only one example of how things could have been far worse for me.

My mother lost her battle to tame me. I fought back every step of the way. I would not be cowed, bullied, undone. I may have won this battle, but I lost my mother, and she lost me.

Sexual Surveillance

Many twentieth-century mothers have violated their adolescent daughters' boundaries with impunity. They have secretly read their daughters' locked diaries, steamed open their mail, listened in on their phone calls. Thus, daughters become used to being patrolled by an intimate avenger. Such invasive maternal behavior does not always end when a daughter becomes an adult. For example, therapist Karen Fite describes how as an adult she met her legally blind mother in a public restaurant. Her mother's hand suddenly shot out and "reached in under her daughter's blouse to see if she was wearing a bra."

Many mothers also conduct their own surveillance of a daughter's sexuality. As I remember the litany, it went something like this: "Why were you late, where did you go, whom were you with, are you lying to me, are you still a virgin, you're no better than a tramp . . ." Some mothers collaborate with a more highly eroticized, *paternal* surveillance by refusing to stop it, or to confirm, privately, that such an invasion is unacceptable.

For example, in an interview, Flora, a forty-year-old massage therapist, describes how her mother "made excuses" for her father when he "interrogated (her) for hours about sex every Sunday morning." Flora's father would repeatedly demand to know what she had done the night before, but would never believe a word she said. To this day, her mother denies that this ever happened. Flora's mother also denies hearing her husband tell Flora that she would end up a prostitute.

In the 1950s, Nancy K. Miller dressed in bohemian all-black and dirty sneakers. Her parents took this for the declaration of sexual and intellectual independence that it was. Her father "thundered" at her:

> If you go to a boy's apartment . . . who will believe you when you testify in the paternity suit? I was always impressed by the leap from the outfit to the jury box . . . .when I started receiving "obscene" phone calls, my mother triumphed: News of my "reputation" had spread.

Collaboration with Incest

According to psychoanalysts Judith Lewis Herman and her mother Helen Block Lewis, daughters in (incestuous) families feel "deeply betrayed" by their mothers. Such daughters feel that they have been "offered as a sacrifice in order to propitiate a powerful male, and they despise their mothers. Many (but not all) sexually abused daughters learn that there is no escape from such abuse within the family. They also learn to expect no help from other women. Some daughters fight back or exact revenge—but mainly against their mothers.

For example, from the time she was five, Rose Wilson was raped almost daily by three men: her father, her step-grandfather, and her uncle. In 1988, after eleven years of such abuse, the sixteen-year-old Rose Wilson shot her mother Martha in the head. Rose explains: Her mother Martha refused to protect Rose and did nothing to stop the beatings or the rapes. Martha also told Rose: "I lived with it, so you can live with it," and allegedly encouraged her husband, Roger Wilson, to beat Rose. Martha laughed as she watched Roger Wilson grab Rose by the neck and throw her over a chair. A jury was unable to agree on a verdict; so Rose's father was never jailed; her step-grandfather, Thomas Cooper, received probation. Rose's uncle, George Nickels, was sentenced to only four years in jail in Illinois. As of 2001, the daughter remains in jail. Her mother remains dead.

Christine Ann Lawson notes that borderline mothers

do not physically sacrifice their children. Emotional sacrifice is much more common. For example, a witch mother who discovers that her husband has sexually molested her daughter may punish the daughter by sending her away. Indirectly, these mothers punish the husband by taking away the object of his desire . . . a witch mother can be insanely jealous of her daughter, may not be able to tolerate displays of affection between her daughter and husband, and may accuse the father of incest. A patient explained that whenever her mother witnessed her father playing with her, her mother flew into a rage and accused the father of being "sick."

The witch mother may be unable to tolerate such displays of affection because she feels left out and abandoned. Such mothers may say to themselves, "he never plays with me like that, we never have that kind of fun together. He is my husband. I should come first. There's something wrong with him." Jealous rage can lead to murderous rage toward the child.

Maternal Envy

Girls and women rarely acknowledge the possibility that their own mothers may envy them. Such knowledge is terrifying and threatens the symbiotic connection. Psychotherapist Betsy Cohen suggests that the daughter of an envious mother wishes to "deny the obvious, to protect herself from a truth that is too painful to bear." The daughter still needs her mother—"precisely because she never had a nurturing mother." In my view, maternal envy teaches many daughters how *not* to be a threat to other women. In addition, maternal envy teaches daughters to be passive, fearful, conformist, obedient—as well as similarly cruel to other women. Cohen's women patients say: "I'm afraid to be powerful because my mother might retaliate." Or, "Right in my own home, I was taught that success is not safe."

Therapists Karen Fite and Nikola Trumbo confirm this. They write: "Daughters who have become successful in the world experienced (maternal) ambivalence toward this success." Their mothers had difficulty just being proud of and happy for their daughters. They note, instead, "maternal resentment toward or envy of their daughters' successes." This dynamic is sometimes also true when a daughter successfully becomes a mother.

Many women have told me how their passage into newborn motherhood was met with maternal criticism and competition. For example, when Maria, a divorced twenty-four-year-old secretary, gave birth, her mother took over. Maria's mother "did everything. I'd try to get a bottle, she would already have one ready." When Maria's daughter was a little older, her maternal grandmother took charge of toilet-training and other socialization tasks. Maria says: "If I wanted to discipline my own child, I didn't get the chance. Mom was already doing it." Maria worked, attended college, and lived with her parents. She would often come home from work and find her daughter and mother gone. "She wouldn't tell me when they were going anywhere. She took complete control." Maria's mother also criticized Maria for being an "absentee mother." "But," Maria says, "whenever I did something with my child, my mom would say she didn't like the way I did it."

Heather, a gynecologist, became a mother when she was in her late thirties. Her mother ran a public relations firm. Heather says: "Every time my mother was visiting and I was breast-feeding, she would say, 'Don't you think she needs a bottle? How do you know you have enough milk? Maybe your milk's not good. You need a rest. It's not fair to the child not to let anyone else feed her.' "

When I gave birth to my son, I did not want my mother physically near me. Within a week, I wanted no one more. That's when *she* did not want to be anywhere near *me*. Each time I'd invite her over, she'd say: "He's all yours, enjoy him. But, if you admit you can't do it and decide to give him up, I'll take him, but you won't be able to have any say in his upbringing." I found all this very strange—until Lois told me the following story.

When Lois was twenty, she married Charles, a French businessman. They moved to Paris. When Lois was pregnant, her parents came to visit, but they fought so bitterly with Charles that he moved out. The stress sent Lois into premature labor. At the hospital, her husband and her parents continued their quarrel, each now blaming the other for Lois's predicament. The baby was not expected to live. "That's when my mother walked out on me and went back home with *her* man," Lois tells me. "She left me with *my* man (that's how she put it) when I was completely vulnerable. I still feel a stab of pain when I think of it." Charles also walked out, leaving Lois alone in a foreign country with a newborn who, if he lived, would be seriously disabled. When Lois tried to tell her mother how she felt, her mother insisted that, since Lois wanted her husband by her side, she had no choice but to leave. "How could she think that?" Lois asks. "Didn't she know I needed her?"

A true Demeter, my own mother softened toward me, a little, after I became a mother—but not much. She fought with me over how to raise my son and refused to be a part of a Holy Family of grandmother, daughter, and grandchild. She did that only with her sons and with one particular nephew; she preferred them to me. They needed her. I, apparently, did not.

How different is this from the experiences of physician and novelist Nawal El-Sadawii as a daughter in Egypt? El-Sadawii writes:

> When I was a little girl I was very good in school, more intelligent than my brother who was one year older than me. But, as a male child, both the family of my father and the family of my mother loved and spoiled him. At the end of the year I passed the examination very well and he failed. He was rewarded for his failure by playing and eating, I was rewarded by working in the kitchen and the house with my mother.

Traditional Mothers, Accomplished Daughters

In the past, slave, immigrant, impoverished, and working-class mothers had no leisure time, no health care, and little formal education. They expressed their "genius" by surviving and by rearing children who survived and in their cooking, quilting, gardening, sewing, and strong emphasis on religion and education.

Psychologist Gwendolyn Keita reports that she grew up in an all-female extended family household. She was taught that

> Women can do anything they want to do and have to be able to take care of themselves . . . this was [not about feminism, this was] about being black and poor. My family had to work to make ends meet and we all learned everything we could to save money.

Dora Yum Kim, a Korean-American community activist, describes the sacrifices that her mother, Han Shim Kim, made so that her daughter could obtain an education. She did not allow Yum Kim to work in the family restaurant. She supported her daughter's desire to read and study. Yum Kim tells her biographer, Soo-Young Chin, that "When I was growing up, I lived in the library. None of my girlfriends had the time." After Yum Kim married, her mother "almost pushed me out the door, encouraging me to work and practically raising my older children."

The writer Alice Walker was inspired by her (working-poor)

mother's "radiance" when her mother gardened. Walker's mother may have worked as a maid and laborer, but she also made time to create. When Walker's mother gardened "she [was] involved in work her soul must have . . . Whatever she planted grew by magic." Walker found strength and a legacy in this.

Teresa Bernardez, the Argentinian-American psychiatrist, remembers her (upper middle class) Argentinian mother as having exerted a "profound influence" on her life. Bernardez's mother was "deeply religious," "thoughtful," and "just." Bernardez writes:

> She had an extraordinary sense of the injustice done to women but she didn't fight her condition nor defy the social order. She did defy the conventional way of raising a girl. I was allowed to run around in the streets until late and I was dressed in comfortable clothes that didn't inhibit exploration and physical activity . . . From my mother I got a deep sense of the spiritual, transcendent, and magical meaning of life.

Poet and writer Toi Derricotte remembers her (middle-class) mother and aunts in the kitchen, cooking collectively, ritualistically, providing a "holding" environment for a family. Derricotte writes: "I understood that there was a factor that could turn being black into something quite comfortable, and turn being white into a bad fate."[1]

Faith Ringgold, the (middle-class) artist, describes a positive relationship with her mother, whom she describes as a "brilliant" Harlem fashion designer. Ringgold writes: "My mother was a treasure. I openly adored her. Not only did she raise me carefully and lovingly but she was also my best friend." Ringgold's mother artistically "collaborated" with Ringgold on her quilts and dolls; she also offered to take Ringgold's two young daughters to Europe so that Ringgold could "paint, undisturbed."

I have cited some autobiographical accounts; a number of psychotherapists have also seen differences in the way white women and women of color experience the mother-daughter relationship, express anger, and bond with each other. Psychologist Beverly Greene observes that black women express anger in interpersonal settings more freely than white women do. (We have seen that this may be true for adolescents too.) In some ways, because black women face racism and sexism in both the white and black communities, they often function as a source of strength for each other. According to Teresa Bernardez,

> Black women have a longer history of solidarity precisely because of the discrimination against them and their low social status . . . Latino women's inhibitions of anger have different sources. Their situation is complicated by the fact that despite having both racism and sexism directed against them, their status as mothers in the Hispanic community is

higher than in Anglo families where motherhood not only does not confer special status but is linked with decreasing mental health . . . thus, although Latino women's inhibitions of anger are as severe as the white women's (and further emphasized by traditional religious norms), the relationships between mothers and daughters are in general more affectionate, more intimate, and less ambivalent.

According to psychotherapists Karen Fite and Nikola Trumbo, who interviewed women about their mothers:

The four women of color we talked with were both less likely than white women to describe their mothers as betraying them and also more likely to describe their mothers as strong, competent and in charge . . . Nonetheless, women of color seemed to more frequently experience their mothers as supportive of them and encouraging of their strengths.

Thus, we have some evidence that some non-white mothers tend to support their daughters' economic and educational ambitions.

A number of religious women, both Jewish and Christian, have also described exceptionally supportive mother-daughter relationships. One religious Jewish woman says:

My most positive, satisfying, and intimate relationships are with my mother and with my daughter. I get the best advice and the most support from these two women. I think that this is true for many other religious women as well.

While very positive mother-daughter relationships may exist for many women, we have also begun to learn how fiercely some white mothers have opposed and punished ambitious daughters for their accomplishments.

Envious Traditional Mothers and Accomplished Daughters
While an envious mother might criticize and compete with her daughter's mothering skills, such a mother might also persecute an ambitious daughter—especially one who is successful in the world. An envious mother may criticize her daughter's failure to succeed at traditional female tasks, such as cooking, gardening, entertaining. She may also systematically refuse to acknowledge that her daughter is successful and may, instead, continue to denigrate her worldly success, attempt to use that success to assuage the demons of her own wounded vanity (this is also known as being a "stage mother"), or demand that her successful daughter give up the world in order to become her mother's domestic servant. Some traditional mothers may also abandon or institutionalize a successful daughter if and when that daughter happens to fall on hard times in a cruel world.[2]

Florence Nightingale (1820-1910), was the founder of

modern nursing. According to British psychoanalyst Nini Herman, Nightingale's mother, Fanny, opposed her second daughter's nursing ambitions. Fanny accused Nightingale of being a prostitute (at the time, many nurses were) and of "consorting with a low and vulgar surgeon." Fanny raged in public about how her daughter would "disgrace herself." In 1851, after years of maternal persecution (and persecution by an older sister as well), the thirty-one-year-old Nightingale left home. She later said that "if she had influence enough" no mother would bring up a child herself; there would be "creches for the rich as well as the poor." Once Nightingale gained world fame and a series of British Cabinet commissions, her mother and sister rushed to London to "bask in her glory." When her mother was seventy-eight years-old, "frail, almost blind," and semi-senile, Nightingale reluctantly agreed to move back home. However, Nightingale's "conditions" for accepting *this* commission included being left entirely alone in a suite of six rooms to work "incessantly and never leave her room except to visit her mother." Nightingale writes that the "hardest years of her life (were) not the Crimean War, nor her twenty-two-hour days, afterwards, for five years, at the War Office." Far harder were the nearly six years during which she lived with her mother.

According to MIT's Professor of Literature, Cynthia Griffen Wolff, Edith Wharton (1862-1937) was an "unplanned and unwelcome surprise to her mother who was already in her thirty-eighth year when the baby was born and who already had two, much-loved older sons." Wharton's mother was cold to her and rejected her. As Wharton grew older, her mother "subjected her to an unremitting barrage of criticism . . . learning to live with a mother who seemed displeased by her very presence was one of the bitter portions of (Wharton's) youth." Wharton lacked her mother's beauty and her obsession with outward appearance.

> It is difficult to imagine what sort of daughter might have managed to placate Edith's mother. Lucretia Jones seems to have been pleased with none of the actual traits her daughter possessed. A bad situation was made even worse, then, when it became evident that the child possessed ferocious intelligence. If there was one thing more thoroughly forbidden to "nice" girls than carnal knowledge, it was intellect. And when the child began to make up stories at a prodigiously early age, her mother was flabbergasted.

For Wharton, writing stories was a way of challenging her mother's superficiality and niceness. It also gave Wharton "power in a situation where she felt otherwise completely vulnerable." Nonetheless, like Nightingale's mother Fanny, Wharton's mother disapproved of her daughter's creativity.

> For a woman to pursue the life of a professional

artist was something akin to harlotry. (In this regard, even the learned James family would not have offered a girl like Edith much support: the James parents were delighted to have intellectual sons, but dismayed by Alice, a daughter with intellectual and artistic ambitions.)

However, writing ultimately healed Wharton, shielding her from the consequences of maternal rejection, a passionless marriage, and a psychiatric depression.

Camille Claudel (1864-1943) was a great sculptor. She also worked with and became the lover of August Rodin, a man who was twenty-four years her senior. Rodin recognized Claudel's extraordinary talent and happily helped himself to that talent and to her youth, beauty, sexual availability, and adoration as well. According to the art historian Anne Higgonet, Claudel did the actual modeling of parts of Rodin's most famous works, such as *Gates of Hell* and *Burghers of Calais*. She also sculpted her own stunning pieces. Rodin tried to do so but was unable to launch an independent career for his protégé because she was a woman and his girlfriend as well. Claudel's only family champion was her father, Louis-Prosper. However, once her sexual liaison with Rodin became known, Claudel was banished from her parents' home; her mother, Louise, viewed her daughter's behavior as an affront to her own provincial propriety. Claudel thereafter lived in a run-down villa for which Rodin paid the rent. After a decade,

Rodin abandoned Claudel for another woman. Claudel still had no way of making a living, and absolutely no family support.

In the words of art historian Anne Higgonet, Claudel became increasingly "reclusive and paranoid . . . she shut herself in an unkempt studio, collected cats, annoyed the neighbors. She raved about Rodin . . . the imbalance in their relationship had been magnified into madness." Her mother had no tender feelings for her and did not wish to nurse her or to keep her at home. Claudel's father died on March 2, 1913. Within three days, Claudel's brother Paul, the well-known Catholic religious poet, obtained a legal certificate to have his sister psychiatrically institutionalized against her will. On March 10, 1913, Paul had Claudel seized and imprisoned *for the rest of her life—for the next thirty years.* In letters to her mother, Claudel repeatedly begged to be released. Her mother, Louise, answered only one letter, by writing to Claudel's doctor: "She has all the vices, I don't want to see her again." Claudel's life was turned into a powerful, haunting movie in which Isabelle Adjani played the title role.

The life of the American actress Frances Farmer is known to us from her writing and also from a film starring Jessica Lange. In the 1940s and 1950s Farmer went to Hollywood and became a star—but she also became a communist and a bohemian. Farmer's mother was delighted to have a star in the family, but not an outspoken renegade and "slut." Farmer's mother had her institutionalized and eventually lobotomized. While institutionalized, Farmer was repeatedly gang-raped by soldiers from the nearby base who were allowed in for this express purpose.

The same mother who may persecute a daughter of genius, may be kind to her only when she becomes ill and is dependent upon her mother for care-taking. For example, the mother who brutally whipped Agnes Smedley "talked tenderly" to her for the first time when Smedley broke her arm. Smedley writes: "Thus I learned that if you are sick or injured, people love you; if you are well they do not."

The eminent British writer, Harriet Martineau (1802-1876), had a cold and demanding mother who was kind to her only once: when it became clear that the twelve-year-old Martineau would become permanently and totally deaf. Illness alone evoked "motherly sympathy," not genius. This is Demetrian psychology at work. Demeter will mother, but only when her daughter is completely merged with and dependent upon her.

Maria Callas (1923-1977), the twentieth-century opera great, was shaped by a demanding stage mother. Callas writes that her mother, Evangelia, had wanted a son, not another daughter. Evangelia refused to hold the newborn Callas for days. Evangelia also preferred her older and "prettier" daughter Iakinthy ("Jacqui") to Callas, whom she at first rejected and mocked, and whom she later overworked musically. Callas writes that Evangelia

Robbed me of [my] childhood . . . (and of a high school education) . . . I was deprived entirely of the joys of adolescence and of its innocent (irreplace-

able) pleasures . . . child prodigies never have genuine childhoods.

However, Callas also credits her mother for instilling in her
a "fury" to succeed, as well as strict discipline. For years, Callas
remained protective of her mother, both during World War II
in Athens and after her operatic success. Callas sent money
home and paid for Evangelia to visit. She drew the line, however, when Evangelia wanted to come and live with her and her
husband, Gian Battista Menighini. Callas was afraid that her
mother would take over the household and ruin her happiness
and peace of mind. Evangelia began demanding more
money—she, too, wanted to live like a millionaire-star; Callas
refused. Evangelia cursed Callas in a vile way and began talking
to the press against her own daughter. Callas was prepared to
support her mother if Evangelia kept quiet, but Evangelia
craved publicity and could not stop herself. When Callas left
her husband, Evangelia commented:

> Now she no longer needs him. Women like Maria
> can never know real love . . . I was her first victim . . .
> Maria will marry (Aristotle) Onassis to further her
> boundless ambition; he will be her third victim.

Callas mourned the absence of a relationship with her
mother and sister. She found a "good surrogate mother" in her
first opera teacher, Elvira de Hidalgo, and again in her much

older "maternal" husband, who devoted himself entirely to her career, just as Evangelia had. (Callas also found many "bad mothers," who, like Evangelia, were obsessed with Callas' fame, and who resented, envied, and used Callas.) Ultimately, Callas depended entirely upon the kindness of strangers. In 1954, Dallas music critic John Ardoin interviewed Callas:

> If you can't trust your husband or your mother, to whom do you turn? When I go back to Paris, you know who takes care of me and who I know will always be there? My maid Bruna, who adores me and who has been a nurse, sister and mother to me. She is only two years older. When I was in the hospital she didn't want the nurse to touch me, for she was ashamed to humiliate me, to have a nurse clean me. Imagine that such a person should exist today . . . They are very rare. But she shouldn't have been there. It should have been my mother and my sister . . . . The people who have been the closest to me have hurt me the most.

When Callas lost her voice and became a depressed recluse living in Paris, her mother and sister did not try to reconcile with her, nor did they offer to visit or nurse her. Callas herself did not dare reach out to her mother; she was afraid that she would only "reject her," now that she was no longer a performing star. Only after Callas died did her sister and mother finally surface—in order to make their claim on her fortune.

I have heard many stories like these, from other accomplished women, friends as well as patients. For example, Cindy, a sixty-five-year-old sculptor, told me that her mother "only went as far as the eighth grade." Cindy's mother remained "suspicious about education" and "hostile" to Cindy's enormous ambition. "My mother wanted me in the kitchen with her to listen to her complain. When I said I wanted to paint or draw instead, she would scream and curse me." Cindy apologizes for her mother. "This was a long time ago. She didn't know any better."

In 1970, my mother attended my first major feminist lecture. She called me the next day and said: "You don't look so good, have you seen a doctor lately?" and "Who's going to marry you if you say things like that?" She would greet each new book of mine in the same way: "What? Another book against the men?" And "Don't think you're so special. *I* could write a book too." (I encouraged her to do so; I wish she had.) Only after her death did a friend of hers tell me that, on a bus trip across the country, my mother would rush to each public library to see if they had any of my books.

Once, long ago, I must have been my mother's little girl, someone she dressed, whose hair she braided—but then she left me, and I left her, and we kept on leaving each other. No matter what I did to try to gain her love or approval, it was never enough, because all she wanted was me for herself, me, merged, me as her shadow, me, devoured. She loved me, but in this primitive way. I failed this love.

The poor woman simply wanted me to be more like her. She had been a stay-at-home mother for as long as she could and a school secretary afterwards; she had put her family, not herself, first. Couldn't I be more like her? If I wasn't, didn't this mean that *I* did not approve of *her*? Maybe she thought I despised her for who she was: "only" a wife and mother. For a long time, I did. Or, rather, I took it for granted, but assigned no positive value to it—which is exactly how she treated my work.

She continued to bully me in private. She called this "going to work on you." Working me over, is what it felt like. To her, this choice of phrase meant continuing to improve her maternal product. She did not understand that what she was doing was trying to destroy her progeny. "Come and visit me, come alone," she would say. That's when she would show me her Medusa Head. I could no longer bear to be turned into stone, paralyzed by poison, while she raged on endlessly. "When will you learn . . . why do you dress the way you do . . . think the way you do . . . keep the friends you keep . . . insist on writing books . . . don't come to me for help . . . I am finished with you." Eventually, I no longer went to visit her alone, it was too unpleasant.

Professor and author Dana Crowley Jack analyzes "Medusa's stare." In the ancient world, a female face surrounded by serpent hair meant many things: female divinity, female wisdom and healing power, female genitalia. In Jack's view, Medusa is "so terrifying" because she represents woman's

capacity to fasten an angry, unyielding female gaze

on others. If others meet her gaze, the force of her subjectivity turns them into "things," into objects of her perspective, and thus freezes their inner worlds. A hostile stare can alter one's self-experience. Caught in the spotlight of another's searing gaze, self-experience shifts from perceiving to being perceived, from subject to object.

No matter what I wrote or how many pretty speeches I delivered, I could never get my Medusa to lower her eyes, nor could I inspire a longing for freedom in her.

A daughter also *becomes* what she most fears: her mother. No matter how hard we try to escape this, nature provides incontrovertible evidence: a similar skull-shape, a smile, hair texture, eyes, the way we laugh, our turns of phrase. Like my mother, I am quick to tell others what to do, why my way is "better." Unlike my mother, I do not restrict myself to my own children; the world is my oyster.

My mother's family responsibilities banished all spontaneity from her life. She had no exit, no solitude, no worldly channel for her enormous energies and intelligence. She took pride in being able to dominate others, especially her children, but her husband too; she had no capacity to show affection.

My mother was very ambitious. I used to say that she could run a small country, but that's exactly what she thought she was doing as she presided over our family of five. And, although she berated me, bitterly, for my "wild" ways, she never forced me to help her with the housework; she disparaged, but she allowed me to do my non-stop reading and writing and drawing and thinking.

From time to time, my mother visits me in my dreams wearing one of her pastel chiffon dresses, beaming. She is, finally, becoming my fairy-tale guardian angel.

Did I love her? Oh, I did—I still do, her death continues to bring us closer. Only now do I really begin to know her. She is gone, and yet I think about her more now than when she was alive. She is more present, closer. I hear her more clearly, I know just what she would say in any given circumstance. I have learned her lines, I know them well. I have come to understand that my mother is the one person I have most tried to please, the one person whom I could never please—and she might say the exact same thing about me.

My mother did not inherit any money. She lived entirely on a small pension; she pinched every penny. She stopped buying new clothing back in the early 1950s. When I visited, my mother would insist on modeling some of her immaculately kept clothing for me. "See," she would say, "if you keep something long enough, it comes back into fashion." (She was right.) When she died, she was still living with the same inexpensive furniture she had bought in the 1940s and 1950s.

My mother was determined not to burden her children as she herself had been burdened. Thus, she deprived herself of every luxury and of many necessities, in order to assist her children financially while she was alive and to leave each of us some money. I think she wanted to give us what her parents could not give her and to spare us her fate as her parents' nurse and provider. How generous! I was utterly inattentive, oblivious. I thought I'd have to borrow money for her funeral. I had no idea that she *chose* to continue living in the 1950s for the rest of her life because she planned to save and invest every last penny as a triumphant legacy for her children and grandchildren.

"Come, let's go shopping," my mother would say. I would go, but I usually disappeared into the nearest bookstore for hours, where I would wait for her while she fingered fruit, grabbed blouses, challenged merchants on their prices. In a sense, I was the shrinking violet, she, the mighty magnificent forager and provider.

I wear her ageless skin of silk, while she lies in the earth decomposing. I write this to keep her with me.

She would always tell me: "Don't trust women, they can be your worst enemy."

Ma—this book is for you.

7.

SISTERS AND THE SEARCH FOR BEST FRIENDS

Women long for a relationship with a Good Mother—certainly if they have had such a relationship with their own mothers, more so if they have not. A woman looks for Good Mothers in other women not only because she emotionally depends upon replicating the daughter-Good Mother relationship, but also as a way of weaning herself away from it, by gradually replacing her mother with best friends. Similarly, women look for Good Sisters among their friends—certainly if they have already had the experience of a Good Sister, more so if they have not. Having best friends (women often have more than one) and being close to a sister or sisters are both very important to a woman and, therefore, fraught with tension.

Despite the early feminist idealization of "sisterhood," in reality, sibling relationships are weighed down by primitive hostilities and competition. A woman's relationship to her sister may range from indifference comparable to Electra's indifference to the plight of her sister Iphegenia, to passionate, life-long competition for parental love and worldly success. It can be a bond that disfigures or a bond that sustains.

Like the importance of birth order, sibling relationships have been underestimated. Until recently, parent-child relationships have dominated our psychoanalytic and psychological understanding of human development. However, in the last twenty years, a number of books and conferences have focused on the importance of sibling relationships. For example, in 1991 Laura Tracy, in *The Secret between Us: Competition among Women,* discusses a week-long seminar led by psychiatrist Jean Baker Miller and her colleagues, which Tracy attended, along with forty-nine other women. At one point the participants were asked to join either a "mother" or a "daughter" group, and Tracy joined the "mother" group. The women in this group were mothers, and the mothers of daughters. Tracy writes:

> But that was not all we were. We discovered that each woman who chose to join the "mother" group was an older sister—every one of us, no exceptions. And we realized that returning inside to join the "daughter" group provoked in us an almost palpable anxiety. We thought they (the "daughter" or younger sister group) would yell at us . . . They did. When we

rejoined the "daughter" group, the room was filled with hostility, despite the fact that during the two days preceding this exercise we had formed ourselves into a large and supportive community. (Although many in the daughter group were also mothers and the mothers of daughters), the "daughter" group, it turned out, was composed of younger sisters . . . In choosing to identify as either "mother" or "daughter," we all unconsciously acted on our sibling position, rather than on our very conscious parental status.

In her book, *Between Sisters: Secret Rivals, Intimate Friends,* Washington, D.C. journalist Barbara Mathias reports the following:

A woman recently learned from her elderly aunt that when she was two and her sister was six, their mother was seriously ill and the two girls had to be separated. "Because I was the youngest and most difficult to care for, I was sent to grandmother to live until my mother was well; my sister was allowed to stay with my mother . . . For years thereafter, this woman perceived her older sister as "privileged" and resented whatever good came her way. She carried this same sense of "sour grapes" with her women friends when they appeared to her to be getting a better deal in their lives with their children, jobs, and husbands.

What's important is that this woman had never been told of the temporary separation. However, the "feelings between the sisters mushroomed well into the next generation."

Sisters may be similar; they may also be quite different. They may complement each other; they may either enjoy or suffer their differences. Sisters may engage in lifelong competition without ever acknowledging it and without ever disconnecting from each other. Sisters may remain ambivalent about each other; sisters may disconnect. Some sisters may function as each other's lifelong friends and most ardent supporters.

Toni McNaron, the Minnesota English and Women's Studies professor and author of *The Sister Bond: A Feminist View of a Timeless Connection*, writes, for example, about Emily Dickinson's life with her sister Vinnie. In their household Emily wrote; Vinnie cooked, sewed, and was "the domestic creature."

We have no record of Vinnie's feelings about this arrangement, but she acquiesced, seemingly out of a deep love for Emily . . . In letter after letter, Emily makes it abundantly clear that without her sister she would wither emotionally and artistically.

McNaron notes that parents influence the sister bond. "Where parents have actively worked against close ties, sisters have most often failed each other emotionally."

In *Psyche's Sisters: Re-imagining the Meaning of Sisterhood,* Christine Downing writes:

> We are stuck with our particular sister as we never are with a friend . . . the relationship is permanent, lifelong, one from which it is almost impossible entirely to disengage. (The) permanence helps make it the safest relationship in which to express hostility and aggression . . . (Therefore), the bond between same-sex siblings is very likely the most stressful, volatile, ambivalent one we will ever know.

Sisters sometimes fail each other in dreadful ways. For example, in Tennessee Williams' play, *A Streetcar Named Desire,* Stella is married to Stanley Kowalski, a man who brutally dominates her—just as Blanche, Stella's older sister and something of a mother figure, once did. Stella tells Blanche: "You never did give me a chance to say much . . . So I just got into the habit of being quiet around you." Blanche drinks. She has lost the family plantation and been run out of their hometown for whoring. Ah, but Blanche/Tennessee is also bewitching, a wordsmith, a believer in Last Chances. Stanley, cunning, feral, wants to be Stella's One-and-Only; he does not want Blanche moving in on his territory. Although Stanley is threatened by Blanche's "airs," he also smells her vulnerability—and he strikes. Stanley ruins Blanche's last chance at marriage by telling the interested suitor about her shady past. He orders Blanche, who is homeless and broke, out of *his* house. And then Stanley rapes Blanche, which sends her over the edge. Stanley denies the rape and tells Stella that Blanche is lying and crazy. Finally, Stanley arranges to have Blanche institutionalized. Stella sides with her husband against her sister. Stella says, "I couldn't believe [Blanche's] story and go on living with Stanley." Precisely. Stanley represents Stella's only future—which she chooses over her past, ruined life with Blanche.

Sisters make similar choices every day, although they are not always this dramatic. For example, forty-five-year-old Christa, whom I interviewed, trains and shows horses. She lives alone, but is on the road half the year. Her sister and her mother are both married women. Christa says:

> My sister is a few years older than me. She lives near my mother. My sister is a beautiful woman who has always dressed beautifully. She has a beautiful home and beautiful children . . . They'll probably have beautiful and perfect children too! My mother beams when she talks about my sister. I'm quite happy, but my sister and my mother constantly worry about me. When is "poor Christa" going to find another husband? Never! I live alone and I have lovers. Why does Christa spend so many hours at work? Because I love what I do. What a shame

> Christa has no children. I never wanted any. It's like
> I have two mothers and neither of them understand
> or approve of me.

In general, men as well as women tend to fear, not welcome, difference. A sibling is both the same and also different. *Close-but-different* may feel especially threatening. A sister's greater success may shame and enrage the sister who views herself as less gifted and less blessed. Sisters may denigrate each other's choices and feel especially threatened when a sister chooses to lead a very different kind of life.[1]

According to Barbara Mathias, most of her female interviewees denied competing with their sisters.

> I kept running into blind alleys when I asked the
> question "do you compete with your sister?" Over
> and over again, I heard the finite, impassioned
> answer, "no," or "never," or at the very most, "that
> was over a long time ago." I could have accepted
> those answers at face value except that in most of the
> cases, with few exceptions, the women went on to
> describe childhoods filled with competition and
> adult years laced with covert envy. After one woman
> told me, "no, we don't compete," she immediately
> spun a list of her sister's "advantages" that she
> "wished" she shared, everything from being more
> popular to having a better education. Another

woman claimed that she and her three sisters never harbored any rivalry, but then described how they called one of the sisters "moo-cow" because "she was so bossy."

Natalie Sadigur Low, a clinical instructor in Psychology at Harvard, found that sisters rarely admit to jealousy. Since the sister pairs that she described were educated, middle-aged women, Low conjectures that they were too "astute" to acknowledge having such childish emotions. Or it may be that the competition was sublimated and displaced so as to be targeted no longer at sisters, but rather at colleagues in the workplace or friends, or even at husbands or lovers.

In *Among Women*, Louise Bernikow writes about her own tendency to deny the most blatant competition among sisters.

I held to this imaginary sisterhood (between my mother and my maternal aunt) in spite of the bickering, the mockery, the competition . . . the guilt that bound them to one another, the rivalry over who had the cleanest house, cooked the best meals, had daughters who made the best marriages, husbands who earned the highest income. I clung, still, to my desire for a phantom sister when my best friend, in adolescence, bonded with me against her own sister, used me, in a way, as a reproach—see, my friend is a better friend to me than *you* are—and I shared with her the youthful sadistic pleasure of excluding the sister.

Novelists such as Erica Jong, Amy Tan, and Jane Smiley depict serious character differences and competition between sisters.

In *Fear of Flying*, Erica Jong's hero, Isabella, describes fighting with Randy, her married sister. Randy condemns Isabella's poetry as "masturbatory and exhibitionistic"; she also condemns Isabella for refusing to have children. Jong writes:

> "Randy," I pleaded, "I *have* to think writing is the most important thing in the world in order to keep *doing* it, but nothing says that *you* have to share my obsession, so why should I have to share *yours?*"
>
> "You think you're so goddamn clever, don't you? Just because you were a grub and a grind and did well in school . . . I had as much talent to write as you and you know it, only I wouldn't *stoop* to revealing myself in public the way you do . . . I don't want to fight with you . . . It's just that you're still my little sister and I really think you've gotten off on the wrong track! I mean you really ought to stop writing and have a baby. You'll find it *so* much more rewarding than writing."

Amy Tan, in *The Joy Luck Club*, depicts how two "inseparable" sisters use their daughters, Waverly and June, to fuel their lifelong competition against each other. The sisters compare their daughters' every physical attribute and intellectual accomplishment. Waverly's mother boasts about

> how smart Waverly was at playing chess, how many trophies she had won last month, how many newspapers had printed her name . . . when I (June) failed to become a concert pianist, or even an accompanist for the church youth choir [my mother] finally explained that I was late-blooming, like Einstein, who everyone thought was retarded until he discovered the bomb.

Jane Smiley's Pulitzer-Prize-winning novel, *A Thousand Acres*, is about an Iowa farming family in which two sisters, Ginny and Rose, are marked by an "incestuous triangle" with their father, and by Rose's subsequent theft of Ginny's boyfriend. Ginny, the eldest sister, is so angry at Rose, the middle sister, that she decides to poison her. Rose never eats the poisoned food. As Rose lies dying of cancer at thirty-seven, Ginny confesses her murderous intention, and Rose assures Ginny that the boyfriend was not worth it. Rose asks Ginny to take care of her two daughters. Ginny realizes how much she misses Rose only after Rose is dead. Ginny sees Rose everywhere.

> If I only knew the trick . . . I could look around this familiar hallway with Rose's eyes, and if I could do

that, then I could sense everything she had sensed in the last few years. That, it seemed, would be one way to stop missing her.

Anger itself reminds me of Rose, but so do most of the women I see on the street, who wear dresses she would have liked, ride children on their hips with the swaying grace that she had . . . Rose left me a riddle I haven't solved, of how we judge those who have hurt us when they have known no remorse or even understanding.

The sister bond may be a lifelong or eternal one; it may not necessarily be a loving bond. People often assume that if two sisters are close this means that they are nourishing each other in a positive way. This is not always the case. For example, in an essay entitled "Competition: A Problem for Academic Women," Evelyn Fox Keller, philosopher of science and author, and Helene Moglen, a Professor of Literature and Women's Studies, note that

> Relationships between real sisters are frequently very close, fostering considerable mutual dependency and deep love. But those relationships also foster intense antagonisms, so much so that the success of a sister is often equated with the failure of oneself. Indeed, envy (and their intense discomfort with it) seems to be the emotion talked about with

the most urgency by the women with whom we have spoken. It is this primarily, they say, that makes competition with women so much more acute and painful ("close to things that are really very scary") than competition with men . . .

When one attempts to trace envy between siblings (perhaps, given the intensity of the mother-daughter bond, especially the envy between sisters) to the quest for a parent's love, it is almost as if that love (whatever its quantity) is seen as capable of supporting the life of only one child. Rivalry then can feel deadly indeed.

Toni McNaron describes the sister bond between Florence Nightingale and her older sister, Parthenope, their mother's favorite. Florence was "her father's darling." As Florence "struck out in ever wider directions, Parthenope clung more closely to her mother for protection and solace." When Florence decided to leave home, Parthenope's health "declined." Parthenope subsequently joined her mother in condemning Florence as an "unnatural" woman.

Needless to say, by this time Florence had little tenderness for Parthenope, and even wrote and published a short, ostensibly fictional, work about a devouring sister. In their old age, however, when Parthenope was genuinely ill and after each had made some efforts to reconcile, Florence of her own volition came and nursed her sister until her death.

Sisters may control or hurt each other in subtle, rarely visible ways. Some may do so through a raised eyebrow, a turned back, or a sharp, sarcastic tone. Barbara Mathias describes an interview with the literary critic Paula Marantz Cohen, who, in her work on the Austen and Bronte sisters, focuses on the "sarcastic voice" between sisters.

> "It's a way of blunting rivalry, placing or distancing oneself from everything," Cohen explained to me. "Jane Austen and her sister Cassandra did it and I hear the sarcastic voice that I use with my own younger sister. Sarcasm takes advantage of the rivalry and parodies it. The sister converts the rivalry and it is so obvious. She publicizes it."
>
> Cassandra, who dutifully read her sister's manuscripts before publication, at one time had the uncomfortable task of requesting from her sister a second copy of *First Impressions* (the original title of *Pride and Prejudice*). She was supposed to have read it much earlier, and apparently had "lost" her original copy. As expected, Jane sent a second copy of the original manuscript with a sarcastic note: "I do not wonder at your wanting to read *First Impressions* again, so seldom as you have gone through it, and so long ago."

A number of biographers have also explored the relationship between the writer Virginia Stephen Woolf and her older sister, the painter Vanessa Stephen Bell. Initial biographies viewed the two as very close and supportive of each other's talents. However, the sisters were also very competitive. After reading Vanessa Bell's *Recollection from Virginia's Childhood* and Jane Dunn's biography, *A Very Close Conspiracy*, Barbara Mathias concludes that Vanessa

> always felt in Virginia's shadow. Undoubtedly, Virginia was the more articulate, intelligent, and generally successful of the two . . . Though Vanessa was eventually enriched and happy raising her own family, her self-deprecation and uncertainty about her work in comparison to her sister's was to remain with her through her entire adult life. (Virginia retaliated.) "When someone had remarked that Vanessa had a harder time practising her art because she had to stand all day at her easel," writes Dunn, "Virginia promptly ordered a tall desk to be made for herself at which she could stand to write."

Vanessa envied Virginia. Being envied means that one is under attack and rendered helpless by it. To be envied by someone upon whom one is psychologically dependent isolates and paralyzes the envied one. According to Professors Ann and Barry Ulanov, in *Cinderella and Her Sisters: The Envied and the Envying,*

The envied grow increasingly desperate, for nothing succeeds in warding off envy. If they renounce any hope of being seen and accepted as themselves, they are accused of being cold and aloof. If they try to share their good, they are attacked for showing off or being patronizing. If they try to defend by explaining, they are not listened to, for explanations will not fill up an empty envier. Even if some of the melodrama is lacking, they are in the position of hostages being held by terrorists. There is nothing they can do to appease their captors. Least of all do the enviers want to lose hold of the envied, to let the hostages get away.

Goodness figures centrally in the last great temptation for the envied one: to deflect the attack of envy by altogether disowning the good that is the target of the attack. "That is not mine," one says at such a point . . . "I am no different from you. I do not have anything you would want. Why, I am really no better than you!"

In a recent biography, *Who's Afraid of Leonard Woolf? A Case for the Sanity of Virginia Woolf,* the Australian painter and playwright Irene Coates suggests that Virginia Woolf's bouts of madness and eventual suicide were not related only to Virginia's sexual abuse in childhood or to the death of her mother Julia when Virginia was thirteen or to the death of her next-oldest half sister and presiding mother figure, Stella, when Virginia was fifteen. Coates believes that these early-life tragedies rendered Virginia vulnerable to and dependent upon her next oldest sister—and final mother figure—Vanessa, who then continuously, maddeningly, distanced herself from Virginia.

In Coates's view, Vanessa wanted Virginia "to be in her orbit. But not get too close." Vanessa both envied and sought to control Virginia. Virginia inherited a small fortune; Vanessa did not. At one point, Vanessa perceived Virginia as getting too close to Vanessa's philandering husband Clive—but Vanessa also disapproved of Virginia's incipient lesbianism. In Coates's opinion, Vanessa attempted to control, punish, and "gaslight" Virginia by persuading her, and others, that Virginia was mad.

For example, according to Coates, Vanessa arranged Virginia's first psychiatric incarceration, behind Virginia's back— then denied having done so. According to Coates, at that point, Virginia's illness consisted mainly of having aroused Vanessa's fear that Virginia was having a "lesbian relationship with Lady Ottoline Morrel, a dark dramatic looking woman who had off-beat parties . . . but Vanessa was wrong, Lady Ottoline was straight."

Vanessa forces Virginia into a dreaded (and dreadful) psychiatric rest cure. According to Coates:

Evidently Vanessa had felt herself increasingly to be losing control; and, as the elder sister, this was an intolerable situation. She remedied it by having

Virginia incarcerated . . . Vanessa had now become extremely anxious to shift the burden of her responsibility for her sister onto someone else as soon as possible. A husband was essential, perhaps partly to deter Virginia from becoming a lesbian.

In Coates's entirely unorthodox view, Leonard Woolf was, in reality, a whoremonger, bully, petty class-climber, misogynist, and autocrat. According to Coates, with Vanessa's blessing, he presumably took over Vanessa's job as Virginia's controller and scapegoater. In Coates's view, the primal, wounding tension between the sisters is the game that Vanessa used to play on Virginia in childhood, one that reduced Virginia to impotent rage. Vanessa would distance herself from Virginia and then get a male intimate to see things from Vanessa's point of view—against Virginia. Vanessa first used their brother, Thoby, in this way, then her husband Clive, and finally Virginia's husband Leonard. Coates writes:

> I am arguing that an important factor in Virginia's mental instability was an underlying tension between Vanessa and herself . . . This co-dependence could reduce Virginia to mental breakdown when the game was played against her and she, feeling entirely innocent, was rejected . . . Virginia's love for Vanessa was the love of the younger for the older . . . Her breakdown in 1904 may have been not

only her desperate reaction to her father's death . . .
but to Vanessa's rejection as she once again tried to
cling to her . . . With the publication of a selection
of Vanessa's letters in 1993, we have a much clearer
idea of their relationship . . . We can see Leonard
taking over many aspects of Vanessa's attitude
towards her sister.

Based on my own interviews, it is my impression that women
of color and working-class women tend to report a strong and
positive relationship to their sisters. However, this is true only
if no one sister is perceived as getting too far ahead of any
other sister. If the world remains hostile and unpredictable,
then sisters may remain merged with a Demetrian mother and
may also provide active listening comfort and domestic and
child-care services to each other; under these conditions, a
powerful, pleasurable, and lifelong sister bond may be forged.
But if a sister tries to rise above her sisters or if she marries a
too-possessive man, all this may change.

Some women do not hesitate to describe their adult sisters
as manipulative, envious, immature, competitive, and cruel.
Some sisters do not forgive each other for daring too much—
or for refusing to dare at all. One of my interviewees, Harriet,
is a thirty-five-year-old chiropractor, who reports that her
mother "set her daughters up to compete against each other."
Harriet says:

I can't take how we talk behind each other's backs. I don't want us to continue our mothers' sick divide-and-conquer game. I won't talk about one sister to another and I try to stop each one when she does this. Even though they know what bad feelings it causes, my three sisters can't stop doing it. It's a poison in their system.

Larraine, a forty-year-old journalist, sought me out to discuss her relationships with her sisters. She says:

My two sisters hated me. They were light-skinned, I was too dark. They persecuted me because of my skin color. If I was dark I was also supposed to be dumb. In fact, I read all the time. When I got a scholarship to college, they stopped talking to me. They persecuted me on both counts.

Larraine's sisters could not forgive her for daring to succeed academically. Sisters are just as quick to criticize each other for refusing to marry or for marrying the wrong kind of man. Sheila is a thirty-year-old Japanese-American businesswoman. She tells me:

When I married a white man my sister stopped talking to me. I think she was afraid for me, but she was also jealous. When he left me and took our daughter with him, my sister felt vindicated. "So you thought you could escape the Butterfly Syndrome?" My sister thinks that my daughter is not worth fighting for because she looks too white. My sister is married to a traditional Japanese man who bosses her around.

When asked, Larraine and Harriet still said that they loved their sisters. This is not surprising. Most primary relationships are complicated, and filled with contradictory emotions. Nevertheless, most women find it too frightening to *say* that their relationships with either their mothers or their sisters are hateful. Maggie, one of author Laura Tracy's interviewees, concludes that her sister Maureen has always hated her:

> She was always jealous. She always tried to hurt me. Our father died about two years ago. Maureen was named executor of his estate. About six months ago, she called to tell me she had some of his things and that I could take my pick whenever I had time. So I went to her apartment where she showed me a shopping bag filled with junk, stuff she should just have thrown away. In the meantime, looking around her apartment, I saw all the furniture and paintings my father had accumulated that we should have shared. When I asked about them, Maureen said that he would have wanted her to have them since I always

was the favorite and got so much more when we were kids. I didn't know what to say at that point, except to feel that I never wanted to see her again.

Only one of my interviewees (I shall call her Abigail) said that she hated her sister. Abigail is a fifty-two-year-old Los Angeles producer. She was diagnosed with multiple sclerosis and is now wheelchair-bound.

> I am an invalid. I can't practice my profession. My colleagues were my friends. Now that I'm no longer a "colleague," only a few bother to remain in touch. My husband makes sure that my nurses are paid. He travels a lot. My younger sister, who lives three houses away, has *never* visited me, not once. As I was getting sicker, my sister was working on our mother to write me out of her will. My sister probably told her I was going to die anyway so what's the point. I'm usually in pain. Stress is dangerous for me. I haven't got the health or the money to fight her. My sister knows I'm helpless.
>
> My sister used to hate me because I was good in school and she wasn't. Later on, she said she disapproved of my having a career. Maybe she just didn't like the idea of any woman being successful since she wasn't. Maybe she thought I was happier than she was. I probably was. My sister is using this time of

my greatest vulnerability to punish me for having been born.

As I thought about the sister bond, I realized how quiet many adult women are about their sisters—at least among their colleagues and in their adult social circles. For example, I have known some women for years who never once mentioned that they even *had* a sister or sisters or that their sister lived in the same building or the same neighborhood. I have a friend who has a twin sister whom she never mentions and another who never mentions her sister who committed suicide. Some women do mention their sisters, but only in passing; their sisters are phantoms in my life. I wonder whether such phantom sisters ever think of me as the phantom friend: we each relate to the same woman—but in seemingly parallel universes.[2]

In adulthood, are sistered women quiet about their sisters as a way of leaving childhood behind? Or as a way of making psychological room for best friends? Does having a real sister disappear make it easier for a best friend to replace her? How odd, then, that so many women still experience sibling-like rivalries with their best friends.

We have seen how passionate and how vengeful pre-adolescent and teenage girls can be to each other. Natalie Angier described how many pre-teen and teenage best friends can behave.

If a girl feels betrayed by a friend she will try . . . to

truly hurt her friend, as she has been hurt . . . To express anger might work (but only if) the betrayer accepts the anger and responds to it with respect. But if she doesn't acknowledge her friend's anger or sense of betrayal, if she refuses to apologize or admit to any wrongdoing, or if she goes further, walking away or snubbing her friend . . . A girl may aim to hurt . . . (through) indirect, vengeful aggression, with the object of destroying the girl's position, her peace of mind, her right to be.

In *Just Friends: The Role of Friendship in Our Lives,* sociologist Lillian B. Rubin notes that best friendships among adult women are sometimes similar to sibling relationships and can lead to the kinds of jealousies and rivalries that recall the scenes of childhood between siblings. One forty-three-year-old woman told Rubin:

> I love (my friend) Bonnie as much as I've ever cared about anyone in this world, but I've never had a relationship, even with my husband, that's so complicated. I don't think of myself as a terribly competitive person, but with her I can get into what feels like an all-out war inside me. She can make me angrier than just about anyone too, except my husband, of course. I've tried to figure it out because it makes me feel bad, and the best I can get is that it's a lot like I felt with my sister when we were kids. Only

I love Bonnie, I really do; I don't think I ever loved my sister, not then and not now.

Rubin quotes another interviewee who has resolved the bad relationship she had with her real sister by finding a Good Sister in a friend:

> One of the things I get from Elaine is the kind of love and approval I never got from my older sister. There was always too much jealousy between us . . . I wanted to tag around after her, but she didn't want me around . . . I was always dying to wear her clothes . . . just to feel like a big girl, but she'd never let me. With Elaine, she'd give me the shirt off her back.

Although a woman may choose friends who do *not* remind her of her sister, women also choose friends who *do*. One of McNaron's interviewees credits her good relationships with her sisters for teaching her how to form good female friendships.

> I have loved some women more passionately [than I have my sisters] . . . but my sisters have remained beloved longest. They allowed me to trust and love women as my parents did. [My] sisters helped me to learn how to treat friends . . . to love who friends become, to work in groups with women, to support women.

The journalist Barbara Mathias' interviewees also saw a relationship between how their sister bond influenced their ability to form female friendships. Mathias writes:

> Many said they chose the "opposite" of their sisters because they couldn't possibly duplicate their relationship. Others were a little more critical and said they didn't want to have friends like their sisters because they didn't want to repeat the problems or further complicate their lives. These women often spoke of their friends as "chosen sisters" and realized that there was a need to have more intimacy and sympathy than their sisters might provide. Often such a chosen relationship is an idealized one, especially since it isn't based on any history and doesn't carry the emotional load that comes with a past . . . One woman noted that she looks for women who have the sense of humor her sister has. Another admits she is attracted only to intelligent, hard-driving women, like all the women in her family.

Laura Tracy agrees and concludes that women

> choose our friends to correct the relationships we experienced with our "real" sisters. Even when we don't have sisters of our own, we long for sisterhood . . . Yet the notion of feminist sisterhood often leaves

us with an aching sense of distress. It denies what
women know: that we can be spiteful, mean, and
malicious . . . When we think of each other as sisters,
we dwell in the dream of sisterhood. We deny real
life with our real sisters. For most of us, for nine out
of ten women with whom I talked, sisterhood is not
a dream at all. Sisterhood is painful, incomplete,
and occasionally humiliating. It is marred by distrust, disapproval, rejection, bitterness, envy, jealousy, despair, and hatred . . . Sisterhood is marked by
fierce love . . . however, the destructive competition
women experienced with their sisters doesn't really
go away. It returns in the way friends behave with
each other.

Thus, adult best friends may perceive each other not as they
truly are, but, unconsciously, as shadow-mothers and shadow-
sisters. Some interviewees described their best friends and
female intimates as overbearing mothers, dependent daughters, or as resentful, envious, sneaky sisters.

Do some best friends expect to be unilaterally mothered?
Callie, my interviewee, works as a secretary and attends graduate school. She is twenty-four. She says:

I supported my best friend, Louise, for a year. Her
family refused to help her after she lost her job. I
treated her as if she were my own blood. I paid the

rent and bought the groceries. She'd promised to repay me. She didn't, not even after she found a job. She insisted that she was still the victim of her family's vendetta against her. I couldn't take it anymore. I could not continue to be her safety net. I had financial and personal crises of my own. Because the landlord said he wouldn't rent to us again, I went out and found my own apartment. At the last minute, the landlord changed his mind. Now, Louise has the apartment all to herself. She has a new roommate coming in.

I'm out, her hands are washed clean of me. She has my apartment, my Con-Ed account, my Segal-Medeco lock on the door, my gas account, my installed phone. She has my old room, my closet. I have to move to a much smaller apartment in a bad neighborhood. I have no roommate, no lock on my door. She didn't volunteer to help me move. We have to divide the plants. Thank goodness we had no pets.

Callie feels that Louise has treated her the same way that Louise treats her own mother.

Why did she treat me so terribly when I had treated her so well? I feel that she's turned me into her mother, someone she has always drained and leached dry. I feel she has used my strength against me. And if I won't continue to use my strength to feed her helplessness, she's just as happy to see me go. I still love her. But I can't continue to be a part of her using me. I will continue to be a good friend to other women, only this time, there are rules.

Sometimes, even successful women have a hard time tempering their envy toward their best friends. For example, Nan, my interviewee, is a forty-six-year-old lawyer. Her best friend is a judge. "She's almost always there for me when I'm down," Nan says. "She's not as available when I'm up." Once, Nan received a major award. "I asked her to be my guest at the dinner. She canceled at the last minute. I was so hurt. She insisted she 'meant nothing by it.'" Another time, when Nan had been promoted to partner in her law firm, she asked this best friend out to dinner to celebrate. "She came," Nan explains, "but she brought two friends along, whom I did not know, and spent most of the evening talking to them."

An envious best friend may also compete against her friend more directly. For example, Leah is a fifty-year-old religious Jew. She told me the following tale.

Many years ago, another woman and I decided it was time to start a volunteer organization to help battered women in our own religious communities. At the time, our rabbinic leaders absolutely refused to admit that such abuse existed. For a decade, my friend and I worked together as a team. We saw each other almost every day, we talked on the phone two or three times a day. We always met with each woman together. We did not charge anyone money for our advice or advocacy. And then, my friend began giving interviews to the media. At first, I didn't notice it. Let her do it, it's her thing. I don't enjoy that. Usually, she'd tell me about an article before it appeared or she'd bring it over. Gradually, she stopped doing this. Then, on her own, without any discussion, but in the name of our organization, she started working with two male politicians, who were both somewhat shady.

Leah found out about this, not from her friend, but from a newspaper article. Initially, Leah thought that sheer frustration was driving her friend to recklessness.

We both were frustrated, only she was ready to make deals with devils and I wasn't. I privately gave her some vital information about these politicians. I implored her to stop working with them. I told her that *I* could not work with them. Again, without telling me, she found a new woman-partner. I was devastated. How could I have misjudged her character? I took no pleasure in it when one of these politicians turned on her, and the other was indicted on charges. Perhaps I was a fool, but she was very clever. She hid her ambitiousness well. She needed a way to get rid of me in order to shine more brightly on her own. I was aghast. How could she sacrifice our friendship and our work together! For what? So that she could be the "only" or the most important woman in our community on this issue? Now, she's trying to position herself as the "religious" expert on this issue among less religious women.

Women long for intimacy with other women, but fear that a female intimate is also, potentially, a betrayer. Only she can poison people's minds about you. She has been by your side; you two have been an "item." If she says something about you, your mutual friends might think it is true. She has always had your best interests at heart. If *she* is breaking with you, you must have done something truly offensive. This longing for female intimacy coupled with a fear of female betrayal might explain why so many adult women remain so "girlishly" reluctant to disagree with or confront a female intimate outright, directly, with any unpleasant truths, such as: I envy you; I disapprove of you; I am threatened by you; I disagree with you; I must win all our competitions; I don't think you love me as much as I love you; I'm afraid you'll leave me; I prefer the company of others; I have to withdraw from you.

Another interviewee, Kelly, is a sixty-two-year-old grand-mother. Her closest friend is afraid to fight with her. Kelly says,

One day, I finally told my friend, "I have to talk to you, I want you to come over." I had actually made a long list of things I needed to say to her. I had it on a clipboard which just infuriated her. After I'd been talking for a half hour she got up and said, "I can't stand this. If I stay here something terrible will happen." Basically, what she thought was that either she would kill me or I would kill her. She walked out on me. Then she went home and she called me and she said, "You can never do that to me again."

Maryanne is nearly twenty years younger than Kelly, yet she has a similar tale. Maryanne belongs to a "devoted group of four friends."

We play bridge, we go to the movies together, usually without our husbands. After years of tip-toeing around each other, for the first time, one of us tried to say what was bothering her about a second woman. The second woman stood up and said: "I can't stand this anymore. It's killing me, you're killing me." What she was really saying was: "I'll kill you if you say these things to me, you will hurt me so badly, that I will hate you and that will destroy our friendship. I cannot listen to you say these things to me because then I won't be able to love you any-more."

Thus, like girls, many adult women intimates are not used to saying *exactly* and directly what they think, and are offended, frightened, when another woman does so. Like girls, adult women intimates value their connection to each other so much that they are willing to sacrifice direct and honest communication.

But, if female friendship is so important to women, why do women, especially best friends, sometimes steal each other's spouses or lovers? In 1949, in *The Second Sex,* Simone de Beauvoir describes women as each other's natural rivals in matters of coquetry and love. Beauvoir does not exempt best friends. On the contrary.

The theme of woman betrayed by her best friend is not a mere literary convention; the more friendly two women are, the more dangerous their duality becomes. The confidante is invited to see through the eyes of the woman in love, to feel through her heart, her flesh; she is attracted by the lover, fascinated by the man who has seduced her friend. She thinks that her loyalty protects her well enough to permit her giving free rein to her feelings, but she also dislikes playing a merely inessential role, and before long she is ready to yield, to make advances (to her best friend's male lovers). Many women prudently avoid intimates once they are in love. This ambivalence makes it hardly possible for women to repose much confidence in their mutual feelings.

The shadow of the male always hangs darkly over them.

My interviewee Charlotte defines a best friend as "someone who sleeps with your husband." Charlotte is thirty-nine, has an MBA, but has not worked for some time. She tells me:

> I got married when I was twenty-five. By 1993, we had two children. My husband works fourteen-hour days and earns at least $750,000 a year. By the time I was thirty-three, I had to cut back on my career so I could be there for our children. In 1995, we moved, and I became friendly with a woman in our new neighborhood who's about ten years *older* than I am. I confided in her and considered her a best friend. Guess what? About a year into our friendship she had begun having an affair with my husband. She used everything I told her to her own advantage. Now, he's left me for her. They are getting married. My husband is fighting for custody of our children so that he won't have to give me any money. Our oldest, a boy, is already saying he wants to live with his father. Why would this woman want to totally destroy me?

Typically, Charlotte is quick to blame her best friend, not her husband. Also, note how much more haunted she sounds about her best friend's betrayal than about her husband's plan to impoverish her and to repossess the children.

Elsa, a potter, describes a very similar occurrence that took place in the 1960s. She says:

> My best friend was a divorced woman who could not have children. I refused to discriminate against her because she was a divorced women. I kept inviting her to family and social events. In retrospect, I should have shunned her the way the other married women did. My friend not only made off with my husband. What was worse, was her systematic campaign to become my son's mother. She stopped working. She started baking birthday cakes for my son, something that I'd always done. I always used to make shaped birthday cakes, one year it was a fire engine, the next year a Volkswagen bus. She made bigger cakes. My son started calling her "Mom." Little by little, my son wanted less and less to do with me.

The theme of a best friend stealing one's boyfriend (or girlfriend) is not uncommon. Such borrowing or stealing is reminiscent of what sisters often do to each other. It is something that women are also used to *getting away with*.

I was a teenager and young woman in the 1950s and 1960s. Back then, it was common for girl and women friends to cancel dates with each other at the last minute if a boy happened to call; we all did this to each other, so we all had to accept it when it happened to us. Back then, if a married woman was on the phone with her best friend and her husband came home, she hurriedly, automatically, hung up in order to give her man her undivided attention.

Historically, this dominant (white, middle-class) pattern of ditching your female friends when a man came to call, was less characteristic of (white) unmarried career women, crusaders, and lesbians, and also women of color, immigrant, and impoverished women, who, since their men were dead, in jail, sick, unemployed, underpaid, or missing in action, relied more on female kin or symbolic kin in order to survive.

By the late 1990s, I assumed that the custom of dropping a woman friend for a man—any man—had gone the way of the whalebone corset. I was wrong. But I was also right. Today, many more women, of all ages, especially feminists and women over forty, do value the importance of female friendships.

As I interviewed women, I would ask "What is your definition of a best friend?" Some women would describe their best friend as a cross between Mary Poppins and a Godmother; some described their best friends as "companions," as "the ones who witness your life and remember everything that happened," "my only non-judgmental confidantes," and as "replacement mothers whom you can trust with your secrets."

Jaclyn Geller, the author of *Here Comes the Bride: Women, Weddings, and the Marriage Mystique,* writes that because friendship is a relationship that is not legally or ceremonially ritualized, friendship remains "private." "Thus, it can develop organically, or on its own terms." According to Geller, her friendship with another woman

> achieved a depth of intimacy and mystery . . . [like those Cicero] defined as "a complete identity of feeling about all things in heaven and earth: an identity that is strengthened by good will and affection:" (A typical ancient, Cicero considered such bonds to be far more powerful than blood relations.) . . . I still recall the ease with which my friend and I slipped into a blissful existence in which rigorous debate coexisted with unconditional support, and mutual admiration for each other's seriousness was offset by a sense of the absurd. While I do dream of growing old with her in a house in New York filled with books and mutual friends (and if she has her way, a few children), there is no need to make promises . . .

I could not get through life without my women friends. My world would be a cold and savage place without the women of ideas, talent, principle, intelligence, beauty, discipline, and courage, whom I am privileged to know as friends. However, there are many kinds of best friends, and there are many ways of being one. I only wish that someone had explained this to me earlier in life, so that I could have made the necessary distinctions and modified my own enormously unrealistic expectations.

I now understand that, like marriage, one must consciously work at friendship; it is not a given; it cannot be taken for granted. The relationship will not always feel good; the price of remaining connected may sometimes be too high. We may outgrow a spouse, a lover, or a friend. Some women would rather remain connected than grow—if it means growing apart. Good friendships do not always last; they cannot always survive certain violations or differences. We may fail at friendship too.

Sometimes we may not be able to bear losing (or winning) the routinely unacknowledged competition between close friends and sisters. Laura Tracy explains that women feel disloyal when they compete with friends and sisters whom they also love. Tracy suggests that this is one reason that women deny that such competition exists. On the one hand, women do not believe that loyal friends should compete with each other; according to Tracy, when sisters and friends compete, they experience that competition as immoral, unethical, and disloyal. Of course, not being able to compete openly—or anyway to acknowledge that one is doing so—is another form of disloyalty, both to oneself and to others. Tracy notes:

> Noncompetition as the basis for friendship conflicts with genuine friendship. Noncompetition . . . is actually unethical: when we practice it, the connection between us is violated just as much as when we are excessively competitive.

Tracy suggests that female friendships might actually be "more frightening" than family relationships. Here is where we experience "the naked outlines of commitment. It is with our friends that we test our courage to attach." According to Tracy, if we express unique selves, we might risk losing our (very different) friend. If we express ourselves uniquely and in "messy and complicated" ways, if we compete anyway but refuse to acknowledge that we are doing so, we also risk failing the demands of friendship.

I have been thinking about this subject for some time now. I am in no way insecure about my intellectual accomplishments. Yet, despite everything I have now learned, I would probably feel quite threatened if my closest friends suddenly started writing books (or stopped writing books) or radically changed their views, addresses, friendship networks, intimate partners, jobs, or daily lives. And, as much as I have loved creating circles of friends, I would probably feel quite threatened if my closest friends became equally close with each other. Or closer to each other than they are to me. I do not oppose change or growth. I am only saying that, like other women, it would probably threaten me too. Once one thing changes, other things might also change, and I might be abandoned as a friend. While I might understand this intellectually, emotionally, I'd be sad, perhaps devastated. Friendships do end; friends do grow apart.

Tracy notes a pattern in her own life. She writes:

Thinking about my own friends, I realize that a pattern emerges. A very good friend usually became a mere acquaintance in five or so years. Sometimes she became even less. I realize that my life is littered with women I no longer know, or see, or talk to, women with whom I once shared intimate conversations and intimate life.

I have had many different kinds of friends. Some were "friendly" colleagues and, therefore, competitors, who, like me, had access to information that we all depended upon. Who could better understand one's problems than someone who shared them? Some friends were intellectual "drinking" buddies and party-mates; no more, no less. Being together, publicly, confirmed our joint social and intellectual standing in the world. When the Good Times ended, we did not see each other as regularly as before. Some friends were only groupies who used everyone to meet "stars," constantly on the move for richer feeding grounds. Some friends were comrades-in-battle, not companions-on-the-road; when the battles (or our capacity to battle) ended, we drifted apart, but I remember such comrades often, and with great affection. Some friends live clear across the country or in other countries; my phone bill is high. Over the long haul, a few comrades and companions became enemies, and some, presumed to have been enemies, have become friends.

Good friends can also lose each other to ordinary tragedies. One succeeds economically, one's friend fails; one remains healthy, the other (or their child) becomes sick. Youth runs out; a person becomes consumed with daily survival: one's own, no one else's.

Over time, many of my good friends began to disappear. They killed themselves, or died, or fell on hard times and were ashamed to keep asking for help and stayed away, pained by the difference in luck and circumstance. Some friends grew mad (I *have* seen the best minds of my feminist generation go mad); some became ill in other ways. Some women who became ill had partners, both male and female, who choreographed and administered medical and communal support for them; many more did not have any support. Cancer, AIDS, immune system breakdowns, hip and joint replacements—these plagues slowly, almost imperceptibly diminished and frayed formerly vital political and intellectual friendships.

Like so many others, I too, became ill and was severely disabled for six years with undiagnosed and untreated Lyme's Disease and with Chronic Fatigue Immune Dysfunction Syndrome. Only two friends remained connected to me as if they were my female kin; no female relative did.

Many more women than men excel at visiting the dramatically sick: those in traction, those with a guaranteed date of recovery, and those who are wealthy, who have estates and social connections to bequeath. Chronic illness is far more demanding: one is at home, one might not "look" sick. There is no promise of recovery, which is frightening. Often, there are no secondary social or economic gains to be had. A chronically ill person who is always, or who is often, in severe pain becomes boring, less scintillating than she was.

I, who understand this, have not turned visiting sick women into a personal crusade. I am aware when a friend slips below the line of social visibility. I will call, persistently; I will even visit, responsibly; but I cannot take her on. I have lost so many years to illness. Life is short; one seizes it with both hands; it is gone soon enough.

I, who understand this, cannot find a way back into certain friendships. I remain uneasy with those who never visited me or who did not find a way of remaining connected to me in some small way. One dear friend never visited; I simply never saw her again. From time to time, I received postcards from foreign ports of call, and annual newsletters about her world travels. Years later, I learned that she had survived multiple surgeries for cancer. I wrote. I was willing to correspond, but I was not ready to meet. In all our years apart, I'd become a ghost, or she had; I wasn't certain I could re-connect. (After I wrote this paragraph, I called this friend; we spoke of our love for each other, and promised to get together. When one is psychologically ready to connect, it is easy, not hard, to do.)

While women do value other women as friends, some women *also* continue to put women friends second, men first. Sixteen-year-old Sara protests this reality. Sara reports that she began to lose girlfriends by the eighth grade.

My friends started worrying about how they looked,

were they thin enough, should they start getting facials before it's too late. Then, suddenly, four friends developed what I call "The Thousand-Light-Years-Away Stare." Their minds were elsewhere. My mom says the same thing happened to her in the 1970s, it's just the way things are. I refuse to accept this. I tell my mom that I will not behave this way when I find a boyfriend. Actually, I already have a boyfriend. My mom just doesn't know about him. Now, I have only one girlfriend left. We don't believe that boys come first, girls last. She also has a boyfriend. But we're definitely in the minority.

My friend Dale, who is sixty-five, was widowed at a young age. Her children are now grown. After many years alone, Dale found a man who'd just left his wife of many years. Dale devoted herself to this affair. Dale called to invite me to a party to meet her lover. She said that she had asked six of her closest women friends, some of whom would be traveling from around the country, to this party. The night before the party, Dale called me, crying, to say that The Man had broken up with her, so she was canceling the party. "Are you crazy?" I said. "Your closest women friends are in town. Let's party." The next afternoon, she called me again, and, in a pleading, little-girl's voice, said: "I want to invite him too. Anyway." And so we all got to meet the man who was about to leave Dale. Dinner time approached. "Why not come out with us for dinner?" we asked her. "Oh," Dale said, "I can't do that. This is his last night here and he's asked to spend it with me. Sorry." Of course, we all understood, but it was 2000, and our friend's inability to conduct herself with any dignity or honor cast a sad pall over our dinner.

Sometimes, when best friends disappoint each other, revenge might be exacted through sexual means. For example, Laurie is a forty-three-year-old violinist. She tells me about a failed friendship with Ruth, a conductor, whom she adored.

> Ruth's husband liked threesomes. Ruth went along with this in order to keep him. Ruth started telling me that her husband was really attracted to me. Finally, we all got stoned and went to bed. It was awful. I felt totally used. I felt that Ruth had used me to keep her husband, and that he'd used Ruth to get me. Afterwards, Ruth became quite distant, but her husband started calling me, secretly. I ended up sleeping with him once. I did it because I was very hurt and very angry at Ruth. I had only done what she herself had asked me to do. And she withdrew from me because of it. She couldn't say "no" to her husband, but she could persecute me, not him, because of her anger at him.

Sometimes, love hath no fury like a woman scorned. Patricia is a thirty-eight-year-old biochemist.

This woman was the straw that finally broke the back of my marriage. As they say, I was the last to know. She was my assistant. She was very smart, made of steel. She insinuated herself into my life. She tried to make herself indispensable. She succeeded. Slowly and surely, she drove a wedge between myself and my husband. He wanted me to fire her, I defended her to him. I said that his jealousy was irrational and that her job with me was non-negotiable. My husband walked out. It turned out that he knew something I had not permitted myself to realize. My assistant had set her cap for me. She continued making herself indispensable. When I started seeing a new man, she confronted me in a fury. She said it was "Her, now, not another man." I was outraged, and scared. I turned her down. She left immediately, with a thousand details pending. She refused to train her replacement. This woman meant to punish me because I was not interested in having a love affair with her.

Sometimes, if a woman feels she can't compete with a close friend professionally, she might resort to flirting with her friend's spouse as a way of feeling important or equal, or as a way of punishing her friend for being more successful in the world. Also, if a woman has had no positive female role models and has also been mistreated by men, she might be more, not less, likely to undermine her relationships with other, potentially supportive women. Thus if one's mother has not been kind, it might be difficult for a woman to accept such kindness from a strange woman—at least not without testing or sabotaging it.

For example, Zarinda is a forty-year-old African-American city planner. She befriended Frances, a twenty-five-year-old woman who lived on her block. At the time, Frances had not completed high school, and was the mother of two children. Zarinda says:

> She called me her Big Sister. She seemed to have no girlfriends. Her mother was dead. I would babysit for her so she and her husband could have some time out together. I counseled her to go to school. Sometimes, she would call me in the middle of the night crying. We talked almost every day. I have a large extended family. This is what women do for each other. But, behind my back, Frances began calling my boyfriend (who sometimes babysat with me), to tell him she was interested in him. When I confronted her she said: "You don't need him but I do." I stopped talking to her. Now, when I meet a woman with no girlfriends, I am instantly suspicious.

A best friend may sometimes need to challenge or end the friendship as a way of dealing with unacceptable (or unreciprocated) longings for further intimacy. Sometimes, sleeping with your best friend's man is a way of getting back at her for preferring him to you; sometimes, it might have no meaning at all.

Toni Morrison's novel, *Sula*, challenges us on just this point. Her protagonists, Nel and Sula, are the only children of

> distant mothers and incomprehensible fathers. Because each had discovered years before that they were neither white nor male, and that all freedom and triumph was forbidden to them, they had set about creating something else to be.

As girls, Nel and Sula are inseparable. Sula leaves home and goes to college. Nel stays, marries Jude, becomes a mother, works for pitiful wages, starts growing old quickly. Sula returns, an educated, glamorous, and sexually promiscuous woman. Perhaps there was no place in early twentieth-century America for someone like Sula to go except back home, to the bottom. Perhaps Sula has returned home to resume her friendship with Nel. Sula proceeds to sleep with everyone's man, including Nel's husband Jude. Sometime thereafter, Jude leaves town. "That was too much. To lose Jude and not have Sula to talk to about it because it was Sula that he had left her for."

Thereafter, Nel refuses to talk to Sula. When Sula lies dying of cancer, alone and in pain, Nel finally visits her. Nel says: "We were friends." Sula responds: "Oh yes. Good friends." Nel says: "And you didn't love me enough to leave him alone. To let him love me. You had to take him away." Sula's response is powerful: "What do you mean take him away? I didn't kill him, I just fucked him. If we were such good friends, how come you couldn't get over it?" Nel does not answer. She just leaves. Sula thinks: "So she will walk on down that road, her back so straight . . . thinking how much I have cost her and never remember the days when we were two throats and one eye and we had no price." Only after white people find and bury Sula, does Nel visit the cemetery. Too late, she cries out:

> All that time, all that time, I thought I was missing Jude. And the loss pressed down on (my) chest . . . "We was girls together . . . O Lord Sula, girl girl girl-girlgirl." It was a fine cry—loud and long—but it had no bottom and it had no top, just circles and circles of sorrow.

8.

WOMEN IN THE WORKPLACE

Girls and women are as competitive as men, but mainly toward each other. However, unlike men, middle-class white women and all those who aspire to that position have learned that *open* competition among women (except in a beauty or a cooking contest) is taboo. Although women have increasingly entered what were once male-only professions, many women still experience each other's overt, visible, direct, or covert competition as not only dangerous, but demonic too.

According to professors Evelyn Fox Keller and Helene Moglen, "competition denied in principle, but unavoidable in practice, surfaces in forms that may be far more wounding, and perhaps even fiercer and more destructive." Thus, class, race, and gender, glass ceilings, and glass walls, pink-collar ghettos, female poverty, and other marketplace realities are further complicated by a woman's tendency to deny that she *is* participating in a forced competition and by her own internalized sexism.

In practice, sexism might mean that women are harder on other women than men are. Ivy E. Broder, a professor of economics at American University, has found, for example, that women economists rejected female proposals for National Science Foundation funding more often than men did. In Broder's view, one reason women appear to be harder on each other than men are on each other may be due to

> the small percentage of female academics in economics. Many women perceive a fixed number of "female slots," leading to a feeling of competition among women; or women may believe that, unless they judge other women harshly, their own credibility will be questioned . . . Similarly, minority members within a group (in this case, women academics in economics) who have achieved a certain status may hold other members of that group to a higher standard. Finally, another explanation twists the interpretation slightly and argues that women are objective about other women, but men are easier on women. This could happen if men want to encourage the advancement of women relative to men or if they hold women to lower standards or expectations and therefore give higher ratings when they are favorably inclined.

Clearly, patriarchy and its various economic systems have set the rules: only a minimal number of women can be allowed to succeed as if they were men. Those who do succeed must either be exceptional—and exceptionally adept in holding other women at bay—or else must cater to the men at the top. Some women do both. Such responses to tokenism demoralize all women.

Would women in top positions treat other women more fairly and kindly if there were more women at the top? Columbia University's professor Robin J. Ely compared relationships between women at *sex-integrated* law firms, where there were many women partners, and at *male-dominated* firms where there were very few women partners. Ely hypothesized that subordinate women would experience more supportive mentoring and less soul-devouring competition in those firms where many women can succeed and where senior women had enough power to share, as compared to what subordinate women experienced elsewhere. To a large extent, Ely proved her thesis.

At large male-dominated law firms with only a few female partners subordinate women did not like the senior women and rated them negatively. Subordinates found the token women partners to be inaccessible, male-like, male-oriented, intolerant, and competitive toward female subordinates. One of Ely's interviewees described two of the women partners in her firm as "horrible examples" for junior women:

> [They are] very, very deferential to men. I don't like
> that . . . their demeanor is just very flirtatious. One
> of them, everyone feels, is a manipulative bitch who
> has no legal talent . . . she's talked about all the time
> as having slept with numerous partners. It doesn't
> even matter if it's not true, if that's the way she's per-
> ceived, she's a bad role model.

Ely's interviewees understand that this is a patriarchal divide-
and-conquer tactic—but it's one that works. The female-female
competition is subtle, deep, tension-producing, wracking. But
it is entirely due to "the law firm's promotion structure and to
the fact that it had yielded few senior women." Only men, not
women, had enough power to safely and genially mentor and
groom subordinates. One interviewee says:

> It's very unfair to say, "well, women are always
> fighting with each other, they're not getting along
> with each other," when it's the nature of the situa-
> tion that you're never dealing with a woman who is
> so firmly entrenched in her authority that you follow
> her lead with the same degree of deference that you
> would follow a man in that position . . . there aren't
> enough [women].

In male-dominated law firms, women tended to compare
themselves "directly (and only) with other women as a way of

gauging their own success and relative opportunities for advancement." Women in sex-integrated firms compared themselves both to men and to other women.

In addition, at the sex-integrated firms, junior women liked the senior women and rated them positively. Some felt "telepathic" connections; the women giggled, supported, and mentored each other. Although competition still existed, women described it as a "positive sum" game as opposed to a "zero sum game." In one instance, one of two friends but not the other was promoted to partner. Instead of experiencing envy, resentment, sabotage, and disconnection, the two friends

worked together to gain an understanding of why the interviewee had not been chosen to fill the position. As a partner, her colleague was now privy to information that could help the interviewee understand and reverse the perceptions that had kept her from receiving the partnership offer. By sharing this information, her colleague made the interviewee's future candidacy for partnership much more viable.

Ely's work confirms the view that many of women's difficulties with each other at work are caused by male domination and the consequent tokenism for women. A sex-integrated firm with many female partners encourages cooperation and healthy competition among women.

In a way, the top Ivy League universities are similar to Ely's male-dominated law firms. One professor at such a university told me how she'd been hounded by another academic woman.

> This woman has writer's block. Therefore, she decided to specialize in viciously attacking any book written by another woman in her field. She singled me out but she did not stop with bad reviews of my books. She began to attack me at conferences, on panels, both in public and behind my back. She refused to meet with me until even her own friends suggested that she was "just jealous" because she has remained unable to produce even one book.

A leading African-American scholar described how devastated she had been when the only other African-American woman on staff at her university continually rebuffed her.

> I called up this other Afro-American woman to meet her, to bond with her, to find out how to work together. She says: "I don't care to meet you. Why should I? It's obvious the Chairman prefers you to me, you've already gotten more attention from him at one meeting than I've gotten in ten years. You don't need me and I want nothing to do with you." And with that she hung up." No one ever sees this woman outside her classroom, no one has ever seen

her *hair* (it's always covered), she has trouble walking up the steps, the place is killing her, but still she wants Daddy's attention. She only knows how to compete with another woman for it, not how to bond with another woman. So we're both absolutely alone.

Competition among women for token positions at prestigious male-dominated universities is very intense. Would women work more effectively with each other in an all-female work setting?

According to Bowling Green State University's Professor Paige P. Edley, "studies show that 35% more people work for small women-owned organizations in the United States than work for the entire Fortune 500 world wide. Studies show that 36% of all U. S. companies are owned by women." According to Edley, studies of woman-owned and female-staffed businesses suggest that women workers communicate "indirectly," "tiptoe around open conflict," are "cliquish, petty, and catty." However, the very women who engage in "cutthroat competition" also "do not want to hurt each other." Or, if they do, they do not want to admit it to themselves or to each other.

Edley, a professor of Organizational and Interpersonal Communication, studied a woman-owned business, "Nan's Interiors," which employed ten women and three men. Edley found that the women on staff "silenced themselves" in terms of "dissent," "creativity," and "deviance." The women acted as if they believed that their relationships at work were essentially "nurturing" and family-like; they described each other as "like" mothers, daughters, and sisters.

Nan, the owner, was "depicted as a caring mother figure who provided a flexible and supportive work environment for women, especially other mothers." In reality, Nan employed married mothers because they had husbands whose companies, not Nan, provided health-care benefits. Nan simultaneously worried "that maybe the married women were 'not hungry enough' to increase her profit margin." Unlike female flight attendants, who, in one study, "trained themselves not to experience anger," Nan's designing employees did "experience and express anger." However, they "re-labeled it as PMS." This allowed them to "maintain the illusion of the happy family." Money demands, creative disagreements, and dissent, were all suppressed. No staff member was supposed to confront or challenge Nan.

> For example, when an employee was labeled deviant, she would be publicly humiliated in weekly meetings via what employees referred to as "the hot seat" (Joanne), "the whipping post" (Theresa), "lynching" (Shelly), and being "embarrassed publicly" (Delores). Besides being publicly humiliated, other treatments of deviants included the owners' close supervision, close attention to time cards and invoices, as well as Nan's cutting commissions,

"looking over [one's] shoulder" (Theresa), and "just mak[ing] me nervous" (Tina). Being labeled as deviant could also get them fired or "washed out," Nan's term for not assigning new clients to a former designer whom she had deemed deviant or "a troublemaker."

Nan prided herself on "never firing designers." She merely "washed them out." Nan described one such "washed out" designer as a "prima donna." Others described this same woman as a "very nice person who got screwed," mainly because she had insisted on meeting her own—not Nan's—creative standards. Nan viewed the washed-out designer not as a creative asset but as too much of an individualist. Edley nevertheless concludes that Nan's female employees' self-silencing was also a form of resistance, since it allowed them to achieve a measure of job autonomy and job security.

In summary, the (women) made excuses for the times they had difficulty working together, and explained away any conflicts with the essentialist argument [which] bound the women together and allowed them to create an idealized climate for women. In exchange for suppressing their voice, employees could pride themselves as being team players . . . and attain a sense of voice.

In other words, the unwritten job description at Nan's Interiors did not include accepting-and-not-complaining about sexual harassment or sex discrimination. Apparently, none existed. Rather, in order to keep their jobs, the women were expected to lie to themselves about employer-employee power differences and to sacrifice their own creative standards.

Like men, many women thrive under such conditions because their need to belong to a family-like team and keep their jobs outweighs all other needs. Others (I am one) might view Nan's unwritten job description as just one more onerous patriarchal script.

Many women demand nurturing rather than visionary or effective leadership from their female employers—or their employees. Thus, women like Nan and like Nan's employees are often willing to sacrifice excellence and diverse creativities for the semblance of family-like nurture on the job.

Perhaps the women at Nan's Interiors enjoyed working with other women so much that sacrificing independent creative vision was a small price to pay. Perhaps women reward each other in other psychologically important ways.

In a study of middle-level corporate managers in a Fortune 500 company, California business and management professors Anne S. Tsui and Charles A. O'Reilly studied age, race, gender, education, job tenure, and company tenure as predictors of job ratings. They found that the most favorably rated work dyad was a female-female pair, one a superior, the other her subordinate. (Shades of our mother-daughter primate ancestors and of the tendency toward dyadic intimacy among girls and women!)

Woman subordinates with woman superiors reported the lowest level of role ambiguity, were rated to be most effective, and were liked most by their superiors. The subordinates in mixed-gender dyads were rated as performing more poorly and were liked less well than the subordinates in same-gender dyads. Furthermore, subordinates in mixed-gender dyads also reported higher levels of role ambiguity and role conflict. Additional analyses suggest that men with women as superiors reported the highest level of role ambiguity. Men and women with men as superiors showed little difference . . . white subordinates with black superiors reported the highest level of role ambiguity and role conflict. Black subordinates reporting to white superiors, on the other hand, reported the lowest level of role ambiguity.

Those work conditions which most closely approximate the societal or familial status quo seem to be most comfortable for managers. Of course, this study did not consider how stable or long-lasting these working dyads are, nor did it measure productivity.

In a recent study of 825 black and white women executives at some of the most prestigious companies in America, Ella L. J. Edmondson Bell, a Professor of Business at Dartmouth College, and Stella M. Nkomo, a Professor of Business at South Africa's UNISA Graduate School of Business Leadership, found that "the combined effects of race and gender create very separate paths to the doors of corporate America." They also concluded that, despite crucial differences, black and white women executives experienced similar patriarchal gender discrimination. But widely different experiences make it difficult for women of different races to achieve the illusion of family-like relationships in corporate America.

Perhaps women work well together if they meet each others' expectations for sex-role conformity. Perhaps a woman's work-related competence is less important to other women (and men) than is her capacity to balance sex-role stereotypes over and above job competence. One study, cited by Illinois psychologist Roya Aymon, documents the view that women managers

> who were more inclined to hold feminine values (e.g., emotional, considerate) and those who were more inclined to hold predominately masculine values (e.g., aggressive, independent) reported mal-adjustment and discomfort in managing their work group. However, women managers who were able to maintain a balance between being emotional and considerate versus independent and assertive seemed to report better adjustment as managers.

Nevertheless, a good manager must be assertive, and some-times even ruthless. An assertive woman manager might be viewed as bitchy and non-maternal. The fact that she might be trying to do her job well is precisely what other women may hold against her.

Industrial psychologist W. J. Camara tells of a woman accountant who sued her company when she was denied partnership. One must assume that the decision-makers were mainly men, although they may have relied upon (or hidden behind) the attitudes of other women at the firm. The decision

> relied upon the fact that her demeanor was too much like that of a man and that she did not wear enough makeup and jewelry. This woman, like many others, was faced with a dilemma. When the woman behaves in accordance with her sex stereotype, it is seen as "too soft," too much like a woman, while the script for her managerial role says "tighten the belt and act like a man." Thus, she has to make a choice. In the case of the woman manager in the accounting firm, she acted like a man, "an aggressive go-getter," and she was judged as "a dragon lady" (i.e., overly masculine).

Perhaps some of the difficulty women have with each other at work is due to how well or how poorly each woman is able to co-navigate her sex role stereotype and her work competence—and how others, both women and men, judge her balancing act. Perhaps certain work settings enhance or diminish a woman's need for such balancing acts.

For example, in a subsequent study, Robin Ely analyzed the data from her study of women lawyers at male-dominated and sex-integrated law firms. She found that male-dominated female lawyers tended to express more sexist or stereotyped views of gender than did sex-integrated women lawyers. Male-dominated female lawyers believed, for example, that male lawyers were superior to female lawyers and that a female lawyer can succeed only by "sexualizing" her relationships to top men; to a lesser extent, a female lawyer may also succeed by minimizing or denying the existence of rampant sex discrimination, devaluing female "connection" virtues, distancing herself from feminist values and from other women, and by being as aggressive as the male lawyers, but not too mannish. This includes putting family concerns second.

In contrast, sex-integrated female lawyers viewed some women as very aggressive and some men as very sensitive. Moreover, some women viewed what women bring to law as an improvement over what happens when "men run in packs (and) tend to act like small boys." One interviewee said:

> I think that women are bringing to the practice the sense that you don't have to be so aggressive—you can be cooperative and still do things for your client. You don't have to fight every inch of the way. Being cooperative may actually help your client in the long run because you won't spend as much time fighting over things that aren't worth fighting over, and so you won't spend the client's money.

In Ely's view, those in sex-integrated firms experienced less ambivalence about their gender identity. Those at male-dominated firms reinforced the notion that "women are deficient, breed resentment among women, and interfere with the development of positive in-group relationships."

These studies suggest that whereas women are hardest on each other under conditions of extreme male domination, women do enjoy each other and work well together under certain conditions: in dyads, in small female-dominated firms (as long as they are willing to subscribe to the myth of the happy family), and in large sex-integrated firms where there are many women at the top.

We may not be able to change certain workplace realities either quickly or radically. Therefore, how women view and treat each other—given workplace limitations—matters, both psychologically and morally.

Women's sexism does not only mean that women dislike or devalue each other. It also means that women expect other women to fulfill unrealistic family or fantasy needs.

Professors Keller and Moglen describe for example, an academic gripe session in which women doctoral students said they felt "betrayed by their female mentors." Keller and Moglen understand that the faculty women have endured both second-class citizenship within the academy and the "patronizing judgments" of their "scornful" male colleagues for so long that they do not "actually experience themselves as powerful . . . [H]ow can they effectively assert power if they actually feel impotent?"

Most women have been trained to obtain power indirectly, "affiliatively," with and for others rather than directly, openly, for themselves. Similarly, most women have been trained to uphold an unjust status-quo peace, not to struggle against it for new forms of justice. A woman may have a lot of power "for a girl," but may still experience herself as powerless. This is a way of conforming to the stereotype for her gender. The Keller and Moglen students believe that the faculty women

> are unable to accept the power they have both within the university and in their professions. "They have access to resources and belong to influential networks," one asserts. "They publish papers, participate in conferences, write book reviews, hire, and fire. And still they cling to their images of themselves as oppressed victims, courting us as friends by identifying with our impotence!" These students believe that they need mentors and even, in their own words, "moms who are adults, able to act as well as to care for us. If they won't help us, who the hell will?"

According to Keller and Moglen, the extent to which academic women view each other as (failed) mothers or (too-greedy) daughters suggests to them that working women still "remain haunted by the residue of unresolved conflicts from another domain."

Childhood-based explanations of complex adult behavior

are always limited. Nevertheless, perhaps any competition between two women might, at an unconscious level, trigger memories of a daughter's guilt and terror over having abandoned or been abandoned by her mother, having competed with or having lost her mother in a competition for the same man—or a sibling rival.

My own interviews confirm what other studies have found: women in the workplace behave in sexist ways and tend to hold double standards in terms of gender. Women can demoralize each other by treating men and women differently. Consider La Toya, a forty-two-year-old head nurse. She says:

> One of the male doctors had a tantrum. He was prescribing too much medication for a patient and he freaked out when I said so. I went down to talk to my director of nursing and the medical nursing coordinator and they told me not to worry about it, that it's okay—that he yells at them too. So in other words, it was all right for him to talk to me that way. Women patients smile at male doctors, and then bitch and complain to the women nurses. We're overworked, the hospital is understaffed. If you ask another nurse: "where are the supplies?" either she won't answer you or she'll snap at you. We take the pressure out on one another.

The same woman who will work for a man with a towering

ego might sabotage his female counterpart. This situation is complicated, since many women who do succeed *are* difficult to work for. Some individuals are simply difficult. More often, the situation is complicated by unspoken, unacknowledged, psychologically internalized double and triple gender standards. A physician-businesswoman once told me that some women physicians whom she employs resent her because she insists that all her physicians "understand that the role of M.D. is more important than the role of Mr. or Mrs."

Women also expect other working women (but not men) to understand things in a sympathetic fashion and to behave in less misogynistic ways than men. These expectations often lead to feeling betrayed when a woman acts "just like a man"—especially if she had previously acted "just like a best friend."

Corporate consultant Judith Briles conducted a survey of hundreds of business executives.

> About sixty-five percent of all respondents reported that they had been unethically treated by a man; forty-seven percent reported unethical treatment by a woman . . . women were more likely to behave unethically to other women than to men.

According to Briles, women did not behave unethically in order to get ahead, as men did; rather, women did so because "they were jealous, envious, or even afraid someone (female) was after their jobs." Briles discusses several cases in which jealous female superiors had their more talented subordinates fired—in one instance, even jailed—and cases in which jealous, incompetent subordinates tried to shame their female superiors in ways they would never use with male superiors.

Rita Lavelle, for example, held a highly visible position in the Environmental Protection Agency. She and five other senior agency heads all worked for a woman, "Anne." According to Rita, Anne became increasingly "jealous and hostile" toward Rita because Rita "was performing so well at a time when Anne was not." Although Rita remained an excellent team player, Anne failed to praise her for her loyalty and programmatic excellence; in fact, Anne criticized Rita for wearing drab clothing and scant makeup and for failing to flirt with various male politicians.

When the agency came under fire, Anne set Rita up as her scapegoat. In order to save herself, she first attacked Rita in anonymous news headlines. Then, after arranging immunity for herself, she accused Rita of various "crimes." The Justice Department prosecuted Rita for having lied under oath "about an innocuous date." Rita had to pay for her own lawyers, and she was found guilty and jailed.

> Anne, financially secure, her attorney fees paid by tax dollars, remarried to a wealthy high government official, continues life in Washington as a (heroically perceived) "victim" of the Department of Justice and the White House . . . [Rita asks] "Why did she do this

to me? Because she felt threatened for her own job, and I think that she thought I might be the replacement."

One of my interviewees, Hope, told a chilling story of how she was betrayed by her employer and mentor, Cindy. Hope is a forty-one-year-old corporate executive and the mother of two young children. Cindy, fifteen years her senior, was friendly with Hope's parents and had once been Hope's babysitter.

> Cindy brought me into business with her. We then moved on and up together, into a larger fifteen-person company that Sharon had formed. I thought of Cindy as my mentor, as a kind of mother. Why would she want to harm me? For two years, Cindy kept telling me that Sharon refused to promote me. I was quite surprised because I was bringing in a lot of business. Quite recently, I discovered that Sharon was in my corner. Cindy was the one opposing me. In fact, Cindy was taking the credit for the business I brought in. Things got worse.
>
> I'd been trying to get pregnant. I was very tense about this. Cindy didn't help matters by warning me, "if you get pregnant, Sharon will probably fire you. The company is not big enough to be able to afford a mommy track." It turns out that Sharon never said

this. But, because I believed Cindy, the minute I became pregnant, I left the company. Within the year, I learned that Sharon had hired three new people, including a pregnant woman, and the mother of an infant. I called Sharon, and we had our first heart-to-heart.

Maybe Cindy was jealous that I was married and she wasn't. Maybe she was jealous because I believed in children, and she didn't. Maybe she needed to have something that I couldn't have, a job at Sharon's company. Maybe Cindy was jealous that I brought in more business than she did, maybe her ego couldn't stand it. Whatever her problem was, Cindy spoiled a good job for me. For awhile, she made me feel that I could never trust another woman again. But, once we cleared the air, Sharon decided to rehire me and to fire Cindy.

Incompetent or less competent subordinates can also behave in jealous, threatened ways toward anyone they perceive as more competent than themselves. For example, according to author Rosabeth Moss Kanter, a "very dignified woman manager" was the only woman at a high management level at a certain company. She supervised both male and female subordinates, including one "aggressive but objectively low-performing woman subordinate." The manager refused to cover for the subordinate, who, in turn, began to hurl invectives at her, accusing her of being a "bitch, a stuck-up snob," and other unpleasant labels. The manager stood quietly, maintaining her dignity, then left the room, fearing physical violence.

The subordinate had found a way of shaming her superior. Few people supported the woman manager. Her male peers either were silent or justified the subordinate's outburst. ("She needed to get that off her chest.")

A male friend told the manager that he heard two young men, who were passed over for the job she was eventually given, commenting on the event: "so miss high-and-mighty finally got hers!" The humiliation and the thought that colleagues supported the worker rather than her was enough to make this otherwise successful woman consider leaving the corporation.

Subordinate, incompetent, jealous women will also use their workplace social friendships against a competent female superior. The subordinate is exercising female psychological power to punish another woman by socially shaming her. Corporate consultant Briles describes a manager, Tina, who invited her staff to parties at her well-appointed home. Tina observed, "The more Linda (a subordinate) saw of what I had, the worse it got." Tina had twice reported that Linda was performing poorly. Linda retaliated by playing on her co-workers' feelings of hostility toward female authority. She cajoled, bullied, and browbeat those who hesitated to join her in her revenge, which was a department walk-out.

> Linda organized a lunch with others in Tina's department. They didn't come back from lunch. Tina was thrown into a panic when they didn't return. The work had to be done but there was no support to do it. Tina called around to find the employees. She (finally) located a junior staff member who broke down and cried on the phone. She said everyone was afraid of Linda.

A woman's unconscious desire to be protected by a Fairy Godmother, coupled with her unconscious fear that an Evil Stepmother will emerge instead, remains a constant and unacknowledged tension among women at work. Thus, women's expectations of each other at work are often unrealistic, sexist, and characterized by unspoken ambivalence, regardless of who objectively holds more power. For example, Patti, a thirty-six-year-old television actress, trusts no one, but she trusts women even less. She says:

> If a man is my agent, he wants to cheat me and have sex with me too. At least I know what to expect from a guy. And I know how to deal with a guy. I'm not

sure how to behave with a woman agent. I don't like women who are male-impersonators. I'm hard as nails, but I don't like hardness in other women. I don't like women who are soft. I have no respect for women agents or directors who are anything like my mother: the type who can't find anything, her desk is a mess. I don't like this type of woman, I don't care if she can pull in the money, in my book she's basically a con artist. She usually talks too fast because she's afraid she's an impostor and that you might be on to her.

If a woman has not grown up surrounded by women leaders in the public realm and if she has not experienced generous, non-envious love from female relatives in childhood, she might have a hard time trusting any woman "in charge" to really know what she's doing or to exercise her authority in a fair, benevolent manner. This might explain why women at work have to repeatedly prove that they know what they're doing—not just to men, but to women too.

Sexist views include viewing other women in the workplace as pseudo-family members. A woman who holds such views runs the risk of trusting female strangers more than she should. She might expect other women to behave ethically, honestly, not to lie, and to remain connected to her as if they were relatives. Many business and professional women have been blind-sided by such expectations.

According to Briles, a business consultant, Carolyn, was not being supported by her male managers. She was, therefore, over-eager to work with Katharine, a free-lance consultant, on a series of seminars for women only. Carolyn did not check Katharine's references. Carolyn's "need to trust" cost her more than a hundred and fifty thousand dollars.

> Katharine led people to believe that she had certain connections and commitments from others, when in fact she did not. She was so good at getting other people to believe the fantasies she spun out that she got networks of people involved in the project . . . "If this had been a man, I would have questioned a lot more" said Carolyn. "But because it was coming from a woman, I wanted to trust (I did no research) . . . I think that fundamentally, women trust women more, or more easily, than they trust men. They do that on a subconscious level."

Dixie, sixty-three, is a successful art dealer. She has galleries and homes in New Mexico, East Hampton, and San Francisco.

> In my business, I am constantly on the road. I've lost touch with most of my non-business friends. Therefore, I was so happy to get a call from someone I knew before I ran a 50-person operation. Gigi was opening a nightclub. She began to come over to cook elaborate French dinners for me, just like old

times. Then she cried and poured her heart out. She was in trouble—but success was just around the corner.

Dixie decided to invest in her old friend's nightclub venture.

I figured, why not? I was sentimental. I was proud to have someone in my life who knew me "when." She turned out to be a con-artist. Hell, I bought into it. My business guard was totally down. This woman and I knew each other when we were broke. We were drinking buddies. She took me for a lot of money before I put a stop to it. Funny thing. Once I got out of our business relationship she never called me again.

Precisely because such things happen every day, many women professionals have come to dislike and fear women clients or colleagues who are too emotionally effusive or emotionally needy or who do not behave in professional ways.

Emotionally needy women tend to overwork a professional woman—and then turn on her. Also, if a woman professional has learned how to mask her emotions and keep her needs to herself, she might find it demoralizing, threatening, to work with or for such an emotionally needy woman.

Denise is a fifty-five-year-old psychiatrist who has sometimes consulted with me. She says, "I have learned that it is crucial for me to set limits with my female staff and female colleagues. Just because I am a good listener does not mean that I can listen to everybody." These days Denise quickly introduces the issues of boundaries and limits. Especially with her incest patients.

> From 1985 on, this specific group of patients demanded my home number, and expected me to be available to them around the clock. The guilt-tripping was incredible. "My mother looked the other way, now you have to make up for that. And if you don't, you're the bad mommy."

Denise now tells each such patient, "I am not your mother. I cannot be available in an open-ended way. I can *work* well with you. But no more than that. If they want to work with me, they get the message."

For such reasons, some women still prefer to work with men. Men are less emotionally complicated. What you see is what you get, warts and all. Jaime, a thirty-eight-year-old lesbian co-mother and a carpenter says,

> With men I know where I stand, with women I never do. They're so indirect. One minute they're kind, the next they're cruel. And all that emotional garbage. It's hard to get respect from women. My female bosses never said "bad work" or "good work." Their evaluations of my work were always so indirect.

I looked for validation from women bosses. I got invalidated. My male boss only says "good" or "bad." That's all I need.

Some women are disconcerted by how much (other) women still remain oriented to male but not female power; perhaps they find it easier to reject sexism in other women than to change it within themselves. For example, Stacey, a forty-six-year-old office manager, reports having experienced many difficulties in this area with her women subordinates. She tells me,

I was supervising fifty women secretaries and clerical workers. I tried to instill some pride into these employees. I encouraged them to return to school. I told them to consider moving up in the company. I said, "You don't need to be taken out for lunch on Secretary's Day, this company would collapse without you." There was nearly a mutiny over that. They wanted more than a free lunch. They wanted the general manager's fatherly attention, once a year. Some were very ingratiating to him in devious ways. But they resented me. Not only was I their boss, I also got to spend a lot of time with the general manager. They hated me because they knew I discussed them with him. But this was part of my job description.

Stacey fairly bridled with pride over her daily intimacy with a man whom her female subordinates could only interact with once a year. Had I mentioned this to her, she probably would have been surprised, or denied it entirely.

Janet is a forty-year-old matrimonial lawyer. She reports similar difficulties with female subordinates and clients.

As a divorce lawyer, I have trouble with *all* my clients, but especially with my female clients. Many of my women clients think that paying a lawyer entitles them to win everything. They don't understand that paying only allows them to fight, and that it's no guarantee of winning, or of winning 100%.

Janet's male clients understand this. They are also used to battling for money and tend not to personalize a battle for money the way many women do.

Men are more up-front about money, more assured about discussing it. They propose various payment plans with me. It's a new millennium, and women are still running around hysterically, throwing themselves on my mercy, feeling cheated. My women clients experience the economic realities of being divorced as unfair punishment. They're right, but they put themselves into male hands. Now they expect me, another woman, to rescue them, and when I do, they are angry that they have to pay for my services. They think that because I'm a woman, I should "understand" their situation.

Sixty-six-year-old Ilona says of a politician she once worked for,

> This woman drove herself. Her staff loved her. But none of us could handle how she verbally abused all her aides, the women and the men. Sometimes, in sheer frustration, she would also hit one of us. She never said she was sorry. We were the ones who went around feeling embarrassed. This high-powered woman also expected us to work 'round the clock but she never said thank you. She was always in a bad mood. I know that male politicians act this way too but experiencing a woman as no better is what drove me out of politics.

Ilona is right—and yet, this is another example of women holding other women to different and higher standards than the standards they use for men. Also, as I've noted, women often have unacknowledged and unrealistic expectations about how a woman professional is supposed to behave. Finally, women are so used to having their own boundaries routinely violated at home both by men and by other women that they often repeat such invasive behavior in business and professional relationships. Women are not always aware that they are doing so. In business, male professionals often know how to set limits without personalizing the process. This is harder for women to do. I have observed women at work treating each other as if they were also each others' mothers, sisters, or best friends. And, as discussed, many women still (unconsciously) experience themselves in the resentful, one-down daughter position, no matter what their objective position at work might be.

Some women professionals are women-haters. Madeline, a thirty-six-year-old social worker, described a horrifying encounter with a "macho" woman gynecologist.

> I never had any trouble with my male gynecologist but when he retired, I decided I wanted to see a woman. It turned out to be the worst gynecological encounter of my life. This woman postured, paced, staked out her territory, talked at great length about how much money she had. Her manner was cutting, abrupt, superior. I was there for a routine check-up and Pap smear. Suddenly, as she was examining me, I began to cramp up, as if I was undergoing a surgical procedure. I was. This woman had decided that I needed a uterine biopsy and simply performed one. Without telling me. When I protested the pain, she said: "You're a big girl, you can take it." I was in such bad shape that I had to have my husband leave work to take me home. I will never see a woman doctor again.

Of course, had Madeline seen a sadistic, male physician, she might not have drawn the same sweeping conclusions about an entire gender.

Bobbi and Gloria, my interviewees, are lawyers with whom I have worked. Bobbi, forty-seven, practices law in Chicago. Gloria, fifty-four, has an office in Manhattan. Although they specialize in very different areas, both have similar struggles with their female clients.

> Bobbi: I have always prided myself on being able to win the hardest of cases. What I can't do is take my clients' every phone call, or listen to their psychological problems. I would rather focus on winning a woman's case—I'm a lawyer, not a shrink. But my women clients seem to want a shrink. Often, given what they're going through at the hands of insurance companies and the medical establishment, they're entitled to freak out. But not at me. I can't help them in this area. I've begun to ask all my female clients to see a shrink, just to keep their anxiety level down so they won't sabotage their own case.

> Gloria: When a woman gets to me, she's probably already burned out by abusive or incompetent male lawyers on top of an abusive husband. Then, she turns around and treats me abusively, something she

never dared do to any of her male lawyers or to her husband. Does she think I am not as skilled, even more skilled than my male opponents? Does she think that a woman's labor is not as valuable as a man's?

Gloria's female (but not her male) clients routinely declare bankruptcy in order not to have to pay her. Some threaten to sue her for malpractice as a way of punishing Gloria for wanting to be paid. She concludes:

> Only a handful of my women clients have ever bothered to thank me for getting them custody or child support. But most women don't. From their point of view, hey, they're facing reduced circumstances, aging, child-care burdens—or a life without their children, and here I am with my bill.

In order to please others at work, a woman professional must not only offer suggestions instead of issuing direct commands; she must also act in warm and encouraging ways. For years, women have been recognized as excellent middle managers because they *do* know how to do this. However, those who don't (or won't), are often feared and disliked.

A highly competent professor might be disliked by her female students because she refuses to play Mommy. Such a professor might resist behaving in maternal ways either because mothers are so devalued by culture or because her male counterparts—who set the standards—rarely treat students in maternal ways. In addition, such a professor might also want to model high *intellectual* standards as the best way to nourish her students. Fifty-one-year-old Penelope teaches metaphysical poetry. She says,

> I do not approve of what some of my colleagues do in order to cultivate a student following. One woman creates cults around herself. She mothers her students. She does not teach them. I want to model intellectual daring for my female students. They are used to this from a male professor, but are far more resistant to it from a female professor.

Penelope notes that most of her male students love her classes.

> There are some exceptions, but most of my female students think I'm cold, heartless, selfish, and obsessed with my subject. They might admire these same traits in a male professor. They fear it in me. Their loss. But mine too.

Fifty-four-year-old Danielle runs a chain of abortion clinics. She is intensely dedicated and tireless. From time to time, Danielle calls me to "vent."

So many of my female employees are incompetent and very thin-skinned. Last week, we were dealing with a municipal workers' strike. I had to be sure that the women whose late-term procedures we began on Day One absolutely had a way of returning to us on Day Two, even if it meant renting a bus for them.

When Danielle asked one of the new nurses to tell her what plans had been made, there was dead silence for fifteen seconds.

So then I said: "Call me back once you have the arrangements in place." That was it. I probably sounded frustrated and annoyed. That did it. This woman began telling people that I'd chewed her out. Then, she did not come to our office Christmas party because, she said, I'd been too obnoxious to her on the phone.

Many feminists of my generation tended to view women as victims. We were not wrong. This was a response to the societal tendency to blame a woman for having provoked her own abuse. Also, most feminists had found that it was too difficult to champion the cause of a less-than-perfect-victim. Rape victims, for example, would not be believed if they were not nuns or virgins. Given the prevailing prejudice, we noted that a man can sin, and sin badly, and still be viewed as worthy of compassion.

Not so a woman. Therefore, many feminists refused to deal with certain wrenching complexities.

A victim of incest, rape, or battery may turn to alcohol or drugs to dull the pain; she may *also* be seriously depressed, paranoid, anxious, or even schizophrenic. I am not saying that such a woman is not worthy of our support (she is) or that she deserves to be punished (she does not). I am saying that those who work on her behalf must become far more realistic. For example, her supporters must understand that, while some victims of violence continue to *feel* that they are still being victimized, in reality they may also be behaving like avenging furies. The "furious victim" may not always remember that she has acted this way. Also, some women have become so hardened by abuse from which they could not escape that they have learned to use force and fear in order to survive or get their way.

Claire, whom I also interviewed, is a forty-six-year-old formerly battered woman who now runs a shelter for battered women.

> I know that part of my job description includes being emotionally overwhelmed at all times. I am used to being verbally and legally attacked by male batterers, and their lawyers, and by various fathers' rights groups.

However, Claire was *not* prepared to deal with verbal and

physical attacks from the women residents. Claire worked hard
to arrange visitation for a battered mother who had been
abusing her three young children. She continues:

> Just because a mother has been beaten and has
> turned to alcohol, does not give her the right to turn
> around and mistreat her own children. They are
> even more vulnerable than she is. One woman was
> paranoid and physically violent. With no warning,
> she hit me. Hard. She didn't stop. She kept cursing
> me too. Her two children witnessed the whole inci-
> dent. This is making me sick. Way more than when
> men have broken into the shelter.

Fifty-four-year-old Vanessa has a similar story. She is a Professor of Social Work.

> A few years ago, I had a very smart, but very dis-
> turbed woman in my clinical social work seminar.
> She introduced herself as an incest survivor whose
> family had tried to institutionalize her. I had no
> reason to doubt her, but she made the same speech
> each time the class met. She demanded that all
> women, starting with the women in my class, with-
> draw from men and refuse to become mothers. If I
> dared to disagree, she would immediately challenge

my feminist credentials. She silenced my other students who, like me, were afraid of her but who also felt sorry for her. In a way, she was acting like her abuser father. Just as he'd hijacked her mental health, she'd hijacked this class and kept us in a state of tension and anxiety.

In the last thirty years, at tremendous cost and despite horrendous opposition, women have brought legal actions against on-the-job economic discrimination and sexual harassment. Sometimes other women have been very supportive of such plaintiffs; often they have not been. In an era of heroic feminist sisterhood, most women, myself included, did not anticipate that any women would continue to disbelieve and sabotage women who alleged workplace sexual harassment or employer-rape.

In 1978, Lin Farley published *Sexual Shakedown: The Sexual Harassment of Women on the Job.* Farley describes a pattern in which female employees either minimized or "laughed about" being touched or propositioned by a male employer. In fact, some women employees seethed with envy when the male harasser chose another woman, not themselves, to harass; such women tended to ostracize any woman who dared complain about what every woman believed she had to accept in order to keep her job. Here is how two of Farley's interviewees described their experiences. Meg (a pseudonym) was then sixteen and working at a hamburger chain:

The next awful thing was that in front of a whole bunch of other women working there he [the general manager] announced in this loud voice that he had this dream that he made love to me. All the other women started snickering. I got the impression they thought I was getting it on with him or something, but to make it worse he kept it up. He would also hang around me and help me do things, which a manager never did. Like he'd help me wrap the hamburgers and he'd stand real close and press against me. I hated it but it made the other women resentful. When I first got the (hourly) raise [25 cents] I was so happy I told everybody, but then all this other shit [the sexual harassment] started and a lot of the women got really burned up. They wouldn't help me any more and it was real uncomfortable. I wanted out real bad but I didn't think I could get another job.

Liza (a pseudonym) and another Farley interviewee, was working as a telephone solicitor for a land-development corporation. She was in her freshman year at Cornell.

When one man forced himself on the pretext of showing me work that in reality needed no explaining, I finally said, "Why don't you knock it off?" The man played dumb, accusing me of an overactive imagination. I backed off, especially since I had seen him doing the same things to the other women. They didn't seem to object; it made me feel crazy. The man continued. One day he slapped [me] on the behind. I just didn't know what to do because I'd told him and he didn't stop, so I just didn't go back. I didn't talk to anybody. All the women were white. They were also older and this was their real job for the rest of their lives, while I was just an outsider. I think now that's why they didn't object, but at the time it just didn't dawn on me. I just thought it was because I was black. I lasted a month.

Thirty-eight-year-old Lurleen, a secretary, brought rape charges against her boss, who was also a leading citizen in a small southern town. Lurleen's life was never the same.

He got off. That wasn't the hard part. The hard part was how the other women began to treat me at work, before the charges became formal. They didn't look me in the eye. They didn't invite me to sit down at their table in the cafeteria anymore. My rapist's mother and wife threatened to blackball me and my children from every club in town if I didn't back down. I refused to back down. My own mother said she wished I hadn't done this. In the end, the rapist kept his reputation and his marriage. I lost my job and could not get another one.

Alice is a fifty-year-old Christian minister who is well known as an innovative preacher. She accepted a congregational position and then discovered that the bishop was having a number of sexual relationships with his female congregants. When she tried to deal with this in a principled way, the women turned on her. She says:

> Now, I understood why my two office assistants felt they could get away with doing extremely incompetent work. They were sleeping with the Bishop. As was the wife of our most powerful male congregant. At the meeting, the wife walked up to the Bishop, slithered her arm around his neck. I knew the meeting was already over. I was fired. I was not allowed to tell the congregation why. I was given no exit interview, I was not allowed to write a letter to the congregation either.

Some women behave in a similar fashion when a woman alleges sexism at work. For example, Darla is a forty-year-old government engineer. She is the only woman at her level. When Darla encountered blatant sexism (non-stop chauvinist jokes were the problem), she sent a letter to the offender informing him that there were "laws barring such behavior."

The agency sent Darla home for two weeks and then hired an outside consultant to investigate the matter. Darla's attempt to defend herself led the other, lower-ranking women in her agency to "persecute" her:

> Three women literally cornered me. One did the taunting. She calls herself "The Mother of You All" because it makes her feel important to make coffee for the guys. She's a secretary. Another woman is an administrator but she does thankless jobs like maintaining the kitchen. She assumes a very controlling attitude. She posts signs telling people to clean up after themselves, she viciously throws away people's food on Friday-clean-the-fridge-day. These two tried to make me feel like I wasn't a real "woman." "There's a way of handling yourself with a man, maybe you should learn how," was their message. A third woman was really a company "man" in skirts whose mandate it was to make sure that there would be no lawsuit. She said I might be "crazy." Their cruelty frightened me. I didn't speak to anyone for several months.

Both Alice and Darla were persecuted or not respected by lower-ranking women who resented and felt threatened by another woman in a position of authority—one who was also trying to change the rules.

I first began doing my interviews for this book in 1981. Pamela, an elected politician, was one of my earliest interviewees. At the time, she was in her early sixties. She described what it was like to run for office in the early 1970s in a district where most women thought of themselves primarily as wives and mothers and resented, disliked, and did not vote for women.

> I was a pioneer. When I began, women were used to emptying the wastepaper baskets and answering the phones. Women wouldn't dare support me publicly, but they did come up to me to whisper: "We hope you win," even though they said they would have to vote as their husbands did. I won. The second time round, the opposition was very clever. They knew they couldn't get me on my record, so they decided to mount a basic character assassination. They used traditional female gossip grapevines to slander me in a way that cannot be combated. "She's a whore, she cheats on her husband, she's a rich bitch." They created an undercurrent. There was no way to confront this and be believed. It was the best way for women to vote "no" to pushy women in politics.

This time when Pamela went from door to door the women would not talk for long nor did they invite her in. They were cold. Pamela felt shunned. She was shocked by how women were willing to believe whatever they were told about another woman. This time Pamela also faced women hecklers in her audiences. She said, "The man I was running against had a wife. She brought her mother to the debates. The two of them started screaming at me: 'You've got a big mouth, your teeth are crooked, your glasses are ugly!' " Pamela lost the election. She adds: "Let me say that the many women who worked with me on my campaigns and who were on my staff were wonderful, completely supportive, a dream."

Nina was also a pioneer political lobbyist. I interviewed her when she was in her seventies. She describes what it was like for her in the 1970s and 1980s to work as the paid executive director for a Jewish organization which was, essentially, run by wife-volunteers:

> I was always the "first woman." Men helped me and mentored me. Men recognized my talents and groomed me. I always felt that competing with women was like shooting fish in a barrel. If you couldn't win competing with men, then what had you won? I thought it might be wonderful to work with women. I wanted to turn this organization into the equal of any men's organization. The wives would not let me do it, it was sand in their teeth. They did not want me to act as if I were the equal of a man because they were not. In the world of Jewish men's organizations, bullies and egomaniacs cer-

tainly exist, but there's also a level of kindness that doesn't exist among women. Men laugh themselves silly. Not these women. The wives undermine each other. They insult each other. They turn on each other. One of their own had her husband leave her. Suddenly, the others were saying "Oh, she was always too abrasive."

All-female Christian volunteer groups are not necessarily any kinder to women. Megan is a thirty-five-year-old nurse (a professional) who works in a facility which is run by nuns (the volunteer "wives") and controlled by the Catholic Church.

We're mostly Catholic girls but the nuns treat us like dirt. Our nursing supervisors are nuns. Most of them yell at us all the time. They think we should be married with six children but if we are, they don't like it that we're working. If you are married and have no children, the nuns never stop asking, "What's wrong with you, are you sterile?" Some of the Sisters are more hostile than others and some are just crazy. A typical staff meeting goes like this: Sister John hands a medical form to Sister Margaret to pass on to me but Sister Margaret ignores me when I ask for it. She hides it in her habit and says she can't find it, don't I already have it? One of the other nurses hates me. I asked her why. She said that I was the Mother Superior's pet. "Don't you remember how Mother put her arm around you at the Christmas party and said: 'This one is my favorite.' "

As among men, power struggles among female peers can be very fierce. I was recently on a women's studies plenary panel with two other women speakers and a woman moderator. It was a very hot day. I was suffering from a relapse of Lyme's Disease and was on antibiotics and feeling fragile. The panel was set up in a school gymnasium on a narrow, high platform. I was the second speaker. When I had finished speaking, I nearly fell off the platform onto the floor below, but, luckily, I fell on the platform. I saw stars and thought I was going to faint. The moderator, whom I did not know, graciously helped me to get up. She was very solicitous. The woman who had spoken first and whom I had known for many years looked the other way. She had a faint look of disgust and satisfaction on her face. The last speaker almost knocked me down a second time as she dashed past me for her too-limited time at the microphone. These two women do admirable work, but they were unable to act in a civilized manner toward one of their own who had, quite literally, fallen.

Such minor, nasty behavior among women academics is not unusual. (Again, men are no better.) My interviewee, Kay, is the head of her university's social science department. When we spoke, she was in her mid-fifties. She told me:

Forget about academic women helping each other. Some do, but mainly, it's cutthroat. The mediocre female talents hate and resent the more stellar female talents. They gang up on them and do them in. I no longer say I'm a feminist. For the last twenty years, I have seen accomplished and generous women destroyed by other women. The more talented woman may not be a loyal member of whatever "politically correct" clique controls the department. Or she may not be sleeping with the right woman. I have seen lesbians do this to lesbians and to hetero women. I have seen hetero women do this to hetero women and to lesbians. Feminist academics have no true standards, only personal interests. Just like the boys.

In 1999, Jenny Onyx described a similar phenomenon. Onyx was the supervisor on a management project. In the interests of "sisterhood" she relinquished a good deal of her power to four other women, two of whom were life-partners. The project was soon "seriously off the rails." Onyx's skills and supervisory position were increasingly "trivialized" and "marginalized" by the other women. Onyx withdrew. Without her "support and energy, the project collapsed within the year." Onyx thereafter "thrived within the bureaucracy." One woman left—but not without "mounting a particularly vicious case against Onyx." A second woman, her partner, never spoke to Onyx again.

> [Among women], power becomes centralized into
> an informal elite or oligarchy. In the absence of
> formal rules or authority a power vacuum is created
> which is filled by those who have the time, energy,
> and skills to act, usually linked by an informal net-
> work based on friendship rather than skill, and with
> no formal accountability. In our case, Barbara [the
> woman who sued Onyx], with her partner, was able
> to form a strong informal pressure group. Within
> the collective, the emotional is as important as the
> rational.

Some women also use the "intimacy card" and informal
emotional networks at work as a way of manipulating, controlling, or paralyzing their potential female opposition. A woman
may hope that by engaging in bonding and intimacy with
female colleagues, she can guarantee that those colleagues will
"watch her back" and not treat her as an enemy. However,
engaging in such intimacy rituals can also blind women. Dawn
is a fifty-six-year-old breast-cancer surgeon. After her husband
left her, she says,

> I was in a terrible state of anxiety. That's when I went
> into practice with Martha. In the beginning, I was
> grateful for her support. Martha offered to "be there"
> for my children when I was working late. She moved
> into the guest cottage so that she could be there when

I was working. It was heaven, or so I thought, for about a year.

Although they were business partners, Martha started competing with Dawn for patients. Long-time patients began to tell Dawn that Martha had approached them, behind Dawn's back, to suggest that she might be a better physician for them. Dawn continues,

> When I finally realized what was happening, I told her that I wanted to split up. Martha refused to move out of the guest cottage for nine months. She insisted that she had the right to continue to relate to my children whether I liked it or not. We stopped speaking. Then, one day, I went up to her at a professional conference. I said, quietly, that matters could not continue, that she had to cut her losses and move on. She took one step back and, at the top of her lungs, began to yell: "This woman is harassing me!" Over and over again.

Many working women long for maternal kindness and attentiveness as much as—perhaps even more than—men do. Like men, women also enjoy being flattered. Perhaps women artists are especially vulnerable. Helene, my interviewee, is a forty-nine-year-old playwright. She related this story:

After a reading of one of my plays, a woman in the audience, Emma, came over and told me that my work had changed her life. She offered to type my manuscripts. I said no. She offered to accompany me to readings. I said no. The second time we met, at another performance, Emma said that she knew a director who might be willing to stage a production of one of my plays, did I want her to pursue this? Of course I did. Before she was done with me, Emma managed to alienate my female agent and had taken her place. As my agent, she managed to destroy my long-time relationship with my female editor. What a fool I was! I thought she was rescuing my career.

Slowly, imperceptibly, people whom Helene had known for years stopped calling, either because they didn't want to deal with Emma or because Emma had somehow managed to turn them against Helene. She continued:

Then, behind my back, Emma started using my contacts to shop a play of her own around! She told my people that my work was not commercial enough, but that her work was. Looking back, I see how hungry I was for this kind of support. I paid a high price. The lasting damage was to my relationships with the people whom she'd turned against me.

There is a certain kind of woman who needs to replace and destroy her envied competitor totally, at home as well as at work. Such a woman needs to force her competitor out of her marriage as well as out of her job. And it doesn't stop there. She, the "winner," also needs to make sure that the "loser" isn't believed when she turns to other women for sympathy or moral support. The winner needs to line up all the support for herself against any allegations of foul play. Becoming intimate with her prey is usually this kind of woman's first step in a hostile takeover campaign. Noel, one of my earliest interviewees, told me the following story. For years, Noel ran a prestigious and well-funded university science department. I interviewed Noel when she was fifty-eight. She says:

> You don't expect women to behave this way. I think betrayals by women have been more significant because I expect this of a man. I do not expect this of a woman. I expect women to be better than that. I expect women to be like I am. My nemesis, Hillary, heard me lecture. She enrolled as my student, then completed her advanced course work elsewhere. Then, one day, Hillary simply dropped in. ("I was in the neighborhood and thought I'd come over.") She disarmed me, totally, by befriending my children. I began to treat her like a relative. Thinking back, it's as if she started to consume me through my children. Today, if a woman would try this again, I'd take

it as a danger signal. It's like being surrounded by an intimate enemy who's gets closer and closer, gets in deeper and deeper, until you trust her—and then she turns on you. I was the last to know.

Hillary applied for a position in Noel's department. She coyly insisted that Noel interview her. Noel hired Hillary. And then, inexplicably, Hillary tried to turn everyone against Noel. Hillary planted doubts, suspicions against Noel among previously friendly colleagues. Hillary would never talk to Noel directly, only indirectly, through others whose minds she was carefully poisoning. For example, Hillary told others that the reason she couldn't talk to Noel directly was because Noel was difficult, that she made her feel too uncomfortable. Hillary began to stop others from coming to Noel directly also. She'd say: "Poor Noel is working so hard, she has enough on her mind. Tell me what the problem is." People believed Hillary since they perceived the two woman as being very close. Slowly, Hillary began to destroy Noel's peace of mind. She would lobby against Noel's proposals before department meetings. According to Noel, Hillary "literally never agreed with anything I said and she could never stop resenting my power. She could have supported me, and I would have given up the world to her." When it became clear that she couldn't destroy Noel, Hillary resigned. Noel says,

But that wasn't enough for her. She literally called everyone in my department and tried to get them to resign too. This was her last-ditch effort to pull the whole house of cards down. You must understand that I knew nothing while this was happening. I first heard about this when a *male* colleague, a subordinate, called me after Hillary had leaned on him to resign. None of my women colleagues or subordinates called me to tell me what was going on. Years later, one woman, Blanche, admitted that Hillary had convinced her that I thought very little of Blanche, so she didn't feel confident enough to approach me herself.

In Noel's opinion, what Hillary did had to be a conscious strategy of manipulation and conniving. Although Noel survived and prospered, she was also devastated and suffered a major depression. She says: "Hillary had presented herself as my friend. I believed her. I felt betrayed, undone. How could I trust my own judgements, or perception of reality? I am now much more suspicious, much less trusting, less gullible."

Many women professionals resent, envy, fear, and disapprove of any woman who is too direct, too emotional or passionate, too generous. For example, Rachel is a fifty-year-old psychotherapist. She was devastated when her group of women psychotherapists "ex-communicated" her. Rachel has been working in near-isolation ever since.

For years, I belonged to a group of mental health

care professionals: psychiatrists, psychologists, social workers, grassroots counselors. We met once a month. It cut the isolation we each experienced in full-time practice. Everyone defined herself as progressive, political, and, to varying degrees, as feminist. We discussed our cases and our lives. We brought food. It was a combination of peer group supervision, consciousness-raising, and a woman's support group.

One of Rachel's patients was a battered wife. Her batterer had stalked her when she was in a shelter. Then he stalked her in her new and (she thought) secret apartment. One night he'd appeared and threatened her on her street corner. Later that night, he broke in and beat her up, badly. The woman was hysterical. Rachel continues:

I turned to my group, not just for advice but for tangible support. I pleaded with them to help me help her. Did someone have access to a house or an apartment in another part of town, or in the country? Did anyone have influence over the D.A.? Who knew a super-competent lawyer who might represent this woman for no fee? I know I was asking for a lot, but my parents are both Holocaust survivors. Rescue is not just a word in a book to me.

According to Rachel, the group turned on her. Group members said she was "inappropriate," too needy, too pushy, that she "needed to work on herself." Rachel admits: "Maybe I am dramatic and overly emotional. Maybe I did put them on the spot. Maybe they didn't like what they saw about themselves. But they criticized me, not themselves." And then Rachel suddenly realized that she was the only Jew in the group. And that she was probably the only one who had to work for money. The other women had wealthy husbands or lived on an inheritance. Rachel felt she had no alternative but to leave. The group subsequently bad-mouthed her in the community. Rachel was devastated. She did not have the stomach to form a new group.

> For years, I could never even talk about this, except to my husband. I don't really have a name for what happened. One day, you think you're part of a community, the next moment, you're all alone, no one you used to know looks you in the eye, no one says anything specific, but you just never see anyone again. It's like having your entire family get wiped out, only they're still alive, and seeing each other. You're the one who's really been wiped out.

9.

WOMEN IN GROUPS

Some say that traditional, patriarchal women are at their best in groups. To some extent, this is true. Small groups of women as well as larger all-female auxiliaries work together as volunteers in cultural and religious institutions, in hospitals and in soup kitchens, and collect food and money for the poor. In so doing, women also uphold (an unjust) status quo—for which they receive important secondary benefits, such as each other's social companionship, relief from boredom, and the opportunity to participate in significant work. Women volunteers also achieve social standing without having to meet objective professional standards and without having to compete against each other—or against men—professionally. Women of all classes and races have excelled at such affiliative and compassionate volunteer work.

Historically, women have worked together in groups to feed,

nurse, house, and petition for the release of men and children, endeavors otherwise known as "humanitarian." Some all-female groups have also worked for women's causes, such as obtaining female suffrage, literacy, higher education, and asylum from pimps, violent husbands, employers, and state jailors, for maternal health care, and for wage increases and improved working conditions on the all-female assembly line.

Historically, women-only groups have organized food, rent, and trade-union strikes and participated in patriotic, fascistic, racist, anti-racist, nationalist, internationalist, colonialist, anti-colonialist, capitalist, socialist, communist, democratic, and totalitarian movements and regimes. Women have also worked on many single-issue campaigns such as Mothers Against Drunk Driving, The Mothers of the Plaza de Mayo, Women's Strike for Peace, and Women of Greenham Common.

Since men have refused to admit women into what were, until recently, virtually all-male work and play forces, women had no choice but to work separately and mainly with each other. Women also *fight* to work mainly with other women; in some ways it was easier.

To some extent, this is still true. Most men are still not comfortable taking orders from women, who in turn feel more comfortable, even safer, asserting both direct and indirect authority over other women than over non-intimate males. Women also enjoy working with others who communicate in complex, sensitive, expressive ways and who can approximate or improve upon family-like female intimacy.

Clearly, women *as women* do not naturally gravitate toward one political viewpoint over any other. But, once one woman stands up to be counted, she has the psychological and social power to attract at least one other woman into a working dyad. Once a small clique of women decides on a project, it too has the power to attract other women who may be as drawn toward the magnetic possibility of affiliation with other women as toward any particular social or political goal. This constitutes a great social-emotional power and skill, which women may use for altruistic or for selfish purposes.

Feminist scholar and activist Janice Raymond has written about the attractions of all-female convent life for European women of all classes. In her view,

> The convent also was one of the few female institutions in which older women became tutors and out-of-the-ordinary mentors for younger women who were drawn to their companionship . . . The presence of women for each other, committed to the same tasks and legitimated by godly motives, created a rich community life . . . Nuns saw themselves as able to change the world, as having a spiritual, social, and intellectual mission to the secular world . . . It helped them to engage in a battle that few women had fought—the battle for souls.

Nevertheless, convent life is not ideal. Raymond remembers being censured as a nun for "forming particular friendships":

One of our peers, who evidently saw us engaged in this rather innocuous act of [holding hands], felt it her spiritual duty to report us. That evening, in the refectory, we were both publicly chastised and berated for endangering these rare days of freedom for the rest of our sisters because we had passed the boundaries of permissibility. In private, after the public exposure, my companion was browbeaten by the novice mistress into "confessing" her "illicit affection" for me. The novice mistress attempted to elicit a similar confession from me, but I was not to be intimidated by her representation of our holding hands as simulating intercourse! My friend, who was traumatized by the censuring and the innuendos of abnormality . . . left the community a year later.

Raymond also discusses Chinese "marriage resister" women who lived together in supportive and powerful communities. Like nuns, such women tended to be more literate, occupationally skilled, and less lonely than married mothers, who suffered the domination of their mothers-in-law and rivalries with co-wives and concubines.

Until recently the traditional work done by women in groups may not have been viewed as important enough to study. Psychologist Paula Caplan noted that

The phrase "group of women" has until recently tended to elicit images that trivialized women, such

as "hen parties," bridge clubs, the Junior League.
Notable exceptions were volunteer organizations,
the goals of which were usually to help either men or
other people regardless of sex. What was missing was
a strong, respected image of women coming together
in groups to help themselves and each other.

Second Wave feminist scholars have discovered, however, that
women historically, have enjoyed strong bonds, which enabled
them to engage in world-changing work.[1] These researchers
discovered that socialist and lesbian friendship networks also
made it possible for women of different classes to work
together on behalf of women's education and in settlement
houses and labor movements on behalf of immigrant and
working poor women. Literature and Women's Studies professor Ann Snitow, in "A Gender Diary," writes eloquently
about contemporary feminist "individualist" longings for "community" which such scholarship may have satisfied:

> We sometimes long for the community the women
> we were studying took more for granted, although
> we couldn't help remarking on the ways those sus-
> taining communities—say of union workers, or peas-
> ants, or ghettoized racial groups—used women's
> energy, loyalty, and passion as by right, while usually
> denying them a say in the group's public life, its his-
> torical consciousness.

Interestingly, historian Sheila Rowbotham notes that many nineteenth-century European women's strikes were leaderless. She believes that the "intense personal struggle to escape from male authority" made many women suspicious of any authority, but also rendered them passive and dependent once authority was asserted, even by another woman. For example, in Rowbotham's view, the spectacular British suffragist Sylvia Pankhurst often eclipsed other women. Pankhurst

> was in the ridiculous position of instructing [other women] not to depend on her. When they were going on a demonstration to Trafalgar Square she said, "I am going with you. I want you not to cling round me, but to do your own business . . . I am certain that the more there are of us, the more difficult it will be for our opponents."

Although we may be hungry for examples of women's noble collective actions, we must be careful not to (unthinkingly) idealize *all* women, who, like men, may function in groups in ignoble ways as well. What do we know about how twentieth-century women function in mixed-gender and in female-only groups?

According to Minnesota psychiatrist Pearl Rosenberg, both male and female leaders exhibit subtle gender-related behavior in groups. Rosenberg notes that, like men, women leaders maintain greater eye contact with men than with women; tend to be more supportive and to give more positive responses to the comments of male group members than to the comments of female members; seem to pay more attention or listen more thoughtfully to a male speaker than to a female speaker; and seem to give men more detailed and more careful instructions about what is to occur than they give women. In addition, both male and female leaders appear to call men by their names more frequently than they do women and seem to support men's suggestions for changing the trend of the group discussion more often than they support women's suggestions.

Thus, women in a mixed-gender group cannot expect special or even equal treatment from either male or female leaders. What do we know about female dynamics in female-only groups? Although it is true that women in group *therapy* groups may represent a different population than women in other kinds of groups, we may also learn a great deal about how women interact in groups in general by understanding how they interact under such controlled circumstances.

For example, according to Canadian psychotherapist Lilly J. Schubert Walker, all-female therapy groups are different from mixed-gender therapy groups. All-female groups are, at least initially, more affiliative, less competitive, and more verbally and emotionally active.

In female groups, women talk more freely, more frequently, and more intimately. Mixed groups focus

on the development of male-female relationships by
discussing and resolving interpersonal issues and
conflicts; female groups emphasize the development
of trusting, caring, close female relationships by
encouraging the sharing of intra-personal issues.
The initial trust-building stage evolves more slowly
in a mixed group and appears to be more quickly
attained in a female group.

Nonetheless, women may also use the power of a group to
control, humiliate, or eject its members, as well as those whom
they do not accept as members.

In her novel *The Group*, Mary McCarthy paints a savage portrait of an intimate group of mainly upper-class American college women in the 1930s. These women are snobbish, selfish,
and cruel. They allow Kay, who hails from more humble begin-
nings, to count herself as one of them. Ultimately, Kay has a
nervous breakdown and kills herself. This was not entirely an
accidental death. Norine, a member of the group, had been
having an affair with Kay's husband, Harold; some members of
the group knew about it.

McCarthy's women are easily bored and sexually adven-
turous. Norine justifies her affair with Harold this way: she has
always felt sexually deprived, and she has envied the group in
general and Kay in particular for their "sexual superiority." Perhaps the group members feel entitled to help themselves to
anything that belongs to another woman, especially one of a

poorer class; perhaps they feel that *telling* Kay about Harold's philandering would harm Kay but their voyeuristic, complicit silence will not. The idea of siding with Kay against her philandering husband or exposing Norine's disloyalty does not occur to anyone.

I am not sure how much has changed since McCarthy's day. When a group of women betrays or colludes in the betrayal of an individual group member, there is really no higher authority to stop them, no legal or religious council who can rule on the matter in a binding way. This is a no-man's land, where anything goes. (Things can get just as wild in all-male groups.)

According to one of my interviewees, seventy-three-year-old Nina, who had been employed as one of three professionals in a Jewish organization, the wife-volunteers were always squabbling and "treating each other badly." Nina found a basic, bottomless envy (and powerlessness) among the volunteer-wives. They had never worked for a living. They felt threatened by any woman who had—or could. Wife-volunteers often acted as if they were superior to the hired help, but their need for nonstop "honor and credit and ego-massage" suggests an enormous economic and psychological insecurity. When Nina successfully represented the organization in public, the wife-volunteers experienced Nina's success as a

> real slap in the face to them. They do not like to give
> any woman credit. Each of these volunteers knows

that she couldn't keep herself in pantyhose much less ultrasuede alone. Men don't behave this way because being a volunteer is not the be-all and end-all of their existence.

Frustrated, belittled, outraged, heartbroken, Nina quit.

On the other hand, many women respect and depend upon their all-female groups and try to act in kind and responsible ways. They cherish the social skills involved in not offending another group member. Emilia (another interviewee) is one such woman. She is in her early seventies and is an experienced club woman. Emilia cautions me:

> You have to be careful what you say and how you say it. Women can be so sensitive, and you do want to bring them along. You don't want to frighten them off. You want them to get along with each other, help each other out, get the tasks accomplished. This requires patience, gentleness, a measured approach. We succeed. Each year, we bring in money for good causes. I think all the women appreciate each other.

Brittany, whom I also interviewed, agrees. Brittany is in her late fifties. She is a wife, a mother, and the owner of a clothing shop. She says:

> I love our professional women's club. Everyone is on

her best behavior. No one wants to hurt anyone. You can't afford to risk offending someone with whom you might do a healthy business or whose family is well established. There is too much to lose. None of us take kindly to fits of temper or bouts of despair. Some things are to be kept private. We try and put our best faces on for each other.

Both Emilia and Brittany have lived in the same city all their lives. Their social relationships are long-term and based on business and family-related hierarchies. Both women understand that "people" resources are finite. Women like Emilia and Brittany know that they are not supposed to confront each other or to fight with each other in direct ways because this would endanger the status quo. In contrast, many younger, professionally mobile women in large cities have no problem with burning their "people" bridges behind them on their way up. Such women function in increasingly successful ways in a man's world and have adopted some male-like styles. For example, Blythe is the forty-eight-year-old president of a publishing house. She says:

If I see someone I'm attracted to or a job I want, I tend to go right up, directly, and say that I'm interested. Some women still have a hard time with this. I get funny looks. Other women experience me as ruthless, selfish. They feel they must attack or destroy me for putting my desires right out there. I hate women who can't say what they mean. This is why men see us as sneaky. Out with it! That's my motto.

Other, younger women tend to agree. Avery is twenty. She describes how another young woman behaved when she attempted to join Avery's sorority:

The girl didn't have the guts to approach us all together and ask outright. Instead, she started lobbying us, one by one, driving each one of us crazy, making each of us feel guilty if we decided to reject her. Pretty soon, this girl's indirect, manipulative, but non-stop approach had us all acting indirectly. With each other. About her. Her persistence made us feel helpless, or powerless to reject her. Like we'd ruin her life or something.

As the member of an all-female group, a woman might experience her own inclination toward dyadic primacy or toward a small clique over loyalty to the whole group as a permanent source of tension. She may also be ambivalent about admitting how important an all-female group is to her, given that her primary loyalty is supposed to be toward her husband (or spouse), children, and parents.

We have discussed how women unconsciously tend to treat

other women as potential mothers. According to Argentinian-American born, Michigan-based psychiatrist Teresa Bernardez, women in groups similarly tend to project their longings for a Good Mother and their fears of a Vengeful, Withholding Mother onto an entire all-female group or onto a group's female leaders. In addition, any expression of anger or the introduction of any tabooed subject may result in the group's scapegoating of one or two of its members. In her article, "Conflicts with Anger and Power in Women's Groups," Bernardez observes:

> Women in groups tend to scapegoat one or two group members as a way of refusing to acknowledge unacceptable, dangerous feelings. The scapegoats become the sacrifices for each and every member of the group who support each other in a collective refusal to acknowledge one's own shadow side, risk anger, or take power.

We may recall to what lengths young girls will go to suppress conflict, difference, and direct expressions of anger in order to remain connected. According to Bernardez, women in groups also self-censor and expect others to express "dissatisfaction without angry affect." A woman's expression of anger is often experienced by other group members as an attack and as justification enough "to reject the angry communication" without "evaluating the complaint on its merits." Rather than acknowledge her own (forbidden) anger, unrealistic expectations, or other powerful emotions, each group member might instead begin to

> experience the group as "noxious," unpleasant, ungiving . . . as if it were an entity or person with the undesirable attributes of an unloving and critical mother; it is somewhat safer to express anger against such a collective entity, since it is neither the therapist nor the members individually who are recognized as objectionable . . . Scapegoating is the end result of an assault on the woman who is most likely to expose the group's timidity or to raise the dangerous conflict to the forefront before the group is ready to deal with it.

In addition to avoiding the expression of anything in an angry manner, women's groups tend to repress and deny knowledge of prejudices whether their own or those of other members. In Bernardez's view, this is partly because women want to accept everyone. Bernardez has found that African-American, Hispanic-American, and white-American women have to first test their anger on "less conflicted grounds" before the group can "advance to the exploration of prejudice." Thus, a member who "takes this issue upon herself before the group is ready runs the risk of being ostracized by black and white alike."

Whatever the provocative or admirable characteristics of the scapegoat, whether she is taking a victim's stance or the tack of courageously exposing the group's denial, the fundamental unconscious agreement of the group is to eliminate, silence, and punish the person who presents the unpalatable truth. In their punitiveness, the members may behave precisely in the fashion they criticize in the scapegoat, all the while feeling supported by other members and by their sense of outrage.

Many women bring a dyadic emotionality into groups. Unless a woman is a loner, an athlete, or socially eccentric, she is not comfortable entering a group alone; most women prefer to enter at the request of a sponsoring member or with a best friend in tow—protection against being gossiped against or rejected. In addition, women in groups approach each other indirectly, in order to maintain non-offending connections.

Some women dislike another woman's indirect and manipulative style; some admire it. For example, Vivian, a forty-four-year-old corporate manager, detests her friend Nikki's social management style. Vivian told me:

Aside from my mother, Nikki is the single most manipulative woman I've ever known in my life. But, unlike me, she gets along with everyone. Nikki told me that "that's the way you get things done." I replied that there are "incompetent women in our school volunteer group who should be told so outright. Instead, you leave them out of the schedule. You placate them. You give them minor jobs. You do their work for them rather than tell them straight up." Instead of arguing, however, Nikki responded "Yes, that's right. I do." What bothers me is that she acts like she's everyone's friend when she really isn't.

Historically, women have expected to compete directly against each other only in women-only areas, that is, in contests involving their dogs, cats, horses, flowers, cooking, swimsuit appearances, or in terms of fertility. Today, in contrast, an increasing number of women expect to compete against each other directly as professionals. Some women are very good at this. But many women are still uncomfortable in doing so because—at least on an unconscious level—they still feel that they are supposed to compete with other women only *through* and on *behalf of* others: their family, religion, or social class. Not on their own behalf.

For example, many women compete against each other with a vengeance through their children. For a certain kind of woman, her children are statements about who she is, proof of her ability to mold living beings according to her will. Of course, such mothers would argue that they are doing this with their children's futures in mind. And that is also true. As mothers, women can be quite aggressive on behalf of their children. For example, the headmistress of Spence, a private school in New York, as quoted in the *New York Times*, described how parents

> lobbied for their seven-year-olds to be assigned to classes with children who weren't their friends but whose parents were rich and prominent—in the hopes that the children would become friends and so would the parents . . . Mothers would be upset because they weren't put on a committee with someone who would give them that social leg up . . . mothers would throw a hissy fit.[2]

My interviewee Dominique is twenty-nine. With barely contained anger, she describes her perfectionist, social-climbing mother.

> We were three girls. We were not allowed to fail our mother by ever failing in school or by having less-than-appropriate friends. We had to have perfect manners. We were expected to succeed. We did. It was unthinkable not to. If Mom thought any one of us was doing anything "inappropriate," our perfectly composed mother would get very quiet, then start screaming at the top of her voice. She'd say terrible

things. Sometimes, she'd faint. The contrast between her enormous composure and her screaming or playing dead was frightening. When we were little, mom would show us off. "Show uncle Harry your riding trophy." Now that we have children of our own, nothing's changed. She shows off our children as if they were her productions too.

Women group members sometimes display this same vicarious/aggressive out-of-control maternalism in areas that have nothing to do with children. Thus, many women feel entitled to vigorously and aggressively protect the "weak" woman with whom they (secretly) identify. The protector woman's passion will be blind, all-consuming, righteous, fierce, because she is not aware that she is really fighting for herself (that is taboo). She is fighting for someone else; her crusade is altruistic.

Bernardez describes a similar kind of unconscious altruism or maternalism among women in therapy groups. Rather than acknowledge their own ambition or anger, group members might project it onto two members who are "chosen" to act out the conflict. The others

> may watch, take sides in relative safety, and contain the dispute, since this strategy may allow the group to protect the "combatants" . . . (The group has) successfully split off their anger onto the protagonists, and now they anxiously await the outcome, moralize

about it, protect or chastise the protagonists, and attempt to help the participants resolve their differences as if the problem existed only between the two of them. This configuration is particularly appealing to women who have a stake in resolving conflict in amiable terms and who have constructed their self-identity predominantly through being helpful to others.

Many women have learned how to appease and benefit from male intimates who are raging, exploitative, and selfish, or they may often adopt a similar bottoms-up (and primate-like) appeasement technique toward a raging and exploitative woman. This is a form of deluded female machismo. Appeasing women feel that they are in control because their exploiters need them; a woman who is needed has a "position." She's been hired. Thus, such women tend to reflexively protect a woman bully or con artist, as if she were both husband and child.

The maternalizing woman focuses on the bully's presumed fragility. This makes the maternal protector feel stronger than the terrorizing bully—as well as safe from her rage. The same woman who might distrust or disapprove of a competent woman's authority might protect an incompetent woman with whom she unconsciously identifies. For example, Alyssa is a forty-five-year-old syndicated columnist whom I interviewed. She tells me that she had once belonged to a group of women who put up with a very abusive and demanding woman just because she and her husband were famous. This woman used everyone. She had us grocery-shop for her, pick up her clothes from the cleaners, baby-sit her animals, invite celebrity guests to parties to which we were not invited. Even though she was exploiting all of us, people talked about her as a helpless invalid who needed our support. I withdrew from the group. The Queen Bee was furious. She told me, and everyone else, that I was a "bad" person. I don't know what she said but it was years before anyone in that group ever called me again. They treated her as if she really was their queen and I was the disloyal deserter.

Julia (whom I also interviewed) is a fifty-year-old architect. She provides another example of how female group members often identify with and aggressively protect the exploiter-as-wounded-victim.

Whenever I would get into a power struggle with Ellen, another member of our group, Rhea, would aggressively insert herself right into the middle of what was a dialogue and turn it into a trialogue. For example, Ellen constantly tried to take all the credit for our successful benefits by minimizing the efforts of the other three women who really did the work.

When I dared to say so, Rhea told me to stop, because this annual benefit was "all" poor Ellen had to hang onto. Rhea felt threatened whenever anyone blew the whistle on any immoral behavior among intimates. Rhea usually sided with whomever she perceived as having done something hurtful. She seemed afraid of Ellen's capacity to shut Rhea out too. Rhea protected Ellen because she saw Ellen as both "fragile" and as a core member. Rhea's mission was to keep the dysfunctional group together.

This identification with and maternalistic protection of the victim-abuser occurs among lesbians too. Kerry Lobel found that individual lesbians, as well as lesbian communities, have tended to side with the lesbian batterer, not with her victim, especially if the batterer is, herself, an incest victim or the child of alcoholic parents. Donna Cecere describes her experience of being battered by a female lover.

The discomfort and anger experienced by the [lesbian] community [about lesbian battering] has, at times, been leveled against the victim. I was as guilty of this form of denial as anyone . . . some dykes tried to explain away [my being battered] by pointing out all the "stress factors" in my relationship. There was an age difference. We were [from] different racial

and class backgrounds . . . perhaps we were unconsciously acting out "roles" . . . my ex's previous lover,
seeking shelter one night, afraid for her life, was
turned away, ironically, by the same institution that
later employed my ex as a counselor while she was
abusing me.

In 1999, Erica Marlowe (a pseudonym) published a piece in
an academic journal about what happened when she was raped
by another lesbian.

I told my lover what had happened and she accused
me of cheating on her and asked why I wasn't worried about bringing AIDS into the relationship.
After that I said nothing. [According to myth],
women don't rape other women. [Therefore], I was
not raped. I must have wanted it. I could see how
manic my rapist was; I should have protected myself
. . . the books on trauma still call the rapist "he" and
the victim "she" . . . We do not pay sufficient attention to the fact that two percent of us (are) attacked
by women. We want things to be simple. We want to
declare one side the perpetrator, the oppressor, the
other side the victim, the oppressed . . . It takes
courage to admit that as women we have power, and
as women we abuse it, deny it and lie about its consequences.

In a paper on domestic violence in same-sex relationships, Celia B. Dutton-Greene found that between seventeen and fifty-two percent of lesbians report having been abused by a partner. Fifty-seven percent experienced sexual victimization, forty-five percent reported physical aggression, and sixty-five percent experienced verbal/emotional aggression. Verbal threats were the most common form of psychological abuse. Partner pushing, grabbing, shoving, throwing things, and slapping were the most common forms of physical abuse. According to Dutton-Greene,

> The reality of lesbian battering challenges the idea that lesbian relationships are more peaceful, non-violent, and egalitarian than heterosexual relationships. Those within the community may be reluctant to provide more ammunition for the homophobic majority to use against them for oppressive purposes. A victim may also be reluctant to betray the lesbian and/or gay community which is already under attack. Victims might also lose much needed support if alienated from their community for publicly acknowledging the abuse.

Barbara is fifty-six and unemployed. When she heard what I was writing about, she asked me to interview her about the years she had spent in a group of straight and gay women. She told me:

I loved the woman whose idea it was to bring us together. We all did. It meant a lot to women to be able to say that they knew or had spent time with this woman artist who was something of a local celebrity. I guess it meant a lot to me too.

Barbara suffered as a result of the difference between her own idealistic expectations and her lived experience. She says that her "hero bullied and yelled at us." Admiration, bordering on adoration, coupled with fear and the need to remain connected made it impossible for most of the involved women ever to confront this hero-as-bully. Barbara concludes:

> They didn't want to admit that reality did not live up to their dreams. Only a few women ever yelled back or walked away. I was one of the few who ever confronted our hero about her bad behavior, but I did so only privately. Most women would put up with her, feed her ego, then use the connection to their own advantage in other social circles.

Like men, women do not want to be held accountable for the consequences of their actions. Men's power often allows them to escape the results of their wrongful actions with impunity and with no loss of honor. Since women are routinely punished for the very things for which men are rewarded and are *not* rewarded for doing what is expected of them as women, what many women do is try not to hold *themselves* accountable for what they do to other women. How? By remaining purposefully unclear about what they are doing—as if not knowing, not owning, and not naming their own unacceptably hurtful behavior means that they haven't done anything bad.

According to Bernardez, in women's therapy groups it is often those women who "appear superficially kind and attentive but who deny their share in the anger of the group" who will have the most difficulty in permitting a candid exploration of dangerous emotion.

> They tend to stop and silence others [with] harsh voices, by appealing prematurely to mutual understanding, respect, and solidarity . . . Without chastising the members who behave in this way and while endorsing their goals as an ideal to be reached eventually, the group therapist must persist in clarifying the fear behind such attempts and in acknowledging how difficult it is to allow a not so perfect expression of forbidden feelings.

Most women have a repertoire of techniques with which to weaken, disorient, humiliate, or banish other female group members. A woman won't often physically knock another woman down. Instead, she might use silence as a way of unnerving or gaslighting her opponent. The gaslighter will refuse to look at the targeted woman when she speaks, will not engage her in dialogue, will not hear what she says. The gaslighter might subtly but continually move to a more favored woman in the group as a way of rendering the targeted woman ultimately invisible—even to herself. The key to the gaslighter's power is the group's unwillingness to name what she is doing or to stop her.

Thirty-six-year-old Carmen, who runs a health club, gave me an example of such gaslighting. She described what happened in a women-only discussion group at her spa:

> Watching these women operate was an eye-opener. When Maggie wanted to get rid of Maria, here is what she did. When Maria spoke, Maggie always looked away. Sometimes, Maggie even began a separate, simultaneous conversation when Maria was speaking. When Maggie did respond to Maria, it was only to criticize her or put her down. Maria would speak and Maggie would go on as if Maria had not spoken.

Such group dynamics are not unusual. Things can really heat up when an entire group, not just one member, wants to punish a woman who has offended a group norm.

I saw this happen once when I attended an invitation-only conference in Europe. Another invitee from a European country was incredibly pompous and self-important. Claude (as I shall call her) insisted on delivering her paper, which had already been translated into English and distributed to us all, in her native language. She demanded—and got—an interpreter who, for forty-five minutes, translated every phrase that Claude herself had just read aloud slowly, in a language that most of us did not understand. The assembled group of female peers got its revenge. For the next two days not one woman spoke to, sat with, walked with, or broke bread with Claude. This happened almost instinctively; it was not premeditated. I took pity on Claude and made it a point to have a meal and take a walk with her. However, Claude seemed oblivious to the group's revenge. It was lost on her. Both Claude's arrogance and the cruelty of the group were upsetting.

In all-female groups, friendly, familiar small talk may also function as a way of minimizing the importance of a women-only gathering. Judy is a twenty-nine-year-old librarian. She joined a woman's book discussion group.

> The one-on-one conversations went on forever, sometimes even after we began to discuss the book. Maybe such "small talk" is a good way of re-establishing our personal connections, but it is also a way of not taking ourselves seriously. It's like nothing that one woman could say was important enough for all the women to hear.

Faith, a fifty-six-year-old financial consultant, has an entirely different perspective on the same phenomenon:

> I was a member of one of the very earliest feminist

consciousness-raising groups. Most of us could not stop ourselves from spending the first half hour in private conversations. It put us at our ease, but it also cut down on the time we would have as a group. Some women tried to pass rules to enforce silence among us until the group discussion began, to ensure that women would not interrupt each other, have private side conversations, or talk for too long. Some women started bringing in stopwatches to time us. Even though we understood the problem, this solution felt awkward and fanatic. Some women tried to force the silent women to speak. Were we wrong! But this took place before we understood that silent women have their own ways of taking over.

Just as women have had to learn how to charm, flatter, seduce, and bond with men, women have also had to learn how to charm, flatter, seduce, and bond with other women. To succeed, a woman does not offer another woman sexual, reproductive or domestic services; what she offers is emotional intimacy and attentive presence, which is experienced as benevolent mothering.

I have seen women form mini-royal courts, even cults, around one woman. The primary goal of such women is to gain status through affiliation with a pretty, popular, well-connected, wealthy, or powerful woman. Unspoken, unacknowledged, is the fantasy that all good (maternal) things will flow from such an affiliation. This is similar to the fantasy that looking good and being seen guarantee that only good things (Prince Charmings) will follow. Women who affiliate by serving and flattering another woman may also envy and resent her. In *The Snow White Syndrome: All about Envy*, California psychotherapist Betsy Cohen notes that

> Another way not to admit your envy is to rush at the person you envy, shouting, "Look how great *you* are!" You idealize the other person and make her more wonderful than she is. If she is so terrific, then she is out of reach of real competition. If you can never match her, if she is "too good to be true" then she is not true, and you can thus avoid real feelings of envy toward her. If you focus on how wonderful the other person is, you do not have to feel any ill feelings toward her or yourself.

The woman who murdered the singer Selena, was the president of Selena's fan club. Groupies, whom stars also need and use, are in reality quite dangerous to the stars. Cohen quotes someone who both resents and fears her groupies. Cohen's interviewee says:

> I resent that some enviers denigrate my accomplishments, almost as much as I resent the other type of enviers fawning on me and getting vicarious thrills.

The vicarious types (fawners) are worse because they confuse me, and because if I mistake them for real friends and honest admirers, I get badly hurt when I realize that they will not tolerate any failure in me and still be friends, and are secretly hoping for me to fail.

The opera great, Maria Callas, lost her voice—and the love of her life—before she was fifty. Callas retreated to her Paris apartment, where she took drugs (probably sleeping pills) and became a recluse. According to one of her recent biographers, Nicholas Petsalis-Diomidis, only when Callas found herself in such a weakened and vulnerable position did she allow a "rather mediocre pianist, Vasso Devetzi . . . to attach herself . . . to take the edge off the loneliness." Devetzi provided Callas with drugs; Callas became dependent upon Devetzi, who then used that dependency to assert a high-handed "moral claim" to the Callas legacy. Devetzi did what I have seen other women do, namely, "use (their) assumed authority as . . . a confidante" and servant, to steal precious archival material, including personal papers, money, clothing, jewelry, and a hoped-for place in history.

Because Devetzi was in attendance, on site, guarding her treasure, she was able to *appear* to Callas's long-estranged mother and sister as a merged female intimate who knew what Callas really wanted. (Women are very susceptible to such appearances.) In Petsalis-Diomidis's words, Devetzi "overpowered" Callas's sister Jacqui and had herself appointed the director of a Callas Foundation to "perpetuate the artistic reputation of Maria Callas," which essentially allowed Devetzi to extort, swindle, and pocket literally millions of dollars. The foundation was subsequently found to exist only on paper. Devetzi desperately forged documents, but to no avail. Only Devetzi's own death (but thirty years later) saved her from being engulfed in a humiliating legal action and scandal.

In short, Devetzi got away with it, in part because she was able to convince the women in Callas's family that she had actually taken their place. A woman's ability to merge and affiliate with another woman can be used for good—or it can be part of a vampiric scam.

If a woman enters a traditional all-female social circle as a man's wife or daughter, she will assume her husband's or her father's status among the other wives and daughters. Hierarchy will prevail. There are rules, limits, boundaries, specific expectations. Both cruelties and kindnesses may occur. Things are far more chaotic when a woman joins an all-female group, not as a wife or daughter but simply as a woman among women.

In a boundaryless and ruleless all-female social group, an emotionally and socially ambitious/needy woman's goal might be to become the female equivalent of a primate alpha male. This is accomplished not by earning the most money—or by possessing the largest number of young and beautiful women—but by systematically becoming intimate with the most important woman (or women) in the group by mothering her (or them) by grooming upwards, primate-style. In this way the ambitious newcomer makes herself indispensable to her (or them). Simultaneously, the newcomer might also bond with the least important woman (or women) in the group, whom she might need to assist her in a future takeover. Such ambitious women may use their social groups as leverage against others and may break down another individual's confidence so that she will submit to the will of the group.

Many women I have known have reported on their experiences—some satisfying, others disappointing—in all–female groups. My interviewee Shaneika is a forty-nine-year-old minister who temporarily put her congregational work on hold in order to join an exciting social-justice group. She told me:

> I entered this group with such high hopes. Finally, here was a group of highly committed African-American women. I was totally vulnerable. I was unprepared for the excessive and destructive emotionality. In this instance, some women adopted male-like personae to break you down into confessing your victimization. They wanted you to cry and wallow. Anyone who maintained the slightest dignity or invulnerability to intimidation was suspect. This group turned out to be more fundamentalist than democratic.

Angela is a thirty-one-year-old formerly prostituted woman who now works as a waitress. She has lived in an almost all-female world from the time she was twelve years old.

"Horizontal hostility" is very extreme among prostitutes. If you are in a pimp's stable, you have to fight each other for the right to service the pimp or his special friends. When I escaped from this life, I entered a program that was supposed to "rehabilitate" me. The women who ran it did not let me sleep. They insulted me around the clock. They said it was in my interest to "break down" so that I could break with my addiction to prostitution. I left them.

Amy is thirty-nine. We first met when she asked me to testify on her behalf. Amy once belonged to a "therapeutic" cult. Amy's therapist moved Amy into her own home, where she expected Amy to schedule her appointments, write checks, pour the coffee, do the dishes. Amy's responsibilities expanded to include that of "bedmate." At the time, Amy was flattered.

I thought I was in love with her. She assured me that whatever she did was only to help me. I watched as she began to use other patients as secretaries, fundraisers, house cleaners, sex-mates. No one protested, everyone felt honored to be able to serve her. Then, she fell in love with another patient. This time it was a man. She kicked me out. I had a breakdown again. She called the mental hospital and told them she was my therapist and that they should keep me there as long as they could, because I was really crazy and dangerous. When I got out, I found a new therapist.

When I understood how she had been taking advantage of all her patients, beginning with me, I tried to tell one or two of my old therapy friends what had really happened. My old therapist threatened to hex me if I dared call anyone else. I believed her.

I tried to call some other women who I'd been in group with. They hung up the phone. One actually crossed to the other side of the street when she saw me coming. Four of my group therapy buddies had been instructed to write and phone my parents, my new employer, and my new friends, to say that I was evil, and very sick. The first fair hearing I got was from the male patient whom she'd had the affair with but only after she got rid of him too. He was in even worse shape than me. I finally sued her and won. But by then she'd hurt many more people.

She still practices. She no longer says she is a therapist. Now, she's an educator. She continues to fly all over the world to deliver lectures and do workshops and train trainers. She has become very rich. Here's what I don't understand. Why didn't anyone in her own profession stop her? Why did she continue to have so many women colleagues? And women funders? And women patients? Didn't anyone know what was happening? Was everyone afraid of her?

These are haunting questions. On the one hand, women are trained to respect, prefer, and bond with men over other women; on the other hand, they long to merge with a Good Mother and with a Good All-Female Family. They are willing to sacrifice honesty, spontaneity, and principle—as well as to overlook the serious mistreatment and rejection of other members—in order to retain their connection to a group. Whenever a daughter is mother-wounded or mother-deprived, her yearning for a better experience with a new mother figure will render her susceptible to Vasso Devetzi-like maternal impostors and con artists.

Betsy Cohen, the psychotherapist, writes: "Beware the person who 'only wants to help,' because people often hide their self-interest. If someone wants to help you, while wanting nothing for herself, she may be deceiving herself and might bear a grudge later. She might secretly end up envying you for receiving so much kindness." The situation is complicated by the fact that such "helper" women may also be warm, engaging, and maternal. Nevertheless their capacity to control a group of women with non-stop half-truths, exaggerations, outright lies, cannot be overestimated.

Such a woman might lure other women with juicy gossip, flattery, and her willingness to listen. She might start by identifying the key members of a circle and catering to them. She will do personal errands, make herself available as a listener and problem-solver virtually around the clock. Many women are so starved for this kind of attention that few will allow their suspicions to deprive them of the much valued grooming.

Such a woman might use the information gained in confidence to impress other women. ("So-and-so has disclosed her problems to me. She says I am the only one who understands her.") She might, at the same time, begin to undermine the very person who has confided in her in order to make herself seem more important. Thus she might say: "So-and-so is having a really hard time. I am doing my best to be 'there' for her. But she's far more insecure than you might believe." Once such a woman is perceived as indispensable to the core members or leaders in a group, other group members will welcome and accept her slightly soiled information as dogma. Here is where she can become dangerous.

A woman I know—I think of her as a professional "admirer"—tried to poison the social and political well at which I drank for more than twenty-five years. Over a fifteen-to-twenty-year period, she told me and everyone she (and I) knew how wonderful I was. Whenever I gave a local, public lecture, there she was, beaming. She had the knack of turning up and lingering. Whenever I attended a colleague's lecture, there she was, beaming again. Soon enough, she expected to be invited along afterwards. Socially, she had a tin ear. For example, at first, my colleagues did not want her to join us. She would invite herself along anyway. She started driving to these events so that she could offer to drive the tired lecturer home. She made herself endlessly useful. Although she is a very smart woman, she is not a public person nor has she achieved a public reputation of her own. But her managerial abilities coupled with her genius as a "groupie" have stood her in good stead. On one occasion she waited outside a theatre and when one of my colleagues came out, she bounded up the steps saying: "My car is here, let me take you home." My colleague became terrified. At least she knew enough to avoid her. Others, myself included, did not. But, over time, I did become more wary of her. This was my downfall. As she made herself helpful to women whom she had met through me, she began to bad-mouth me. Not exactly bad-mouth. She told half-truths and some outright lies. For example, she started telling people that I had disparaged a very close friend. I hadn't, but the rumor cost me that friendship for a long time. The woman created enormous bad will for me among a group of women whom I loved. Eventually, I found that it took too much time to undo her gossip. Also, over time, I was forced to view my former companions as too easily duped, too desperate for attention. Just as I had been. Eventually, I dropped out of the group entirely.

For some women, being accepted into a group is not enough. They have to get rid of—or replace—the very woman who first introduced them. Many women have described in painful detail how a woman whom they had befriended ultimately tried to destroy and replace them socially. My interviewee Erin is a fifty-six-year-old photographer and social-justice activist. She told me:

I started an international network when practically no one else was yet thinking about women's problems in this area. It was based on my own research but it was a totally volunteer and activist organization. I definitely enjoyed professional benefits. I traveled widely. I attended important conferences. Of course, I had to raise the money to do this. I could not do all the work alone, so I invited two other women to join me. Did I say "join" me? That's a laugh. What they did was get rid of me. They started applying to foundations for grants to attend the conferences instead of me. They didn't include me in their grants. At first, I thought: great, they're not waiting for me to fund-raise for them. But, then they'd go to those conferences and drop little hints about why I wasn't at a particular conference. They said I was mentally ill. They also said I was dying of something mysterious and quite awful. Sometimes they said that I had lost my fighting spirit. For a long time, I had no idea this was going on. When I first got wind of it, I confronted them. They denied it. Then, when I really got sick, they used it as the perfect time to get rid of me. While I was still in the hospital, they told me that they would be co-chairing the group from now on. They honestly believed that they would be better for the network that I ever was. But I miss the women whom I would otherwise still be seeing from around the world.

Fifty-one-year-old Dagmar, a grandmother and active church member, has a similar story. Dagmar admitted that she had made a big mistake by expecting that a woman whom she had introduced into her country club circle would, in return, be decent to her, if not loyal:

> I thought she would come and tell me if a rumor was circulating against me. The opposite occurred. It turned out that a close friend of mine was the one who, all along, had been competing with me the hardest. These two bonded. I lost two women, one of whom had been important to me for a long time. But I also lost all the people the two of them borrowed from me and never "returned." Does this even make sense to you?

Alas, it does. In each of the above instances (myself, Erin, Dagmar), all it took was one woman to damage another woman's relationship to a *group* of women. In each instance, no group member found anything suspicious about a newcomer who flattered and paid attention to her; no group member ever alerted the unsuspecting, gossiped-against woman. This is understandable. Most women are busy people who have little leisure time and even less disposable income with which to communicate with women all across the country or around the world. Also, most women have not been trained to carefully interrogate the bearer of idle gossip or to resist repeating what they've heard. Like men, women have also learned how to look the other way when their spouses, employers, or social allies engage in unethical, psychologically pathological, or criminal behavior toward *someone else*. After all, it is not happening to them, and they are not necessarily eyewitnesses when it happens to someone else.

Most women are emotionally needy and are therefore emotionally greedy. Like girls, women remain reluctant to stop a group from scapegoating or excluding an individual woman because they are afraid the group might turn on them next. Like men, most women fail to display the requisite courage in standing up to a lynch mob at full throttle.

If two group members become locked in a power struggle, like men, the other women wait to see who's going to win so that they can be on the winning side. Many men remain connected to male allies who impoverish orphans and widows, beat or abandon their wives, even commit genocide, as long as the money's good, and no one has publicly proved in a court of law that a crime has been committed. However, most men do not necessarily experience their allies as intimates.

Most women remain *intimately* connected to both contenders in a group power struggle, at least while it is still going on. Sometimes women take sides, but they tend to do so in twos or threes, not as individuals. Sometimes women refuse to take sides. What women most often refuse to do is tell one group member that another is bad-mouthing her or take a *principled* stand against a group member who is doing something immoral. (To most women, doing so feels like betraying a family member.)

Like men, women are affiliative. Unlike men, women may have a more primary loyalty to a dyad or to a small clique than to the larger group. Both men and women create hierarchies in groups; men are often clearer and less troubled about this; women require a greater illusion of equality and more moment-by-moment mutual grooming. In some ways this makes women more democratic, expressive, and anarchic than men.

To some extent all-female groups resemble all-female primate groups. While dyads dominate, cliques also dominate, hierarchies also exist, as do sudden takeovers, fights, and ejections. Belonging, interacting, and affiliating are more important than succeeding or being right.

Psychotherapist Patricia Doherty cites a Harvard Business Review article by Judy Rosener, which confirms the view that women's social and affiliative styles may be seen in how women conduct business.

> A second wave of women . . . is making its way into top management, not by adopting the style and habits that have proved successful for men . . . These women managers tend to form flat organizations, not hierarchies as men do. Rosener calls this leadership style "interactive leadership" because "the women actively work to make their interaction with subordinates positive for everyone involved." More

specifically, these women encourage participation, share power and information and enhance others' self-worth and get others excited about their work.

Some might argue that, on the contrary, women are more difficult to work with in groups—too sensitive, too demanding, too self-censoring, too wounded, too unrealistic, and therefore emotionally dangerous and socially destructive. In the view of some feminist psychotherapists, women would benefit from exploring these issues in feminist group therapy.

By the mid to late 1980s, a number of books and articles had appeared on the subject of competition and relationship difficulties among women.

In 1987, Vancouver counseling psychologists Lorette K. Woolsey and Laura-Lynne McBain published a paper entitled "Issues of Power and Powerlessness in All-woman Groups." They were concerned with the intense anger that female group members felt and expressed toward each other. They found that such conflicts could *not* be successfully mediated by counselor-leaders; all attempts to do so only seemed to increase the level of hostility to more destructive proportions. Most "confronters" focused their anger on women whom they perceived to be more competent than themselves; confronters had a distorted view that the group had rewarded the competent women with more time, attention, and recognition for their abilities.

Woolsey and McBain discovered, in agreement with psychiatrist Teresa Bernardez, that most female group members expect to receive continuously large supplies of nurturance, support, and sympathy from all-female groups and from any woman leader. According to Woolsey and McBain, "powerless" (I would say, "envious") women view power as a scarce resource. They are jealous of the recognition given to others and move against them in indirect ways. Those who become aggressive feel that their very being has been annihilated by the greater creativity or accomplishment of another woman. According to Woolsey and McBain, women who feel powerless tend to disguise their rising hostility. They do not attack openly. They do not acknowledge their own backbiting and gossiping or the harmful consequences of their prolonged avoidance of conflict.

Some people mistrust the patriarchal arts (or institutional and pharmacological sciences) of psychology, psychiatry, psychoanalysis, and psychotherapy and do not view them as safe ways to "look within." Some people believe that God and family or legal, political, and social action are all the "therapy" they need.

Although all-female social groups might satisfy a woman's need for affiliation at any price and although feminist consciousness-raising groups, bibliotherapy, education, and collective action might also do so, *psychologically* working through certain issues might require an all-female therapy group. For example, according to psychotherapists Patricia Doherty, Lita Newman Moses, and Joy Perlow, such an all-female group might allow a woman to "explore her early struggles with her mother," but with a difference. This time, the woman

> becomes the focus of the group's attention, curiosity, and concern. When other group members respond empathically and welcome all sides of her, the woman's tie to past images of her self is altered. In the safety of the group, the woman group member can reclaim the cutoff and unwanted aspects of herself. She is able to mourn the mother who wasn't and gain more clarity about the mother who was. With this increased understanding of her past experiences, the woman is able to loosen the bonds that have (psychologically) imprisoned her.

Psychotherapists Josephine M. Cunningham and Elizabeth B. Knight agree.

> The group experience can offer a very powerful mentoring process. In addition to experiencing the two female therapists as role models and mentors, the group itself becomes a mentor, which provides a strong support system (similar to the mother-group) and serves as a conduit of information, encourages self-promotion, and openly acknowledges competition.

According to Bernardez, the all-female therapeutic group has advantages and possibilities not available to the all-female consciousness-raising or social-action group.

> The presence and interventions of a therapist allow for: (1) the exploration and analysis of transference reactions to the therapist, of particular importance in the critical relations of women with their mothers and with maternal authority; (2) the examination and resolution of unconscious conflict in the participants; and (3) the dynamic understanding of group functioning, which tends to clarify group conflicts and increase group coherence and individual responsibility.

In Bernardez's view, there are profound advantages in daring to acknowledge our shadow or dark side and in interacting with a female role model who understands that risking "fine-tuned" expressions of anger can, potentially, lead to "a more genuine acceptance of one another, and a less fearful discourse." In her words,

> The presence of a female group therapist who provides a different image of authority makes it possible for women to acquire a comfort with power and authority so rapidly that one would suspect that the internalization of these conflicts is not as profound

as had been assumed at first. This is one of the reasons why the female leader in a therapy group who models the capacity to lead without fear, who trusts her own authority and doesn't surrender it to men, and who is equally free to be angry at men and to love them, is already a formidable asset in the treatment of women.

I have never done volunteer work in an all-female but non-feminist group. I have, however, run all-female therapy groups. I have also been a member of many feminist non-therapy groups.

Some feminists have engaged in a good deal of navel-gazing. They have transformed political consciousness-raising sessions into group therapy. Other feminists have resisted looking within and scorned psychological ways of thinking partly on the ground that psychology has a misogynist history and partly because they wished to outrun any personal trauma through fast-paced public group activities.

In the next chapter I will explore the issue of whether feminist women in groups have exhibited radical or psychologically ethical behavior or whether they have behaved more traditionally, like most other women.

10.

PSYCHOLOGICAL ETHICS

In 1967, after enduring years of second– and third–class citizenship at home, at school, at work, and in other political movements, a large number of American women said "no" to such inequality and found each other. For about five to ten years, women's psychological isolation from each other miraculously ended. For many "the Movement" became their first and only home. Most feminists believed that the revolution would happen in their own lifetimes.

Women (and some men) in feminist groups have accomplished a great deal. Within a span of thirty-five years, a visionary feminism has managed to challenge, if not transform, world consciousness. Feminist ideals are battling patriarchal institutions and ideology, the world over. For example, rape as a *weapon*—not a *spoil*—of war is now viewed as an international human rights violation. Feminists have also mounted brave and

436

determined battles against such local practices as honor killings, dowry burnings, female genital mutilation, against the global trafficking in women as sexual slaves, and, more generally, against rape, incest, domestic violence, and economic inequality. Feminists have also campaigned for women's religious, medical, educational, and legal rights. There are more women in government today than ever before. Some are feminists; some are not; some have been elected or appointed precisely because they are anti-feminists.

I believe that certain feminist ideals will, eventually, triumph—but so will some of those of our opponents. I also believe that feminists will have to keep fighting for our ideals, which may never become "givens."

Feminists are still fighting for a woman's right to a safe and legal abortion. The war over a woman's right to control her own body remains a very hot war, both here and abroad, involving violence against clinics, erosion of access and funding, and attrition by lawsuit, legislation, and propaganda. Every year, world wide, nearly 100,000 women continue to die from unsafe illegal abortions. Abortion providers continue to be menaced, bombed, and killed.

Who were the women who spearheaded the Second Wave of feminism?

Although many 1967-era radical feminists came from ruling-class families, many thousands more had grown up in working- and middle-class "political" families or had learned to think politically on their own in pre-feminist terms. Many were pro-labor, pro-socialist, pro-pacifist, pro-communist, pro-anarchist, but many also supported wars of national liberation or were concerned primarily about individual career advancement. Most feminists were educated, read a lot, created and consumed High Culture, opposed racism, capitalism, imperialism, organized religion, and capital punishment. Most were horrified by the McCarthy hearings and by the execution of the Rosenbergs. They had joined the NAACP or were involved in Fair Play for Cuba committees. Some went down to Mississippi for Freedom Summer to register voters in 1964; some were involved in the civil-rights movement in the North and in the anti-war movement. Some feminists had been members of Students for a Democratic Society or supporters of the Weather Underground. "Politicals" understood that one might have to pay a high price in "going up against the state." "Non-politicals" had entirely different expectations when they entered the feminist arena.

We—and the rest of America—had never seen anything like us before. We were smoldering figures of sin and soul; we were "bad" in the African-American sense. As the song goes, we were "dancing in the streets" of America. The early radical feminists were like rock stars, or action heroes, but in the flesh and On The Road. We were—like guys! No, we were more than that. We, who had been destined for lesser lives had miraculously escaped the small-town prisons in our heads to become cultural commandos in the Big City. In the beginning we were mainly white, but we came from every race, tribe, and class;

overnight—or so it seemed—we were everywhere, one vast egalitarian cocktail party on the barricades.

As members of a much later generation might say, we were, for about five years, truly awesome. Cracked, belligerent, misguided, strangers to ourselves and to each other, radical feminists were nevertheless also giants on the earth.

The feminists of my generation empowered each other in ways that nothing else ever did or could. We took each other— and therefore took ourselves and our own ideas—seriously. For most of us, this had never happened before, not with other women, not with most men. Feminists were each others' role models, teachers, midwives, and momentary mothers, but since the mother-daughter relationship had been painful and humiliating for many of us, we called each other "sisters."

I expected so much of other feminists—we all did—that the most ordinary disappointments were often experienced as major betrayals. Like most women, feminists expected less of men and forgave them, more than once, when they failed women. Feminists expected far more of other women, who paradoxically had less (power) to share than men had. We held grudges against other women in ways we dared not do against men. We were not always aware of this.

The honeymoon had been so unbelievably romantic that most feminists denied or minimized the obvious differences among them and the inevitable difficulties. This was pure insanity and utter genius, given that feminist political philosophies ranged from anarchism and socialism right on through to right-wing capitalism and various forms of ethnic and religious tribalism and nationalism. Feminists occupied very different places racially, economically, sexually, socially, and educationally. If this wasn't challenge enough, feminists also had in their midst the usual assortment of scoundrels, sadists, bullies, grifters, con artists, impostors, poseurs, careerists, liberals, rage-aholics, loners, eccentrics, champion hair-splitters, spoilers, sore-losers, drug addicts, alcoholics, the dim-witted, the incompetent, and the incomparably lazy. And then there were the egomaniacs, psychopaths, schizophrenics, manic depressives, and suicides.

In most ways, feminists were psychologically no different from any other group of women or men. However, although feminists insisted that all women had been damaged, wounded, victimized, or tortured, they acted as if what they were saying did not apply to themselves and would in no way compromise feminist efforts.

Feminists were no worse—but no better—than any other group of human beings, male or female. The fact that women's rights activists would bring the same human behavior—well trained in sexism—to the liberal or revolutionary table should come as no surprise. Even after "the troubles" (I borrow the phrase from our Irish friends) were well under way, I absolutely refused to believe, as feminist pioneer Ti-Grace Atkinson had quipped, that "Sisterhood is powerful—it can kill sisters." Although we knew that this was true, most feminists denied that it was *really* true.[1]

Let me share some hard-won perspectives.

First, most people do not keep doing the same thing. Young people may embrace ideals and principles that are quite demanding. Not everyone can "keep on keeping on" for the rest of their lives. In some ways, Second Wave feminism had its day, did its work in the world—it's over. On the other hand, let me suggest that the Second Wave of feminism is not yet altogether over; our successors are still continuing this Wave's work.

Second, political animals are a notoriously cantankerous lot. Even if the FBI and the CIA did infiltrate the feminist movement as fatefully as they infiltrated civil rights, new left, and anti-war movements (and I believe they did), feminists also functioned as unpaid, un-recruited, patriarchal "agents" against themselves. How could anyone have expected feminists always to work and play well together? People in other movements have not done so.[2]

Third, as we have seen, men routinely compete with, steal from, shoot, and kill each other. Most women are aggressive, not in this way but in indirect ways, mainly against other women. Young girls, teenagers, and adult women insult, taunt, shame, gossip about, slander, bully, and ostracize each other.

Although we were feminists, psychologically we behaved like women, not like revolutionaries.

In 1963, in *The Feminine Mystique*, Betty Friedan described the malaise that gripped suburban housewives as the "problem that had no name." In the late sixties and early seventies, a new problem "that had no name" had begun to plague feminists. In cities up and down the east and west coasts (and in between), feminists were fighting. The confrontations were angry and very personal. Feminists accused each other of classism, racism, homophobia, elitism, careerism, male-identification, and excessive man-hating.

Interestingly, feminists did not accuse each other of having internalized *sexist* attitudes. This was unfortunate. It allowed feminists no opportunity to acknowledge, understand, or work on sexism as a problem that needed to be overcome.

Although many feminists had worked in the civil rights movement, this did not mean that they had triumphed over racism. Racism still existed, both in the world and in their heads—just as internalized racism still existed among African-American civil rights workers. Psychologically, one works on racism day by day. It's a process. One also *does* anti-racist political work. One does not engage in mere dramatic showdowns. White feminists often called each other racists as a way of demoralizing and destroying each other, not as a way to begin doing anti-racist *work* together.

The "politically correct" accusations were often valid, but women's unacknowledged sexism turned such political accusations into psychological kamikaze missions. Feminists "heard" their mothers in the accusations—or the envied prom queen from Hell—not each other; they heard their older or their preferred sisters telling them what to do. Feminists withdrew or began to associate only with those with whom they agreed or, terrified, caved in and confessed and admitted their various high crimes and misdemeanors.

Some feminist orators were punished by their comrades in consciousness-raising groups for public speaking or for appearing in the media. Authors were attacked for refusing to publish their work anonymously and, paradoxically, for trying to keep their private lives "private."

For example, when Kate Millett's *Sexual Politics* was first published in 1970, Millett was a bisexual married woman with a Ph.D. In her next book, *Flying*, Millett painfully describes how certain lesbians began to demand that she "come out." Out-lesbians bullied and "guilt-tripped" her. But other heterosexual married women and closeted lesbians also terrorized her, and not only about public lesbianism. Among other things, they accused her of not publishing *Sexual Politics* anonymously. Millett writes:

> I wonder if they will kill me. Somehow I am about to
> be assassinated for the crime of individualism . . .
> [Jenny says] it is bourgeois to write. . . . She glares at
> me like I am the kind she will shoot when she has
> power. . . . All money from publications go to a cen-
> tral committee, you may apply to them for groceries
> and carfare but the neediest women in the city will
> get funded first.

Millett launched a feminist film company to portray the

extraordinary events as they happened, but in her words the "dream" quickly becomes a "nightmare." Millett rents the equipment, assumes all economic responsibility—for which she is resented and punished. The battles are "savage," the interrogations "fascist."

> We were a capsule scenario of every oppressed unit
> on earth, a nest of oppressed women screaming at
> me like machine guns. . . . each day of the shooting
> I made more strenuous efforts to be gentle, inoffen-
> sive, never assert anything, becoming so vague they
> screamed harder, needing orders.[3]

Trashing did not take place only among radicals. National Organization for Women (NOW) leaders, Democratic party operatives, certain elected politicians, and middle-class profes- sionals behaved in very similar ways.

New York writer Nancy Friday describes what happened in the mid-1970s in a group of white, educated, middle class, het- erosexual women writers, in a group called "Woman's Ink." A power struggle erupted, and an "insidious whisper campaign" ensued:

> There were midnight telephone calls, secret meet-
> ings of the so-called Steering Committee, the objec-
> tive of which was to blackball this one assertive
> woman, to exclude her in the style of Three Little

Girls Can't Play Together . . . to this day I am not
sure exactly what crime The Accused One had committed, the pretty blond one whose head was on the
guillotine. Certainly, the real argument was over
power, something we couldn't say out loud, being
women raised by women. . . . We had not been
taught to compete in a healthy way.

Instead of open, honest argument, this group of seasoned,
card-carrying feminists preferred to destroy their own organization that might have helped them all professionally.

One woman had the audacity to question the
group's leaders. . . . She had broken the no-compete
rule. It was a nasty piece of business, that campaign
to spray her, an ugly little war waged by grown
women. There was no enemy "out there," no evil
men upon whom we could dump our badness. The
enemy was within, a cruelty that each of us had felt
at one time or another, seething inside, just waiting
for a victim. And here she was: Spray her!

According to the pioneer leaders of NOW—Betty Friedan,
Ti-Grace Atkinson, Karen DeCrow, Sonia Johnson, Ginny Foat,
and others—feminist leaders in both NOW and the National
Women's Political Caucus (NWPC) not only brokered, but
rigged elections. Ballots were allegedly stolen, and voting mem-

berships were sold at the door. Whistle blowers were threatened and silenced, either by guilt-tripping or by slander. Microphones went famously dead, workshops were pre-packed, backroom deals were cut—and woe to anyone who tried to stand in the way of the deal "on principle" or for the sake of fairness or democracy.

Progressive and radical organizations are notoriously prone to in-fighting. What complicated this tendency was the fact that many NOW members had, psychologically, "married" NOW; they had turned NOW into a Total Institution, the equivalent of a family or a religious order. When they lost, they lost everything, for all time. This was not a game. It was all they had, everything that mattered, and there were no rules of engagement or disengagement. By the mid-1970s, Betty Friedan claimed that control of both NOW and NWPC had been unfairly and perhaps illegally wrested away from her. She concluded that NOW was suffering from a

> power struggle so acute and so vicious that, finally, only those who can devote twenty-four hours a day to the movement can play—women who have made the women's movement their sole profession, their career, their sole road to glory, even their personal life.

New York lawyer and ex-NOW President Karen DeCrow told journalist Ellen Hawkes:

> Until you've seen a contested NOW election, you

haven't seen anything. I had a bodyguard with me when I ran for reelection at the 1975 Philadelphia conference, and I thought, my God, am I going to need armed guards to be head of the sisters! When I left in '77 I felt I would have no trouble being a litigator because I'd been through the NOW wars. I'm frequently in a legal situation where someone will say, 'How can you stay so cool?' I smile sweetly and think back on NOW. If you can live through NOW, you can battle both the Fortune 500 and the worst sex-discrimination cases.

In 1976, Friedan published "An Open Letter to the Women's Movement" in which she begged feminists to stop "manipulating each other covertly" and to stop "denying the reality of our conflicts and [to] provide formal, open, democratic channels for their resolution."

A cannibalization of leadership has set in at the core of the women's movement, both in NOW and in the radical women's groups and the women's centers. Our organizations and our alternate institutions die from internal bleeding long before they succumb to external pressure.

No one in the mainstream listened to Friedan's passionate plea. By then it was probably already too late.

For nearly fifteen years I too believed that most feminist

leaders were sisters. One strives to believe the best about one's own group, not the worst. As we have seen, most women, myself included, prize connection over disconnection and fear confronting powerful and charismatic intimates with unpleasant truths. But then something happened, something bad, something I could neither deny nor minimize, something I could not even comprehend.

In 1980, I was a well-paid consultant on women's issues at the United Nations. Certainly I needed the money, but I also wanted to find and bring together feminists from all over the world who were in positions of power or influence in their countries. I wanted to assemble a feminist government in exile. Some people thought I was joking; others knew that I was serious. And then reality set in. The man who had hired me began to proposition me. Only in retrospect did I understand that this man routinely expected to—and probably did—sleep with every woman he hired. I was in a bind. I did not want to quit. And I did not want to sleep with him. I actually thought that he'd hired me for my brains.

How foolish could I be?

At midnight, twenty-four hours after my contract was finalized, my bell rang. It was the Boss Man, come to collect his fee. I let him in. He raped me. Calling the police would have led nowhere—he had diplomatic immunity. I was therefore determined not to let him drive me off the field of battle. I made sure I was never again alone with him in the same room. Boss Man made my working life miserable. I did not pursue a lawsuit. At that time, to the best of my knowledge, no woman had ever sued a U.N. diplomat. My sexual harassment and rape took place eleven years before Anita Hill's public ordeal and fourteen years before Catherine Claxton won her (groundbreaking) lawsuit against Luis Maria Gomez, the high-ranking Argentinian official who had sexually assaulted her in his U.N. office.

I remained committed to coordinating the international feminist conference that I'd envisioned and to editing and introducing the published Proceedings. I told every feminist I knew that I was doing this. In 1980, at the conference, my rapist wandered through the halls drunk and began sexually harassing other women. On *their* behalf, I finally found my voice. I told a group of about ten women about my sexual harassment and rape. I asked them to join me in privately confronting, not suing, my harasser and rapist. Many black African women were willing to do so. To my surprise, my friend Inge (a pseudonym), whom I had invited to the conference, successfully lobbied these women against confronting my rapist, on the grounds that since he was black such a confrontation might be perceived as reverse (feminist) racism. Inge was not at all worried about (feminist) sexism.

Within a year I learned that Inge was working on an international feminist anthology of her own. Apparently that was not enough for her. In 1983 Inge also usurped my place and wrote the Foreword to the Proceedings of the Conference that *I*, not she, had organized. Inge had collaborated with my rapist in order to corner the market on global feminism for herself and her allies, and he had rewarded her in this way. There was more. Unbeknownst to me, Inge had also scooped up fifty percent of the women whom I had so carefully found, funded, and brought together. Inge had invited them to contribute to a *second* anthology of her own.

I was aghast. Had Inge not cooled out the confrontation with my rapist and simply asked me for my phonebook, I would have handed it over instantly. I did not own these women. Inge had an absolute right to ask them to contribute to her anthology. Why did she feel she had to steal them from me in order to work with them? Why did she need to usurp my place? And having done so, why did she need to "disappear" me from the international feminist networks that were coming into existence?

In this instance, Inge had done what women do to each other in incest-families: collaborate with the rapist, obtain some reward, and ostracize his victim when she tries to "tell."

In 1983, when the Proceedings of *my* conference with Inge's Introduction was published, I threatened to sue both her and my rapist. But, instead, I quickly suggested a private, feminist mini-tribunal. I invited two of Inge's most powerful feminist allies to join us. To their credit, they came and they made sure that Inge came too. I also brought two feminist leaders along, one of whom had herself also been systematically "disappeared" by Inge. We were all magnificently sober.

Behind closed feminist doors, I "cried rape" and "feminist collaboration." I did not want my rapist to go to his grave thinking he could divide the likes of us—or at least the likes of those we were *supposed* to be. However belatedly, I wanted us to confront my rapist privately and together. For more than four hours Inge remained silent, sullen. From time to time she punctuated the air with theatrical sighs. When asked to speak, she said: "I don't remember a lot from that year." She also said: "When I was a child, my mother was abusive to me." Inge and her protectors finally agreed to confront my rapist together with me—only we never did. Inge did not try to find my rapist. Inge's most powerful protector did place several phone calls to him, as she had promised to do, but they yielded no immediate results, and that was the end of it.

I did not try to find him. I was gripped by the strangest passivity.

Please understand: I am not talking about civilians here, but about prominent feminist leaders, myself included. I had expected us to be able to deal with rape—and with how some women collaborate with rapists—in more principled, feminist ways. Inge refused to acknowledge what she had done; had she done so it may have assuaged my suffering. Yes, a woman can be raped on the job; true, she might have no redress; but surely the other women on the job (in this case those of us who stood for justice for women) could believe the raped woman, try not to turn her disadvantage into a career advantage for themselves, try to help her move against her rapist in non-legal ways. From the raped woman's point of view, this might make all the difference.

What could we have done? Would it ever have been enough? None of us were able to live up to our own rhetoric or to face our failure to do so. In retrospect, I am not sure whether Inge's protectors really believed that I had been sexually harassed and then raped, as opposed to having been a reluctant, but technically willing partner in a love affair gone sour; nor am I sure that they could bring themselves to admit that they themselves were in an intimate, complicated, personal, political, and economic alliance with a charismatic and immoral monster.

Perhaps it was too late for Inge's protectors to change course. They also knew that I would not go public with this—not because I was afraid of Inge or of them, but because I did not want to expose any of us as vulnerable, inadequate, or immoral, at a time when the "ball was still in play." We were not sitting on our hands, we were fighting for women's rights, however imperfectly.

Am I blaming my feminist sisters and letting my rapist off the hook? Am I doing what so many women do: blaming other women for being unable to stop sexually violent men, scapegoating other women because it is safer to do this than to confront violent and powerful men? I hope that I am not, but to the extent that I am, let me emphasize the following: The blame belongs to the rapist, to the United Nations, which employed and protected him (and others like him), and to a system of laws that allows rapist-diplomats to remain immune from civil and criminal prosecution. No woman raped me, no feminist or progressive system of laws failed me. Having said this, I must also say that given this reality, how women treat each other under such circumstances matters more, not less.

Now, only after writing this book do I understand that Inge simply viewed herself as my competitor for a highly limited, much prized resource and did what millions of women do to each other in similar circumstances. I was so blinded by the myth of sisterhood that I had expected feminists to transcend 10,000 years of human history and the laws of nature and culture as well. Now I understand that ideology alone is not enough, that even ideologues may behave in stereotypically sexist and unethical ways toward women.

It is important to note that, at the end of the day, Inge got away with it. No one stopped working with her or funding her or protecting her. This is the way of the world, and I will expose and oppose it wherever it exists. It is little enough to do.

There is an Inge in every village and city, an Inge in most all-female social circles. She is the kind of woman who feels cheated. She is talented, ambitious, unhappy, envious, shrewd, and manipulative. She experiences excellence in others as a form of persecution and so justifies her every immorality toward others as a form of self-defense.

I have always wondered what Inge might have said about me in order to cover her tracks. That I was "difficult?" (that's an ever-popular way of putting any woman in her place) or that I was "politically incorrect?" Recently, one brave soul, new to our immediate feminist world, told me exactly what Inge had said about me to at least one influential feminist who had then repeated what she'd been told to three other women. Inge said, "You must stay away from Phyllis. She is too dangerous to even talk to because she'll sue you at the drop of a hat for anything you might say, including 'it's a nice day.'"

In this case feminist women simply behaved like *women*. This was our weak point, not our source of strength. The absence of psychologically self-aware and consciously ethical behavior among most feminists has weakened our capacity to resist patriarchy and our ability to recognize and defend ourselves against the bullies and opportunists in our midst.

The original Cultural Revolution in communist China was intended to eradicate the existing class system and privileges. Americans favor our class systems. (We also like to deny that classes exist.) Nevertheless, many feminists have sought to redistribute privilege and eradicate difference by trying to psychologically destroy any feminist who is different from themselves. Thus, countless feminists have been verbally bullied, shamed, slandered, and ostracized not only by their patriarchal opponents, but also by smaller self-appointed "politically correct" feminist cliques—who keep whatever power and privilege they have accrued for themselves and their friends.

Feminists conducted an entirely American version of the Chinese Cultural Revolution. As Americans, we had inherited a tradition all our own of intolerance toward intellectuals and independent thinkers. On the one hand, some feminists created cults in which they worshiped a chosen feminist leader as if she were the Queen of Heaven or a

Good Fairy Godmother—but one who they believed would crumble without Her followers' fanatical devotion. On the other hand, feminists, like other women, were starved for attention and were, therefore profoundly envious of any women who received more attention than they did. As philosopher Claudia Card has noted,

> Attention is to the soul what air, water, and food are to the body—they keep it vital. Loss of attention may be more demoralizing than loss of control . . . invisibility produces attention starvation.

For most women, being seen, having others pay attention to you, is imagined and experienced as more desirable and more powerful than commanding an army or seizing control of the means of production and reproduction.

Like everyone else, feminists did not automatically trust or respect women. We thought we should. We said we did. Feminists called each other "sisters." Thus, we had no vocabulary for the destructive things that happened between feminists, quite apart from our political differences. Resentments built, then exploded into take-no-prisoner emotional showdowns. Blood boiled, tempers flared, hearts broke. And then some feminists never spoke to each other again. There was no safe space to talk about what we were doing to each other.

Feminist activists, such as Anselma Dell'Olio and Jo Freeman did try to analyze the "trashing" phenomenon while it was going on. Sadly, their analyses did not end the problem. For example, in 1971, Dell'Olio wrote:

> Every Second-Wave feminist has a theory about why the movement lost steam. Mine was that our refusal to wash our dirty linen in public, i.e., to examine and thus politicize the new experience of (non-sexual) competition between/among women, brought us to an intellectual and emotional impasse. Our inability to create a philosophical life jacket for the burgeoning numbers of movement burnout victims forced them to retreat from activism and heal themselves as best they could. Female ambition and achievement had long been demonized by the patriarchy in the name of the feminine mystique, but now once again by the hostility, aggression, and masked rage of some women.

The anthropologist Joan Cassell published a study about how women behaved in feminist groups. Cassell observed how feminists in groups "penalize superior ability." A woman so accused said:

> I've been put down by men all my life for my brains and aggressiveness. I will not be put down by other women. I've had that all my life—that's why I went into the women's movement.[4]

Envy, jealousy, unacknowledged competition, trashing, slander, ostracism, and other psychologically traditional behaviors among women who happened to be feminists did not end in the 1970s. It continued throughout the 1980s and 1990s; it continues today. For example, the author Naomi Wolf described the late 1980s feminist "sisterhood" as she'd encountered it on her college campus as authoritarian, "horizontally hostile," downwardly mobile, and with a worm's eye view of realpolitik. While working in a rape-crisis center Wolf observed feminist "backstabbing," denying one's own "dark" side, rewarding the weakest, punishing the strongest, ruling by excluding, taking no prisoners.

Mississippi lesbian feminists Wanda Henson and Brenda Henson of Camp Sister Spirit used to run the feminist bookstore and crisis center in Gulfport, as well as the Gulf Coast Women's Music Festival. In the mid-1990s, the Hensons bought land in Ovett, Mississippi. In 1993, they became the subject of world-wide headlines when they and their supporters were shot at point-blank range and a dead dog and other dead animals were hung on their mailbox and placed in their driveway. Because of these attacks, the Hensons also became embroiled in a federal hearing conducted by Representatives Barney Frank and Gerald Nadler, and in local lawsuits as well.[5]

In a recent interview with me, the Hensons described how all through the 1990s, some lesbian feminist volunteers competed with them for the same funding sources; falsely pretended that they "represented Camp Sister Spirit," a feminist education and cultural retreat, when they did not—for the express purpose of making themselves seem important and to obtain the funding monies. These same con artists also slandered the Hensons. Other so-called supporters blamed the Hensons for "bringing the troubles on themselves."

> They said we did not represent southern lesbians well because of the way we talked and looked on Oprah's show. They went to a meeting of The Lesbian Avengers and said 'Don't help those women, they are not really threatened and if they are, they brought it on themselves and they make things bad for the rest of us.' It was easier to find fault with us than to feel guilty for turning their backs in times of trouble.
>
> The worst betrayal came after we had agreed years ago to make our festival and later the land, free of S/M (Sado-masochistic) violence. One of the caretakers was taken in by an S/M activist and threw away her friendship with us, her job as a caretaker here, and the trust we had for her. She later tried to file an unemployment claim against us (though she, like us, had been a full-time volunteer). Of course, there was no way she could get it but she wanted to expose us to state scrutiny, which she did. We were put under a microscope. When she left, it was like a divorce because of the amount of trust we had for her. We

have not really opened up to a 'friend' ever since,
not at that level of trust. I think it is high time we
held each other accountable for betrayal.

In 1999-2001, in New York City, Merle Hoffman, my dear
friend and the founder and president of Choices Women's
Medical and Mental Health Center, one of the first and largest
abortion facilities in the country, was shut down by a politically
motivated anti-abortion Health Commissioner. Sensational
ongoing national and international news coverage about what
a recently hired (and promptly fired) Choices physician had
done at another major city hospital (about which Hoffman
knew nothing) was all the excuse the Commissioner needed.
Simultaneously, Hoffman's landlord had hired the county
leaders and their lawyers to evict Hoffman—not because the
landlord was morally opposed to abortion, but because he himself had plans to bankrupt her and take over her business. At
the same time, officials of the Catholic Church were pressuring
the Health Department to keep Choices closed. Few feminists
or pro-choice activists called or offered any assistance or sympathy. Hoffman says:

> I was totally alone—fighting three major fronts with
> no visible support from my "allies" in a movement I
> had helped build and lead for thirty years. I did
> receive one call from The Feminist Majority. New
> York City NOW sent a letter to the Health Commis-

sioner and NARAL (on whose board I had served for eight years) sent a basket of flowers—for the funeral? Not one politician, not one feminist leader, not one pro-choice activist—not one—came out and defended me to the press or the public. Everyone ran for cover. Patients, women, were being hurt by my closing. This was a major frontal assault on abortion rights, but they may have just felt "well she's so strong—let her take care of herself." Finally, after being closed down for three weeks, continuous attacks in the press, and teetering on financial disaster, I managed to reopen, save my license, and go on.

But there is still a residue. Planned Parenthood, an organization that had been referring patients for services to Choices for over twenty-five years, stopped sending them simply because of the bad press. It was a short time later that I learned that Planned Parenthood's strategic goal was to pick up the patients that were lost during my closing. The saddest part is that four days before she closed me down, the Commissioner of Health was at an upstate meeting of pro-choice activists where she announced that she would be going to Choices that week "hunting for bear." No one at that meeting—none of the providers, people who knew me for thirty years told me. No one picked up a phone.

In this situation there was no feminist solidarity—only capitalist competition and female psychology as usual. Perhaps feminists cannot be expected to support a *for-profit* venture like Choices—although this makes no sense, given the strong feminist support for legal abortion and for women's economic advancement.

For thirty-five years many feminists have refused to reevaluate and refine our initial understanding of sisterhood—or to do so publicly, rigorously, and intellectually. Perhaps feminists have not wanted to look at how we ourselves treat other women; perhaps we do not want to expose a gender or a movement that remains so profoundly under siege; perhaps feminists do not want to appear disloyal to intimates who have neither betrayed the faith nor disappointed their friends.

Before I began research for this book I was not consciously aware that women were aggressive in indirect ways, that they gossiped and ostracized each other incessantly, and did not acknowledge their own envious and competitive feelings. I now understand that, in order to survive as a woman, among women, one must speak carefully, cautiously, neutrally, indirectly; one must pay careful attention to what more socially powerful women have to say before one speaks; one must learn how to flatter, manipulate, agree with, and appease them. And, if one is hurt or offended by another woman, one does not say so outright; one expresses it indirectly, by turning others against her.

Of course, I refuse to learn these "girlish" lessons.

The feminist movement has been the most romantic and liberating experience of my life, yet upon reflection, I realize that it has also, strangely, been like a prison experience. I have seen women at our worst when we should have been at our best. Slowly, and against my will, I have been learning how to keep my guard up among women. I understand that I cannot expect automatic or unconditional love, approval, or support from other women, and that I must expect instead their disapproval, envy, unacknowledged competition, fair-weather friendship, opportunism, cowardice, or indifference. I am trying hard to balance my new expectations against my earlier ones. I am trying to become realistic. Wrongfully, I too felt that other women were my fairy godmother(s)—but they are not. Nor are they my evil stepmothers. They are only human beings with profound limitations, who also have the capacity to comfort and protect those who do not threaten them.

We have seen that women are aggressive, but in indirect ways and mainly toward other women. Since women depend upon each other for intimacy, they do not acknowledge that this is the case. Instead, girls and women often refrain from telling each other what they really think for fear of being offensive or "different." Authentic or independent thought or emotion might lead to disconnection, ostracism, and loss of status. Rather than risk this, girls and women talk behind each others' backs.

Truth and peace do not often coexist. Telling the truth offends, startles, endangers, and upsets the status quo. People prefer, first, to benefit from the status quo; they express their critiques of it afterwards, indirectly, behind closed doors, behind backs. As we have seen, women excel at this.

Truth-tellers are considered dangerous. They do not play the game: they blow the whistle on it. Groups tie bells around their necks to warn others off, or, more often, they leave on their own, sickened by a level of corruption and compromise that most people find perfectly acceptable and useful. It is important that, one by one, women learn how to stand up to and disconnect from a woman who lies, gossips, and bullies others into looking the other way or into joining her.

We have seen how gossip, slander, and ostracism are major weapons of indirect aggression. For centuries, Jewish religious thinkers have advised Jews not to gossip. Some religious Jews have taken this advice too far. For example, they might even refuse to tell someone the truth about anything, lest it be misconstrued as gossip. Of course, men gossip too, but it is not their primary weapon against each other. Women are slandered by both men and other women. Therefore I would like women to think about how we might not gossip against each other.

How do you stop a rumor? Do you ask each person: "Have you heard something really bad about me?" (You would sound paranoid.) Do you say: "I want you to know that the rumor is not true"—when you don't even know what exactly the rumor is. Once a woman is weakened, rendered vulnerable, by one rumor, she becomes an easy target for subsequent slander.

We have seen how women in communities all over the world can and do destroy other women's reputations, often with fateful consequences, and for pitiful gain, through gossip, which is also a form of misrepresentation. Women fight each other both directly and indirectly for food, but for baubles too. The biographies of kings and queens are thick with the details of deadly intrigue. Ladies-in-waiting and royal mistresses fight for the ear of the crown for personal and class advancement and on behalf of various causes. Betrayal of other human beings in the service of one's cause is no stranger to the female gender, or to any ideology. In fact, as we have seen, no one ideology, including feminism, can guarantee that its followers have *psychologically* transcended or resisted their own internalized prejudices.

Lying, in order to manipulate others, is an art. A liar-artist often believes her own lies—What she's saying must be true, no one has ever stopped her, she's been able to get away with false, unethical reports, she's even been rewarded for them. Emboldened by reward, she thinks that what she's saying *has* to be the truth; otherwise, the Empress is buck-naked, and the castle is a mere pack of cards, a fantastic sleight-of-hand trick—except that all the slandered women remain slandered. In one's own very small circle, the psychological executions are real.

To be envied is no small thing. In a profound and graceful psychoanalytic, literary, and theological work entitled *Cinderella and her Sisters: The Envied and the Envying*, professors Ann and Barry Ulanov write:

> To be the object of envy is a terrible experience . . .
> the envied one feels cut off at her roots, severed
> from personal connection to the resources of her
> own being . . . envy can be seized upon politically as
> a force to promote ideology.

To be envied by those who themselves are also talented and ambitious is to be vulnerable to their spoiling you. For example, Abel had Cain, Mozart his Salieri. Psychologically, enviers wish to be the one God loves most, the Chosen One, the one whose being radiates excellence. Many women wish to star in this role, and many do. The male universe has room for many more stars; the female universe is therefore much smaller, and the competition quite fierce for the limited number of starring roles.

Some women cannot bear to experience themselves as lesser lights; in order to shine more brightly, they must rid the stage of greater lights. Originality, creativity, generosity, excellence, especially in the service of humanity (otherwise known as goodness or integrity) offends and threatens them. Envious people experience excellence in others as a form of persecution.

In the Talmud, slander is likened to murder. Perhaps, like murder, the damage can never be undone.[6] Those who murder reputations and life-sustaining opportunities are, perhaps, protesting what they experience as a less than blessed fate. Given that the Chosen Ones seem to have so much more, the envious damned feel justified in diminishing or ruining the Good.

Gossip can have a life of its own. It is a form of oral history that can be intergenerationally codified. Being the target of gossip can render a woman vulnerable, fair game for further gossip and scapegoating.

There are two kinds of gossip. One is a way of identifying oneself as a member of a cherished clique and of sharing one's love for another clique member by talking about her in her absence. Such gossip is harmless as long as the absent woman is liked or loved by those who are gossiping about her. "So and so is not feeling well. I wonder what we can do to help her?" Or "So and so won the competition. How proud I am to know her."

It is quite another thing to gossip about a woman who is not present in order to belittle, slander, ostracize, endanger, and get others to assist you in defeating and demoralizing her. As we have seen, this is something women usually do in order to uphold the patriarchal status quo. For example, calling another woman a "slut," "crazy," "difficult," an "enemy," is a way to get her out of the way, punish her, break her spirit, because you envy her. According to Ann and Barry Ulanov

> Envy . . . encourages gossip and (the) subtle but persistent withholding of any affirmation of another's self. Envy undermines the ground on which we stand. A few envious persons in a small community can destroy the whole, fraying connections, leaving holes through which only too many can fall.

Women may sometimes be able to stop female-initiated slander in its tracks by refusing to listen to it, refusing to repeat it, and by refusing to instigate it.

This is hard to do.

What might help is a commitment not to believe everything you hear, but in fact to disbelieve it, especially if it's something negative about another woman. It is important that a woman develop the courage to stand up to a slanderer or a bully, knowing that she risks being the next to be slandered or intimidated. According to historian and San Francisco columnist Ruth Rosen,

> Bullies gain power because they practice an intimate kind of terrorism. A bully is a self-centered person who must have his or her own way. If challenged, the bully reacts with angry outbursts or enraged confrontations. Bullies dominate because others capitulate rather than endure the bully's wrath . . . Like sexual harassment, (bullying) creates a hostile working environment.

The women whom I interviewed about woman's inhumanity to woman mainly talked about how *other* women had disappointed or betrayed them. Few were able to recall the ways in which they had disappointed or betrayed other women. No one admitted to remaining part of or profiting from a group in which members were gossiped about or ostracized. Many women whom I interviewed felt connected to me afterwards for a long time, perhaps forever, because I'd allowed them to say important, forbidden truths.

And I, have I never been inhumane to other women? I first asked this question in the Introduction; I will answer it more fully here. For years in my lectures I would sometimes create the desired atmosphere by reading a poem by Judy Grahn, Audre Lorde, Pat Parker, Marge Piercy, Adrienne Rich, or Monique Wittig, among others. In Judy Grahn's magnificent poem, *A Woman Is Talking to Death*, Grahn's narrator is being interrogated.

> Have you ever held hands with a woman?

> Yes, many times—women about to deliver, women about to have breasts removed, wombs removed, miscarriages . . . women who were vomiting, over-dosed, depressed, drunk, lonely to the point of extinction . . .

> These were many women?

> Yes. Many . . .

> Have you ever committed any indecent acts with women?

> Yes, many. I am guilty of allowing suicidal women to

die before my eyes or in my ears or under my hands because I thought I could do nothing.

Thus, I too have failed to personally save most of the women who turned to me—turned to me, not to another, because they thought that my written or spoken words meant that I could or would save them. I rarely had the patience or the humility to put my other commitments on hold to do so.

Have I ever been rejected by women? I've been rejected many times. As a girl, my inability to play dead, to say one thing but mean another, my bloodied but unbowed spirit of adventurousness and sheer exuberance, marked me as a target among girls from the start. I could not keep my mouth shut or my spirit humble. I was not broken. I said forbidden things. Eventually, I did forbidden things. I always wanted other girls to like me, but I lacked the ability to dissemble, keep a low profile, express myself cautiously, neutrally.

Although I have never slept with a friend's mate, I have sacrificed many female friendships on the altar of all my causes. I have never stopped to help another woman bring up a child, I did not routinely visit the sick or attend the dying but chose, instead, to write books, deliver speeches, mount barricades.

Although I have never testified against a woman who alleged injustice, I did not respect or obey my own mother who devoted her life to her children.

Although I have never consciously stolen an idea or a job

away from another woman, I have expected unwavering loyalty and primary affection from close female colleagues and friends. I have often felt betrayed when I turned out not to be "their one and only." I am insecure and therefore possessive and jealous.

While I have refrained from engaging in gossip about women, I myself talk about women all the time. However, the gossip which I oppose is that which slanders another woman ("she's a slut") in the service of the patriarchal status quo and in an effort to have others shun her. I do not oppose talking about women for other reasons.

I have worked with and for women who are very different from me. I pride myself on this, and yet in the past I have also been afraid that if an intimate held strong opposing views that he or she would desert me or I them.

I have devoted my life to a search for justice, and for intellectual and artistic freedom. I still have exceedingly thin skin when others criticize me, especially other women. Despite everything, I would still like women to like both me and my work. It has sometimes taken me months, even years before I was able to see that something I had initially experienced as an overwhelming attack was not really an attack at all, or that it was an attack, but not malevolent or even personal, that it did not have the power to either silence or kill me; I did not have to respond to it as if it were a life-threatening event.

My mother raged at and criticized me brutally. Thus, I cannot bear raging, critical women near me. Only recently have I been able to acknowledge that my own bold ideas and my passionate, direct style are probably very threatening to other women. Perhaps other women experience me as raging at them. Perhaps I have also disappointed some women deeply by not sharing their views, or by not being as invulnerable, personally, as my ideas may be.

Finally, I remain unable to reconnect with those women whom I once loved, enjoyed, respected, but who in the past found it opportune to believe false rumors about me and to ostracize me. I still cannot reach out, take the first difficult step. In this I recognize my own enormous limitations. Perhaps this book is my way of reaching out—although I am now far too realistic to expect any romantic reunions.

We have seen how women have internalized sexist values and how they judge other women in patriarchal ways.

We have seen how girls and women gossip about each other—and how gossip destroys reputations, breaks spirits, embitters, impoverishes—sometimes even ends lives.

We have discussed the ways in which unacknowledged mother-daughter and female sibling interactions color many subsequent female-female interactions both socially and in the workplace.

We have seen how women in all-female groups unconsciously expect other women to mother them, do not acknowledge their own envy or competitiveness, allow hostilities to fester, intensify, and remain unresolved. This is true despite women's dependence upon their female intimates for emotional grooming and despite the high value they place upon loyalty among intimates.

We have also seen how girls and women revitalize their dyadic or clique bonds by ousting and ostracizing their own members and how the power to do so keeps group members in line.

Despite women's psychologically matricidal and matrophobic tendencies, we have seen that many women can *also* be fiercely, maternalistically protective of each other—especially of a female intimate whom they perceive as wounded and psychologically fragile, and on whose behalf similarly fragile women can act in very aggressive, permissibly altruistic ways.

We have seen how reluctant both girls and women are to stand up to the bullies in their midst, how women fail to recognize such bullies, and how they do not know how to confront, neutralize, avoid, or rehabilitate a female bully, slanderer, boundary-violator, or rage-aholic, especially if she is *also* maternally seductive, charismatic, or socially powerful.

In this chapter, we have discussed the ways in which women in feminist groups have also behaved in psychologically traditional rather than in psychologically radical ways.

I would now like to share some thoughts about what might constitute more ethical, compassionate, and radical psychological behaviors among human beings. Such guidelines are not for feminists only.

Although many women may be economically and politically

second- or third-class citizens and while they may as individuals feel psychologically weak and powerless, they may still exercise enormous emotional and social power over one another. Woman's inhumanity to woman is painful, powerful, and paralyzing. I would like women to learn to use their power in generous, not envious ways.

This is not meant to be a "how to" book. Still, I would like to think that the information and analysis I have presented here can be used to help women treat each other more respectfully and compassionately.

A woman might begin by acknowledging some fairly obvious truths. Like any man, she is a human being; as such, she is capable of aggression, competition, prejudice, crafty servility, insufferable vanity, envy, jealousy, cruelty, pettiness. A woman also has a "shadow" side—just as a man does. Still, many women learn to pretend that they are not really aggressive or competitive, because such traits are not socially desirable in women. But if a woman pretends to herself that she is kind to other women when she is not, she will have no reason to learn how to resist her own normal, but emotionally primitive, human inclinations.

Once a woman acknowledges that normal women are aggressive and competitive, she may become more realistic about what to expect from other women and clear about her own limitations as well.

If people wish to change their behavior, they must acknowledge their own unconscious prejudices. They cannot change their behavior if they do not see or name what they are doing. As bell hooks has noted:

> We must challenge the simplistic notion that man is the enemy, woman the victim. We all have the capacity to act in ways that oppress, dominate, wound (whether or not that power is institutionalized). It is necessary to remember that it is first the potential oppressor within that we must resist—the potential victim within that we must rescue—otherwise we cannot hope for an end to domination, for liberation.

Like the concept of brotherhood, sisterhood must be practiced daily, not merely invoked apocalyptically. Like the practice of friendship, the practice of sisterhood is an ongoing, complex commitment. Such a commitment requires the courage of perseverance. As Massachusetts professor Janice G. Raymond, the author of *A Passion for Friends: Toward a Philosophy of Female Affection*, has noted:

> Friendship is a process of "repeated acts." In this sense, friendship is a habit that reoccurs in the face of betrayals, ruptures. . . . It is a creative habit that, to take Mary Daly's words and use them in another context, "does not happen through wishful

thinking but through arduous practice, through repeated acts."

Each woman must understand that women have probably been internalizing sexist values for thousands of years; this value structure cannot disappear immediately. This means that no individual woman is responsible for solving this immense problem by herself, or even in her lifetime. I would like women to understand that the practice of sisterhood is a psychological and ethical discipline.

Loving your sister as you love yourself—the quiet, daily practice of sisterhood—requires a strong and independent mind and spirit. To practice sisterhood, a woman must first love her (own) self. She must be clear about her psychological boundaries and be able to guard them well. Only then will she have the capacity to respect and not violate another woman's boundaries.

Sexism is not only about mistrusting or disliking women. It is also about idealizing or demonizing women either as fairy godmothers or as evil stepmothers. Sexism is about expecting women to be family-like intimates. Women must learn to resist the illusion of instant intimacy and the assumption that a newfound intimate is a true friend or ally.

A woman does not have to like another woman in order to respect her or to work together. She does not have to *be* like her either. On the contrary, diversity and difference are preferable to uniformity and conformity.

As we have seen, women often confuse a difference of opinion, character, or circumstance with unfair criticism and rejection. Women are not used to remaining connected to those with whom they disagree or who are different in other important ways. Certainly many mothers, daughters, sisters, and close friends struggle over this. To many women criticism signifies disconnection and abandonment, the transformation of the Other as Good Mother into the Other as Evil Stepmother. This is one reason why women tend to tell each other one thing directly, but quite another thing indirectly, behind backs.

Many women are not trained (as men are) to work with nonintimates. Nevertheless, a woman must learn how to resist personalizing her differences with other women, especially on the job. She must be educated to do so.

Many women have been taught that a good woman is someone who remains connected to an abusive intimate. Let me suggest that women must also learn how to remain connected to women who are both different from themselves and not intimates. To do so productively will require radically new approaches that may be found only through trial and error.

Indirect aggression is often more harmful than direct aggression. There are many more things to do when you are indirectly aggressive. You can verbally taunt and shame a woman, but you can also whisper, gossip, slander, and ostracize her behind her back; you may also influence everyone you know to "cut her dead," socially, without having to give your victim any explanation; you can also befriend your former friend's enemies, turn her own allies against her, and appropriate those allies as a resource for yourself. Such aggression interferes totally with a woman's peace of mind.

Sexism is complicated. It means that a woman will unconsciously enact and uphold certain double standards. For example, women are trained to have compassion for men, to forgive men when they fail them, to allow men second and third chances. Women must behave in a similar fashion toward other women.

Women are also trained to respect male accomplishments and to express gratitude towards men when they do something that they are supposed to do, for example, protect and employ women. A woman is not taught to respect another woman's accomplishments or to express gratitude toward another woman when that woman assists her. A woman must learn how to thank another woman for every small act of kindness—as opposed to expecting everything from her and being angry when she doesn't get it all.

Just as a woman is trained to make a man feel welcome, so too must a woman learn how to treat other women politely, ceremoniously, and in ways that make women feel truly welcome.

A woman may hold a grudge against another woman for a long time. She might instead learn how to express her anger verbally, directly, and only once, to the woman who has offended her—and then let go of that anger.

Men are trained to disagree with each other in violent ways, and they are trained *not* to take competition or difference personally. Women are trained to smile and agree with each other, even if they secretly disagree. Women often view this as getting along with others, or as a way of creating harmony and peace in a rancorous world. However, this is one of the reasons why many women do not fight for justice; to do so, they would have to challenge the status quo, which means offending other people and opposing their views.

Often, a woman becomes offended and emotional very quickly. She may be oversensitive to criticism because she has been excessively and unjustly criticized by both women and men from a very young age; she has also been treated as if she were invisible. Women have been readied to hear unjust criticism where none exists. Because mothers and other female relatives have so often brutally forced a girl to conform to a too-narrow gender role, many women experience all disagreements as personal and highly dangerous. Many women do not hear how they sound when, feeling (unjustly) attacked, they attack in return. Therefore, I would like to see women learn how to hear each other gently, respectfully. Each female dyad, every all-female group, will have to find its own unique ways of doing so.

At the same time, a woman must become strong enough to hear outside, diverse, critical voices. Asking another woman what she really thinks is not the same as asking her to support you, right or wrong, or to falsely flatter you. A woman has to be able to endure opposing views without collapsing and without feeling personally betrayed by those who hold such views.

A woman will say: "I asked my friend to read my report and she destroyed me with her comments." Do you want your friend to agree with you or to fortify you with her views that may be different from your own? Sometimes, a woman intellectual may ask a female colleague to critique her work; if the critic does not use just the right voice, she may be experienced as vicious merely for doing what she has been asked to do. Women must learn that such critiques, if they are not petty or envious, can strengthen your work and enrich your life. You must try to welcome this kind of dialogue. If you disagree with someone else's views, you do not have to adopt them.

It is important that a woman find her own voice and that she discover ways of projecting it into the universe. A woman must learn how to express her views clearly and firmly without being afraid that this will offend, fatally injure, or drive her intimates away. Difference does not have to mean disconnection. Each woman must find her own way of balancing a woman's over-sensitivity with a woman's right to hear authentic female voices and a woman's obligation to become that authentic, spontaneous female voice.

A woman must be encouraged to put what she wants into words, to ask for it directly, not to wait for someone to guess what she wants. If a woman cannot get what she wants, she does not have to pout, blame herself, give up, disconnect, or become enraged. She must learn that she can get what she wants another day or at another job or with another person. Women must be encouraged to move on as well as to stay the course.

A woman must find ways to encourage other women, not to

turn them to stone with a Medusa stare, ways to disagree without annihilating the next woman. Men have sports- and business-based rules for this. As yet, most women don't.

While men are the number one killers of other men, paradoxically, men are also geniuses at buddying up. One reason for this may be men's early experience in bonding through competitive team sports. Non-athlete women do not choose the strongest woman to be on their team; they do not understand that her strength will work for—not against—them. Men will often bypass the weakest men for this same reason.

Women who are involved in competitive team sports learn that they can't win alone; that, in fact, they have to become openly and directly aggressive both for their own sake and for the sake of their team. Women learn that competing head-on for the gold is desirable; that if they lose one day, they won't die, it's not all over, they may very well win the next day; that falling down, getting bruised, getting dirty won't kill them. Becoming physically strong, feeling their physical power, can translate into strength and confidence in other areas of their lives.[7]

It is important for a woman to learn how to walk away at the end of the day without having her self-esteem—or her very identity—undermined by losing a game, a job, a friend, or a spouse. Women must also learn how to compete with other women and how to befriend their competitors as well. Competitors are not necessarily your enemies for life; they may also become your allies.

Perhaps many women are at their best when they relate mainly to intimates, engage in emotional grooming, maintain an egalitarian dyad or one in which a dominant-subordinate status quo prevails. Also, many women may dislike open team competition and may experience winning as too emotionally unsatisfying, abstract, impersonal, gender-inappropriate. I am not saying that women cannot be altruists—only that within each tribe, class, race, and religion, a woman may express or facilitate both aggression and altruism differently than her male counterpart.[8]

Many women will say: "She's my friend, she'll back me, she'll lie for me, no matter what I do." This kind of personal loyalty must be tempered by an equal loyalty to justice and honor. Many women have been trained to choose peace as the path of least resistance. This usually means accepting the status quo and on its behalf, punishing anyone who challenges it. Like men (whom I do not exempt from most of this conversation) women must also be trained to choose justice, which tends to challenge the status quo and which may be achieved only at considerable cost. A woman must be taught to take sides in matters of injustice, as well as to remain a neutral bystander on many issues.

Perhaps women need to discuss the subject of woman's inhumanity to woman in a safe space. I suggest that women do so in a special educational environment, not in a therapy group. Such a group will probably require two female leaders. This book can be a resource for such groups.

The leaders must state formally that women unconsciously expect constant nurturing from other women (and from all-female groups) and that this expectation is irrational. In reality, normal women are quite aggressive and competitive toward other women. Women have been taught to deny this. The denial leads to grudge-holding, rumor-mongering, slander, and ostracism. This sort of indirect aggression is painful to experience, since most women also depend upon other women for emotional intimacy, friendship, and social approval.

The leaders must explain that women have internalized sexist views. Being able to talk about this may relieve anxiety and guilt and liberate positive energies. For example, the writer Valerie Miner describes the relief that she and other writers in her group felt when they were able to "speak the forbidden."

> We began talking about outside people of whom we were jealous. Then Sandy admitted that she was jealous of Judy's fame, of the fact that she is invited to give so many talks, even though Sandy herself isn't particularly interested in being a public speaker. Paula said she was also jealous of the public appearances—until she started to get invitations and to feel oppressed by them. Judy said that she was jealous of Sandy's royalty advances from a major publisher. I said I was jealous of the grants the other three had received. Sandy said she was jealous of the fact that I

had published four novels when she hadn't yet published one. And so on. As we talked, the air got easier to breathe. I found myself stretching comfortably on the floor of Paula's studio.

It is important to encourage women to express what they think and feel *directly*, openly, in the here-and-now. Women will learn that doing so will not kill anyone and that truth-telling does not have to lead to female disapproval or rejection.

Psychologists Lorette K. Woolsey and Laura-Lynne McBain found that such educational groups can be successful. For example, one such group (composed of graduate students in counseling psychology) found ways to support both their stronger and their weaker members; although conflicts still arose, a level of respectfulness toward women who were different from each other was achieved. Woolsey and McBain view this as due to their presentation of a "clear theoretical framework."

What do women want? Dear Brother Sigmund, women need other women to be there for them, in sickness and in health, to comfort them when they are in pain, and to share their joy and triumph. Like me, women who write need like-minded spirits to read our work while it is still in progress; this is the greatest kindness. I myself was blessed by a group of readers without whom my courage might have failed me as I brought this work of twenty-one years to an end.

This group was composed of sixteen souls: the philosopher

and feminist Ti-Grace Atkinson; the education philanthropist Sanda Balaban; my extraordinary assistant Gavriel Z. Bellino; the lawyer and my companion, Susan L. Bender; the feminist organizer and theoretician Charlotte Bunch; the psychologist and author Paula Caplan; logician and copyeditor Leigh Cauman; my son Ariel Chesler who is a feminist law student; the film-maker and journalist Anselma dell'Olio; my agent Carolyn French of the Fifi Oscard Agency; the Orthodox Jewish feminist leader and my Torah study partner, Rivka Haut; the Harvard psychiatrist and author Judith Lewis Herman; the entrepreneur and publisher of *On The Issues* magazine, Merle Hoffman; anthropologist Barbara Joans; my editor Dan Weaver; and the feminist historian Barbara Winslow.

I am also deeply grateful to the following people for their expertise and support: Helene Kostre, Harvey Rossell, Rebecca Tinkelman, Joanna Wilczyska, David Zimmerman, and the community of the Park Slope Jewish Center.

Every woman who writes or who serves truth and justice in some other way is utterly dependent upon such people. Let me be clear. These readers did not just praise and agree with me. They carefully read my words and ideas; they challenged me. The work is far better because they did so. I alone am responsible for its failings.

I have been blessed by Carolyn French, an agent who is a retired professor of literature and who recognizes good writing when she sees it, and by Dan Weaver, an editor who believed in this project from the start, fought for it, and quietly, deftly, improved it.

Anselma Dell'Olio, Ti-Grace Atkinson, Charlotte Bunch, Barbara Joans and I all go way back to 1967 in feminist America.

Dell'Olio is a film-maker and journalist who has been living, loving, writing, and agitating gloriously, in Italy, for the last quarter of a century. She was the first among feminists to have written about woman's inhumanity to woman.

Atkinson, who is currently an adjunct professor of Logic and Philosophy at Harvard, was one of the earliest leaders of the National Organization for Women. Together with her comrade Flo Kennedy, Atkinson has been a tireless trouble-maker (this is meant as a compliment), and the veteran of many a feminist war.

Charlotte Bunch is the Director of the Center for Women's Global Leadership at Rutgers. Bunch is our highest-ranking feminist diplomat in the world. She travels constantly and has attended and contributed to most of the important international feminist conferences of the last twenty years. Nevertheless, she set her own work aside, sat on my couch sipping tea, and read one chapter until late in the night, took another chapter home and returned it quickly with comments and materials.

Sanda Balaban first wrote to me in 1997. Young, bold, strong-minded, ambitious, she became the first reader for *Letters to a Young Feminist*. Once again, Balaban came over many times and read this work in progress. She called it a "master-work," but she also urged me to make certain changes. I did so; she was right.

This group read drafts of the entire manuscript or selected chapters. They engaged in passionate, critical dialogue with me about the ideas contained herein. Should I name names or not? Some thought that I was obliged to do so, others that I would diminish the work if I did. Some demanded that I take on the various "politically correct" mafias; others feared for me personally were I to do so. What about all the women who love each other? Was I being fair to them? Would I write another book about women loving women?

I spoke to most of my readers in person or on the phone. I communicated with two readers (Ti-Grace Atkinson and Anselma Dell'Olio) primarily via email. I would read their words either late at night or perhaps early in the morning. An uncanny intimacy arose. When I met with Dell'Olio in person in New York—there she was in living flesh—I told her to hurry back home to Rome, that I missed the hushed excitement of our eerily old-fashioned and yet undeniably futuristic communication. Dell'Olio brought a spiritual dimension to this work. She told me that I was "on the path that all great souls must walk." She taught me that Saint Teresa of Avila and Mother Cabrini were both "mercilessly slandered" and, in Teresa's case,

> denounced to the Inquisition (even by her own nuns!). Did this make her life easy? Of course not. But she kept on going, cleansed herself of resentment so as not to waste precious energy. Of course,

she prevailed. At one point, Padre Alcantara, a holy man who is widely recognized, visits Teresa and declares her visions and ecstasies the real thing. This pretty much single-handedly saves T's bacon from being barbecued by the Inquisition, which was breathing down her neck HER WHOLE LIFE! Anyway, she tells him her woes. He says: "One of the greatest trials a human being can experience is the opposition of good people."

Dell'Olio assured me that anyone who would take this subject on is "divinely inspired, no question." She consoled me. She *prayed* for me. A mountain of sorrow rolled off my heart when Dell'Olio confirmed certain outrageous slanders about me and shared some similar experiences of her own. Dell'Olio wrote:

There is such grace in our relationship because our correspondence forces me to pay attention to my own behavior, reminds me to walk my talk. For this I am very grateful. I'm glad to hear the full story of your rocky road, it helps to know what you've been through. I have been through my own purgatories, been maligned and gossiped about and excluded. I slogged, then stumbled, then glided, then sailed, to the best of my abilities, and lo and behold, life presented me with greater gifts than ever I dreamed of, including the stunned, stupefied, gaze of the slanderous perpetrators. No matter how it feels, you are NOT on the outside looking in. You are the center of your unique and irreplaceable universe, and no one can keep your good from you.

There is a Simone Weil quote I used to carry around with me in my wallet for years, to the effect (not verbatim) that a person of spiritual quality sees to it that the evil stops when it comes to her: she will not pass it on, but neutralizes and dissolves it back into the nothingness from which it came. Period.

Atkinson and I engaged in a more secular, political, and philosophical dialogue, but one that also focused on the absence of ethical behavior among women, including feminists, and on our desire to speak our "different" truths clearly, but to treat each kindly and ethically. I initially needed her assistance with certain feminist dates and concepts. Atkinson was very generous with her time and resources. However, as I pursued certain leads, it became clear that I could not do them justice in the time I had left; someone else, not I, would have to revisit and expose these painful historical events. Atkinson had put her own work aside to help me; she was understandably frustrated that I would not be able to do this. Thus we disagreed with each other. We said so. Neither of us died. In fact, the reverse occurred. Atkinson wrote:

In many ways it has been 'fortuna' that we got into

such a long discussion about the past. Yes, there was/is much pain. But our talk was/is desperately important to me. Obviously. I am very proud of our discussion . . . . We have been struggling. Admittedly, with some rough edges. We MUST continue, since apart from the benefits for the two of us, I feel that we are a mini-laboratory for the Movement. THIS is what we (and I have to include myself in this indictment) never could do in the Movement. So I want to thank you for this.

I'm not saying our format for dialogue has been perfect. But the most important thing for me is that we're trying and struggling with honest communication about important things. In some ways, it appears (but it may not be) the opposite of consciousness-raising, in that we are trying to express our thoughts without first worrying about whether or not they "fit."

What we've been doing is often hard on the ego for anyone/everyone involved. I believe you have to want (your goal) very, very badly to engage in it. And our egos are SO fragile. But when we confuse our egos with the truth, guess what loses out?

I hope that this book blesses and inspires my readers as I have been blessed by these sixteen people.

Earlier, I wrote that women are both Demeter and Persephone, both Clytemnestra and Electra. Let me now say that women are also Cinderella, Cinderella's sisters, and her step-mother too. When we envy our sister, or our daughter, and therefore humiliate her, we drive others away; as the professors Ulanov ask, "who would seek out Cinderella's sisters as com-panions?" The Ulanovs view Cinderella as a "female Christ figure, hardly divine, but a true suffering servant and scape-goat." They see her as Kierkegaard's "Knight of Faith, (and) the scriptural Abraham," because "in spite of all difficulties she "remains convinced that her wish will surely be fulfilled." Boldly, the Ulanovs suggest that we are all, to some extent, like Cinderella's sisters, when we, both the envied and the envying, "cannot surrender" to the "extraordinary relationship God offers."

> Cinderella sits in her ashes, utterly undefended except by her good heart. She will be hurt . . . . We all must be, good or bad . . . . No matter how savagely treated by the world around it, (an unenvious good-ness) does not . . . join its torturers, either in reprisal or in conquest. She goes about her business, looking everywhere for the good. When it comes she accepts it and enjoys it. Cinderella . . . . does not shake her fist at heaven. Taunted by her sisters as Job was by his friends . . . . Cinderella shows a stubbornness like Job's. She insists on her own dreams. She surrenders to the daring of the possible.

The Ulanovs suggest that the "way to have being. . . is to share it. Recognizing the good entails realizing that it does not summarily banish evil but rather enters even where evil is." They urge us to trust in the "endurance of the good, despite the attacks of the bad" because it is present within us, "keeping us alive."

And I, dear reader, agree.

ENDNOTES

INTRODUCTION

1. Women (and men too of course) might consider funding their local shelters for battered women and their legal representatives that are perpetually under-funded. Scholarships for girls, not just for boys, are important for our future. Funding abortions for poor women, breast cancer research, and social services for women who suffer from AIDS (who are increasingly poor women of color) and for women who suffer from other chronic or terminal illnesses are all important. As women, they are often deserted or neglected by their families. My personal plea is to fund talented women artists, thinkers, and social-justice activists, since their male counterparts in these areas already receive the lion's share of the resources.

2. Those who focus on this subject include: Dorothy Allison, Natalie Angier, Margaret Atwood, Teresa Bernardez, Judith Briles, Susan Brownmiller, Anne Campbell, Paula Caplan, Claudia Card, Joan Cassell, Betty de Chant, Kim Chernin, Betsy Cohen, Gloria Cowan, Mary Daly, Anselma Dell'Olio, Rachel Blau Du Plessis and Ann Snitow, Louise Eichenbaum and Susie Orbach, Bernice Fischer, Karen Fite and Nikola Trumbo, Jane Flax, Ginny Foat, Jo Freeman, Nancy K. Friday, Judith Kegan Gardiner, Judith Lewis Herman and Helen Block Lewis, Nini Herman, Marianne Hirsch, Sarah Lucia Hoagland, bell hooks, Dana Crowley Jack, Evelyn Fox Keller and Helene Moglen, Christine Ann Lawson, Kerry Lobel, Eva Margolies, Barbara Mathias, Toni A. H. McNaron, Nancy K. Miller, Valerie Miner and Helen Longino, Kate Millett, Toni Morrison, Pat O'Connor, Letty Cottin Pogrebin, Jan Raymond, Ruth Rosen, Lillian Rubin, Joanna Russ, Leora Tannenbaum, Laura Tracy, Alice Walker, Monique Wittig, Naomi Wolf, and Laurette K. Woolsey and Laura-Lynne McBain, among others.

There are many more researchers (scholars of aggression, primatologists, evolutionary theorists, anthropologists, cognitive, developmental and gender psychologists, psycho-linguists, psychoanalytic
theorists, experimental psychologists, management and corporate
psychologists, sociologists), whose work did not focus on woman's
inhumanity or hostility to woman. Nevertheless, their experimental
or observational work has been utterly invaluable in confirming,
expanding, deepening, and correcting my own understanding of
this subject. You will find their names in the References section of
this book.

CHAPTER ONE

No notes.

CHAPTER TWO

1. Interestingly, in this study, when girls reached eleven, they
   increased their use of direct physical aggression—and not surprisingly, also decreased their level of indirect aggression. However, by
   the time the girls turned fifteen, their use of direct aggression had
   decreased—and their level of indirect aggression had, accordingly,
   increased—to their previous eight-year-old level.

CHAPTER THREE

1. In 1996, Florida Atlantic University psychologists Samantha Walker,
   Deborah R. Richardson, and Laura Green did not find such differences among college age students; in 2000, S. Walker, L. Green,
   and L. Richardson did not find such differences among elder
   adults.

2. For example, in 1987, M. W. Matlin wrote, "By the time they reach
   adulthood, most women agree with most men that males are superior"; and in 1988, H. M. Lips wrote that "Not only are males viewed
   as different from females; they are viewed as superior to them."

3. In 1996, Glick and Fiske published a study in which they presented both a theory and a scale that parallels concepts of "ambivalent racism," differentiates racist from sexist prejudice, and measures what they call "Ambivalent Sexism" (ASI). This inventory is different from other measures of sexism in that it includes both "hostile" (HS) and "benevolent" sexism (BS).

    Hostile sexism items tapped the categories of Dominative Paternalism (e.g., "The world would be a better place if women supported men more and criticized them less"), Competitive Gender Differentiation (e.g., "A wife should not be significantly more successful in her career than her husband"), and Heterosexual Hostility (e.g., "There are many women who get a kick out of teasing men by seeming sexually available and then refusing male advances"). Each subcategory was represented by approximately fifteen items.

    Benevolent sexism items tapped the categories of Protective Paternalum (e.g., "Every woman should have a man to whom she can turn for help in times of trouble"), Complementary Gender Differentiation (e.g., "Many women have a quality of purity that few men possess"), and Heterosexual Intimacy (e.g., "People are not truly happy in life unless they are romantically involved with a member of the other sex"). Each subcategory was represented by approximately fifteen items.

4. Karen Jo Koonan and Terry Waller (1989) report:
    "During the voir dire in the first trial, one of the jurors denied having any experience with domestic or spousal violence and also denied having any "preconceived position" about battering or abuse. Following the defendant's conviction of second degree murder, it was revealed that that juror had in fact been the victim of an abusive spouse and in evaluating this case, had compared the defendant's experience to her own. The

conviction was reversed by the First District Court of
Appeals, which held that a juror's failure to reveal her
personal experiences with domestic violence constituted juror misconduct. People v. Blackwell, 191
Cal.App.3d at 925 (1987).

CHAPTER FOUR

1. I am indebted to Nini Herman for her 1989 work on mothers and
    daughters. In her, I have certainly found a kindred spirit. A friend
    in London gave me a copy of this book, which has never been pub-
    lished in America, many years after I had first written about
    Demeter and Persephone in *Women and Madness* (1972); in an
    Introduction to a collection of *Wonder Woman* comic strips entitled
    "The Amazon Legacy," published by Holt, Rinehart, Winston which
    was also published in 1972; and in two subsequent journals articles.
    In 1985, I first wrote about psychological matricide, using the myth
    of Clytemenstra and Electra. This appeared in Dale Spender's *For
    the Record: The Making and Meaning of Feminist Knowledge,* London:
    The Woman's Press. In 1988, I presented a paper on this subject
    that was published in 1990, in a special issue of *The Journal of
    Women and Therapy.* It was entitled: "Mother-Hatred and Mother-
    Blaming: What Electra Did to Clytemnestra." If only I had known
    about Nini Herman's most excellent work, I would have both bene-
    fited from it and used it in my 1990 journal article. (Actually, I
    would have brought it with me to the 1988 conference, which took
    place in Vermont; it would have served as a worthy companion and
    comrade-in-arms when the assembled feminist therapists either
    challenged or remained puzzled by what I was saying.)

    Nini Herman's work in this area and my own are similar, in
    some ways, but I feel the need to carefully differentiate myself intel-
    lectually. In a sense, this is a mother-daughter dynamic—is it not?

    Nini Herman is at her best when she writes about accom-
    plished daughters and their unfortunately destructive mothers.

Like Freud, Herman uses myth to create or explain psychoanalytic concepts—which she then applies to the biographies of women who are not on her couch or in her consulting room. It is tempting to do this, as long as we remain clear that the result is more art than science.

2. Interestingly, Hamner fails to note that Medea killed her sons (Hamner's mother did not physically kill her), and that Clytemnestra was herself killed by a son (Hamner did not kill her mother). Still, Hamner is right to situate her own drama on the classic Greek stage.

CHAPTER FIVE

1. I do not wish to take Freud's comments out of context; hence, I am quoting from this essay more fully. Freud writes:

> She became keenly conscious of the wish to have a child, and a male one; that what she desired was her father's child and an image of him, her consciousness was not allowed to know. And what happened next? It was not she who bore the child, but her unconsciously hated rival, her mother. Furiously resentful and embittered, she turned away from her father and from men altogether. After this first great reverse she forswore her womanhood and sought another goal for her libido. In doing so she behaved just as many men do who after a first distressing experience turn their backs for ever upon the faithless female sex and become woman-haters. . . . After her disappointment, therefore, this girl had entirely repudiated her wish for a child, her love of men, and the feminine role in general. It is evident that at this point a number of very different things might have happened. What actually happened was the most extreme case. She changed into a man and took her mother in

place of her father as the object of her love. Her relation to her mother had certainly been ambivalent from the beginning, and it proved easy to revive her earlier love for her mother and with its help to bring about an over-compensation for her current hostility towards her.

2. Chodorow argues that women become biological mothers in order to capture—or re-capture—an intimacy with their mothers that they once had—or never had, but cannot have with other adults, including a spouse.

3. Klein also published a piece on the *Oresteia*. I rushed to read it. Surprisingly, Klein did not discuss the psychology of Electra and Clytemnestra in this piece, "Some reflections on the *Oresteia*."

4. Herman and Lewis write about the consequences of male-preference in mothers; others have written about the causes of such male-preference and about female-preference as well. Carol Jahme, in her book *Beauty and the Beasts: Woman, Ape and Evolution* has an interesting discussion about why a maternal preference for a child of a particular gender might exist:

> It has been suggested that a human mother might, depending on her own status, evolutionarily favour boys over girls, or vice versa. If a woman is high-status it seems likely her children will be high-status too. Theoretically high-status men usually have more opportunities to reproduce than high-status females. . . . In evolutionary terms it is an imperative to have as many descendants as possible. If we accept that humans are patrilineal, dominant women benefit from sons because they have the potential to grow up to be high-status men and have more chances to reproduce.
>
> Lower-status women will have lower-status children

> and because women usually have a chance to reproduce, whereas low-status males do not, it is better for a low-status mother to have daughters as a means of having descendants. Sociological studies have shown a trend for low-income single mothers to have daughters.

Unfortunately, it is not clear what sociological data Jahme is relying upon.

5.   In 1988, Jessica Benjamin called for an "intersubjective view" in which women approach "the other as a separate person who is like us yet distinct."

6.   I wrote about this briefly in Dale Spender's excellent book, *For the Record: The Making and Meaning of Feminist Knowledge* (1985); This was in response to Spender's essay about *Women and Madness*.

7.   These two young feminists have real feminist mothers and mentors against whom they did not dare rebel. Had they been able to do so, they might have written another kind of book.

CHAPTER SIX

1.   On the other hand, Derricotte has also observed how "happy" certain white families seemed, "how much more accepting and lenient with their children." She attributes this, in part, to their "being without the stresses that race brings into their family."

2.   Mothers cannot control everything; most control very little. In order for genius to flourish, in either men or women, great luck is required. In addition, both male and female genius require literacy, leisure, money, intimate and institutional support, and continuing access to the right circles. Women of genius also specifically require encouraging fathers. In the past, few mothers were able to prevail against husbands who refused to allow their daughters to be educated or to enter public life. In addition, many women of genius, even with empowering fathers, mothers, and other intimates, have been systemically crushed in their own lifetime, their work and importance systematically "disappeared."

CHAPTER SEVEN

1. The Biblical Cain slew his brother Abel because Abel's offering was accepted by God, while Cain's was not; Abel was "successful" and for this, his brother killed him.

2. I have no sisters, only brothers, whom I rarely mention. They are violent and dangerous men. My life and character are so different from theirs that I have actually come to consider them "former brothers." For now, silence is my only refuge; words fail.

CHAPTER EIGHT

No notes.

CHAPTER NINE

1. Here I include historians Sheila Rowbottham, Eleanor Flexner, Carol Smith-Rosenberg, and Blanche Wiesen Cook; literature professor Lillian Faderman; sociologist Kathy Barry; scholar Dale Spender, playwright Claire Coss, and film-maker Midge MacKenzie.

2. Yazigi, Monique P. "Reading, Writing, and Social Climbing." *New York Times*, October 3, 1999.

CHAPTER TEN

1. This is similar to the young girls whom Linda A. Hughes studied in Chapter Two. Hughes studied how girls behaved when faced with a forced choice competition. She found that when girls disqualified one opponent they were really being "nice mean," since the disqualified player would now be replaced by another girl. Thus, girls convinced themselves that winning and disqualifying someone really amounted to a form of altruism.

    Hughes, Linda A. (1998). " 'But that's not really mean': Competing in a cooperative mode." *Sex Roles, 19* (11/12).

2. According to historian Barbara Winslow, social justice and revolutionary movements often cannibalize themselves. Winslow describes the various feuds and fallings-out among First Wave American feminists (Victoria Woodhull and Stanton and

Anthony), and among their British suffragist counterparts, the
Pankhursts in England.

> The Women's Social and Political Union is the story
> of a family-built organization that turned on itself (the
> two boys die); one daughter is exiled to Australia, the
> other, Sylvia, gets expelled. Under Christabel's leader-
> ship, people are expelled or shunned.

3. Let me note that sometimes the woman being "trashed" *was* unac-
    ceptably arrogant, interpersonally tone-deaf, egomaniacal, awkward,
    eccentric, bullying, or simply had poor personal hygiene. Like most
    women, feminists had no room at their Inn for her. They fancied
    themselves revolutionaries, not mothers. Also, like other women,
    many feminists were afraid to associate with the "wrong" kind of
    people, given the penalties levied against women for doing so.

4. According to Cassell's study, the accused woman said that she felt
    the group "relied upon her brains and verbal ability in times of con-
    flict, especially conflict with men," but when there were no men to
    feel oppressed by, then she was "accused of oppressing other
    women." Women were so used to criticizing each other that they
    could not stop doing so. According to Cassell:

    > Chairing the weekly meeting required control, flex-
    > ibility, and political skill. A too controlling chair was
    > criticized for being authoritarian; a laissez-faire one
    > heard complaints about an overlong and chaotic
    > meeting. It was a classic double-bind: the chair was
    > damned if she led and damned if she did not. . . .
    > (Chairing) was, in fact, so unpleasant a task . . . that a
    > number of women consistently refused to volunteer.

5. Chesler, Phyllis (1994). "Sister, Fear Has No Place Here." *On The
    Issues*, Fall.

6. This idea is found in the Babylonian Talmud that was eventually compiled in the sixth century. These comments were most likely authored between the second and fourth centuries.

> Rabbi Johanan said on the authority of Rabbi Simeon b. Yohai: "Verbal wrong is more heinous than monetary wrong, because . . .Rabbi Eleazar said: 'The one affects his [the victim's] person, the other only his money.'" Rabbi Samuel b. Nahmani said: "For the former restoration is possible, but not for the latter. . ."
> A Tanna (A rabbi from the Tannaitic period) recited before Rabbi Nahman b. Isaac: "He who publicly shames his neighbor is as though he shed blood." ("kol hamalbin pnei chavero barabim keilu shofech damim") Whereupon Rabbi Nahman remarked to him, "You say well, because I have seen it [sc. such shaming], the ruddiness departing and paleness supervening." (Baba Metzia 58b).
> The Rabbis compare the act of shaming someone to the act of shedding blood (i.e., murder) because the blood drains from the face of the person. Perhaps they recognized that shaming someone can often cause long term or permanent damage to the psyche, reputation and/or livelihood. Similarly, "the talk about the third [persons] kills three persons: him who tells [the slander], him who accepts it, and him about whom it is told." (Arachin 15b).

7. Studies suggest that both female and male athletes are highly affiliative and are less stressed and frustrated when faced with the need to make quick decisions. Some other athletic "virtues" women might learn to apply elsewhere in their lives: how to jockey for the ball, not merely for attention; how to experience one's body as strong and capable of both aggression and resistance; how to work as a team toward a common goal; how the needs of the whole team

supersede—without negating—the needs of the individual athlete; how to feel part of something larger than oneself, or than one's self merged with only one other; how to enjoy one's body for what it does rather than for how it looks.

8. Given the right historical opportunity, many women are quite capable of behaving "like men" or like men of their own or of different classes. Working-class, slave, and impoverished women, and women of all classes during war, have always proved capable of behaving, not only like women, but also "like men" in terms of direct aggression or productive team-spirit.

REFERENCES

INTRODUCTION

Allison, Dorothy (1983). *The Women Who Hate Me*. Brooklyn, New York: Long Haul Press.

Bernikow, Louise (1980). *Among Women*. New York: Harmony Books.

Brown, Elaine (1992). *A Taste of Power: A Black Woman's Story*. New York: Anchor Books, Doubleday.

Caplan, Paula J. (1981). *Between Women: Lowering the Barriers*. Toronto: Personal Library.

Cowan, Gloria and W. J. Quinton, (1997). "Cognitive style and attitudinal correlates of the Perceived Causes of Rape (PCR) Scale." *Psychology of Women Quarterly, 21*, 227-245.

Cowan, Gloria., C. Neighbors, J. DeLaMoreaux, and C. Behnke (1998). "Women's hostility toward women." *Psychology of Women Quarterly, 22*, 267-284.

Cowan, Gloria (2000). "Women's hostility toward women and rape and sexual harassment myths." *Violence Against Women, 6* (3), pp. 238-246.

Daly, Mary (1984). *Pure Lust: Elemental Feminist Philosophy*. Boston: Beacon Press.

Dugger, Celia (2000). "Kerosene, weapon of choice for attacks on wives in India." *New York Times*, December 26.

Fanon, Frantz (1965). *A Dying Colonialism*. Haakon Chevalier, Trans. New York: Grove Press, Inc.

Fanon, Frantz (1967). *Black Skin, White Masks*. Charles Lam Markmann, Trans. New York: Grove Press, Inc.

Fanon, Frantz (1968). *The Wretched of the Earth: The Handbook for the Black Revolution that is Changing the Shape of the World*. New York: Grove Press, Inc.

Fite, Karen and Nikola Trumbo (1984). "Betrayals among women: barriers to a common language." *Lesbian Ethics, 1*(1).

Freire, Paulo (1970). *Pedagogy of the Oppressed.* Myra Bergman Ramos, Trans. New York: Herder and Herder.

Friday, Nancy K. (1985). *Jealousy.* New York: William Morrow and Co.

Friday, Nancy K. (1996). *Our Looks, Our Lives: Sex, Beauty, Power, and the Need to Be Seen.* New York: HarperCollins.

Goodman, Ellen and Patricia O'Brien. *I Know Just What You Mean: The Power of Friendship in Women's Lives.* New York: Simon and Schuster, 2000.

Grahn, Judy (1972). "A Woman is Talking to Death." In Elly Bulkin and Joan Larkin, eds. *Lesbian Poetry: An Anthology.* Watertown, MA: Persephone Press.

Herzl, Theodor (1972). *The Jewish State: An Attempt at a Modern Solution to the Jewish Question.* Sylvie D'Avigdor, Trans. London: H. Pordes.

Hoagland, Sarah Lucia (1986). "Lesbian ethics: Some thoughts on power in our interactions." *Lesbian Ethics,* 2(1).

Hoagland, Sarah Lucia (1988). *Lesbian Ethics: Toward New Value.* Palo Alto, California: Institute of Lesbian Studies.

hooks, bell (1981). *Ain't I a Woman: Black Women and Feminism.* Cambridge, MA: South End Press.

Leland, John (2000). "Silence ending about abuse in gay relationships." *New York Times,* November 6.

Levi, Primo (1988). *The Drowned and the Saved.* New York: Simon and Schuster.

Memmi, Albert (1966). *The Liberation of the Jew.* Judy Hyun, Trans. New York: The Viking Press.

Memmi, Albert (1971). *Portrait of a Jew.* Elisabeth Abbott, Trans. New York: The Viking Press.

Mitscherlich, Margarete (1987). *The Peaceable Sex.* New York: International Publishing Corporation.

Pogrebin, Letty Cottin (1986). *Among Friends: Who We Like, Why We Like Them, and What We Do About Them.* New York: The McGraw Hill Companies.

Russ, Joanna (1997). *What are We Fighting For? Sex, Race, Class, and the Future of Feminism.* New York: St. Martin's Press.

Smucker, Phillip (2001). "Egypt's battle against female circumcision: A new US-Egypt-funded survey shows more women here are against the practice." *Christian Science Monitor*, February 27.

Tannen, Deborah (2001). *I Only Say this Because I Love You: How the Way We Talk Can Make or Break Family Relationships Throughout Our Lives.* New York: Random House.

Tierney, John (2000). "Negotiating sexual politics on 'Survivor.' " *New York Times.* August 22.

Weisser, Susan Ostrov and Jennifer Fleischner, eds. (1995). *Feminist Nightmares: Women at Odds: Feminism and the Problems of Sisterhood.* New York: New York University Press.

Wittig, Monique (1987). *Across the Acheron.* David Le Vay, Trans. London: Peter Owen.

Wittig, Monique (1969). *Les Guérillères.* David Le Vay, Trans. New York: The Viking Press.

CHAPTER ONE

Abbott, Shirley (1983). *Womenfolks: Growing Up Down South.* New Haven: Ticknor & Fields.

Aguilar, Delia D. (1997). "Lost in translation: Western feminism and Asian women." In Sonia Shah, ed.: *Dragon Ladies: Asian-American Feminists Breathe Fire.* Boston: South End Press.

Albert, Alexa (2001). *Brothel: Mustang Ranch and Its Women.* New York: Random House.

Anderson, Duncan Maxwell (1986). "The delicate sex: How females threaten, starve, and abuse one another." *Science*, April, 42+.

Andrews, Josephine (1998). "Infanticide by a female black lemur, eulemur macaco, in disturbed habitat on Nose By, North-Western Madagascar." *Folia Primatologica, 69*(suppl 1), 14-7.

Angier, Natalie (1999). *Woman: An Intimate Geography.* Boston and New York: Houghton Mifflin.

Björkqvist, Kaj (1994). "Sex differences in physical, verbal, and indirect aggression: A review of recent research." *Sex Roles, 30*(3/4), 177-88.

Björkqvist, Kaj and Pirkko Niemelä, eds. (1992). *Of Mice and Women: Aspects of Female Aggression.* San Diego, CA: Academic Press., Harcourt Brace Jovanovich. Hereafter, Björkvist and Niemelä: *Of Mice and Women.*

Björkqvist, Kaj and Pirrko Niemelä (1992). "New trends in the study of female aggression." In Björkqvist and Niemelä: *Of Mice and Women.*

Björkqvist, Kaj, Kirsti Lagerspetz, and Ari Kaukiainen (1992). "Do girls manipulate and boys fight?" *Aggressive Behavior, 18,* 117-27.

Björkqvist, Kaj, Karen Österman, and Kirsti Lagerspetz (1993). "Sex differences in covert aggression among adults." *Aggressive Behavior, 19.*

Briton, Nancy J. and Judith A. Hall (1995). "Beliefs about female and male nonverbal communication." *Sex Roles, 32*(1-2), 79-90.

Burbank, Victoria K. (1987). "Female aggression in cross-cultural perspective." *Behavior Science Research, 21:*70-100.

Buss, David M. and Joshua Duntley (1999). "The evolutionary psychology of patriarchy: Women are not passive pawns in men's games." *Behavioral and Brain Sciences, 22*(2).

Campbell, Anne; Steven Muncer; and Daniel Bibel (1998). "Female-female criminal assault: An evolutionary perspective." *Journal of Research in Crime and Delinquency, 35*(4), November, 413-28.

Cook, H. B. Kimberley (1992). "Matrifocality and female aggression in Margariteño society." In Björkqvist and Niemelä: *Of Mice and Women.*

Cowan, Gloria (2000). "Women's hostility toward women and rape and sexual harassment myths." *Violence against Women, 6*(3), 238-46.

Cowan, Gloria and W. J. Quinton (1997). "Cognitive style and attitudinal correlates of the Perceived Causes of Rape (PCR) Scale." *Psychology of Women Quarterly, 21,* 227-45.

Cowan, Gloria, C. Neighbors, J. DeLaMoreaux, and C. Behnke (1998). "Women's hostility toward women." *Psychology of Women Quarterly, 22,* 267-84.

Cummings, Laura L. (1994). "Fighting by the rules: Women street-fighting in Chihuahua, Chihuahua, Mexico." *Sex Roles, 30*(3/4), 189-98.

Curtis, Deborah J. and Alphonse Zaramody (1997). "Social structure and seasonal variation in the behaviour of eulemur mongoz." *Folia Primatologica, 70,* 79-96.

Dolgin, Kim Ci and Stephanie Kim (1994). "Adolescents' disclosure to best and good friends: The effects of gender and topic intimacy." *Social Development, 3*(2), 146-57.

Dugger, Celia (2000). "Kerosene, weapon of choice for attacks on wives in India." *New York Times,* December 26.

Eder, Donna and David A. Kinney (1995). "The effect of middle school extra-curricular activities on adolescents' popularity and peer status." *Youth and Society, 26*(3), 298-324.

Farley, Melissa, Isin Baral, Merab Kiremire, and Ufuk Sezgin (1998). "Prostitution in five countries: Violence and post-traumatic stress disorder." *Feminism and Psychology, 8*(4), 405-26.

Fossey, Dian (1983). *Gorillas in the Mist.* Boston: Houghton Mifflin.

Glazer, Ilsa (1992). "Inter-female aggression and resource scarcity in a cross-cultural perspective." In Björkqvist and Niemelä: *Of Mice and Women.*

Goodall, Jane (1977). "Infant killing and cannibalism in free-living chimpanzees." *Folia Primatologica, 28,* 259-82.

Goodall, Jane (1986). *The Chimpanzees Gombe: Patterns of Behavior.* Cambridge, MA: Harvard University Press.

Goodall, Jane (1991). *Through a Window: Thirty Years with the Chimpanzees of Gombe.* Boston: Houghton Mifflin.

Harris, Mary G. (1993). "Cholas, Mexican-American girls, and gangs." *Sex Roles, 30* (3/4), 189-98.

Hines, J. Nicole and Douglas P. Fry (1994). "Indirect modes of aggression among women of Buenos Aires, Argentina." *Sex Roles, 30*(3), 213-36.

Hoffmann, Bill (2000). "Men have half a mind to listen." *New York Post,* Wednesday Nov. 29.

Holmström, Reijo (1992). "Female aggression among the great apes." In Björkqvist and Niemelä: *Of Mice and Women.*

hooks, bell (1981). *Ain't I a Woman: Black Women and Feminism.* Cambridge, MA: South End Press.

Hrdy, Sarah Blaffer (1981). *The Woman that Never Evolved.* Cambridge, MA: Harvard University Press.

Hrdy, Sarah Blaffer (1981). " 'Nepotists' and 'altruists': The behavior of old females among macaques and langur monkeys." In P. Amoss and S. Harrell, eds.: *Other Ways of Growing Old.* Stanford, CA: Stanford University Press.

Jahme, Carole (2001). *Beauty and the Beasts: Woman, Ape and Evolution.* New York: Soho Press.

Johnston, Marc A. and Charles B. Crawford (1999). "Stigmatizing women's aggressive behavior: Who does it benefit and why?" *Behavioral and Brain Sciences, 22*(2).

Jolly, Allison (1998). "Pair-bonding, female aggression, and the evolution of lemur societies." *Folia Primatologica, 69* (suppl 1).

Jost, J. T. and Mahzarin R. Banaji (1994). "The role of stereotyping in system-justification and the production of false consciousness." *British Journal of Social Psychology, 33,* 1-27.

Kenton, Edgar (2000). Study mentioned in Hoffmann, Ibid. *New York Post.*

Lagerspetz, Kirsti. (1989). "Biologinen ihmiskäsitys (The biological concept of man)." In M. Kamppinen, P. Laihonen, and T. Vuorisalo, *Kulttuurieläin: Ihmistutkimuksen biologiaa. (The Cultural Animal. Essays on the Biology of Culture).* Helsinki: Otava.

Lorde, Audre (1984). *Sister Outsider.* Freedom, CA: The Crossing Press.

Maher, L. and R. Curtis (1992). "Women on the edge of crime: Crack cocaine and the changing contexts of street-level sex work in New York City." *Crime, Law and Social Change, 18,* 221-58.

Manson, Joseph H., Lisa M. Rose, Susan Perry, and Julie Gros-Louis (1999). "Dynamics of female-female relationships in wild cebus capunicinus: Data from two Costa Rican sites." *International Journal of Primatology, 20*(5).

McGrew, W. C. and E. C. McLuckie (1986). "Philopatry and dispersion in the cotton-top tamarin, saguinus (o.) oedipus: An attempted laboratory simulation." *International Journal of Primatology, 7,* 401-22.

Miller, E. M. (1986). *Street Woman.* Philadelphia: Temple University Press.

Mirikitani, Janice (1987). *Shedding Silence: Poetry and Prose.* Berkeley, CA: Celestial Arts.

Moore, Jim (1986). Quoted in Anderson, Ibid.

Pusey, Anne, Jennifer Williams and Jane Goodall (1997). "The influence of dominance rank on the reproductive success of female chimpanzees." *Chimpanzee Reproductive Sciences* (Online), *227*(5327).

Saltzman, Wendy, N. J. Schultz-Darken, and D. H. Abbott (1996). "Behavioral and endocrine predictors of dominance and tolerance in female common marmosets, Callithrix jacchus" *Animal Behavior, 51*: 657-74.

Schuster, Ilsa (1983). "Women's aggression: An African case study." *Aggressive Behavior, 9*, 319-31.

Schuster, Ilsa (1985). "Female aggression and resource scarcity: A cross-cultural perspective." In D. Benton, Marc Haug, and Paul F. Brain, eds.: *The Aggressive Female*. Montreal: Eden Press.

Shuntich, Richard J. and Richard M. Shapiro (1991). "Explorations of verbal affection and aggression." *Journal of Social Behavior and Personality, 6*(2), 283-300.

Shah, Sonia, ed. (1997). *Dragon Ladies: Asian American Feminists Breathe Fire*. Boston: South End Press.

Smuts, Barbara (1992). "Male aggression against women: An evolutionary perspective." *Human Nature, 3*, 1-44.

Smuts, Barbara (1995). "Apes of wrath." *Discover*, Aug., 35-7.

Smuts, Barbara (1995). "The evolutionary origins of patriarchy." *Human Nature, 6*, 1-32.

Snowdon, Charles T. and Jennifer J. Pickhard (1999). "Family feuds: Severe aggression among cooperatively breeding cotton-top tamarins." *International Journal of Primatology, 20*(5), 651-63.

Spielberger, C. D., G. P. Jacobs, S. F. Russell, and R. J. Crane (1983). "Assessment of anger: The State-Trait Anger Scale." In J. N. Butcher and C. D. Spielberger, eds.: *Advances in Personality Assessment*, vol. 2. Hillsdale, NJ: Lawrence Erlbaum.

Taylor, C. (1993). *Girls, Gangs, Women and Drugs*. East Lansing: Michigan State University Press.

U.S. Department of Justice. (1994). "Violence against women." Washington, DC.

Walker, Alice (1983). "The Black writer and the Southern experience." In her *In Search of Our Mother's Gardens*, New York: Harcourt Brace Jovanovich.

Wasser, Samuel K. (1986). Quoted in Anderson, Ibid.

Wrangham, Richard W. (1997). "Enhances: Subtle, secret female chim-panzees."*Chimpanzee Reproductive Sciences (Online), 227*(5327).

CHAPTER TWO

Angier, Natalie (1999). "Spiking the punch: In defense of female aggres-sion." In her *Woman: An Intimate Geography.* Boston: Houghton Mif-flin.

Archer, J. and A. Haigh (1996). "Do beliefs about aggressive feelings and actions predict reported levels of aggression? *British Journal of Social Psychology, 35,* 1-23.

Archer, J. and A. Haigh (1999). "Sex differences in beliefs about aggres-sion: Opponent's sex and the for-in of aggression." *British Journal of Social Psychology, 38,* 71-84.

Archer, J. and S. Parker (1994). "Social representations of aggression in children." *Aggressive Behavior, 20,* 101-14.

Atwood, Margaret (1988). *Cat's Eye.* New York: Doubleday.

Benenson, Joyce F. and Deborah Bennaroch (1998). "Gender differ-ences in response to friends' hypothetical greater success." *Journal of Early Adolescence, 18*(2), 192-208.

Björkqvist, Kaj (1994). "Sex differences in physical, verbal, and indirect aggression: A review of recent research." *Sex Roles, 30,* 177-88.

Björkqvist, Kaj (2000). "A cross-cultural investigation of sex differences and developmental trends in regard to direct and indirect aggres-sion: An on-going research project." Available online.

Björkqvist, Kaj and Pirkko Niemelä, eds. (1992). *Of Mice and Women: Aspects of Female Aggression.* San Diego, CA: Academic Press, Har-court Brace Jovanovich. Hereafter, Björkqvist and Niemelä: *Of Mice and Women.*

Brown, Lyn Mikel and and Carol Gilligan (1992). *Meeting at the Cross-roads: Women's Psychology and Girl's Development.* Cambridge, MA: Harvard University Press.

Campbell, Anne (1993). *Men, Women, and Aggression.* New York: Basic Books.

Campbell, Anne (1995). "A few good men: Evolutionary psychology and female adolescent aggression." *Ethology and Sociobiology, 16,* 99-123.

Campbell, Anne (1999). "Staying alive: Evolution, culture, and women's intra-sexual aggression."*Behavioural and Brain Sciences, 22*(2).

Campbell, Anne, Steven Muncer, and Daniel Bibel (1998). "Female-female criminal assault: An evolutionary perspective." *Journal of Research in Crime and Delinquency, 35*(4), 413-28.

Crick, N. and J. Grotpeter (1995). "Relational aggression, gender and social-psychological adjustment." *Child Development, 34,* 777-89.

Eder, Donna and David A. Kinney (1995). "The effect of middle school extracurricular activities on adolescents' popularity and peer status." *Youth and Society, 26*(3), 298-324.

Feshbach, Norma D. (1969). "Sex differences in children's modes of aggressive responses towards outsiders." *Merrill-Palmer Quarterly, 15,* 249-58.

Fite, Karen and Nikola Trumbo (1984). "Betrayals among women: Barriers to a common language." *Lesbian Ethics, 1*(1).

Fordham, Signithia (1996). *Blacked Out: Dilemmas of Race, Identity, and Success at Capital High.* Chicago: University of Chicago Press.

Frączek, Adam (1992). "Patterns of aggressive-hostile behavior orientation among adolescent boys and girls." In Björkqvist and Niemelä: *Of Mice and Women.*

Gibbs, J. C. and S. B. Schell (1985). "Moral development 'versus' socialization: A critique." *American Psychologist, 40*(10), 1071-80.

Gibbs, Jewelle Taylor and Larke Nahme Huang (1997). *Children of Color: Psychological Interventions with Culturally Diverse Youth.* (Jossey-Bass Social and Behavioral Science Series, University of California, Berkeley). New York: John Wiley & Sons.

Gilligan, Carol (1982). *In a Different Voice: Psychological Theory and Women's Development.* Cambridge, MA: Harvard University Press.

Goodwin, Marjorie Harness (1990). "Tactical uses of stories: Participation frameworks within girls' and boys' disputes." *Discourse Processes, 13,* 33-71.

Huesmann, L. Rowell, Nancy G. Guerra, Arnaldo Zelli, and Laurie

Miller (1992). "Differing normative beliefs about aggression for boys and girls." In Björkqvist and Niemelä: *Of Mice and Women*.

Hughes, Linda (1988). " 'But that's not really mean': Competing in a cooperative mode." *Sex Roles, 19*(11/12).

Kaukiainen, Ari, et al. (1999). "The relationships between social intelligence, empathy, and three types of aggression." *Aggressive Behavior, 25*, 81-9.

Maynard, J. (1971). *Looking Back*. New York: Avon Books.

Merkin, Daphne (1984). *Enchantment: A Novel*. New York: Harcourt Brace Jovanovich.

Miller, Jean Baker (1976). *Toward a New Psychology of Women*. Boston: Beacon Press.

Österman, Karin (1999). "Developmental trends and sex differences in conflict behavior." Doctoral dissertation in Developmental Psychology. Turku, Finland: Åbo Akademi University.

Österman, Karin, et al. (1994) "Peer and self-estimated aggression and victimization in 8-year-old children from five ethnic groups." *Aggressive Behavior. 20*, 411-28.

Österman, Karin, et al. (1997). "Sex differences in styles of conflict resolution: A developmental and cross-cultural study with data from Finland, Israel, Italy, and Poland." In Douglas P. Fry and Kaj Björkqvist, eds.: *Cultural Variation in Conflict Resolution: Alternatives to Violence*. Mahwah, NJ: Lawrence Erlbaum.

Österman, Karin, et al. (1998). "Cross-cultural evidence of female indirect aggression." *Aggressive Behavior, 24*, 1-8.

Owens, Lawrence, Rosalyn Shute, & Phillip Slee (2000). " 'Guess what I just heard!' Indirect aggression among teenage girls in Australia." *Aggressive Behavior, 26*, 67-83.

Pulkkinen, Lea(1992). "The path to adulthood for aggressively inclined girls." In Björkqvist and Niemelä: *Of Mice and Women*.

Russell, Alan and Laurence Owens (1999). "Peer estimates of school-aged boys' and girls' aggression to same- and cross-sex targets." *Social Development, 8*(3), 365-79.

Salmivalli, Christina, et al. (1996). "Bullying as a group process: Participant roles and their relations to social status within the group." *Aggressive Behavior*, *22*, 1-15.

Savin-Williams, R. (1980). "Social interactions of adolescent females in natural groups." In H. Foot, A. Chapman, and J. Smith, eds.: *Friendship and Social Relationships in Children*. New York: John Wiley & Sons.

Smith, Anna Deavere (2000). *Talk to Me: Listening between the Lines*. New York: Random House.

Tannenbaum, Leora (1999). *Slut!: Growing Up Female with a Bad Reputation*. New York: Seven Stories Press.

Tapper, Katy and Michael Boulton (2000). "Social representations of physical, verbal, and indirect aggression in children: Sex and age differences." *Aggressive Behavior*, *26*, 442-54.

Taylor, Jill McLean, Carol Gilligan, and Amy M. Sullivan (1996). *Between Voice and Silence : Women and Girls, Race and Relationship*. Cambridge, MA: Harvard University Press.

CHAPTER THREE

Banaji, Mahzarin R. and Anthony G. Greenwald (1994). "Implicit stereotyping and prejudice." In Mark P. Zanna and James M. Olson, eds., *The Psychology of Prejudice: The Ontario Symposium*, vol. 7. Hillsdale, N.J.: Lawrence Erlbaum.

Beere, C. A., D. W. King, D. B. Beere, and L. A. King (1984). "The Sex-Role Egalitarianism Scale: A measure of attitudes toward equality between the sexes." *Sex Roles*, *10*, 563-76.

Björkqvist, Kaj (1994). "Sex differences in physical, verbal, and indirect aggression: A review of recent research." *Sex Roles*, *30*, 177-88.

Björkqvist, Kaj, Karin Österman, and Ari Kakiainen (1992). "The development of direct and indirect aggressive strategies in males and females." In Björkqvist and Niemelä: *Of Mice and Women*.

Björkqvist, Kaj and Pirkko Niemelä (1992). "New trends in the study of female aggression." In *Of Mice and Women*.

Briton, Nancy J. and Judith A. Hall (1995). "Beliefs about female and male nonverbal communication." *Sex Roles*, *32*(1-2), 79-90.

Burbank, Victoria K. (1987). Female aggression in cross-cultural perspective. *Behavior Science Research, 21,* 70-100.

Burbank, Victoria K. (1994). "Cross-cultural perspectives on aggression in women and girls: An introduction." *Sex Roles, 30*(3/4).

Buss, David M. (1990). "The evolution of anxiety and social exclusion." *Journal of Social and Clinical Psychology, 9*(2), 196-201.

Butler, D. and F. L. Geis (1990). "Nonverbal affect responses to male and female leaders: Implications for leadership evaluations." *Journal of Personality and Social Psychology, 58,* 48-59.

Campbell, Anne (1999). "Staying alive: Evolution, culture, and women's intra-sexual aggression." *Behavioural and Brain Sciences, 22*(2).

Check, J. V. P., N. M. Malamuth, B. Elias, & S. A. Barton (1985). "On hostile ground." *Psychology Today,* April, 56-61.

Chinas, B. L (1973). *The Isthmus Zapotecs.* New York: Holt, Rinehart and Winston.

Colson, Elizabeth (1953). *The Makah Indians.* Manchester: Manchester University Press; Minneapolis: University of Minnesota Press.

Corbitt, E. M. and T. A. Widiger (1995). "Sex differences among the personality disorders: An exploration of the data." *Clinical Psychology: Science and Practice, 2,* 225-38.

Cowan, Gloria (2000). "Women's hostility toward women and rape and sexual harassment myths." *Violence against Women, 6,* 236-46.

Cowan, Gloria and R. R. Campbell (1995). "Rape causal attitudes among adolescents." *Journal of Sex Research, 32,* 145-53.

Cowan, Gloria, C. Neighbors, J. DeLaMoreaux, and C. Behnke (1998). "Women's hostility toward women." *Psychology of Women Quarterly, 22,* 236-46.

Daly, M. and M. Wilson (1988). *Homicide.* New York: Aldine.

Dolgin, Kim C. and Stephanie Kim (1994). "Adolescents' disclosure to best and good friends: The effects of gender and topic intimacy." *Social Development, 3*(2), 146-57.

Eagly, Alice H. (1978). "Sex differences in influenceability." *Psychological Bulletin, 85,* 86-116.

Eagly, Alice H. and Antonion Mladinic (1989). "Gender stereotypes and attitudes toward women and men." *Personality and Social Psychology Bulletin, 15,* 543-58.

Eagly, Alice H., Antonion Mladinic, and Stacey Otto (1991). "Are women evaluated more favorably than men? An analysis of attitudes, beliefs, and emotions." *Psychology of Women Quarterly, 15,* 203-16.

Eagly, Alice H. and Steven J. Karau (1991). "Gender and the emergence of leaders: A meta-analysis." *Journal of Personality and Social Psychology, 60*(5), 685-710.

Ely, Robin (1994). "The Effects of Organizational Demographics and Social Identity on Relationships among Professional Women." *Administrative Science Quarterly, 39.*

Feldman-Summers, S. and K. Lindner (1976). "Perceptions of victims and defendants in criminal assault cases." *Criminal Justice and Behavior, 3.*

Fiske, Susan T. and Peter Glick (1995). "Ambivalence and stereotypes cause sexual harassment: A theory with implications for organizational change." *Journal of Social Issues, 51*(1), 97-115.

Freedman, S. A., J. K. Swim, and C. Silverman (1997). "The effects of reasonable-person and reasonable-woman jury instructions on perceptions of and decisions about sexual harassment cases." Unpublished manuscript, The Pennsylvania State University.

Fry, Douglas P. (1992). "Female aggression among the Zapotec of Oaxaca, Mexico." In Björkqvist and Niemelä: *Of Mice and Women.*

Gilmore, David D. (1987). *Aggression and Community: Paradoxes of Andalusian Culture.* New Haven and London: Yale University Press.

Ginat, J. (1982). *Women in Muslim Rural Society.* New Brunswick, NJ: Transaction Books.

Ginat, J. (1987). *Blood Disputes among Bedouin and Rural Arabs in Israel.* Pittsburgh: University of Pittsburgh Press.

Glazer, Ilsa (1992) "Inter-female aggression and resource scarcity in a cross-cultural perspective." In Björkqvist and Niemelä: *Of Mice and Women.*

Glazer, Ilsa M. and Wahiba Abu Ras (1994). "On aggression, human rights, and hegemonic discourse: The case of a murder for family honor in Israel." *Sex Roles, 30*(3/4), 269-89.

Glick, Peter (1991). "Trait-based and sex-based discrimination in occupational prestige, occupational salary, and hiring." *Sex Roles, 25*(5-6), 351-78.

Glick, Peter, Cari Zion, and Cynthia Nelson (1988). "What mediates sex discrimination in hiring decisions?" *Journal of Personality and Social Psychology, 55*(2), 178-86.

Glick, Peter, Korin Wilk and Michele Perreault (1995). "Images of occupations: Images of gender and status in occupational stereotypes." *Sex Roles, 32*(9-10), 565-82.

Glick, Peter and Susan T. Fiske (1996). "The ambivalent sexism inventory: Differentiating hostile and benevolent sexism." *Journal of Personality and Social Psychology, 70*(3), 491-512.

Glick, Peter and Susan T. Fiske (1997). "Hostile and Benevolent Sexism: Measuring ambivalent sexist attitudes toward women." *Psychology of Women Quarterly, 21,* 119-35.

Glick, Peter, Jefferey Diebold, Barbara Bailey-Werner, and Lin Zhu (1997). "The two faces of Adam: Ambivalent sexism and polarized attitudes toward women." *Personality and Social Psychology Bulletin, 23*(12).

Glick Peter, et al. (2000). "Beyond prejudice as simple antipathy: Hostile and benevolent sexism across cultures." *Journal of Personality and Social Psychology, 70*(5).

Gluckman, Max (1963). "Gossip and scandal." *Current Anthropology, 4*(3).

Goldberg, P. (1968). "Are women prejudiced against women?" *Transaction, 5,* 28-30.

Goldenbeld, Charles and J. M. Rabbie (1991). "Effects of modelling and norm setting on aggressive behavior of males and females." Paper presented at the 6th European Conference of the International Society for Research on Aggression (ISRA), Jerusalem, Israel, 23-28 June, 1991.

Goldenbeld, Charles (1992). "Aggression after provocation." (In Dutch). Ph.D. dissertation, University of Utrecht.

Haviland, John Beard (1977). "Gossip as Competition in Zinacantan," *Journal of Communication,* Winter.

Herskovits, Melville J. (1937). *Life in a Haitian Valley.* New York: Knopf.

Hibey, R. (1972). "The trial of a rape case: An advocate's analysis of consent, corroboration, and character." *American Criminal Law Review, 11.*

Hines, J. Nicole and Fry, Douglas P. (1994). "Indirect modes of aggression among women of Buenos Aires, Argentina." *Sex Roles, 30*(3), 213-36.

Hirschman, Lynette (1994). "Female-male differences in conversational interaction." *Language in Society, 23*(3), 427-42.

Jack, Dana Crowly (1999). *Behind the Mask: Destruction and Creativity in Women's Aggression.* Cambridge, MA: Harvard University Press.

Johnston, Marc A. and Charles B. Crawford (1999). "Stigmatizing women's aggressive behavior: Who does it benefit and why?" *Behavioral and Brain Sciences, 22*(2).

Kenton, Edgar (2000). Study mentioned in Hoffmann, Ibid. *New York Post.*

Shalhoub-Kevorkian, Nadera (2001). "Redefining and confronting 'Honor Killings' as femicide." In Cynthia Meillón with Charlotte Bunch, eds. *Holding on to the Promise: Women's Human Rights and the Beijing +5 Review.* New Brunswick, NJ: Rutgers. Center for Women's Global Leadership.

Koonan, Karen Jo, and Terri Walker (1989). "Jury Selection in a Woman's Self-defense Case." Oakland, CA: National Jury Project.

Koss, M. P., T. E. Dinero, C. A. Seibel, and S. L. Cox (1988). "Stranger and acquaintance rape: Are there differences in the victim's experiences?" *Psychology of Women Quarterly, 12,* 1-24.

Kressel, Gideon M. (1981). "Sororicide/filiacide: Homicide for family honour." *Current Anthropology, 22*(2).

Lagerspetz, K., K. Björkqvist, and T. Peltonen (1988). "Is indirect aggression typical of females? Gender differences in aggressiveness in 11- to 12-year-old children." *Aggressive Behavior, 14,* 403-14.

Leaper, Campbell, Mary Carson, Carilyn Baker, Heithre Holliday, et al. (1995). "Self-disclosure and listener verbal support in same-gender and cross-gender friends' conversations." *Sex Roles, 33*(5-6), 387-404.

Lips, H. M. (1988). *Sex and Gender: An Introduction.* Mountain View, CA: Mayfield.

Lonsway, Kimberly A. and Louise F. Fitzgerald (1994). "Rape myths: In review." *Psychology of Women Quarterly, 18,* 133-64.

Lonsway, Kimberly A. and Louise F. Fitzgerald (1995). "Attitudinal antecedents of rape myth acceptance: A theoretical and empirical reexamination." *Journal of Personality and Social Psychology, 68*(4), 704-11.

Marche T. A. and C. Peterson (1993). "On the gender differential use of listener responsiveness." *Sex Roles, 29,* 795-816.

Mathias, Barbara (1992). *Between Sisters: Secret Rivals, Intimate Friends.* New York: Delacorte Press.

Matlin, M. W. (1987). *The Psychology of Women.* New York: Holt, Rinehart and Winston.

Mealey, Linda (1997). "Bulking up: The roles of gender and sexual orientation on attempts to manipulate physical attractiveness." *Journal of Sex Research, 34,* 223-28.

Olson, Ernest (1994). "Female voices of aggression in Tonga." *Sex Roles,* 30(3/4), 237-48.

Österman, Karin, et al. (1998). "Cross-cultural evidence of female indirect aggression." *Aggressive Behavior, 24,* 1-8.

Parsons, E. C. (1936). *Mitla: Town of the Souls, and Other Zapotec-speaking Pueblos of Oaxaca, Mexico.* Chicago: University of Chicago Press.

Rabbie, Jacob M., Charles Goldenbeld, and Hein F. M. Lodewijkx (1992). "Sex differences in conflict and aggression in individual and group settings." In Björkqvist and Niemelä: *Of Mice and Women.*

Rabbie, Jacob M., H. Lodewijkx, and M. Broeze (1985). "Deindividuation and emergent norms in individual and group aggression." Paper presented to the European conference "The Social Psychology of Social Problems," Poland, University of Warsaw, 2-6 October.

Rosnow, Ralph L. (1977). "Gossip and marketplace psychology." *Journal of Communication*

Rysman, Alexander (1977). "How the 'gossip' became a woman," *Journal of Communication,* Winter.

Schafran, Lynn Hecht (1993). "Writing and reading about rape: A primer." *St. John's Law Review, 66* (4), Fall-Winter, 979-1045.

Schuster, I. and M. Glazer (1984). "The power of the weak: Arab women in Israel." *Reviews in Current Anthropology, 10,* 37-43.

Schuster, I. and J. Hartz-Karp (1986). "Kinder, Kueche, Kibbutz: Female aggression and status quo maintenance in a small-scale community." *Anthropological Quarterly, 59*, 191-99.

Schuster, L. (1983). "Women's aggression: An African case study." *Aggressive Behavior, 9*, 319-31.

Scutt, Jocelyn A. (1997). *The Incredible Woman: Power and Sexual Politics.* vol. I. Melbourne, Australia: Artemis.

Selby, H. A. (1974). *Zapotec Deviance.* Austin: University of Texas Press.

Suls, Jerry M. (1977). "Gossip as social comparison" *Journal of Communication,* Winter.

Sumner, Margaret. L. (1978). "The social face of antiviolence." Paper presented at the Meeting of the International Society for Research on Aggression, Washington, D.C., September.

Swim, Janet K., K. J. Aiken, W. S. Hall, and B. A. Hunter (1995). "Sexism and racism: Old-fashioned and modern prejudices." *Journal of Personality and Social Psychology, 68*, 199-214.

Swim, Janet K. and Laurie L. Cohen (1997). "Overt, Covert, and Subtle Sexism. A Comparison between the Attitudes Toward Women and Modern Sexism Scales." *Psychology of Women Quarterly, 21*, 103-88.

Tannen, Deborah (1990). *You Just Don't Understand: Women and Men in Conversation.* New York: William Morrow.

Tougas, F., R. Brown, A. M. Beaton, and S. Joly (1995). "Neosexism: Plus ça change plus c'est pareil." *Personality and Social Psychology Bulletin, 21*, 842-49.

Townsend, John M. and Timothy Wasserman (1997). The perception of sexual attractiveness: Sex differences in variability." *Archives of Sexual Behavior, 26*(3), 243-68.

Townsend, John M.(1999). "Male dominance hierarchies and women's intra-sexual competition." *The Behavioral and Brain Sciences, 22*(2), 235-6.

Tracy, Laura (1991). *The Secret between Us: Competition among Women.* Boston: Little, Brown.

Turner, R. H. and L. M. Killian (1972). *Collective Behavior* (2nd edition). Englewood Cliffs, NJ: Prentice-Hall.

Walker, Samantha, Deborah R. Richardson, and Laura R. Green (2000). "Aggression among older adults: The relationship of interaction networks and gender role to direct and indirect responses." *Aggressive Behavior, 26,* 145-54.

West, James (1945). *Plainville, U.S.A.* New York: Columbia University Press.

CHAPTER FOUR

Aragno, Anna (1998). " 'Die so that I may live!' A psychoanalytic essay on the adolescent girl's struggle to delimit her identity." In Gerd H. Fenchel, ed. *The Mother-Daughter Relationship: Echoes through Time.* Northvale, NJ: Jason Aronson.

Arcana, Judith (1979). *Our Mother's Daughters.* Berkeley, CA: Shameless Hussy Press.

Bachofen, Johannn Jakob (1967). *Myth, Religion, and Mother Right.* Princeton, NJ: Princeton University Press.

Bernardez, Teresa (1996). "Conflicts with anger and power in women's groups." In Betsy DeChant: *Women and Group Psychotherapy: Theory and Practice.* New York: The Guilford Press.

Bynner, Witter, trans. (1952). Euripides: *Iphigenia in Tauris,* with an introduction by Richmond Lattimore. In David Grene and Richmond Lattimore, eds. *The Complete Greek Tragedies: Euripides II.* Chicago: University of Chicago Press.

Caplan, Paula J. (1989). *Don't Blame Mother.* New York: Harper and Row.

Case, Ann (2000). Found in Lewin, Tamar (2000). "Differences found in care with stepmothers." *The New York Times,* August 17.

Cashdan, Sheldon (1999). *The Witch Must Die: How Fairy Tales Shape Our Lives.* New York: Basic Books.

Chang, Jung (1992). *Wild Swans: Three Daughters of China.* New York: Anchor Books/Doubleday.

Conway, Jill Ker (1989). *The Road from Coorain.* New York: Vintage Departures.

Crawford, Christina (1978). *Mommie Dearest.* New York: William Morrow.

Daly, Martin and Margo Wilson (1998). *The Truth about Cinderella: A Darwinian View of Parental Love.* New Haven, CT: Yale University Press.

Du Maurier, Daphne (1971). *Rebecca.* New York: Avon Books.

Epstein, Helen (1997). *Where She Came from: A Daughter's Search for Her Mother's History.* New York: Little, Brown.

Esquivel, Laura (1989, 1992). *Like Water For Chocolate.* Translated by Carol Christensen and Thomans Christensen. New York: Doubleday.

Felman, Jyl Lyn (1997). *Cravings: A Sensual Memoir.* Boston: Beacon Press.

Fitzroy, Lee (1999). "Mother/Daughter incest: Making sense of the unthinkable." *Feminism and Psychology, 9*(4): 402-5.

Gornick, Vivian (1987). *Fierce Attachments.* Boston: Beacon Press.

Grene, David, trans. (1953). Sophocles: *Electra.* In David Grene and Richmond Lattimore, eds. *The Complete Greek Tragedies: Sophocles II.* Chicago: University of Chicago Press.

Hamner, Signe (1991). "By her own hand." In Rebecca Shannonhouse, ed. (2000). *Out of Her Mind: Women Writing on Madness.* New York: Modern Library.

Herman, Nini (1989). *Too Long a Child: The Mother-Daughter Dyad.* London: Free Association Books.

Hughes, T. and F. McCullough, ed. (1982). *The Journals of Sylvia Plath.* New York: Ballantine.

Hyman, B.D. (1985). *My Mother's Keeper.* New York: Morrow and Co.

Katz, Naomi and Nancy Milton, eds. (1973). *Fragment From a Lost Diary and Other Stories: Women of Asia, African, and Latin America.* New York: Pantheon Books.

Kerényi, Carl (1967). *Eleusis: Archetypal Image of Mother and Daughter.* Translated by Ralph Manheim. In *Bollingen Series LXV, 4.* New York: Pantheon Books.

Lattimore, Richmond, trans. (1953). Aeschylus: *Oresteia.* In David Grene and Richmond Lattimore, eds. *The Complete Greek Tragedies: Aeschylus I.* Chicago: University of Chicago Press.

Lawson, Christine Ann (2000). *Understanding the Borderline Mother: Helping Her Children Transcend the Intense, Unpredictable, Volatile Relationship.* Northvale, NJ: Jason Aronson.

Leonowens, Anna H. (1953). *Siamese Harem Life.* New York: E. P. Dutton.

Lewin, Tamar (2000). "Differences found in care with stepmothers." *The New York Times,* August 17.

Malcolm, Janet (1993). *The Silent Woman: Sylvia Plath and Ted Hughes.* New York: Knopf.

Middlebrook, Diane. (1991). *Anne Sexton: A Biography.* Boston: Houghton Mifflin.

Morrison, Toni (1998). *Beloved.* New York: Knopf.

Neumann, Erich (1955). *The Great Mother: An Analysis of the Archetype.* New York: Pantheon Press.

O'Neill, Eugene (1931). *Mourning Becomes Electra.* In *The Plays of Eugene O'Neill.* New York: Random House.

Pierpont, Claudia Roth (2000). *Passionate Minds: Women Rewriting the World.* New York: Knopf.

Plath, Sylvia (2000). "Life and Letters: Journals." Karen Kukil, a curator at Smith, prepared these unsealed journals for publication. *The New Yorker,* March 27, 2000.

Richards, Arlene Kramer (1998). "Anne Sexton and Child Abuse." *The Mother-Daughter Relationship Echoes Through Time.* Gerd H. Fenshel, Jason Aronson, editors. Northvale, N.J.: Jason Aronson.

Rossner, Judith (1997). *Perfidia: A Novel,* New York: Doubleday.

Schreiber, Flora Rheta (1973). *Sybil: The True Story of a Woman Possessed by Sixteen Separate Personalities.* Chicago: Regnery.

Sexton, Linda Grey (1994). *Looking for Mercy Street.* New York: Little, Brown.

Sexton, Anne (1981). *The Complete Poems.* New York: Houghton Mifflin.

Sherman, Charlotte Watson (1994). *Sister Fire.* New York: Harper Collins.

Shulman, Alix Kates (1999). *A Good Enough Daughter: A Memoir.* New York: Random House.

Stannard, Una (1995). Privately distributed essay. Stannard is the author of *Mrs. Man.* San Francisco: Germain books, 1977.

Stevenson, A. (1989). *Bitter Fame: A Life of Sylvia Plath.* Boston: Houghton Mifflin.

Toer, Pramoedya Ananta. *Inem.* In Naomi Katz and Nancy Milton, eds.,

(1973). *Fragment from a Lost Diary and Other Stories: Women of Asia, Africa, and Latin America*. New York: Pantheon Books.

Tracy, Laura (1991). *The Secret between Us: Competition among Women*. Boston: Little, Brown.

Warner, Marina (1994). *From the Beast to the Blonde: On Fairy Tales and Their Tellers*. New York: The Noonday Press.

CHAPTER FIVE

Abrams, Kathryn (2001). "Refusing and resisting." A review of Katha Pollitt's collected columns, *Subject to Debate: Sense and Dissents on Women, Politics, and Culture*. *The Woman's Review of Books*, April, *xviii*,(7).

Anderson, Nancy Fix (1987). *Woman against Women in Victorian England: A Life of Eliza Lynn Linton*, Bloomington: Indiana University Press.

Aragno, Anna (1998). " 'Die so that I may live!' A psychoanalytic essay on the adolescent girl's struggle to delimit her identity." In Gerd H. Fenchel, *The Mother-Daughter Relationship*.

Benjamin, Jessica (1988). *The Bonds of Love: Psychoanalysis, Feminism, and the Problem of Domination*. New York: Pantheon Books.

Bernardez, Teresa (1996). "Conflicts with anger and power in women's groups." In DeChant. *Women and Group Psychotherapy*.

Bernstein, Richard (1989). "Susan Sontag, as image and as herself." *New York Times*, January 26, C17.

Chesler, Phyllis (1972). *Women and Madness*. New York: Doubleday.

Chodorow, Nancy (1978). *The Reproduction of Mothering*. Berkeley: University of California Press.

Conway, Jill Ker (1989). *The Road from Coorain*. New York: Vintage Departures.

DeChant, Betty (1996). *Women and Group Psychotherapy: Theory and Practice*. New York: The Guilford Press.

Donovan, Molly Walsh (1998). "Demeter and Persephone revisited: Ambivalence and separation in the mother-daughter relationship." In Gerd H. Fenchel, ed. *The Mother-Daughter Relationship: Echoes through Time*. Northvale, NJ: Jason Aronson.

Fenchel, Gerd H., ed. (1998). *The Mother-Daughter Relationship: Echoes through Time.* Northvael, NJ: Jason Aronson.

Flax, Jane (1980). "Mother-daughter relationships: Psychodynamics, politics, and philosophy." In Hester Eisenstein and Alice Jardine, eds., (1985). *The Future of Difference,* New Brunswick, NJ: Rutgers University Press.

Freud, Sigmund (1920). "The psychogenesis of a case of homosexuality in a woman." Translated by Joan Riviere (1959). In *Collected Papers,* 2. New York: Basic Books.

Freud, Sigmund (1931). "Female sexuality" in *The Standard Edition of the Complete Psychological Works of Sigmund Freud,* vol. 21, London: Hogarth Press.

Freud, Sigmund (1938). "An Example of Psychoanalytic Work." In *The Standard Edition of the Complete Psychological Works of Sigmund Freud, 23,* London: Hogarth Press.

Friedan, Betty (1963). *It Changed My Life: Writings on the Women's Movement,* Cambridge, MA: Random House.

Gardiner, Judith Kegan (1978). "A wake for mother: The maternal deathbed in women's fiction." *Feminist Studies, 4*(2) June.

Herman, Judith Lewis and Helen Block Lewis (1986). "Anger in the mother-daughter relationship." In Toni Bernay and Dorothy Cantor, eds. *The Psychology of Today's Woman: New Psychoanalytic Visions.* Hillsdale, NJ: Analytic Press.

Herman, Nini (1989). *Too Long a Child: The Mother-Daughter Dyad,* London: Free Association Books.

Hirsch, Marianne (1989). *The Mother/Daughter Plot: Narrative, Psychoanalysis, Feminism.* Bloomington: Indiana University Press.

Horney, Karen (1926). "The flight from womanhood." In Horney (1967): *Feminine Psychology,* New York: Norton.

Horney, Karen (1926-7). "Inhibited femininity." In Horney (1967): *Feminine Psychology,* New York: Norton.

Jahme, Carole (2001). *Beauty and the Beasts: Woman, Ape and Evolution.* New York: Soho Press.

Klein, Melanie (1938). "Love, Guilt and Reparation." In *Love, Guilt and*

Reparation and Other Works, The Writings of Melanie Klein, 1. London: Hogarth Press. Reprinted in 1975.

Klein, Melanie (1957). "Envy and Gratitude." In *Envy and Gratitude and Other Works, The Writings of Melanie Klein, 3.* London: Hogarth Press. Reprinted in 1975.

Klein, Melanie (1963). "Some Reflections on the Oresteia." in Klein, ed. *Our Adult World and Other Essays* (Writings III.) London: Heinemann Medicaf.

Lorde, Audre (1984). *Sister Outsider: Essays and Speeches.* Freedom, CA: The Crossing Press.

Merkin, Daphne (1984). *Enchantment: A Novel.* New York: Harcourt Brace Jovanovich.

Meyers, Marilyn B. (1998). " 'Am I my mother's keeper?': Certain vicissitudes concerning envy in the mother-daughter dyad." In Gerd H. Fenchel, *The Mother-Daughter Relationship.*

Miller, Nancy K. (1996). *Bequest and Betrayal: Memoirs of a Parent's Death.* Bloomington: Indiana University Press.

Paglia, Camille (1994). *Vamps and Tramps.* New York: Vintage Books.

Pierpont, Claudia Roth (2000). *Passionate Minds: Women Rewriting the World.* New York: Knopf.

Podhoretz, Norman (1967). *Making It.* New York: Random House.

Rich, Adrienne (1976). *Of Woman Born: Motherhood as Experience and Institution* New York: Norton.

Russ, Joanna. Personal interview in the early 1980s. Russ developed this theme further in *Magic Mommas, Trembling Sisters, Puritans and Perverts. Feminist Essays* (1985) Trumansberg, NY: The Crossing Press.

Showalter, Elaine (2001). *Inventing herself: Claiming a Feminist Intellectual Heritage.* New York: Scribner.

CHAPTER SIX

Ardoin, John (1995). *The Callas Legacy: The Complete Guide to her Recordings on Compact Disc.* Portland, OR: The Amadeus Press.

Ardoin, John (1954). Interview of Maria Callas in *Italia Oggi*, Milan.

Bernardez, Teresa (1995). "By my sisters reborn." In Phyllis Chesler,

Esther D. Rothblum, and Ellen Cole, eds.: *Feminist Foremothers in Women's Studies, Psychology, and Mental Health*, New York: Haworth Press.

Callas, Evangelia (1967). *My Daughter: Maria Callas*. London: Leslie Frewin.

Cardinal, Marie (1984). *Words to Say It*. Pat Goodheart, Trans. Cambridge, MA: Van Vactor and Goodheart.

Chernin, Kim (1998). *The Woman Who Gave Birth to Her Mother : Tales of Women in Transformation*.: New York: Viking Books.

Chin, Soo-Young (1999). *Doing What Had to Be Done: The Life Narrative of Dora Yum Kim*. Philadelphia: Temple University Press.

Cohen, Betsy (1986). *The Snow White Syndrome: All about Envy*. New York: Macmillan.

Comas-Diaz, L. (1988). "Feminist therapy with Hispanic/Latina women: Myth or Reality?" *Women and Therapy* 6(4), 39-61. Also in Betty DeChant: *Women and Group Psychotherapy*.

Conway, Jill Ker (1989). *The Road from Coorain*. New York: Vintage Departures.

Csampai, Attila, ed. (1996). *Callas : Images of a Legend*. New York: Stewart Tabori & Chang.

DeChant, Betty (1996). *Women and Group Psychotherapy: Theory and Practice*. New York: The Guilford Press.

Derricotte, Toi (1999). *The Black Notebooks: An Interior Journey*. New York: Norton.

El-Sadawil, Nawal and Mary E. Willmuth (1995). "A feminist in an Arab world." In Phyllis Chesler; Esther D. Rothblum; Ellen Cole, eds., (1995). *Feminist Foremothers in Women's Studies, Psychology, and Mental Health*, New York: Haworth Press.

Fite, Karen & Nikola Trumbo (1984). "Betrayals among women: Barriers to a common language." *Lesbian Ethics*, 1(1), Fall.

Gage, Nicholas (2000). "Callas's Unsung lullaby." *Vanity Fair*, October.

Galatopoulous, Stelios (1998). *Maria Callas: Sacred Monster*. New York: Simon and Schuster.

Gilman, Charlotte Perkins (1935). *The Living of Charlotte Perkins Gilman: An Autobiography*. New York: Harper and Row.

Greene, B. A. (1990). "What has gone before: The legacy of racism and sexism in the lives of black mothers and daughters." In L. S. Brown and M. P. Root, eds. *Diversity and Complexity in Feminist Therapy.* New York: Haworth Press. Also in Betty DeChant: *Women and Group Psychotherapy.*

Harris, Bertha (1993). *Lover.* (With New Introduction.) New York: New York University Press.

Herman, Nini (1989). *Too Long a Child: The Mother-Daughter Dyad.* London: Free Association Books.

Herman, Judith Lewis and Helen Block Lewis (1986). "Anger in the mother-daughter relationship." In Toni Bernay & Dorothy Cantor, eds. *The Psychology of Today's Woman: New Psychoanalytic Visions.* Hillsdale, NJ: Analytic Press.

Higgonet, Anne (1993). "Myths of creation: Camille Claudel and Auguste Rodin." In Whitney Chadwick and Isabelle de Courtivron: *Significant Others: Creativity and Intimate Partnership.* New York: Thames and Hudson. Claudel's work includes *Brother and Sister, Cacountala, The Waltz, Perseus,* and the *Gorgon.* For a long time, her works remained uncatalogued, in private collections, not part of the historical record.

hooks, bell (2000). *All about Love: New Visions.* New York: William Morrow.

Jack, Dana Crowley (1999). *Behind the Mask: Destruction and Creativity in Women's Aggression.* Cambridge, MA: Harvard University Press.

Keita, Gwendolyn P. and Adele Jones (1995). "Working with feminist foremothers to advance women's issues." In Phyllis Chesler, Esther D. Rothblum, and Ellen Cole, eds.: *Feminist Foremothers in Women's Studies, Psychology, and Mental Health.* New York: Haworth Press.

Lawson, Christine Ann (2000). *Understanding the Borderline Mother: Helping Her Children Transcend the Intense, Unpredictable, Volatile Relationship.* Northvale, NJ: Jason Aronson.

Martineau, Harriet (1877). *Harriet Martineau's Autobiography,* vols. 1 and 2. London: Virago Press.

Mathias, Barbara (1992). *Between Sisters: Secret Rivals, Intimate Friends.* New York: Delacorte Press.

Merkin, Daphne (1984). *Enchantment: A Novel.* New York: Harcourt Brace Jovanovich.

Miller, Nancy K. (1996). *Bequest and Betrayal: Memoirs of a Parent's Death.* Bloomington: Indiana University Press.

Painter, Nell Irvin (1996). *Sojourner Truth: A Life, a Symbol.* New York: Norton.

Parker, Rozsika (1995). *Mother Love/Mother Hate: The Power of Maternal Ambivalence.* New York: Basic Books.

Pierpont, Claudia Roth (2000). "Memoirs of a Revolutionary: Doris Lessing." In Pierpont: *Passionate Minds: Women Rewriting the World.* New York: Knopf.

Pierpont, Claudia Roth (2000). "A Woman's Place: Olive Schreiner." In Pierpont: *Passionate Minds: Women Rewriting the World.*

Plath, Sylvia. Cited in Nini Herman (1989): *Too Long A Child: The Mother Daughter Dyad,* and contained in C. Newman (ed.) (1970): *The Art of Sylvia Plath: A Symposium.* London: Faber and Faber.

Ringgold, Faith (1995). *We Flew over the Bridge: The Memoirs of Faith Ringgold.* Boston: Bulfinch Press.

Scott, Michael (1991). *Maria Meneghini Callas.* Boston: Northeastern University Press.

Smedley, Agnes (1973). *Daughter of Earth.* New York: The Feminist Press.

Stevenson, Brenda (2000). "Distress and Discord in Virginia Slave Families, 1830-1860." In Vicki L. Ruiz and Ellen Carol DuBois, eds. *Unequal Sisters: A Multicultural Reader in U. S. Women's History.* New York: Routledge.

Stone, Laurie (2000). "Shedding Hope." *Tikkun, 15*(5). September/October, 57-9.

Stannard, Una (1995). Private communication. Stannard is the author of *Mrs. Man* (1977): Germainbooks.

Walker, Alice (1983). *In Search of Our Mother's Gardens.* New York: Harcourt, Brace, Jovanovich.

Wharton, Edith (1905, reprint 1985). *The House of Mirth.* With an introduction by Cynthia Griffen Wolff. New York: Penguin Twentieth-century Classics.

Wolff, Cynthia Griffen (1985). *Introduction* to Edith Wharton, *The House of Mirth*. New York: Penguin Twentieth Century Classics.

CHAPTER SEVEN

Angier, Natalie (1999). *Woman: An Intimate Geography*. Boston, New York: Houghton Mifflin.

Atkins, Dale V. (1984). *Sisters: A Practical, Helpful Exploration of the Intimate and Complex Bond between Female Siblings*. New York: Arbor House.

Beauvoir, Simone de (1952). *The Second Sex*. Translated by H. M. Parshley. New York, London: Bantam Books.

Bernikow, Louise (1980). *Among Women*. New York: Harmony Books.

Coates, Irene (1998). *Who's Afraid of Leonard Woolf? A Case for the Sanity of Virginia Woolf*. New York: Soho Press.

Downing, Christine (1988). *Psyche's Sisters: Re-imagining the Meaning of Sisterhood*. San Francisco: Harper & Row.

Fishel, Elizabeth (1979). *Sisters: Love and Rivalry Inside the Family and Beyond*. New York: Quill Trade Paperbacks.

Geller, Jaclyn (2001). *Here Comes the Bride: Women, Weddings, and the Marriage Mystique*. New York: Four Walls Eight Windows.

Jong, Erica (1973). *Fear of Flying*. New York: Signet.

Keller, Evelyn Fox and Helene Moglen (1987). "Competition: A Problem for Academic Women." In Valerie Miner and Helen E. Longino, eds.: *Competition: A Feminist Taboo?* New York: The Feminist Press.

Longino, Helen E. (1987). "The ideology of competition." In Miner and Longino: *Competition: A Feminist Taboo?*

Mathias, Barbara (1992). *Between Sisters: Secret Rivals, Intimate Friends*. New York: Delacorte Press.

McNaron, Toni A. H. (1987). "Little Women and 'Cinderella': Sisters and competition." In Miner and Longino: *Competition: A Feminist Taboo?*

McNaron, Toni A. H. (1985). *The Sister Bond: A Feminist View of a Timeless Connection*. Elmsford, NY: Pergamon Press.

Miner, Valerie (1987). "Rumors from the cauldron: Competition among feminist writers." In Valerie Miner and Helen E. Longino: *Competition: A Feminist Taboo?*

Mitchell, Juliet (2000). *Mad Men and Medusas: Reclaiming Hysteria.* New York: Basic Books, Perseus.

Morrison, Toni (1973). *Sula.* New York: Plume Books.

Rubin, Lillian (1985). *Just Friends: The Role of Friendship in Our Lives.* New York: Harper & Row.

Smiley, Jane (1991). *A Thousand Acres: A Novel.* New York: Ballantine Books.

Tan, Amy. *The Joy Luck Club.* New York: Putnam Publishing Group.

Tracy, Laura (1991). *The Secret between Us: Competition among Women.* Boston: Little, Brown.

Ulanov, Ann and Barry (1998). *Cinderella and Her Sisters: The Envied and the Envying.* Hull, Quebec: Daimon Verlag.

Williams, Tennessee (1947). *A Streetcar Named Desire.* New York: New Directions.

CHAPTER EIGHT

Ashcraft, K. L. and M. E. Pacanowsky (1996). "A woman's worst enemy: Reflections on a narrative of organizational life and female identity." *Journal of Applied Communication Quarterly, 24,* 217-39. In Paige P. Edley.

Ayman, Roya (1993). "Leadership perception: The role of gender and culture." In Martin M. Chemers, and Roya Ayman, eds., *Leadership Theory and Research: Perspectives and Directions.* San Diego, CA: Academic Press.

Bell, Ella, L. J., Edmondson and Stella M. Nkomo (2001). *Our Separate Ways: Black and White Women and the Struggle for Professional Identity.* Boston, MA: Harvard Business School.

Briles, Judith (1989). *Woman to Woman: From Sabotage to Support.* Far Hills, NJ: New Horizon Press.

Briles, Judith (2000). *Woman to Woman 2000: Becoming Sabotage Savvy in the New Millennium.* Far Hills, NJ: New Horizon Press.

Broder, Ivy E. (1993). "Review of NSF economics proposals: Gender and institutional patterns." *The American Economic Review, 83,* September.

Camara, W. J. (1989). "Supreme Court reviews case of sex bias in the workplace." *The Industrial-Organizational Psychologist, 26,* 39-41.

Caplan, Paula J. (1993). *Lifting a Ton of Feathers: A Woman's Guide to Surviving in the Academic World.* Toronto: University of Toronto Press.

Chemers, Martin M. and Roya Ayman, eds., (1993). *Leadership Theory and Research: Perspectives and Directions.* San Diego, CA: Academic Press.

Chusmir, L. H. and C. S. Koberg (1986). "Development and validation of the sex role conflict scale." *The Journal of Applied and Behavior Science, 22,* 392-409.

Dutton-Greene, Leila B. (2001). "Domestic violence in same-sex relationships." Unpublished study. Providence, RI: University of Rhode Island.

Edley, Paige P. (2000). "Discursive essentializing in a woman-owned business: Gendered stereotypes and strategic subordination." *Management Communication Quarterly,* 14, 211-306.

Ely, Robin (1994). "The effects of organizational demographics and social identity on relationships among professional women." *Administrative Science Quarterly, 39.*

Ely, Robin (1995). "The power in demography: Women's social constructions of gender identity at work." *Academy of Management Journal, 38*(3), 589-634.

Farley, Lin (1978). *Sexual Shakedown: The Sexual Harassment of Women on the Job.* New York: McGraw-Hill.

Hochschild, A.R. (1983). *The Managed Heart: Commercialization of Human Feeling.* Berkeley: University of California Press.

Kanter, Rosabeth Moss (1987). "Performance pressures: Life in the limelight." In Valerie Miner and Helen E. Longino, eds.: *Competition: A Feminist Taboo?* New York: The Feminist Press.

Keller, Evelyn Fox and Helene Moglen (1987). "Competition: A problem for academic women." In Miner and Longino: *Competition: A Feminist Taboo?*

Korabik, K. and Ayman, R. (1989). "Should women managers have to act like men?" *The Journal of Management Development, 8,* 23-32. (Cited in Ayman).

Miner, Valerie (1987). "Rumors from the cauldron: Competition among feminist writers." In Miner and Longino: *Competition: A Feminist Taboo?*

Onyx, Jenny (1999). "Power between women in organizations." *Feminism and Psychology, 9*(4), 417-421.

Tsui, Anne S. and Charles A. O'Reilly III (1993). "Beyond simple demographic effects: The importance of relational demography in superior-subordinate dyads." *Academy of Management Journal, 32*(2), 402-23.

CHAPTER NINE

Barry, Kathleen (1988). *Susan B. Anthony: A Biography.* New York: New York University Press.

Bernardez, Teresa (1996). "Gender-based countertransference in the group treatment of women." In Betty DeChant: *Women and Group Psychotherapy.*

Bernardez, Teresa (1996). "Theoretical perspectives: Treatments of choice." In Betty DeChant: *Women and Group Psychotherapy.*

Bernardez, Teresa (1996). "Conflicts with anger and power in women's groups." In Betty DeChant: *Women and Group Psychotherapy.*

Brody, Claire M., ed. (1987). *Women's Therapy Groups: Paradigms of Feminist Treatment.* New York: Springer.

Caplan, Paula (1985). "Women in groups: Introduction." *International Journal of Women's Studies, 8*(4).

Cecere, Donna J. (1986). "The second closet: Battered lesbians." In Kerry Lobel: *Naming the Violence: Speaking Out about Lesbian Battering.* Washington, DC: The Seal Press.

Cohen, Betsy (1986). *The Snow White Syndrome. All about Envy.* New York: Macmillan.

Cunningham, Josephine M. and Elizabeth B. Knight (1996). "Mothers, models, and mentors: Issues in long-term group therapy for women." In Betty DeChant: *Women and Group Psychotherapy.*

DeChant, Betty (1996). *Women and Group Psychotherapy: Theory and Practice.* New York: The Guilford Press.

Doherty, Patricia, Lita Newman Moses, and Joy Perlow (1996). "Competition in women: From prohibition to triumph." In Betty DeChant: *Women and Group Psychotherapy*.

Dutton-Greene, Leila B. (2001). "Domestic violence in same-sex relationships." Unpublished study. Providence, RI: University of Rhode Island.

Faderman, Lillian (1981). *Surpassing the Love of Men: Romantic Friendship and Love between Women from the Present*. New York: William Morrow.

Faderman, Lillian (1991). *Odd Girls and Twilight Lovers: A History of Lesbian Life in Twentieth-century America*. New York: Columbia University Press.

Flexner, Eleanor (1975). *Century of Struggle: The Women's Movement in the United States*. Cambridge, MA: Harvard University Press.

Lobel, Kerry (1986). *Naming the Violence: Speaking Out about Lesbian Battering*. Seattle, Washington: The Seal Press.

MacKenzie, Midge (1975). *Shoulder to Shoulder: A Documentary*. New York: Knopf.

Marlowe, Erica (Pseudonym) (1999). "Five thousand lesbians and no police force." *Feminism and Psychology*, *9*(4).

McCarthy, Mary (1963). *The Group*. (Paperback Reissue edition.) new York: Harcourt, Brace, & World.

Raymond, Janice G. (1986). *A Passion for Friends: Toward a Philosophy of Female Affection*. Boston: Beacon Press.

Rosenberg, Pearl (1996). "Comparative leadership styles of male female therapists." In Betty DeChant: *Women and Group Psychotherapy*.

Rowbotham, Sheila (1972). *Women Resistance and Revolution: A History of Women and Revolution in the Modern World*. New York: Vintage Books.

Schubert Walker, Lilly J. (1987). "Women's groups are different." In Claire M. Brody, ed. (1987). *Women's Therapy Groups: Paradigms of Feminist Treatment*. New York: Springer.

Snitow, Ann (1990). "A gender diary." In Marianne Hirsch and Evelyn Fox Keller, eds., *Conflicts in Feminism*. New York, Routledge.

Spender, Dale (1982). *Women of Ideas and What Men Have Done to Them from Aphra Behn to Adrienne Rich*. London: Pandora.

Woolsey, Laurette K. and Laura-Lynne McBain (1987). "Issues of power and powerlessness in all-woman groups." *Women's Studies International Forum,* *10,* (6).

Yazigi, Monique P. (1999). "Reading, writing, and social climbing." *New York Times,* October 3.

CHAPTER TEN

Arenas, Reinaldo (1993). *Before Night Falls: A Memoir.* New York: Viking.

Baxandall, Rosalyn Fraad (1998). "Catching the fire." In Rachel Blau Du Plessis and Ann Snitow, eds., *The Feminist Memoir Project: Voices from Women's Liberation.* New York: Three Rivers Press.

Baxandall, Rosalyn and Linda Gordon, eds. (2000). *Dear Sisters: Dispatches from the Women's Liberation Movement.* New York: Basic Books.

Brownmiller, Susan (1999). *In Our Time: Memoir of a Revolution.* New York: The Dial Press, Random House.

Caplan, Paula J. (1981). *Between Women: Lowering the Barriers.* Toronto: Personal Library.

Card, Claudia (1989). "Defusing the bomb: Lesbian ethics and horizontal violence." *Lesbian Ethics,* *3*(3).

Cassell, Joan (1977). "Contradictions in a women's liberation action group: A case study." *A Group Called Women: Sisterhood and Symbolism in the Feminist Movement.* New York: David McKay.

Dell'Olio, Anselma (1998). "Home before sundown." In Du Plessis and Snitow, *The Feminist Memoir Project.*

Dell'Olio, Anselma (1971). Unpublished article.

Densmore, Dana (1998). "A year of living dangerously: 1968." In Du Plessis and Snitow: *The Feminist Memoir Project.*

Du Plessis, Rachel Blau and Ann Snitow (1998). "A feminist memoir project." In Du Plessis and Snitow: *The Feminist Memoir Project.*

Eichenbaum, Luise and Susie Orbach (1988). *Between Women: Love, Envy, and Competition in Women's Friendships.* New York: Viking Penguin.

Firestone, Shulamith (1970). *The Dialectic of Sex.* New York: William Morrow.

Fisher, Bernice (1984). "Guilt and shame in the women's movement:

The radical ideal of action and its meaning for feminist intellectuals." *Feminist Studies,* *10*(2), Summer.

Foat, Ginny with Laura Foreman (1985). *Never Guilty, Never Free.* New York: Random House.

Freeman, Jo aka Joreen (1976). "Trashing: The dark side of sisterhood." *Ms.* April.

Freeman, Jo aka Joreen (1998). "On the origins of the women's liberation movement from a strictly personal perspective." In Du Plessis and Snitow: *The Feminist Memoir Project.*

Freeman, Jo aka Joreen (1998). "The tyranny of structurelessness," *The Second Wave,* *2*(1), 1972, p. 20.

Friday, Nancy K. (1998). *Our Looks, Our Lives: Sex, Beauty, Power, and the Need to Be Seen.* New York: HarperCollins.

Friedan, Betty (1963). *The Feminine Mystique.* New York: Norton.

Friedan, Betty (1976). *It Changed My Life: Writings on the Women's Movement.* New York: Random House.

Friedan, Betty (2000). *Life So Far: A Memoir.* New York: Simon and Schuster.

Gornick, Vivian (1998). "What feminism means to me." In Du Plessis and Snitow: *The Feminist Memoir Project.*

Hanisch, Carol (1998). "Two letters from the women's liberation movement." In Du Plessis and Snitow: *The Feminist Memoir Project.*

Harris, Bertha (1993). *Lover,* With a new Introduction. New York: New York University Press. Originally published in 1976 by Daughters, Inc.

Hawkes, Ellen (1986). *Feminism on Trial: The Ginny Foat Case and the Future of the Women's Movement.* New York: William Morrow.

Hennessee, Judith (1999). *Betty Friedan: Her Life.* New York: Random House.

hooks, bell (1981). *Ain't I a Woman: Black Women and Feminism.* Cambridge, MA: Harvard University Press.

Hughes, Linda (1998). "'But that's not really mean': Competing in a cooperative mode." *Sex Roles,* *19*(11/12).

Lobel, Kerry (1986). *Naming the Violence: Speaking Out about Lesbian Battering.* Washington, DC: The Seal Press.

536 • Phyllis Chesler

Margolies, Eva (1985). *The Best of Friends, The Worst of Enemies: Women's Hidden Power over Women.* Garden City, NY: The Dial Press.

Millett, Kate (1970). *Sexual Politics.* New York: Doubleday.

Millett, Kate (1974). *Flying.* New York: Knopf.

Miner, Valerie and Helen E. Longino, eds. (1987). *Competition: A Feminist Taboo?* New York: The Feminist Press. Hereafter, Miner and Longino: *Competition: A Feminist Taboo?*

Miner, Valerie (1985). "Rumors from the cauldron: Competition among feminist writers." In Miner and Longino: *Competition: A Feminist Taboo?*

Pogrebin, Letty Cottin (1987). *Among Friends: Who We Like, Why We Like Them, and What We Do with Them.* New York: McGraw Hill.

Raymond, Janice G. (1986). *A Passion for Friends: Toward a Philosophy of Female Affection.* Boston: Beacon Press.

Rosen, Ruth (2001). "From Bullies to Ladies." *San Francisco Chronicle.* July 30.

Rowbotham, Sheila (1972). *Women, Resistance and Revolution: A History of Women and Revolution in the Modern World.* New York: Vintage Books.

Russ, Joanna (1998). *What Are We Fighting for? Sex, Race, Class, and the Future of Feminism.* New York: St. Martin's Press.

Ulanov, Ann and Barry (1998). *Cinderella and Her Sisters: The Envied and the Envying.* Hull, Quebec: Daimon Verlag.

Weisser, Susan Ostrov and Jennifer Fleischner, eds., (1995). *Feminist Nightmares: Women at Odds: Feminism and the Problems of Sisterhood.* New York: New York University Press.

Wolf, Naomi (1994). *Fire with Fire: The New Female Power and How to Use It.* Random House New York.

INDEX

Best-selling author **Phyllis Chesler**, Emerita Professor of Psychology and Women's Studies and leading exponent of women's rights, has more than three million copies in print, including the classic *Women and Madness*. She is a founder of The Association for Women in Psychology and the National Women's Health Network. A popular guest on national television and radio programs, she has been an expert commentator on the major events of our time, including the Monica Lewinsky scandal, the Baby M case and the Aileen Wuornos serial murder trial. Her books include *Women and Madness; Letters to a Young Feminist; With Child: A Diary of Motherhood; Patriarchy: Notes of an Expert Witness; Feminist Foremothers in Mental Health; About Men; Mothers on Trial: The Battle for Women and Children; Sacred Bond; Women, Money, and Power;* and the forthcoming *Women of the Wall: Claiming Sacred Ground at Judaism's Holy Site.* She has lived in Kabul, Afghanistan, Jerusalem, and Tel Aviv and currently lives in Brooklyn, New York.